【英汉对照全译本】

CONSIDERATIONS ON REPRESENTATIVE GOVERNMENT
代 议 制 政 府

[英]约翰·穆勒 著

段小平 译

中国社会科学出版社

图书在版编目(CIP)数据

代议制政府/[英]约翰·穆勒著；段小平译.—北京：中国社会科学出版社,2007.8

(西方学术经典译丛)

ISBN 978-7-5004-6292-7

Ⅰ.代… Ⅱ.①约…②段… Ⅲ.议会制—研究 Ⅳ.D034.3

中国版本图书馆CIP数据核字(2007)第097670号

出版策划　曹宏举
责任编辑　韩小群
责任校对　朱小青
技术编辑　李　建

出版发行	中国社会科学出版社			
社　　址	北京鼓楼西大街甲158号		邮　编	100720
电　　话	010—84029450(邮购)			
网　　址	http://www.csspw.cn			
经　　销	新华书店			
印　　刷	北京京晟纪元印刷有限公司			
版　　次	2007年8月第1版			
印　　次	2007年8月第1次印刷			
开　　本	630×970　1/16			
印　　张	33.75			
字　　数	363千字			
定　　价	65.00元			

凡购买中国社会科学出版社图书，如有质量问题请与本社发行部联系调换
版权所有　侵权必究

出版说明

为了进一步促进中西文化交流,构建全新的西学思想平台,我们出版了这套《西方学术经典译丛》(英汉对照全译本)。本译丛精选西方学术思想流变中最有代表性的部分传世名作,由多位专家学者选目,内容涵盖了哲学、宗教学、政治学、经济学、心理学、法学、历史学等人文社会科学领域,收录了不同国家、不同时代、不同体裁的诸多名著。

本译丛系根据英文原著或其他文种的较佳英文译本译出,在国内第一次以英汉对照的形式出版。与以往译本不同的是,本译丛全部用现代汉语译出,尽量避免以往译本时而出现的文白相间、拗口难懂的现象;另外出于尊重原作和正本清源的目的,本译本对原作品内容一律不做删节处理,全部照译。以往译本由于时代和社会局限,往往对原作品有所删节,因此,本译本也是对过去译本的补充和完善。

为加以区别,原文中的英文注释,注释号用①、②……形式表示;中文译者注释则以〔1〕、〔2〕……形式表示。至于英译本中出现的原文页码和特殊索引等问题,中文译者在"译者后记"中将予以解释、说明。另外,在英文原著或原英译本中,有一些表示着重意义的斜体或大写等字体,考虑到读者可以在英汉对照阅读中注意到,在本译文中没有照样标出,还望读者理解。

中国社会科学出版社

Considerations On Representative Government

By *John Stuart Mill*

本书根据 George Routledge & Sons, Ltd. 1905 年版本译出

CONTENTS

目 录

CHAPTER Ⅰ　To What Extent Forms Of Government Are A Matter Of Choice ······ 2

第一章　政府形式在多大程度上涉及选择问题 ········ 3

CHAPTER Ⅱ　The Criterion Of A Good Form Of Government ············ 26

第二章　良好的政府形式的标准 ······················ 27

CHAPTER Ⅲ　That The Ideally Best Form Of Government Is
　　　　　　Representative Government ················· 66

第三章　理论上最好的政府形式是代议制政府 ········ 67

CHAPTER Ⅳ　Under What Social Conditions Representative Government
　　　　　　Is Inapplicable ···························· 106

第四章　在哪些社会条件下不适宜采用
　　　　代议制政府 ································· 107

CHAPTER Ⅴ　Of The Proper Functions Of Representative Bodies ············· 128

第五章　代议机关的应有职能 ······················ 129

CHAPTER VI   Of The Infirmities And Dangers To Which Representative

　　　　　　Government Is Liable ·· 160

第六章　代议制政府容易有的薄弱环节和危险 ······ 161

CHAPTER VII   Of True And False Democracy; Representation Of All, And

　　　　　　Representation Of The Majority Only ······················ 194

第七章　真民主与假民主；代表全体和仅仅

　　　　　　代表多数 ·· 195

CHAPTER VIII   Of The Extension Of The Suffrage ···························· 242

第八章　关于扩大选举权 ·· 243

CHAPTER IX   Should There Be Two Stages Of Election? ················ 280

第九章　选举应该分为两个阶段吗？ ·· 281

CHAPTER X   Of The Mode Of Voting ·· 294

第十章　投票的模式 ·· 295

CHAPTER XI   Of The Duration Of Parliaments ································ 330

第十一章　议会的期限 ·· 331

CHAPTER XII   Ought Pledges To Be Required From Members

　　　　　　Of Parliament? ·· 336

第十二章　应当要求议会议员作出保证吗？ ································ 337

CHAPTER XIII   Of A Second Chamber ·· 360

第十三章　关于第二院 ·· 361

CHAPTER XIV   Of The Executive In A Representative Government ······ 376

第十四章　代议制政府拥有的行政权力 ·· 377

— 2 —

CHAPTER XV　Of Local Representative Bodies …………………… 410

第十五章　地方代表机关 ………………………………… 411

CHAPTER XVI　Of Nationality, As Connected With

　　　　　　　Representative Government ……………………… 442

第十六章　与代议制政府有关的民族问题 …………… 443

CHAPTER XVII　Of Federal Representative Governments ………………… 460

第十七章　联邦的代议制政府 ……………………… 461

CHAPTER XVIII　Of The Government Of Dependencies By A Free State ……… 484

第十八章　自由国家的附属国政府 ……………… 485

译者后记 ……………………………………………………… 528

CHAPTER I
To What Extent Forms Of Government Are A Matter Of Choice

All speculations concerning forms of government bear the impress, more or less exclusive, of two conflicting theories respecting political institutions; or, to speak more properly, conflicting conceptions of what political institutions are.

By some minds, government is conceived as strictly a practical art, giving rise to no questions but those of means and an end. Forms of government are assimilated to any other expedients for the attainment of human objects. They are regarded as wholly an affair of invention and contrivance. Being made by man, it is assumed that man has the choice either to make them or not, and how or on what pattern they shall be made. Government, according to this conception, is a problem, to be worked like any other question of business. The first step is to define the purposes which governments are required to promote. The next, is to inquire what form of government is best fitted to fulfil those purposes. Having satisfied ourselves on these two points, and ascertained the form of government which combines the greatest amount of good with the least of evil, what further remains is to obtain the concurrence of our countrymen, or those for whom the institutions are intended, in the opinion which we have privately arrived at. To find the best form of government; to persuade others that it is the best; and having done so, to stir them up to insist on having it, is the order of ideas in the minds of those who adopt this view of political philosophy. They look upon a constitution in the same light (difference of scale being allowed for) as they would upon a steam plough, or a threshing machine.

To these stand opposed another kind of political reasoners, who

第一章　政府形式在多大程度上涉及选择问题

　　一切有关政府形式的学说，都或多或少地存在两种政治制度相互冲突的理论特征。或者，更准确地说，存在关于什么是政治制度的互相冲突的概念的特征。

　　在有些人看来，政府严格地说是一种实用的艺术，它除手段和目的问题外不会引发其他问题。像实现人类目的的其他手段一样，政府的形式被完全看作一件发明创造的事情。既然它是由人所设计的，当然人就有权利选择是否设计，以及怎样设计或遵循什么模式去设计。根据这种看法，政府也是一个应像任何其他事务问题一样加以处理的问题。首先是明确政府被要求促进实现的目的。其次，是研究怎样的政府形式最适于达到这些目的。在做到了这两点，进而确定了将利益最大化和弊端最小化结合起来的政府形式之后，剩下所要做的，就是争取我们的同胞，或者说是这些人（这诸种制度是打算经他们使用的），接受我们私下达成的意见。找到最好的政府形式，说服别人相信它是最棒的，并且如此去做了，去鼓动他们坚持要实行这种制度，这就是采取这种政治哲学观点的人们心中的环环相扣的想法。他们就像对待一部蒸汽拖拉机或一部打谷机那样（可能程度上有所差异）来对待一个政体。

　　与这些人截然不同的是，另一种政治理论家则绝不是把政

are so far from assimilating a form of government to a machine, that they regard it as a sort of spontaneous product, and the science of government as a branch (so to speak) of natural history. According to them, forms of government are not a matter of choice. We must take them, in the main, as we find them. Governments cannot be constructed by premeditated design. They 'are not made, but grow.' Our business with them, as with the other facts of the universe, is to acquaint ourselves with their natural properties, and adapt ourselves to them. The fundamental political institutions of a people are considered by this school as a sort of organic growth from the nature and life of that people: a product of their habits, instincts, and unconscious wants and desires, scarcely at all of their deliberate purposes. Their will has had no part in the matter but that of meeting the necessities of the moment, by the contrivances of the moment, which contrivances, if in sufficient conformity to the national feelings and character, commonly last, and by successive aggregation constitute a polity, suited to the people who possess it, but which it would be vain to attempt to superinduce upon any people whose nature and circumstances had not spontaneously evolved it.

It is difficult to decide which of these doctrines would be the most absurd, if we could suppose either of them held as an exclusive theory. But the principles which men profess, on any controverted subject, are usually a very incomplete exponent of the opinions they really hold. No one believes that every people is capable of working every sort of institutions. Carry the analogy of mechanical contrivances as far as we will, a man does not choose even an instrument of timber and iron on the sole ground that it is in itself the best. He considers whether he possesses the other requisites which must be combined with it to render its employment advantageous, and in particular whether those by whom it will have to be worked, possess the knowledge and skill necessary for its management. On the other hand, neither are those who speak of institutions as if they were a kind of living organisms, really the political fatalists they give themselves out to be. They do not pretend that mankind have absolutely no range of choice as

府形式等同于一部机器,而是把它当做一种自然产物,把政治科学看成(好比说)自然史的一个子学科。在他们看来,政府的形式不是一个选择问题。大体上,我们必须遵循它们的实际情形加以接受。政府不能靠事先的设计来创建。它们"不是设计出来的,而是自然成长的"。和看待宇宙中的其他事实一样,我们对于它们所能做的就是:熟悉它们的自然特性并使我们自己适应它们。在这一学派看来,一国人民的根本的政治制度是从该国人民的特性和生活中生成的一种有机的产物,是他们的习惯、本能和无意识的需要和愿望的一种产物,而绝不是他们深思熟虑的意图的产物。除了用权宜的设计来应对一时之需以外,对于这一问题,他们的意志力起不了任何作用。如果这些设计充分符合民族的感情和性格,它往往就是可持续的,再经过连续不断的聚积,就生成了适用于这国人民的政体,但是,该国人民的特性和情况如果不能自发地产生这种设计,那么,要将该政体灌输于他们则是枉费心机的。

如果我们假定两种学说都是至上独到的话,那么就难确定两者之中谁最不合理。但是,人们在任何争论的问题上所声称的道理,往往是他们真正持有的意见的极不完整的代表。没有人相信,每一国人民都能够设计每一种制度。甚至我们可以运用机械装置的类比来说明这一问题,一个人不会因这一工具本身是最好的就选择该工具,他还得考虑到,他是否具有必须与这工具相结合的其他条件以使工具的运用有利,特别是使用该工具的人是否具有管理工具所必要的知识和技能。另一方面,把制度比作好像是一种活的有机体的人们,也并不真正是他们自称的政治宿命论者。他们并不主张,对于人类要生

to the government they will live under, or that a consideration of the consequences which flow from different forms of polity is no element at all in deciding which of them should be preferred. But though each side greatly exaggerates its own theory, out of opposition to the other, and no one holds without modification to either, the two doctrines correspond to a deepseated difference between two modes of thought ; and though it is evident that neither of these is entirely in the right, yet it being equally evident that neither is wholly in the wrong, we must endeavour to get down to what is at the root of each, and avail ourselves of the amount of truth which exists in either.

Let us remember, then, in the first place, that political institutions (however the proposition may be at times ignored) are the work of men; owe their origin and their whole existence to human will. Men did not wake on a summer morning and find them sprung up. Neither do they resemble trees, which, once planted, ' are aye growing' while men ' are sleeping. ' In every stage of their existence they are made what they are by human voluntary agency. Like all things, therefore, which are made by men, they may be either well or ill made; judgment and skill may have been exercised in their production, or the reverse of these. And again, if a people had omitted, or from outward pressure have not had it in their power, to give themselves a constitution by the tentative process of applying a corrective to each evil as it arose, or as the sufferers gained strength to resist it, this retardation of political progress is no doubt a great disadvantage to them, but it does not prove that what has been found good for others would not have been good also for them, and will not be so still when they think fit to adopt it.

On the other hand, it is also to be borne in mind that political machinery does not act of itself. As it is first made, so it has to be worked, by men, and even by ordinary men. It needs, not their simple

活在其下的政府,他们毫无选择的余地,或者主张,对于不同政体形式所产生的后果的考虑,丝毫不是合适形式的决定中的要素。然而,尽管双方出于能够驳倒对方的目的,他们都极大地夸大了自己的学说,而且双方都抱有对彼此的学说作些更正的态度,但是这两种学说思想方法之间的分歧的确是根深蒂固的。尽管在两者中,任何一个显然都不是完全正确的,但是显然也不是完全错误的,我们必须竭力去弄明白这两种学说的主要实质,并充分利用两者中蕴含的所有真理。

于是,首先,让我们记得,政治制度(这个说法有时是可能被忽略的)是人们的创作;它们的起源和它们的整个存在均取决于人的意志。人们并不会在一个夏天的清晨醒来之后就发现它们已经生成了。它们也不像树木那样,只要种下去就可以自己生长,而人们则不用去管它。因为在它们存在的各个阶段,它们的存在都是人的意志力交互作用的结果。所以,正如由人做成的一切东西那样,它们要么做得棒极了,要么做得糟透了。在它们的制作过程中,人们可能使用了判断力和技能手段,也可能情形截然不同。再者,如果一国人民出于疏忽而不能够或者迫于外来压力而无能力凭借试验性办法——也就是当邪恶作乱时,或当受害者有力量反抗时,对每一种邪恶试验应用矫正之法——来为他们自己构建一种政体,那么毫无疑问,这种政治进步方面的阻碍对他是极大的不利,但不是这并证明,被发现对其他国家民众有用的东西就不会对他们有用了,而且当他们认为适于采用时仍然是没用的。

另一方面,还应该明确政治机器并不会自动运转。正如它最初是由人制成的,所以它同样还应该由人,甚至由普通人去操

acquiescence, but their active participation ; and must be adjusted to the capacities and qualities of such men as are available. This implies three conditions. The people for whom the form of government is intended must be willing to accept it; or at least not so unwilling, as to oppose an insurmountable obstacle to its establishment. They must be willing and able to do what is necessary to keep it standing. And they must be willing and able to do what it requires of them to enable it to fulfil its purposes. The word 'do' must be understood as including forbearances as well as acts. They must be capable of fulfilling the conditions of action, and the conditions of self-restraint, Which are necessary either for keeping the established polity in existence, or for enabling it to achieve the ends, its conduciveness to which forms its recommendation.

The failure of any of these conditions renders a form of government, whatever favourable promise it may otherwise hold out, unsuitable to the particular case.

The first obstacle, the repugnance of the people to the particular form of government, needs little illustration, because it never can in theory have been overlooked. The case is of perpetual occurrence. Nothing but foreign force would induce a tribe of North American Indians to submit to the restraints of a regular and civilized government. The same might have been said, though somewhat less absolutely, of the barbarians Who overran the Roman Empire. It required centuries of time, and an entire change of circumstances, to discipline them into regular obedience even to their own leaders, when not actually serving under their banner. There are nations who will not voluntarily submit to any government but that of certain families which have from time immemorial had the privilege of supplying them with chiefs. Some nations could not, except by foreign conquest, be made to endure a monarchy; others are equally averse to a republic. The hindrance often amounts, for the time being, to impracticability.

But there are also cases in which, though not averse to a form of government—possibly even desiring it—a people may be unwilling or

作。它所需要的并非人们一味的顺从,而是人们积极的参与,而且要使它适应这样一些人们的可用的能力和特质。这需要具备三个条件:人民必须乐于接受意在由他们所用的政府形式,或至少不是不乐意到对它的建立设置不可克服的障碍的地步;为使它生存延续下去,他们必须愿意且能够做必要的事情;以及为使它能实现其目的,他们必须愿意且能够做它需要他们做的事情。"做"这个字应解读为既包括作为的方面,也包括不作为的方面。他们必须能满足作为的条件和自我约束的条件,无论是对维持现有的已确立的政体的存在,抑或是使它能达到目的,这些条件都是必要的。有利于实现这些目的的政体就是这个政体的优势之所在。

若不足这些条件中的任何条件,就会使一种形式的政府(不论它在别的方面可能作出多么善意的诺言)不适合于特定情况。

对第一个障碍,即人民不愿要特定的政府形式,毋需作太多的解释,因为这在理论上是从来不会被忽视过的。这种情形是反复出现的。北美印第安人部落只有在外来的暴力因素的作用下,才促使它遵循正规的文明政府的约束。对侵害罗马帝国的野蛮人也可以这么说,尽管不那么绝对。在野蛮人事实上并非效力于该首领的旗帜下的时候,如果要把他们训练得有规矩地服从哪怕是他们自己的首领,也需要有几个世纪的时间和整个形势的演变。有些民族除了服从某些家族之外,不愿意服从任何政府,这些家族从远古时候起,就拥有为他们提供首领的特权。有些民族,除非被外国征服,否则无法接受君主制;另一些民族则同样程度地反对共和制。这种障碍会达到一时无法克服的情形。

但是还有这样一些情形,一国人民虽不排斥——甚至可能是期

unable to fulfil its conditions. They may be incapable of fulfilling such of them as are necessary to keep the government even in nominal existence. Thus, a people may prefer a free government, but if, from indolence, or carelessness, or cowardice, or want of public spirit, they are unequal to the exertions necessary for preserving it; if they will not fight for it when it is directly attacked ; if they can be deluded by the artifices used to cheat them out of it; if by momentary discouragement or a temporary panic, or a fit of enthusiasm for an individual, they can be induced to lay their liberties at the feet even of a great man, or trust him with powers which enable him to subvert their institutions ; in all these cases they are more or less unfit for liberty : and though it may be for their good to have had it even for a short time, they are unlikely long to enjoy it. Again, a people may be unwilling or unable to fulfil the duties which a particular form of government requires of them. A rude people, though in some degree alive to the benefits of civilized society, may be unable to practise the forbearances which it demands : their passions may be too violent, or their personal pride too exacting, to forgo private conflict, and leave to the laws the avenging of their real or supposed wrongs. In such a case, a civilized, government, to be really advantageous to them, will require to be in a considerable degree despotic : one over which they do not themselves exercise control, and which imposes a great amount of forcible restraint upon their actions. Again, a people must be considered unfit for more than a limited and qualified freedom, who will not cooperate actively with the law and the public authorities, in the repression of evildoers. A people who are more disposed to shelter a criminal than to apprehend him ; who, like the Hindoos, will perjure themselves to screen the man who has robbed them, rather than take trouble or expose themselves to vindictiveness by giving evidence against him; who, like some nations of Europe down to a recent date,

待——一种政府形式,但也许不愿意或不能够满足它的条件,甚至连维持政府名义上的存在所必要的条件可能也无力满足。比如说,一国人民可能更喜欢一个自由政府,但是如果因为懒惰成性,或者漠不关心,或者怯懦怕事,或者缺失公共精神,这样的话,他们就与维护这种制度所必备的努力不协调;如果在这个制度受到直接攻击时他们不为它斗争;如果由于受阴谋诡计所蒙蔽,他们废止了这种制度;如果由于片刻的垂头丧气,或是一时的惊慌失措,或是对某个人的一时着迷,他们被诱使,将自己的自由托付给即使是一个杰出人物的脚下,或者赋予他足够颠覆他们的制度的权力;在所有这些情形下,他们和自由或多或少是不太相称的。即使在短期内,这种制度安排也可能对他们是有好处的,但他们未必能长期享受这种制度的好处。另外,一国人民可能不情愿,或无法履行特定的政府形式所要求于他们的职责。一个野蛮的民族,尽管在某种程度上领受到文明社会的好处,但也许不能做到它所要求的自我克制:他们也许太容易感情冲动,或者他们太看重面子,以至不能放弃私下的争斗而把对事实上的或者所认为的不端行为的报复交给法律去解决。在这种情形下,一个文明政府要对他们真正有好处,在相当程度上,它将必须是专制的——必须是一个他们自己无法实行控制,却能对他们的行动施加大量强制力的政府。又比如,一国人民如果不愿主动地和法律以及当局协作来镇压犯罪的人,那就必定被看作只不过是适于有限度的、留有余地的自由罢了。甚至有这样的人民,他们故意包庇罪犯而不想逮捕罪犯,就像印度人那样,他们宁愿作伪证来包庇曾抢劫过他们的人,而不愿不怕麻烦或者挺身而出进行报复,提交犯罪人的证据;就像直到近日为止的

if a man poniards another in the public street, pass by on the other side, because it is the business of the police to look to the matter, and it is safer not to interfere in what does not concern them ; a people who are revolted by an execution, but not shocked at an assassination—require that the public authorities should be armed with much sterner powers of repression than elsewhere, since the first indispensable requisites of civilized life have nothing else to rest on. These deplorable states of feeling, in any people who have emerged from savage life, are, no doubt, usually the consequence of previous bad government, which has taught them to regard the law as made for other ends than their good, and its administrators as worse enemies than those who openly violate it. But however little blame may be due to those in whom these mental habits have grown up, and however the habits may be ultimately conquerable by better government, yet while they exist, a people so disposed cannot be governed with as little power exercised over them, as a people whose sympathies are on the side of the law, and who are willing to give active assistance in its enforcement. Again, representative institutions are of little value, and may be a mere instrument of tyranny or intrigue, when the generality of electors are not sufficiently interested in their own government to give their vote, or, if they vote at all, do not bestow their suffrages on public grounds, but sell them for money, or vote at the beck of some one who has control over them, or whom for private reasons they desire to propitiate. Popular election thus practised, instead of a security against misgovernment, is but an additional wheel in its machinery. Besides these moral hindrances, mechanical difficulties are often an insuperable impediment to forms of government. In the ancient world, though there might be, and often was, great individual independence, there could be nothing like a regulated popular government, beyond the bounds of a single city-community ; because there did not exist the physical conditions for the formation and propagation of a public opinion, except among those who could be brought together to discuss public matters in the same agora. This obstacle is generally thought to have ceased by the adoption of the representative system. But to surmount it completely, required the press, and even the newspaper press,

第一章

某些欧洲民族那样,如果有人在大街上杀死另一个人,而他们绕着走过,因为这是警察的分内事,则比较安全些。对执行死刑厌恶,但对暗杀却不感到吃惊的人民,需要政府当局掌握比其他的地方厉害得多的镇压权力,因为感受到生活的首要条件便无可凭借了。毫无疑问,刚刚脱离野蛮生活的民族,他们心里的这种可悲状态往往是以前的坏政府种下的恶果:政府教给人们把法律看作是为了其他目的,不是源于他们的利益而制定的,并把法律的执行者变作竟然是比公然破坏法律的人更坏的敌人。但是,尽管不能过多责怪习得这种心理习惯的人们,尽管终将可以由较好的政府来克服这种习惯,然而只要这些习惯还存在,一个有这种倾向的民族,就不能像对法律具有同情并愿意主动协助它贯彻行使的民族那样,遭受如此少的权力控制。此外,对于选举自己的政府,倘若大多数选民缺乏足够的热情,或者他们虽然去投票,却不是源于公共理由去行使选举权,而是为金钱而出卖选票,或者按照控制着自己的人的命令,或者按理私人原因所要讨好的人的意思而投票时,代议制度就谈不上有多大价值,也许仅仅是恶政或阴谋的工具而已。普选如此运作的话,非但不能防止恶政,反而会成为其帮凶。除了这些道德上的阻滞因素之外,技术方面的困难也是政府形式难以跨越的障碍。在古代社会,尽管可能有,并且经常存在着伟大的个人自治,但不会超出单个城邦共同体的界限,存在着一个井然有序的人民政府。因为只是在那些可能被召集到同一广场来商讨公共事务的人们当中,此外,形成和传播公众舆论的物质条件就不存在了。一般认为,一经采用代议制,这个障碍就会得到克服。但是要完全克服它就需要有出版机

the real equivalent, though not in all respects an adequate one, of the Pnyx and the Forum. There have been states of society in which even a monarchy of any great territorial extent could not subsist, but unavoidably broke up into petty principalities, either mutually independent, or held together by a loose tie like the feudal: because the machinery of authority was not perfect enough to carry orders into effect at a great distance from the person of the ruler. He depended mainly upon voluntary fidelity for the obedience even of his army, nor did there exist the means of making the people pay an amount of taxes sufficient for keeping up the force necessary to compel obedience throughout a large territory. In these and all similar cases, it must be understood that the amount of the hindrance may be either greater or less. It may be so great as to make the form of government work very ill, without absolutely precluding its existence, or hindering it from being practically preferable to any other which can be had. This last question mainly depends upon a consideration which we have not yet arrived at—the tendencies of different forms of government to promote Progress.

We have now examined the three fundamental conditions of the adaptation of forms of government to the people who are to be governed by them. If the supporters of what may be termed the naturalistic theory of politics, mean but to insist on the necessity of these three conditions; if they only mean that no government can permanently exist, which does not fulfil the first and second conditions, and, in some considerable measure, the third; their doctrine, thus limited, is incontestable. Whatever they mean more than this, appears to me altogether untenable. All that we are told about the necessity of an historical basis for institutions, of their being in harmony with the national usages and character, and the like, means either this, or nothing to the purpose. There is a great quantity of mere sentimentality connected with these and similar phrases, over and above the amount of rational meaning contained in them. But, considered practically, these alleged requisites

构,甚至新闻报业,这是和古雅典和古罗马广场真正等同的东西,尽管并不在所有方面都等同。曾经出现过这样的社会状态:在其中,甚至一个拥有巨大领土的君主政体都不能继续存在下去,而是难以避免地分裂成几个小诸侯国,这些小诸侯国要么彼此独立,要么是一种像封建关系那样足够松散的纽带联结在一起,因为权力机器并没有完善到将统治者本的命令传达到遥远的地方的程度。甚至他们军队对他的服从,他也依靠自愿的效忠,同样,也不存在使人们交纳足够赋税的措施以维持必要的武力,来达到其在辽阔的领土上的强迫服从。在这些以及类似的例子中,必须明白障碍是有大有小的。它可以大到使政府形式行使得非常糟,当然还不至于达到完全排斥它的存在,或阻碍它从实践上转向其他可能有的形式的地步。这最后的问题主要取决于我们还未谈到的一种考虑,即迥异的政府形式有促进进步的倾向。

现在,对于政府形式适用于由它们统治的人民的三个基本条件,我们已经作了一番探究。遵循可以称之为自然主义理论的政治理论的倡导者们的意向,如果只是要坚持这三个条件的必要性,如果他们的意思只是说,不能满足条件一和条件二,并且,在相当程度上不能满足条件三的政府不能永久存在,那么,他们的理论经由这样的界定,就变得不可反驳了。而超出这个限定范围,对我而言,这个学说是经不起驳斥的。一切有关制度要有历史作为根基,制度必须与民族惯例和性格相适应,以及诸如此类的说法,要么就是针对这一点而言,要么就跟这个意图关系不大。这些以及类似的语句中含有大量的仅仅是纯粹感情方面的信息,超出了包含其中的理性的涵义。但是从实践层面上看,这些政治制度的所

of political institutions are merely so many facilities for realizing the three conditions. When an institution, or set of institutions, has the way prepared for it by the opinions, tastes, and habits of the people, they are not only more easily induced to accept it, but will more easily learn, and will be, from the beginning, better disposed, to do what is required of them both for the preservation of the institutions, and for bringing them into such action as enables them to produce their best results. It would be a great mistake in any legislator not to shape his measures so as to take advantage of such pre-existing habits and feelings, when available. On the other hand, it is an exaggeration to elevate these mere aids and facilities into necessary conditions. People are more easily induced to do, and do more easily, what they are already used to ; but people also learn to do things new to them. Familiarity is a great help; but much dwelling on an idea will make it familiar, even when strange at first. There are abundant instances in which a whole people have been eager for untried things. The amount of capacity which a people possess for doing new things, and adapting themselves to new circumstances, is itself one of the elements of the question. It is a quality in which different nations, and different stages of civilization, differ much from one another. The capability of any given people for fulfilling the conditions of a given form of government, cannot be pronounced on by any sweeping rule. Knowledge of the particular people, and general practical judgment and sagacity, must be the guides. There is also another consideration not to be lost sight of. A people may be unprepared for good institutions ; but to kindle a desire for them is a necessary part of the preparation. To recommend and advocate a particular institution or form of government, and set its advantages in the strongest light, is one of the modes, often the only mode within reach, of educating the mind of the nation, not only for accepting or claiming, but also for working, the institution. What means had Italian patriots, during the last and present generation, of preparing the Italian people for freedom in unity, but by inciting them to demand it ? Those, however, who

谓必要条件,仅仅是赋予实现这三个条件的众多便利而已。当一项制度,或一套制度,有民族的舆论、偏好和习俗来作铺垫时,人民不仅容易被说服来接受它,而且将更容易去学习它,并且从一开始,就会有某种倾向去做需要他们去做的事情,以维护这些制度,使他们能够行动起来,得到最好的结果。任何立法者在琢磨它的方法时,不利用这种已经存在的可供利用的习俗和感情时,就将是一个很大的错误。另一方面,将这些仅仅是扶助和便利的东西提升为必要条件就显得夸张了。对于人们早就习惯做的事情,人们更易于被诱导去做并且更加容易去做,但人们也会尝试着做对他们而言是新颖的东西。熟悉是极大的便利条件。但还有另外一种情形,人们因为老是琢磨着一个问题就会更加熟悉它,即使这个问题一开始是陌生的。有很多例子可以说明,全国人民曾经渴望做没做过的事情。这国人民所具有的应对新事情的能力以及适应新环境的能力的强弱,本身是这个问题的要素之一。这是不同的民族、不同发展阶段的文明彼此明确区分的一个特质。任何特定民族满足特定的政府形式的能力,不能被任何概括性的准则加以判断。特定民族的知识水平和一般的实际判断能力和聪明才智,毫无疑问是这方面的指导。我们还不能忽视另一种考虑。对于好的制度,一国人民也许缺乏心理准备,但是激发他们追求这些制度,就构成了准备工作的必要组成部分。推荐和支持某种特定制度或政府形式,强调它的优点,这不仅仅是为了使他们接受或要求这个制度,而且这是为了执行这个制度而对该民族进行思想教育的模式之一,而这往往是能够采取的唯一模式。在上一代和这一代中,为了做好意大利人民实现自由统一的思想准备,意大利的爱国人士除了鼓动他们去争

undertake such a task, need to be duly impressed, not solely with the benefits of the institution or polity which they recommend, but also with the capacities, moral, intellectual, and active, required for working it, that they may avoid, if possible, stirring up a desire too much in advance of the capacity.

The result of what has been said is, that, within the limits set by the three conditions so often adverted to, institutions and forms of government *are* a matter of choice. To inquire into the best form of government in the abstract (as it is called) is not a chimerical, but a highly practical, employment of scientific intellect; and to introduce into any country the best institutions which, in the existing state of that country, are capable of, in any tolerable degree, fulfilling the conditions is one of the most rational objects to which practical effort can address itself. Everything which can be said by way of disparaging the efficacy of human will and purpose in matters of government, might be said of it in every other of its applications. In all things there are very strict limits to human power. It can only act by wielding some one or more of the forces of nature. Forces, therefore, that can be applied to the desired use, must exist ; and will only act according to their own laws. We cannot make the river run backwards; but we do not therefore say that watermills ' are not made, but grow. ' In politics as in mechanics, the power which is to keep the engine going must be sought for *outside* the machinery ; and if it is not forthcoming, or is insufficient to surmount the obstacles which may reasonably be expected, the contrivance will fail. This is no peculiarity of the political art, and amounts only to saying that it is subject to the same limitations and conditions as all other arts.

At this point we are met by another objection, or the same objection in a different form. The forces, it is contended, on which the greater political phenomena depend, are not amenable to the direction of politicians or philosophers. The government of a country,

取自由统一外,还有其他更好的做法吗?然而,承担这样一种职责的人们,不仅要牢记这制度或政体所带来的好处,而且要铭记为贯彻这个制度,还需要道德层面的、智力方面的以及主动行动的能力。还应该记住,要尽可能地避免鼓动超出这种能力的太高要求。

通过对前面的探讨,我们能得出的结论是:在多次曾提及的三个条件所规定的范围内,制度和政府形式只是一个选择问题。抽象地(正如人们所提及的)探讨什么是最佳的政府形式,不是空想,而是对科学智能的高度的实际运用;在一个国家的现有状况下,如果这种制度能够在相当程度上满足这些条件,那么把最好的制度引进到这个国家就是人们不懈努力、一以贯之所能达到的最合理的目标之一。在政府问题上,如果有贬抑人的意志和目的的作用的言论的话,同样它也可能存在其应用的其他方面中。在所有事情上,人的力量是受到很严格的限制的。只有靠运用某个或多个的自然力量,人的力量才能发挥作用。所以,毫无疑问,可以运用于所希望的用途的力量是存在的;但只有遵循其规律,这种力量才发挥作用。我们无法使河水倒流;但我们并不因此就得出结论:水车"不是人们制造的而是自己生长出来的"。就政治学而言,和在机械学上一样,发动引擎的动力必须在机器之外去寻找;如果无法找到,或者不能克服可以理性预期的障碍,则该发明必将失败。这并非说政治艺术有什么特殊之处;这只是说政治艺术同样要受制于与和其他一切技艺一样的限制和条件。

关于这一点存在另一种分歧,或者以不同形式出现的同一种分歧。他们争论说,大的政治现象所依靠的力量,并不服从政治家们或哲学家们的发号施令。他们声称,在一切实质性方面,

it is affirmed, is, in all substantial respects, fixed and determined beforehand by the state of the country in regard to the distribution of the elements of social power. Whatever is the strongest power in society will obtain the governing authority ; and a change in the political constitution cannot be durable unless preceded or accompanied by an altered distribution of power in society itself. A nation, therefore, cannot choose its form of government. The mere details, and practical organization it may choose ; but the essence of the whole, the seat of the supreme power, is determined for it by social circumstances.

That there is a portion of truth in this doctrine, I at once admit; but to make it of any use, it must be reduced to a distinct expression and proper limits. When it is said that the strongest power in society will make itself strongest in the government, what is meant by power ? Not thews and sinews ; otherwise pure democracy would be the only form of polity that could exist. To mere muscular strength, add two other elements, property and intelligence, and we are nearer the truth, but far from having yet reached it. Not only is a greater number often kept down by a less, but the greater number may have a preponderance in property, and individually in intelligence, and may yet be held in subjection, forcible or otherwise, by a minority in both respects inferior to it. To make these various elements of power politically influential, they must be organized ; and the advantage in organization is necessarily with those who are in possession of the government. A much weaker party in all other elements of power, may greatly preponderate when the powers of government are thrown into the scale ; and may long retain its predominance through this alone : though, no doubt, a government so situated is in the condition called in mechanics unstable equilibrium, like a thing balanced on its smaller end, which, if once disturbed, tends more and more to depart from, instead of reverting to, its previous state.

But there are still stronger objections to this theory of government in the terms in which it is usually stated. The power in society which has any tendency to convert itself into political power, is not power

一国的政府,是事先由这个国家社会权力的分布状况所确立和决定的。社会中最强大的力量将获取统治的权力,并且,除非已出现或伴随有在社会自身的权力分配上的变化,政治结构中的变动是不能持久的。因此,国家无法选择国家的政府形式。它可以选择的只能是细节和实际的组织,但整体的实质即最高权力的核心部分,是由社会综合条件所决定的。

对此我毫不否认,这个学说中存在部分的真理,但要使它变得有用,就必须使它成为一种明确的说法并给予更为适当的限定。当它提及社会中的最强大力量将转化为政府中的最强大力量时,力量是指什么呢?绝不是指体力,否则,纯粹的民主政治将会是唯一能够存在的政体形式。在单纯的体力以外,再考虑两个其他因素即财产和智慧,我们就会离真理更近,但这还远未接近真理。不仅多数经常受到少数的压制,而且,也许在财产方面甚至在个人智慧方面,多数占上风,尽管如此,仍然被这两方面都不如它的少数,用强迫的或其他的方法所压制。要让这些力量的不同因素在政治方面产生影响力,就必须把它们加以组织;而控制政府的那些人必然在组织方面占有利地位。当政府的权力被放入天平时,在其他一切力量因素方面弱小得多的一方可能处于显著优势地位,并仅仅由于这一点,弱小得多的一方可能长期保持优势。很明显,尽管政府是处在机械学上所谓的不稳定的平衡状态中,像用较小的一头倒立着的东西那样,一旦被干扰,平衡就被破坏了,越来越偏离事先的状态,而不是恢复到事先的状态。

但是,对于通常所说的这一政府理论,还存在着更强烈的反对意见。社会力量有一种趋势,即能够把其自身转化为政治力量,

quiescent, power merely passive, but active power ; in other words, power actually exerted ; that is to say, a very small portion of all the power in existence. Politically speaking, a great part of all power consists in will. How is it possible, then, to compute the elements of political power, while we omit from the computation anything which acts on the will ? To think that, because those who wield the power in society wield in the end that of government, therefore it is of no use to attempt to influence the constitution of the government by acting on opinion, is to forget that opinion is itself one of the greatest active social forces. One person with a belief is a social power equal to ninety-nine who have only interests. They who can succeed in creating a general persuasion that a certain form of government, or secial fact of any kind, deserves to be preferred, have made nearly the most important step which can possibly be taken towards ranging the powers of society on its side. On the day when the protomartyr was stoned to death at Jerusalem, while he who was to be the Apostle of the Gentiles stood by ' consenting unto his death, ' would any one have supposed that the party of that stoned man were then and there the strongest power in society ? And has not the event proved that they were so? Because theirs was the most powerful of then existing beliefs. The same element made a monk of Wittenberg, at the meeting of the Diet of Worms, a more powerful social force than the Emperor Charles the Fifth, and all the princes there assembled. But these, it may be said, are cases in which religion was concerned, and religious convictions are something peculiar in their strength. Then let us take a case purely political, where religion, if concerned at all, was chiefly on the losing side. If any one requires to be convinced that speculative thought is one of the chief elements of social power, let him bethink himself of the age in which there was scarcely

第一章

这种力量既不是静止的力量,也不是一味消极的力量,而是积极的力量;也就是说,它是实际上发挥出来的力量。换言之,在所有现存力量中,它只占其中的一个极小的部分。就政治方面来看,所有力量的一大部分来源于意志力,因此,倘若我们在估计中忽视掉任何遵循意志行动的东西,我们又怎么可能估计政治力量的因素呢?认为由于在社会中控制权力的人也终将控制政府的权力,因此认为企图通过左右社会舆论来影响政府的构成方式是枉费心机的。这样一种看法,就是忽略了舆论本身就是一种最厉害的积极的社会力量。就社会力量而言,一个有信仰的人和九十九个仅仅有利益的人是不相上下的。只要能成功地生成这样一种普遍信念,即认为某种政府形式或任何一种社会事实,值得优先选择,那么,就动员社会力量支持他们那一方而言,他们就迈出了可能采取的几乎是最关键的一步。第一个殉教者在耶路撒冷被人用石头砸死的那一天,当初附和着"同意他死"一方的那个人,后来却成为基督的使徒,有谁会认为被砸死的那个人的一方彼时彼地拥有社会中最强大的力量呢?后来的事件不是已经证明他们是那样吗?因为他们的信仰是当时存在的最具影响力的信仰。基于同样的因素,在沃尔姆斯会议的议席上,威顿伯格的一名僧人变成比查理五世皇帝以及在那里集会的所有君主更为强大的社会力量。但这些例子也许可以说,只是涉及宗教方面的,宗教信仰在其力量方面是有些特殊性的。那就让我们列举一个纯粹政治的事例吧,在该例子中,就宗教而言,它总体上处于不利的地位。倘若还有人不认可纯理论的思想是社会力量的主要因素之一的话,就让他追溯一下那个时代吧,在那时,欧洲几乎所有掌控权

a throne in Europe which was not filled by a liberal and reforming king, a liberal and reforming emperor, or, strangest of all, a liberal and reforming pope; the age of Frederic the Great, of Catherine the Second, of Joseph the Second, of Peter Leopold, of Benedict XIV. , of Ganganelli, of Pombal, Of Arauda ; when the very Bourbons of Naples were liberals and reformers, and all the active minds among the noblesse of France were filled with the ideas which were soon after to cost them so dear. Surely a conclusive example how far mere physical and economic power is from being the whole of social power. It was not by any change in the distribution of material interests, but by the spread of moral convictions, that negro slavery has been put an end to in the British Empire and elsewhere. The serfs in Russia will owe their emancipation, if not to a sentiment of duty, at least to the growth of a more enlightened opinion respecting the true interest of the State. It is what men think, that determines how they act ; and though the persuasions and convictions of average men are in a much greater degree determined by their personal position than by reason, no little power, is exercised over them by the persuasions and convictions of those whose personal position is different, and by the united authority of the instructed. When, therefore, the instructed in general can be brought to recognise one social arrangement, or political or other institution, as good, and another as bad, one as desirable, another as condemnable, very much has been done towards giving to the one, or withdrawing from the other, that preponderance of social force which enables it to subsist. And the maxim, that the government of a country is what the social forces in existence compel it to be, is true only in the sense in which it favours, instead of discouraging, the attempt to exercise, among all forms of government practicable in the existing condition of society, a rational choice.

力的不是倡导自由主义和拥护改革的国王,就是倡导自由主义和拥护改革的皇帝,尤为奇怪的是,还有倡导自由主义和拥护改革的教皇;弗雷德里克大帝年代,凯瑟琳二世年代,约瑟夫二世年代,彼得·利奥波德年代,本尼迪克特十四世年代,甘加内里、庞巴尔、阿兰达年代;当时那不勒斯的波旁王朝本身是自由主义者和改革者,而法国贵族中的所有积极活动的人士都充满着这一观点,此后不久这一观点就使他们付出了非常昂贵的代价。的确,这是关于单纯体力和经济力量绝不是社会力量的全部的一个总结性的事例。在英帝国和其他地方,黑人奴隶制的宣告终结,靠的不是物质利益分配上的任何更改,而是道德信念的传播。俄国农奴得到解放,倘若不是来源于一种责任感,至少也得归功于逐渐出现的有关国家真正利益的更为开明的舆论。这就是人们的信念决定他们如何行动。在很大程度上,尽管大众的信仰和信念取决于他们的个人地位而并非取决于理性,但个人地位迥异的人们的信仰和信念,以及接受过教育的人们凝聚起来的权威,对大众施加的影响是不容小觑的。所以,对于一种社会安排,或者一种政治制度或其他的制度,当受过教育的人们能一般地被引导接纳哪一种是好的,而另一种是坏的,前者是值得追求的,后者则是应受指责的时候,那就已经在足以使之存在下去的社会力量的优势赋予了前者,或者在不赋予后者方面作出不少努力了。现存社会力量决定一国政府的这一原理只有在下述意义上是对的:在现存社会条件下,对于一切行得通的政府形式而言,这一学说是有利于而不是有碍于试图对这种政府形式进行合理的选择。

CHAPTER II
The Criterion Of A Good Form Of Government

The form of government for any given country being (within certain definite conditions) amenable to choice, it is now to be considered by what test the choice should be directed ; what are the distinctive characteristics of the form of government best fitted to promote the interests of any given society.

Before entering into this inquiry it may seem necessary to decide what are the proper functions of government: for, government altogether being only a means, the elegibility of the means must depend on their adaptation to the end. But this mode of stating the problem gives less aid to its investigation than might be supposed and does not even bring the whole of the question into view. For, in the first place, the proper functions of a government are not a fixed thing, butdifferent in different states of society; much more extensive in a backward than in an advanced state. And, secondly, the character of a government or set of political institutions cannot be sufficiently estimated while we confine our attention to the legitimate sphere of governmental functions. For though the goodness of a government is necessarily circumscribed within that sphere, its badness unhappily is not. Every kind and degree of evil of which mankind are susceptible, may be inflicted on them by their government; and none of the good which social existence is capable of, can be any further realized than as the constitution of the government is compatible with, and allows scope for, its attainment. Not to speak of indirect effects, the direct meddling of the public authorities has no necessary limits but those of human existence ; and the influence of government on the well-being of society can be considered or estimated in reference to nothing less than

第二章 良好的政府形式的标准

在一定条件下,既然特定国家的政府形式是服从选择的,那么现在要考虑的是这种选择应该由什么来指导;什么是最适宜促进特定社会利益的政府形式的独特特性。

在谈论这个问题之前,似乎需要确定一下什么是政府的固有功能。因为政府只不过是一种手段,而手段的适当性取决于它们的合目的性。但这种陈述问题的方式对于问题的研究所给予的帮助要比可能设想的要小得多,甚至不能看到问题的全部方面。因为,首先,政府的固有功能并非一成不变的,而是在不同的社会状态中呈现出不同的样子,在落后的社会状态中的要比在先进的社会状态中广泛得多。其次,当我们把注意力集中在政府职能的合法范围时,政府的性质或一系列政治制度的性质就不能得到充分的评估。因为尽管在那个范围内,政府好的方面得到了必要的限制,但它的坏的方面却不幸地没有得到限制。政府可能将人类遭受的任何种类以及任何程度的罪恶加在它的子民头上。而社会存在所能有的好处,若超出了政府规定的与这种好处相一致或留有余地来实现的范围,则不能得到进一步的实现。不用说间接的影响,政府当局的直接干预除关系到人类的生存外,不存在任何必要的限制;而政府对社会福利的影响,则简直可能按

the whole of the interests of humanity.

Being thus obliged to place before ourselves, as the test of good and bad government, so complex an object as the aggregate interests of society, we would willingly attempt some kind of classification of those interests, which, bringing them before the mind in definite groups, might give indication of the qualities by which a form of government is fitted to promote those various interests respectively. It would be a great facility if we could say, the good of society consists of such and such elements ; one of these elements requires such conditions, another such others ; the government, then, which unites in the greatest degree all these conditions, must be the best. The theory of government would thus be built up from the separate theorems of the elements which compose a good state of society.

Unfortunately, to enumerate and classify the constituents of social well-being, so as to admit of the formation of such theorems, is no easy task. Most of those who, in the last or present generation, have applied themselves to the philosophy of politics in any comprehensive spirit, have felt the importance of such a classification ; but the attempts which have been made towards it are as yet limited, so far as I am aware, to a single step. The classification begins and ends with a partition of the exigencies of society between the two heads of Order and Progress (in the phraseology of French thinkers) ; Permanence and Progression, in the words of Coleridge. This division is plausible and seductive, from the apparently clean-cut opposition between its two members, and the remarkable difference between the sentiments to which they appeal. But I apprehend that (however admissible for purposes of popular discourse), the distinction between Order, or Permanence, and Progress, employed to define the qualities necessary in a government, is unscientific and incorrect.

For, first, what are Order and Progress ? Concerning Progress there is no difficulty, or none which is apparent at first sight. When Progress is spoken of as one of the wants of human society, it may be supposed to mean Improvement. That is a tolerably distinct idea. But what is Order? Sometimes it means more, sometimes less, but

第二章

照整个人类利益来考虑或评估。

既然我们因此不得不把这样社会的共同利益,一个如此复杂的对象摆在我们面前,来检验政府的好坏,我们就乐意对那些利益做些分类的尝试。这种分类,在某些群体眼中,则可能表明政府形式适合分别促进各种利益的特质。如果我们能够说社会利益是由这样和那样的因素组成,那将会带来很大的便利;其中某个需要这样的条件,而另一个则需要那样的条件,那么,在最大程度上统合了所有这些条件的政府必定是最好的了。因此,政府理论就将在组成一个好的社会状态的种种因素的个别法则的基础上建立起来。

但不幸的是,要对社会福利的种种要素加以列举和分类,以便形成这样的法则却不是一件容易的事。致力于比较全面地进行政治哲学研究的那些前代或当代学者,他们中的大多数大多数都觉察到了这样一种分类的重要性;但就我所知,朝这方面所做的尝试,还只是一小步而已。分类从开始到结束都只是将社会的急需按"秩序"和"进步"(依照法国思想家的说法)这两个方面加以区分;按科尔里奇的说法则是"永久性"和"进步性"。从这两者间显然阵营分明的对立,以及从这两者所诉求的感情的明显不同来看,这种区分似乎很有道理并且很吸引人。但在我的理解中,不管大众话语可以怎样允许,对"秩序"或者"永久性"以及"进步"加以区分,用来详细说明政府所必需的特质,都是不科学的和不正确的。

因为,第一,什么是"秩序"和"进步"呢?就"进步"而言,不存在什么困难,或者不存在乍看起来显而易见的困难。当"进步"被说成人类社会的需求之一时,它可以被理解为"改良"。那是一个相当不同的概念。但什么是"秩序"呢?它的意义有时要宽泛

hardly ever the whole of what society needs except improvement.

In its narrowest acceptation, Order means Obedience. A government is said to preserve order, if it succeeds in getting itself obeyed. But there are different degrees of obedience, and it is not every degree that is commendable. Only an unmitigated despotism demands that the individual citizen shall obey unconditionally every mandate of persons in authority. We must at least limit the definition to such mandates as are general, and issued in the deliberate form of laws. Order, thus understood, expresses, doubtless, an indispensable attribute of government. Those who are unable to make their ordinances obeyed, cannot be said to govern. But though a necessary condition, this is not the object of government. That it should make itself obeyed is requisite, in order that it may accomplish some other purpose. We are still to seek what is this other purpose which government ought to fulfil, abstractedly from the idea of improvement, and which has to be fulfilled in every society, whether stationary or progressive.

In a sense somewhat more enlarged, Order means the preservation of peace, by the cessation of private violence. Order is said to exist, where the people of the country have, as a general rule, ceased to prosecute their quarrels by private force, and acquired the habit of referring the decision of their disputes and the redress of their injuries to the public authorities. But in this larger use of the term, as well as in the former narrow one, Order expresses rather one of the conditions of government than either its purpose or the criterion of its excellence. For the habit may be well established of submitting to the government, and referring all disputed matters to its authority, and yet the manner in which the government deals with those disputed matters, and with the other things about which it concerns itself, may differ by the whole interval which divides the best from the worst possible.

If we intend to comprise in the idea of Order, all that society requires from its government which is not included in the idea of Progress, we must define Order as the preservation of all kinds and amounts of good which already exist, and Progress as consisting in

第二章

些,有时它又要狭窄些,但从不曾意味社会除改良之外的全部需要。

就其最狭窄的意义来说,"秩序"韵味着服从。如果政府成功地使其自身得到人民的服从,那么就说它保有"秩序"。但是存在着各种各样不同程度的服从,并且不是每种程度的服从都是值得赞美的。只有极端专制的政府会要求单个的公民无条件服从当权者的每一道命令。我们必须至少将这些命令限定为一般的、并以慎重的法律形式公布过的命令。这样理解"秩序"的话,就无疑表示它是政府不可或缺的一个属性。那些不能使他们的法令得到服从的人,就不能说拥有统治的权力。尽管这是一个必要条件,但并不是政府的目标。政府应该使自己得到服从,这是以便能够完成某个其他目标必不可少的。我们仍须追求这个其他目标,这个目标是政府从抽象的改良观念出发应当完成的,也是每个不管是停滞不前还是进步的社会都必须完成的。

广而延之,"秩序"意味着通过平息私人暴力来保持和平。作为一般法则,一国民众不以私人暴力解决他们之间的争端,并且养成将他们的争端和对伤害的赔偿诉诸政府当局的习惯,在这种地方,就是存在了"秩序"。但在这种较广意义上使用这个词,和前面讲到的狭义意义一样,与其说是"秩序"表达了政府的一个条件,不如说它表达了政府的目标,或是政府优劣的标准。因为服从政府以及将所有争端诉诸政府当局的习惯可以很好地建立起来,但政府处理这些争议事项以及其他它所关心的事项的手段,在将最好和最坏政府区分开来的整个时期,可能有所不同。

如果我们打算将社会要求它的政府做到而又不包括在"进步"这个概念中的所有一切,都包括在"秩序"这个概念之内,那么我们就必须将"秩序"定义为保持已经存在的所有种类和数量的利益,

— 31 —

the increase of them. This distinction does comprehend in one or the other section everything which a government can be required to promote. But, thus understood, it affords no basis for a philosophy of government. We cannot say that, in constituting a policy, certain provisions ought to be made for Order, and certain others for Progress; since the conditions of Order, in the sense now indicated, and those of Progress, are not opposite, but the same. The agencies which tend to preserve the social good which already exists, are the very same which promote the increase of it, and *vice versâ*; the sole difference being, that a greater degree of those agencies is required for the latter purpose than for the former.

What, for example, are the qualities in the citizens individually, which conduce most to keep up the amount of good conduct, of good management, of success and prosperity, which already exist in society? Everybody will agree that those qualities are, industry, integrity, justice, and prudence. But are not these, of all qualities, the most conducive to improvement ? and is not any growth of these virtues in the community, in itself the greatest of improvements ? If so, whatever qualities in the government are promotive of industry, integrity, justice, and prudence, conduce alike to permanence and to progression; only there is needed more of those qualities to make the society decidedly progressive, than merely to keep it permanent.

What, again, are the particular attributes in human beings which seem to have a more especial reference to Progress, and do not so directly suggest the ideas of Order and Preservation? They are chiefly the qualities of mental activity, enterprise, and courage. But are not all these qualities fully as much required for preserving the good we have, as for adding to it ? If there is anything certain in human affairs, it is that valuable acquisitions are only to be retained by the continuation of the same energies which gained them. Things left to take care of themselves inevitably decay. Those whom success induces to relax their habits of care and thoughtfulness, and their willingness to encounter disagreeables, seldom long retain their good fortune at its height. The mental attribute which seems exclusively dedicated to Progress, and is the culmination of the tendencies to it, is Originality, or Invention.

而"进步"则在于增进这些利益。这种区分确实把要求政府促进的一切都包括在这个或者那个部分之中。但是,一经这般理解,它就不能给政府的哲学提供基础了。在制定政策时,我们不能说,某些规定应当适合"秩序",而另外一些则应当适合"进步",因为在现在所说的意义上,"秩序"的条件和"进步"的条件并不是对立的,而是相同的。倾向于保持已经存在的社会好的方面的力量,就是增进好的方面的力量,反之亦然;唯一不同的是,为了实现后一意图要有比实现前一目标更大程度的力量。

例如,什么是单个公民最有助于保持社会已经存在的全部良好的行为、良好的管理、成功和繁荣的品质呢?每个人都会同意,那就是勤奋、正直、公平和审慎。但是所有这些品质,不就是最有助于改良吗?社会共同体中美德的任何发展不就是最大的改良吗?如果是这样,那么政府中凡是促进勤奋、正直、公平和审慎的特质,就同样能促进永久性和进步性;只是与仅仅保持永久相比,将更需要这些特质来使社会变得明显更为进步。

再举一例,什么是特别涉及到"进步"而又和"秩序"与"保持"的观念并不那么直接相关的人类特殊的属性呢?它们主要是智力活动、进取心和勇气等特质。但是所有这些特质与保持我们所拥有的利益相比,不是和增进它同样十分需要吗?如果人类事务中存在着确定无疑的东西的话,那就是凡是已经拥有的有价值的东西,只有继续用获得它时所用的精力才能将之加以保持。事物如果放任自流就不可避免地导致衰亡。那些因为成功而松懈,放弃了小心谨慎和深思熟虑的习惯,并且不愿意面对不愉快事物的人,很少能长期保持他们的好运巅峰状态。似乎专属于"进步"并且是它的各种倾向的集中表现的智力属性,是"原创能力"或者叫"创造能

Yet this is no less necessary for Permanence; since in the inevitable changes of human affairs, new inconveniences and dangers continually grow up, which must be encountered by new resources and contrivances, in order to keep things going on even only as well as they did before. Whatever qualities, therefore, in a government, tend to encourage activity, energy, originality, are requisites of Permanence as well as of Progress; only a somewhat less degree of them will on the average suffice for the former purpose than for the latter.

To pass now from the mental to the outward and objective requisites of society ; it is impossible to point out any contrivance in politics, or arrangement of social affairs, which conduces to Order only, or to Progress only ; whatever tends to either promotes both. Take, for instance, the common institution of a police. Order is the object which seems most immediately interested in the efficiency of this part of the social organization. Yet if it is effectual to promote Order, that is, if it represses crime, and enables every one to feel his person and property secure, can any state of things be more conducive to Progress ? The greater security of property is one of the main conditions and causes of greater production, which is Progress in its most familiar and vulgarest aspect. The better repression of crime represses the dispositions which tend to crime, and this is Progress in a somewhat higher sense. The release of the individual from the cares and anxieties of a state of imperfect protection sets his faculties free to be employed in any new effort for improving his own state and that of others: while the same cause, by attaching him to social existence, and making him no longer see present or prospective enemies in his fellow-creatures, fosters all those feelings of kindness and fellowship towards others and interest in the general well-being of the community, which are such important parts of social improvement.

Take, again, such a familiar case as that of a good system of taxation and finance. This would generally be classed as belonging to the province of Order. Yet what can be more conducive to

第二章

力"。但是这对"永久性"来说当然是必要的,因为在不可避免的人类事务的变化中,新的麻烦和危险不断产生,而哪怕为了使事情跟以前一样顺利运转,处理这些麻烦和危险也必须用新的智谋和办法。因此,在一个政府中,倾向于鼓励活力,精力和原创能力的任何特质,对于"永久性"和"进步"来说,都是必不可少的。只是前一目标与后一目标相比较,这些性质的程度只要稍微低一点,一般也就够了。

现在,我们从社会的智力条件转到外部条件和客观条件。我们不可能指出政治中有哪些方法,或者社会事务中的哪些安排,只对"秩序"有益,或者只对"进步"有益。对任何一方面有益的就对两者都有益。我们拿普通的警察制度作为例子来加以说明。"秩序"似乎是和社会的这个部分的效率最直接相关的目的。然而,如果它能有效地促进"秩序",也就是说,如果它能够打击犯罪,使每个人都觉得人身和财产得到了保护,那么还有什么事态比这更有助于"进步"的吗?财产的更大安全是更大生产的主要条件和主要原因之一,而更大的生产,也就是"进步"的最常见和最普通的因素,更好地打击犯罪就等于压制了犯罪的倾向,而这就是在多多少少较高意义上的"进步"。将处于不完善的保护状态中的个人从焦虑与不安中解脱出来,就是解放了他的能力,使他能够有精力去为改善自己与别人的处境而努力。而同样的原因,通过使他热爱社会的存在,并且使他在他的同胞中看不到当前的或预期的敌人,能培育出对待他人的亲切感情和友谊,以及对社会共同体的普遍福利的关注,而这正是社会进步的重要组成部分。

再以人们熟悉的良好的税收与财政制度为例。人们一般会把这个案例划归到属于"秩序"范围内的一类。但是,什么能比它

Progress ? A financial system which promotes the one, conduces, by the very same excellences, to the other. Economy, for example, equally preserves the existing stock of national wealth, and favours the creation of more. A just distribution of burthens by holding up to every citizen an example of morality and good conscience applied to difficult adjustments, and an evidence of the value which the highest authorities attach to them, tends in an eminent degree to educate the moral sentiments of the community, both in respect of strength and of discrimination. Such a mode of levying the taxes as does not impede the industry, or unnecessarily interfere with the liberty, of the citizen, promotes, not the preservation only, but the increase of the national wealth, and encourages a more active use of the individual faculties. And *vice versâ* , all errors in finance and taxation which obstruct the improvement of the people in wealth and morals, tend also, if of sufficiently serious amount, positively to impoverish and demoralize them. It holds, in short, universally that when Order and Permanence are taken in their widest sense, for the stability of existing advantages, the requisites of Progress are but the requisites of Order in a greater degree; those of Permanence merely those of Progress, in a somewhat smaller measure.

In support of the position that Order is intrinsically different from Progress, and that preservation of existing and acquisition of additional good are sufficiently distinct to afford the basis of a fundamental classification, we shall perhaps be reminded that Progress may be at the expense of Order ; that while we are acquiring, or striving to acquire, good of one kind, we may be losing ground in respect to others; thus there may be progress in wealth, while there is deterioration in virtue. Granting this, what it proves is not that Progress is generically a different thing from Permanence, but that wealth is a different thing from virtue. Progress is Permanence and something more ; and it is no answer to this, to say that Progress in one thing does not imply Permanence in everything.

对"进步"有益呢？一个促进秩序的财政制度，基于同样的优点，对进步也十分有益。例如经济既均等地保持了国家现有的财富，又有利于创造更多的财富。将负担公平地分配给每一个公民，就是将道德和良知运用于困难的调整工作的范例，也是最高当局评价这些工作的证明。这样的负担分配，无论就强度还是精度而言，都大大地培养了社会的道德情操。这样一种征税模式，并没有妨碍公民的勤奋，或者不必要地妨碍公民的自由，它不仅对保持国家财富有益，而且对增加国家财富有益，并且使个人的聪明才智得到了更加积极的应用。反之，一切阻碍人民增加财富和道德的财政和税收上的错误，如果达到相当严重的程度，就肯定会使人民变得贫困和道德败坏。总之，当我们在最普遍意义上谈论"秩序"和"永久性"时，为了现存利益的稳定，"进步"所要求的只不过是"秩序"在更大程度上所要求的，"永久性"所要求的仅仅是"进步"在较小程度上所要求的。

　　支持那种认为"秩序"本质上不同于"进步"的立场，以及保有现有的和另外获得的好的事物的立场时，就为基本分类提供了足够区分的基础，这时，我们也许应当注意"进步"可能会以"秩序"为代价；当我们正在得到或竭力获取某种美好事物时，也许会放弃别的东西，因此，可能会出现财富增长了，而美德却堕落了的现象。承认这一点，它所证明的不是"进步"在种类上与"永久性"是两种不同的事物，而是说财富跟美德是两种不同的事物。"进步"就是"永久性"以及多一点的东西。并且，说在某件事情上的"进步"并不意味着在所有事情上的"永久性"，并不是针对这点的答案。在某种事物上的"进步"也不再是意味着在所有事情上的"进步"。任何方面的"进步"都包括那个方面相应的

No more does Progress in one thing imply Progress in everything. Progress of any kind includes Permanence in that same kind: whenever Permanence is sacrificed to some particular kind of Progress, other Progress is still more sacrificed to it ; and if it be not worth the sacrifice, not the interest of Permanence alone has been disregarded, but the general interest of Progress has been mistaken.

If these improperly contrasted ideas are to be used at all in the attempt to give a first commencement of scientific precision to the notion of good government, it would be more philosophically correct to leave out of the definition the word Order, and to say that the best government is that which is most conducive to Progress. For Progress includes Order, but Order does not include Progress. Progress is a greater degree of that of which Order is a less. Order, in any other sense, stands only for a part of the requisites of good government, not for its idea and essence. Order would find a more suitable place among the conditions of Progress; since, if we would increase our sum of good, nothing is more indispensable than to take due care of what we already have. If we are endeavouring after more riches, our very first rule should be, not to squander uselessly our existing means. Order, thus considered, is not an additional end to be reconciled with Progress, but a part and means of Progress itself. If a gain in one respect is purchased by a more than equivalent loss in the same or in any other, there is not Progress. Conduciveness to Progress, thus understood, includes the whole excellence of a government.

But, though metaphysically defensible, this definition of the criterion of good government is not appropriate, because, though it contains the whole of the truth, it recalls only a part. What is suggested by the term Progress is the idea of moving onward, whereas the meaning of it here is quite as much the prevention of falling back. The very same social causes—the same beliefs, feelings, institutions, and practices—are as much required to prevent society from retrograding,

第二章

"永久性",每当"永久性"为某个方面特殊的"进步"作出牺牲时,其他方面的"进步"就要对这种牺牲作更大的补偿;而如果它不值得作这样的牺牲时,不仅"永久性"的利益被忽视了,而且"进步"的一般利益也被搞错了。

如果在一开始尝试给好的政府一个科学、精确的定义时,竟然就要使用这些不恰当地加以对比的概念,那么不考虑"秩序"一词的定义,以及说最好的政府是对"进步"最为有益的政府,在哲学上就较为正确些。因为"进步"包括"秩序",但"秩序"并不包括"进步"。"进步"的程度较为深入,而"秩序"则程度要小些。在任何其他意义上,"秩序"只是好的政府所必须具备的条件的一部分,并不代表好的政府的概念和本质。在"进步"的条件下,"秩序"会找到更为合适的位置,因为如果我们增加美好事物的总和的话,那么没什么事情比对我们已经拥有的东西加以正当的照顾更加重要了。如果我们在更为富有之后更努力进取的话,我们的第一条规则应当是,不要无益地浪费我们已有的财富。从这个角度考虑,"秩序"就不只是为了和"进步"相和谐的一个附加目的,而是"进步"本身的一部分和手段。如果某方面的增长是用同一方面或任何其他方面更多的损失换来的,那么就无"进步"可言。从这个角度来理解,有助于"进步"的因素就包括了政府所有卓越的方面。

尽管这个关于好的政府的标准在抽象推理方面是可自我辩解的,但却是不恰当的。因为尽管它包含了真理的全部,却只让人想起一部分。"进步"一词表示的是向前移动的概念,而到了这里却相当于防止倒退。同样的社会原因——同样的信仰、感情、制度和实践——与推动社会进一步发展一样,对于防止社会

as to produce a further advance. Were there no improvement to be hoped for, life would be not the less an unceasing struggle against causes of deterioration; as it even now is. Politics, as conceived by the ancients, consisted wholly in this. The natural tendency of men and their works was to degenerate, which tendency, however, by good institutions virtuously administered, it might be possible for an indefinite length of time to counteract. Though we no longer hold this opinion; though most men in the present age profess the contrary creed, believing that the tendency of things, on the whole, is towards improvement; we ought not to forget, that there is an incessant and ever-flowing current of human affairs towards the worse, consisting of all the follies, all the vices, all the negligences, indolences, and supinenesses of mankind; which is only controlled, and kept from sweeping all before it, by the exertions which some persons constantly, and others by fits, put forth in the direction of good and worthy objects. It gives a very insufficient idea of the importance of the strivings which take place to improve and elevate human nature and life, to suppose that their chief value consists in the amount of actual improvement realized by their means, and that the consequence of their cessation would merely be that we should remain as we are. A very small diminution of those exertions would not only put a stop to improvement, but would turn the general tendency of things towards deterioration; which, once begun, would proceed with increasing rapidity, and become more and more difficult to check, until it reached a state often seen in history, and in which many large portions of mankind even now grovel; when hardly anything short of superhuman power seems sufficient to turn the tide, and give a fresh commencement to the upward movement.

These reasons make the word Progress as unapt as the terms Order and Permanence, to become the basis for a classification of the requisites of a form of government. The fundamental antithesis which these words express, does not lie in the things themselves, so much as in the types of human character which answer to them. There are, we know, some minds in which caution, and others in which boldness, predominates: in some, the desire to avoid imperilling what is already possessed is a stronger sentiment than that which prompts to improve

第二章

倒退是同样重要的。如果人们没有改善生活的期望,生活将依然会是一场反对堕落的无休止的斗争,像实际上现在这样。古人所设想的政治就完全是这样的。人类及其他们的作品的自然倾向是退化,然而,经由得到良好管理的好的制度,可能在一段不确定长度的时间内来抵消这种倾向。尽管我们不再持这样的观点,尽管大部分人提出了相反的信念,相信事物发展的总体趋势是进步的,但我们不应该忘记,人类事务中存在着不间断的、永不休止的走向更加糟糕境地的潮流,由人类所有的蠢事、所有的罪恶、所有的疏忽、懒散和怠惰所组成。这个潮流,仅仅由某些人不断地,以及其他人时不时地,向着美好的并且有价值的目标努力,才仅仅得以控制,并且席卷其面前的一切。以为他们的主要价值存在于由他们的手段实现的实际上的进步,以及以为他们努力停止的结果仅仅就是使我们保持我们现在的样子,就是对所采取的努力以改善和提高人类本性和生活的重要性的严重估计不足。对那些努力的丝毫松懈不仅会使进步停止,而且会使事物发展的普遍趋势倾向后退,而这种倒退一旦开始,就会以越来越快的速度发展下去,变得越来越难以控制,直到它达到历史上常常看到的那种状态,在这种状态中甚至现在还有人类的一大部分匍匐其中,到那时,除了有超人的力量,否则难以扭转这种趋势,难以重新开始向上的运动。

这些理由使得"进步"这个词汇与"秩序"和"永久性"这两个词汇一样不适于构成划分政府形式必要条件的基础。这些词汇所表达的根本对立不存在于事物本身之中,甚至于不存在于与符合这些词汇相对应的人的性格之中。我们知道,有些人小心谨慎,有些人大胆敢为。在某些人中,避免危及既得利益的愿望要比促使改

the old and acquire new advantages; while there are others who lean the contrary way, and are more eager for future than careful of present good. The road to the ends of both is the same ; but they are liable to wander from it in opposite directions. This consideration is of importance in composing the *personnel* of any political body: persons of both types ought to be included in it, that the tendencies of each may be tempered, in so far as they are excessive, by a due proportion of the other. There needs no express provision to ensure this object, provided care is taken to admit nothing inconsistent: with it. The natural and spontaneous admixture of the old and the young, of these whose position and reputation are made, and those who have them still to make, will in general sufficiently answer the purpose, if only this natural balance is not disturbed by artificial regulation.

Since the distinction most commonly adopted for the classification of social exigencies does not possess the properties needful for that use, we have to seek for some other leading distinction better adapted to the purpose. Such a distinction would seem to be indicated by the considerations to which I now proceed.

If we ask ourselves on what causes and conditions good government in all its senses, from the humblest to the most exalted, depends, we find that the principal of them, the one which transcends all others, is the qualities of the human beings composing the society over which the government is exercised.

We may take, as a first instance, the administration of justice; with the more propriety, since there is no part of public business in which the mere machinery, the rules and contrivances for conducting the details of the operation, are of such vital consequence. Yet even these yield in importance to the qualities of the human agents employed. Of what efficacy are rules of procedure in securing the ends of justice, if the moral condition of the people is such that the witnesses generally lie, and the judges and their subordinates take bribes ? Again, how can institutions provide a good municipal administration, if there exists such indifference to the subject, that those who would administer honestly and capably cannot be induced to serve, and the duties are left to those who undertake them because they have some

进旧的和取得新的利益的愿望更为强烈。而另外有一些人的倾向则完全相反,对未来的利益要比对当前利益更为关心。通向这两个目的的道路是一样的,但他们容易在相反方向偏离这条道路。这种考虑在任何政治团体挑选成员时都是非常重要的:在团体中两种人都应当有,这样的话,在一种人倾向极端的时候,就可以有恰当比例的另一种倾向的人来调节。只要注意不要有不协调的地方,那么就没有必要用明文规定来确保这一目的。年老的和年少的,功成名就的和正在为事业奋斗的人,自然和自发地组合在一起,只要这种自然平衡没有被人为的规定所扰乱,一般而言,就可以充分地满足这一目的。

既然最通常被用来对社会急迫需要所作分类的区别不具备所需要的性质,我们就必须寻求某些更加适合这一意图的主要区别。这种区别将由我现在要进行下去的考虑所表示出来。

如果我们问自己,好的政府在其所有意义上,从最低微的意义到最高尚的意义,所依赖的是什么原因和什么条件,我们会发现,最主要的,也即超越其他一切的,是组成社会(政府就是在社会中运转的)的那些人的品质。

我们可以举司法作为第一个例子加以说明。这样做更为恰当,因为没有哪一部分公共事务,其单纯的机构、规则和为了执行操作的细节而做的设计,拥有如此重要的后果。但即使这些与所雇用的人员的品质相比,其重要性也没有那么大。如果人民的道德水平是如此败坏,证人常常说谎,法官及其下属受贿,那么程序规则在保证司法目的上又能起什么作用呢?再者,如果人民麻木不仁,诚实能干的人不愿得到使用,职务由那些谋取私利的人去担任,制度又如何能够提供一个良好的市政管理呢?如果选民

private interest to be promoted ? Of what avail is the most broadly popular representative system, if the electors do not care to choose the best member of parliament, but choose him who will spend most to be elected ? How can a representative assembly work for good, if its members can be bought, or if their excitability of temperament, uncorrected by public discipline or private selfcontrol, makes them incapable of calm deliberation and they resort to manual violence on the floor of the House, or shoot at one another with rifles ? How, again, can government, or any joint concern, be carried on in a tolerable manner by a people so envious, that if one among them seems likely to succeed in anything, those who ought to co-operate with him form a tacit combination to make him fail ? Whenever the general disposition of the people is such, that each individual regards those only of his interests which are selfish, and does not dwell on, or concern himself for, his share of the general interest, in such a state of things good government is impossible. The influence of defects of intelligence in obstructing all the elements of good government requires no illustration. Government consists of acts done by human beings ; and if the agents, or those who choose the agents, or those to whom the agents are responsible, or the lookers-on whose opinion ought to influence and check all these, are mere masses of ignorance, stupidity, and baleful prejudice, every operation of government will go wrong: while, in proportion as the men rise above this standard, so will the government improve in quality; up to the point of excellence, attainable but nowhere attained, where the officers of government, themselves persons of superior virtue and intellect, are surrounded by the atmosphere of a virtuous and enlightened public opinion.

  The first element of good government, therefore, being the virtue and intelligence of the human beings composing the community, the most important point of excellence which any form of government can possess is to promote the virtue and intelligence of the people themselves. The first question in respect to any political institutions is, how far they tend to foster in the member of the community the various desirable qualities, moral and intellectual; or rather (following Bentham's more complete

不关心选择最恰当的议员,而是选择那些为了当选而愿意出最多钱的人,那么最广泛通行的代议制体系又有什么作用呢?如果议员可以被收买,或者如果他们容易冲动的性情得不到公共纪律或自制力的约束,使他们不能进行冷静的思考,并且在议院的议员席上互相殴打,或者互相开枪射击,那么代议机关又如何能够为人民的利益而工作呢?又比如,如果在一群人中,有一个人似乎就要成功了,但本来应该和他合作的人却形成默契的联盟,使他失败,这样嫉妒成性的人民,又怎能以宽容的方式来管理政府或者任何共同关注的事业呢?只要人们的普遍倾向是每个人都只关心自己的私利,不去思考,或者关心他在普遍利益中的份额,那么在这样的事态下,好的政府是不可能的。知识的缺乏在阻碍所有好的政府要素时的影响是不需要举例来说明的。管理由人的行为所组成,如果政府成员,或者选择那些成员的人,或者那些成员的需要对之负责的人,或者那些观点会影响上述所有人的观看者,都只是无知、蠢笨、心怀恶毒偏见的乌合之众,则任何政府都将管理不好。但是,人们按照一定的比例提高这个标准,这样政府的性质将会有所改进,达到卓越的标准——这是可以达到但是还没有达到的标准,在那里的政府官员,本身就是道德高尚、智力不凡的,周围的公众舆论的氛围也是纯洁的和开明的。

因此,既然衡量一个政府是好政府的第一要素是组成社会的人的美德和智慧,那么任何形式的政府都能拥有的最重要的优点就是促进人民本身的美德和智慧。对任何形式的政治制度来说,首要的问题是这些制度在何种程度上在社会成员中培育出各种所需的品质:道德的以及智慧的,或者按照边沁更为全面

classification) moral, intellectual, and active. The government which does this the best, has every likelihood of being the best in all other respects, since it is on these qualities, so far as they exist in the people, that all possibility of goodness in the practical operations of the government depends.

We may consider, then, as one criterion of the goodness of a government, the degree in which it tends to increase the sum of good qualities in the governed, collectively and individually; since, besides that their well-being is the sole object of government, their good qualities supply the moving force which works the machinery. This leaves, as the other constituent element of the merit of a government, the quality of the machinery itself; that is, the degree in which it is adapted to take advantage of the amount of good qualities which may at any time exist, and make them instrumental to the right purposes. Let us again take the subject of judicature as an example and illustration. The judicial system being given, the goodness of the administration of justice is in the compound ratio of the worth of the men composing the tribunals, and the worth of the public opinion which influences or controls them. But all the difference between a good and a bad system of judicature lies in the contrivance adopted for bringing whatever moral and intellectual worth exists in the community to bear upon the administration of justice, and making it duly operative on the result. The arrangements for rendering the choice of the judges such as to obtain the highest average of virtue and intelligence; the salutary forms of procedure; the publicity which allows observation and criticism of whatever is amiss ; the liberty of discussion and censure through the press; the mode of taking evidence, according as it is well or ill adapted to elicit truth; the facilities, whatever be their amount, for obtaining access to the tribunals ; the arrangements for detecting crimes and apprehending offenders ;—all these things are not the power, but the machinery for bringing the power into contact with the obstacle : and the machinery has no action of itself, but without it the power, let it be ever so ample, would be wasted and of no effect. A similar distinction exists in regard to the constitution of the executive departments of administration. Their machinery is good, when the proper tests are prescribed for the qualifications of officers, the proper rules

的分类,干脆就说道德的、智力的和积极的品质。在这方面做得最好的政府,就可能在所有其他一切方面都会做得很好,因为只要它们存在于人民之中,政府在实践过程中的一切可能好的优点都依赖于它们。

那么,我们可以认为,于增加被统治者集体的或个人的良好品质的总和所倾向的程度,就是判断良好政府的一个标准。这除了是因为他们的福利是政府的唯一目标之外,他们的优秀品质也为政府机器的运转提供动力。政府机器本身的性质,也就成了构成政府优点的另外一个要素了。也就是说,政府机器本身的性质就是它适合于利用全部的优良品质的程度,而这些优良品质在任何时候都可能存在,并且使它们成为实现正确目标的工具。让我们再举司法作为例子来加以阐释吧。司法体系一旦形成,司法中的优点就和法庭的人员组成以及影响和控制他们的舆论的价值成比例。好与坏的司法体系的区别就在于它的方法,这种方法就是要将社会中存在的一切道德和智力的价值拿来,施加给执法过程,并使它对司法的结果起充分作用。为了使法官的挑选能得到最高水平的美德和智慧而作的安排,有益的程序模式,允许观察和对任何错误进行批评的公开性,通过媒体进行讨论和批评的自由,按照是否适于导出真相的取证模式,不管有多少都有接近法庭的机会,侦查和逮捕罪犯的程序,——所有这一切都不是权力,而是使用权力来排除障碍的机器。并且这部机器本身不会采取行动,但是如果没有它,不管有多大的权力,都会是徒劳的。行政部门的构成也存在着类似的区别。行政部门的运转机器是好的:有对官员资格的适当考察,对他们升迁的适当规定;事务被方便地分配到处理它们的人员中去,有处理事务的方便有效的程序,在事

for their promotion ; when the business is conveniently distributed among those who are to transact it, a convenient and methodical order established for its transaction, a correct and intelligible record kept of it after being transacted; when each individual knows for what he is responsible, and is known to others as responsible for it; when the best-contrived checks are provided against negligence, favoritism, or jobbery in any of the acts of the department. But political checks will no more act of themselves, than a bridle will direct a horse without a rider. If the checking functionaries are as corrupt or as negligent as those whom they ought to check, and if the public, the mainspring of the whole checking machinery, are too ignorant, too passive, or too careless and inattentive, to do their part, little benefit will be derived from the best administrative apparatus. Yet a good apparatus is always preferable to a bad. It enables such insufficient moving or checking power as exists, to act at the greatest advantage; and without it, no amount of moving or checking power would be sufficient. Publicity, for instance, is no impediment to evil or stimulus to good if the public will not look at what is done ; but without publicity, how could they either check or encourage what they were not permitted to see ? The ideally perfect constitution of a public office is that in which the interest of the functionary is entirely coincident with his duty. No more system will make it so, but still less can it be made so without a system, aptly devised for the purpose.

What we have said of the arrangements for the detailed administration of the government, is still more evidently true of its general constitution. All government which aims at being good, is an organization of some part of the good qualities existing in the individual members of the community, for the conduct of its collective affairs. A representative constitution is a means of bringing the general standard of intelligence and honesty existing in the community, and the individual intellect and virtue of its wisest members, more directly to bear upon the government, and investing them with greater influence in it than they would in general have under any other mode of organization; though, under any, such influence as they do have is the source of all good that there is in the government, and the hindrance of every evil that there is not. The greater the amount of these good qualities which the institutions of a country succeed in organizing, and the better the mode of organization, the better will be thegovernment.

务被处理后有准确和明了的记录;每个人都知道他的职责范围,别人也知道他的责任所在;对部门中的任何疏忽、偏袒以及假公济私都有精心设计的调查方法。但政治监察自己不会行动,就像如果没有骑手,缰绳不能指挥马儿一样。如果进行监察的官员和那些被检查的官员一样腐败和玩忽职守,如果作为整个监察机制的主要动力的公众太无知,太消极,或者太粗心,太麻木,那么,最好的行政机构也不能带来丝毫好处。但是尽管这样,好的机构也总是比坏的要更为可取。它能使目前如此不充分的运转以及监察动力得到最大程度的发挥;没有它,不管多大的运转或监察动力都会是不充足的。例如,公开的宣传——如果公众对所做的事漠不关心的话——既不能阻止坏事也不能鼓励好事,但是如果没有公开的宣传,公众又如何对他们不允许看到的事情加以阻止或者鼓励呢?理想的完美的公众机关的构成,就是在这个机构中,官员的利益和他的职责完全相符。单靠制度是做不到这一点的,但没有为这一目标设计的恰当制度,就更不可能做到这一点。

我们所提到的政府各项行政安排,对政府的一般构成来说仍然更为适用。所有想要成为好政府的政府,就是一个为了管理集体事务而组成的、拥有存在于社会单个成员中的某些良好特质的组织。代议制政体就是这样一种手段,它把存在于社会中的智慧和诚实,以及个人才智和社会成员的美德的一般标准,更加直接地施加给政府,并使他们在政府中的影响要比在任何其他形式的组织中都大。尽管在任何形式的组织下,他们所拥有的影响力是政府中一切好的事物的根源以及阻止一切坏事物的条件。一个国家的制度成功组织的良好的特质越多,以及组织模式越好,政府就会越好。

We have now, therefore, obtained a foundation for a twofold division of the merit which any set of political institutions can possess. It consists partly of the degree in which they promote the general mental advancement of the community, including under that phrase advancement in intellect, in virtue, and in practical activity and efficiency; and partly of the degree of perfection with which they organize the moral, intellectual, and active worth already existing, so as to operate with the greatest effect on public affairs. A government is to be judged by its action upon men, and by its action upon things; by what it makes of the citizens, and what it does with them ; its tendency to improve or deteriorate the people themselves, and the goodness or badness of the work it performs for them, and by means of them. Government is at once a great influence acting on the human mind, and a set of organized arrangements for public business: in the first capacity its beneficial action is chiefly indirect, but not therefore less vital, while its mischievous action may be direct.

The difference between these two functions of a government is not, like that between Order and Progress, a difference merely in degree, but in kind. We must not, however, suppose that they have no intimate connexion with one another. The institutions which ensure the best management of public affairs practicable in the existing state of cultivation, tend by this alone to the further improvement of that state. A people which had the most just laws, the purest and most efficient judicature, the most enlightened administration, the most equitable and least onerous system of finance, compatible with the stage it had attained in moral and intellectual advancement, would be in a fair way to pass rapidly into a higher stage. Nor is there any mode in which political institutions can contribute more effectually to the improvement of the people, than by doing their more direct work well. And, reversely, if their machinery is so badly constructed that they do their own particular business ill, the effect is felt in a thousand ways in lowering the morality and deadening the intelligence and activity of the people.

因此，现在我们已经得到一个用来对任何一套政治制度都会有的优点进行双重区分的基础。这个基础部分由政治制度促进社会普遍精神上的进步程度所构成，包括在智力、美德，以及实践活动和效率方面的进步；部分由它们组织已有的道德、智力以及积极的价值的完美程度所组成，以便在公共事务方面发挥最大的效应。人们是通过政府对其人民以及事情的所作所为，通过它训练公民的手段以及它如何对待公民，它使人民进步还是堕落的倾向，它对人民和依靠人民所做的工作的好与坏，来判断政府的好与坏的。政府马上就成了对人类思想上有巨大影响，成了一套为了公共事务的有组织的安排：就前者而言，它的有益的作用一般是间接的，但并不因此就不是关键的，而它的有害的作用则可以是直接的。

政府这两个功能之间的区别，不像"秩序"与"进步"之间仅仅是程度上的区别，而是性质的不同。然而，我们不能因此认为它们之间就没有密切的联系。能保证在现有的文化状态下对公共事务进行最佳管理的制度，单凭这一点就能将那种状态作进一步的改进。一个民族具有与其道德和智力进步达到的阶段相协调一致的最公正的法律、最完美有效的司法、最开明的行政、最公平和最不繁重的财政体系，就能相当迅速地进入到一个更高的阶段。没什么模式能比政治机构的基本工作更有效地促进民众进步的了。反过来，如果政治机构建造得如此糟糕，以至于它们将各自的事情做得一塌糊涂，就会处处感受到它降低人民的道德水平和压抑他们的才智以及活动能力的后果。但这种差别是真实存在的，因为这只是政治制度用来提高或者损害人类思想的方法之一，并且有益或有害影响的原因和

But the distinction is nevertheless real, because this is only one of the means by which political institutions improve or deteriorate the human mind, and the causes and modes of that beneficial or injurious influence remain a distinct and much wider subject of study.

Of the two modes of operation by which a form of government or set of political institutions affects the welfare of the community—its operation as an agency of national education, and its arrangements for conducting the collective affairs of the community in the state of education in which they already are; the last evidently varies much less, from difference of country and state of civilization, than the first. It has also much less to do with the fundamental constitution of the government. The mode of conducting the practical business of government, which is best under a free constitution, would generally be best also in an absolute monarchy: only, an absolute monarchy is not so likely to practise it. The laws of property, for example ; the principles of evidence and judicial procedure; the system of taxation and of financial administration, need not necessarily be different in different forms of government. Each of these matters has principles and rules of its own, which are a subject of separate study. General jurisprudence, civil and penal legislation, financial and commercial policy, are sciences in themselves, or rather, separate members of the comprehensive science or art of government: and the most enlightened doctrines on all these subjects, though not equally likely to be understood and acted on under all forms of government, yet, if understood and acted on, would in general be equally beneficial under them all. It is true that these doctrines could not be applied without some modifications to all states of society and of the human mind: neverthelesss, by far the greater number of them would require modifications solely of detail, to adapt them to any state of society sufficiently advanced to possess rulers capable of understanding them. A government to which they would be wholly unsuitable, must be one so bad in itself, or so opposed to public feeling, as to be unable to maintain itself in existence by honest means.

It is otherwise with that portion of the interests of the community which relate to the better or worse training of the people themselves. Considered as instrumental to this, institutions need to be radically different, according to the stage of advancement already reached. The recognition of this truth, though for the most part empirically rather than philosophically, may be regarded as the main point of superiority

模式仍然是一个明显和相当宽广的研究领域。

就一种政府形式或一套政治制度影响社会福利的两种操作模式——它作为国民教育机关的操作,以及它作为在已有教育状况下处理社会集体事务的安排——来说,在不同的国家和不同的文明状态中,后一种要比前一种的变化要小得多。它对政府的基本构成的关系也没那么大。在自由政体下是最好的处理实际事务的模式,同样在君主政体下也是最好的,只是君主政体不会太愿意去实行它。例如,关于财产的法律,取证和司法程序的原则,纳税制度和财政管理,在不同的政府形式中就没有必要有所不同。这些事情每一件都有其自身的原则和规定。一般法学,民事和刑事法学,财政和商业政策,本身都是科学,或者说是综合科学或统治艺术的相互独立的部分。在所有这些学科中的最开明的原则,尽管不是在所有政府形式下都会被同样地去理解和执行,可是,如果它们得以理解和执行,那么所有这些政府形式下都会有同样的好处。毫无疑问,这些学说在不同的社会状况和不同的人类思想发展阶段需要做些修正,但是到目前为止,它们中的相当部分都只需要作些细节上的修正以适应充分发展到拥有能够理解它们的统治者的任何社会状况。一个完全不能容纳这些学说的政府,必定是一个自身很糟糕的政府,或者是一个由于如此反对公众情绪,以至于不能依靠诚实的手段来维持其自身存在的政府。

否则,它就是和那部分涉及到民众本身较好或较坏训练的利益相关。考虑到在这方面的工具性作用,制度应当根据早已取得的发展阶段明显地有所不同。对于这一真理的认识,尽管还是从经验上而不是从哲学上的认识,可以被看作是当今政治

in the political theories of the present above those of the last age; in which it was customary to claim representative democracy for England or France by arguments which would equally have proved it the only fit form of government for Bedouins or Malaya. The state of different communities, in point of culture and development, ranges downwards to a condition very little above the highest of the beasts. The upward range, too, is considerable, and the future possible extension vastly greater. A community can only be developed out of one of these states into a higher, by a concourse of influences, among the principal of which is the government to which they are subject. In all states of human improvement ever yet attained, the nature and degree of authority exercised over individuals, the distribution of power, and the conditions of command and obedience are the most powerful of the influences, except their religious belief, which make them what they are, and enable them to become what they can be. They may be stopped short at any point in their progress by defective adaptation of their government to that particular stage of advancement. And the one indispensable merit of a government, in favour of which it may be forgiven almost any amount of other demerit compatible with progress, is that its operation on the people is favourable, or not unfavourable, to the next step which it is necessary for them to take in order to raise them selves to a higher level.

Thus (to repeat a former example), a people in a state of savage independence, in which every one lives for himself, exempt, unless by fits, from any external control, is practically incapable of making any progress in civilization until it has learnt to obey. The indispensable virtue, therefore, in a government which establishes itself over a people of this sort is, that it make itself obeyed. To enable it to do this, the constitution of the government must be nearly, or quite, despotic. A constitution in any degree popular, dependent on the voluntary surrender by the different members of the community of their individual freedom of action, would fail to enforce the first lesson which the pupils, in this stage of their progress, require. Accordingly, the civilization of such tribes, when not the result of juxtaposition with others

学较之过去政治学的主要优越之处。在过去时代,主张在英国或是法国实行代议制是司空见惯的,其所凭依据同样会证明这对贝都因人或马来人来说也是最好的政府形式。从文化和发展的视角看,不同的社会状况向下排列,其最低状况比动物的最高状况稍好一些。同样,向上排列,发展的空间也是相当广阔的,而将来的可能扩展则更大得多。社会只能根据各种影响的汇合,从其中的一个状态向更高的状态发展,在这些影响中,主要的就是它们所从属的政府。在人类已经达到的所有进步状态中,施加于个人的权威本质和程度、权力的配置、统治和服从的条件都是最有力的影响,当然他们的宗教信仰除外。这些影响使他们成为现在的样子,并且使他们变成他们能变成的样子。由于他们的政府与特定的发展阶段不相适应,他们可能在任何一个进步阶段突然停下来。政府的一个绝对必要的优点——为了支持这个观点,可以原谅几乎任何其他在进步中出现的缺陷——就是它对民众的统治是有利于,或者不是不利于民众为了将他们自身提升到一个更高的阶段,所必须采取的下一个步骤。

因此(重复前面一个例子),一个处于野蛮未开化的独立状态的民族——在这种状态中每个人都为自己活着,除非偶然,不受外部的控制——在学会服从之前,实际上是不能在文明方面有任何进步的。因此,在将自己建立在这样一个民族之上的政府,可或缺的美德就是要使自己得到人们的服从。为了使它能做到这一点,政体必须近乎或者相当专制。一个在任何程度上普遍的,依靠其社会不同成员自愿放弃他们个人自由行动的政体,不能将处于这个发展阶段上人所需要的第一课进行贯彻实行,从而,这样的部族的文明,如果不是和那些早已开化的部族比邻

already civilized, is almost always the work of an absolute ruler, deriving his power from either religion or military prowess—very often from foreign arms.

Again, uncivilized races, and the bravest and most energetic still more than the rest, are averse to continuous labour of an unexciting kind. Yet all real civilization is at this price; without such labour, neither can the mind be disciplined into the habits required by civilized society, nor the material world prepared to receive it. There needs a rare concurrence of circumstances, and for that reason often a vast length of time, to reconcile such a people to industry, unless they are for a while compelled to it. Hence even personal slavery, by giving a commencement to industrial life, and enforcing it as the exclusive occupation of the most numerous portion of the community, may accelerate the transition to a better freedom than that of fighting and rapine. It is almost needless to say that this excuse for slavery is only available in a very early state of society. A civilized people have far other means of imparting civilization to those under their influence; and slavery is, in all its details, so repugnant to that government of law, which is the foundation of all modern life, and so corrupting to the master-class when they have once come under civilized influences, that its adoption under any circumstances whatever in modern society is a relapse into worse than barbarism.

At some period, however, of their history, almost every people, now civilized, have consisted, in majority, of slaves. A people in that condition require to raise them out of it a very different polity from a nation of savages. If they are energetic by nature, and especially if there be associated with them in the same community an industrious class who are neither slaves nor slave-owners (as was the case in Greece), they need, probably, no more to ensure their improvement than to make them free : when freed, they may often be fit, like Roman freedmen, to be admitted at once to the full rights of citizenship. This, however, is not the normal condition of slavery, and is generally

而居的结果,那就几乎总是权力来自宗教或者军事威慑(经常是外国军队的威慑)的专制君主的杰作。

又比如,未开化的种族不愿意从事持续的单调的劳动,而且那些最勇敢,精力最充沛的部族要比其他部族更加如此。然而,真正的文明需要付出过这样的代价,没有这样的劳动,人既不能形成文明社会所需要的习惯,也不能为物质世界所接受。这需要非常难得的巧合,并且由于这个原因,需要相当长的时间来使人民变得勤奋起来,除非他们有时被强迫这样做。因此,即使是人身奴隶制度,由于它是勤勉生活的开始,并且被当成社会中人数最多的那个阶层的专属职业,也可能要比那种充满争斗和掠夺的社会更快速地向更自由的状态转化。毫无疑问,这就是只有在社会很早期的状态中才能起作用的为奴隶制辩护的理由。一个开化的民族有大量其他的办法来向那些处在它影响之下的民族传播文明,而奴隶制在一切细节上,都与法治相抵触,而法治是一切现代生活的基础。并且一旦当奴隶主阶级处于文明影响下,会如此腐坏,以至于现代社会在任何情况下采用奴隶制,都会倒退到比野蛮状态更为糟糕的状态中去了。

然而,几乎每个现在已经开化的民族在它们的历史中,都有某个时期主要采用奴隶制。在那种状态中的民族,为了摆脱那种状态,需要一种与野蛮民族完全不同的政治组织。如果他们天生精力旺盛,特别是如果在同一社会内,他们和一个勤劳的、既不是奴隶也不是奴隶主的阶级结合在一起(就像古希腊那样),比较确保他们的进步来说,他所需要自由。当他们自由时,可以马上赋予他们全部的公民资格,像古罗马的自由民一样。然而,这并不是奴隶制的正常情形,而通常是

a sign that it is becoming obsolete. A slave, properly so called, is a being who has not learnt to help himself. He is, no doubt, one step in advance of a savage. He has not the first lesson of political society still to acquire. He has learnt to obey. But what he obeys is only a direct command. It is the characteristic of *born* slaves to be incapable of conforming their conduct to a rule, or law. They can only do what they are ordered, and only when they are ordered to do it. If a man whom they fear is standing over them and threatening them with punishment, they obey ; but when his back is turned, the work remains undone. The motive determining them must appeal not to their interests, but to their instincts; immediate hope or immediate terror. A despotism, which may tame the savage, will, in so far as it is a despotism, only confirm the slaves in their incapacities. Yet a government under their own control would be entirely unmanageable by them. Their improvement cannot come from themselves, but must be superinduced from without. The step which they have to take, and their only path to improvement, is to be raised from a government of will to one of law. They have to be taught self-government, and this, in its initial stage, means the capacity to act on general instructions. What they require is not a government of force, but one of guidance. Being, however, in too low a state to yield to the guidance of any but those to whom they look up as the possessors of force, the sort of government fittest for them is one which possesses force, but seldom uses it : a parental despotism or aristocracy, resembling the St. Simonian form of socialism ; maintaining a general superintendence over all the operations of society, so as to keep before each the sense of a present force sufficient to compel his obedience to the rule laid down, but which, owing to the impossibility of descending to regulate all the minutiæ of industry and life, necessarily leaves and induces individuals to do much of themselves. This, which may be termed the government of leading-strings, seems to be the one required to carry such a people the most rapidly through the next necessary step in social progress. Such appears

它要被废弃的征兆。奴隶,恰当地说来,就是一个还没有学会自我救助的人。毫无疑问,他比野蛮状态更进了一步。他没有经历他仍然需要取得的政治社会所需的第一课。他学会了服从,但他所服从的只是直接的命令。天生就是奴隶的人不能使他们自己的行为和规则与法律相一致,这是他们的一个特征。他们只能做别人命令他们做的事情,并且只有当别人命令他们做时他们才会去做。如果有他们所害怕的人站在边上,以惩罚相威胁,他们就会服从;但只要他一转身,他们就不干活了。决定他们动机的一定不是他们的利益,而是他们的本能,直接的希望或直接的恐惧。专制统治也许可以驯服野蛮,但就它是专制统治而言,只能使奴隶们庸庸碌碌。然而,处在他们控制之下的政府肯定是管理不好的。他们的进步不能来自他们自己,而必须来自外部。他们必须采取的步骤,以及通向进步的唯一道路,就是从意志的统治提升到法律的统治。他们必须学会自我管理,这在它的初始阶段就意味着按照一般的指示行事的能力。他们要求的不是武力的统治,而是指导性的统治。然而,由于他们所处的阶段太低,以至于除了那些拥有武力而受到他们尊敬的人之外,他们不屈从于任何人的指导,所以最适合他们的政府就是拥有武力但又很少使用武力的政府:类似于圣·西门式社会主义那样的父亲般的专制统治或贵族统治,维持着对整个社会活动的普遍监督,以使每个人都能感觉到在他们面前有足够的压力迫使他们服从已经颁布的规则。但是由于规则没法规范行业和生活的所有微小之处,必定会听任并诱导人们去做很多他们自己的事情。这个可以被称作引导绳式政府的政府,似乎就是在社会进步中将人民以最快速度带到下一个必要阶段所需要的。这似乎曾经是秘

to have been the idea of the government of the Incas of Peru ; and such was that of the Jesuits in Paraguay. I need scarcely remark that leadingstrings are only admissible as a means of gradually training the people to walk alone.

It would be out of place to carry the illustration further. To attempt to investigate what kind of government is suited to every known state of society, would be to compose a treatise, not on representative government, but on political science at large. For our more limited purpose we borrow from political philosophy only its general principles. To determine the form of government most suited to any particular people, we must be able, among the defects and shortcomings which belong to that people, to distinguish those that are the immediate impediment to progress; to discover what it is which (as it were) stops the way. The best government for them is the one which tends most to give them that for want of which they cannot advance, or advance only in a lame and lopsided manner. We must not, however, forget the reservation necessary in all things which have for their object improvement, or Progress ; namely, that in seeking the good which is needed, no damage, or as little as possible, be done to that already possessed. A people of savages should be taught obedience, but not in such a manner as to convert them into a people of slaves. And (to give the observation a higher generality) the form of government which is most effectual for carrying a people through the next stage of progress, will still be very improper for them if it does this in such a manner as to obstruct, or positively unfit them for, the stop next beyond. Such cases are frequent, and are among the most melancholy facts in history, The Egyptian hierarchy, the paternal despotism of China, were very fit instruments for carrying those nations up to the point of civilization which they attained. But having reached that point, they were brought to a permanent halt for want of mental liberty and individuality; requisites of improvement which the institutions that had carried them thus far, entirely incapacitated them from acquiring; and as the institutions did not break down and give place to others, further improvement stopped. In contrast with these nations, let us consider the example of an opposite character afforded by another

第二章

鲁英卡斯政府的想法,也是巴拉圭的耶稣会教士的想法。不用说,只有引导绳才能作为训练人民慢慢学会独立行走的唯一可行办法。

再作进一步的说明将会是不合时宜的。试图研究什么样的政府才适合于已知的每一种社会状态,将可以写成与代议制政府无关的一篇详尽的政治学论文。为了我们有限的意图,我们仅从政治哲学那里借用了它的普遍原则。为了确定最适合于任何特定的民族的政府形式,我们必须能够从那个民族的缺点与不足中,找出那些直接妨碍进步的东西,发现(比如说)挡道的到底是什么。最适合于他们的政府就是一个最倾向于提供给他们缺少了就不能前进,或者只能以一瘸一拐的方式前进的东西的政府。然而,我们不能忘记一切以改进或者"进步"作为目标的事物中所必然含有的保留,也即是,在寻找所需要的利益过程中,不破坏或者尽量少破坏已经拥有的利益。处于野蛮阶段的民族应当被教以服从,但不能以将他们变成奴隶的方式来让他们服从。并且(为了使立论更具概括性)能最有效地使一个民族进入到发展的更高阶段的政府形式,如果它这样做的方式是阻碍,或者肯定使他们不适于更进一步的发展,那么对他们来说仍然是不合适的。这样的例子是常见的,并且是历史上最悲哀的事例。埃及的等级体制,中国家长式的专制体制,是将那些民族提升到他们已经达到的文明阶段的十分合适的工具。但是一旦达到那个阶段,他们就由于缺乏精神自由和个人自主性而永远停滞不前了。把他们带到目前阶段的制度使他们完全没有能力得到发展的必要条件,并且由于制度没有崩溃和给其他制度让路,进一步的发展就停滞了。为了与这些民族的例子相比照,我们举另一个不怎

and a comparatively insignificant Oriental people—the Jews. They too had an absolute monarchy and a hierarchy, and their organized institutions were as obviously of sacerdotal origin as those of the Hindoos. These did for them what was done for other Oriental races by their institutions—subdued them to industry and order and gave them a national life. But neither their kings nor their priests ever obtained, as in those other countries, the exclusive moulding of their character. Their religion, which enabled persons of genius and a high religious tone to be regarded and to regard themselves as inspired from heaven, gave existence to an inestimably precious unorganized institution—the Order (if it may be so termed) of Prophets. Under the protection, generally though not always effectual, of their sacred character, the Prophets were a power in the nation, often more than a match for kings and priests, and kept up, in that little corner of the earth, the antagonism of influences which is the only real security for continued progress. Religion consequently was not there, what it has been in so many other places —a consecration of all that was once established, and a barrier against further improvement. The remark of a distinguished Hebrew, M. Salvador, that the Prophets were, in Church and State, the equivalent of the modern liberty of the press, gives a just but not an adequate conception of the part fulfilled in national and universal history by this great element of Jewish life ; by means of which, the canon of inspiration never being complete, the persons most eminent in genius and moral feeling could not only denounce and reprobate, with the direct authority of the Almighty, whatever appeared to them deserving of such treatment, but could give forth better and higher interpretations of the national religion, which thenceforth became part of the religion. Accordingly, whoever can divest himself of the habit of reading the Bible as if it was one book, which until lately was equally inveterate in Christians and in unbelievers, sees with admiration the vast interval between the morality and religion of the Pentateuch, or even of the historical books

第二章

么重要的东方民族——犹太人提供的性质相反的例子。他们同样有绝对君主制和等级制,并且他们组织良好的制度跟印度人的制度一样,明显起源于祭司制度。这些制度为他们做了其他东方民族的制度为他们民族所做的同样的事情,即使他们变得勤奋和守秩序并且给他们以民族的生活。但是他们的国王和他们的祭司,都没有像在其他国家那样,取得独一无二的塑造他们性格的权力。他们的宗教,使天才以及极端虔诚的人被当成或者自己把自己当成从天堂中得到了神灵感应,产生了不可估量、极其珍贵的未经组织的制度——先知会社(如果可以这样说的话)。在他们神圣性质的保护下(一般说来尽管不总是有效),先知是一个民族中的力量所在,经常不仅仅只是国王或祭司的对手,而且在地球的那个小小角落,维持着有影响的对抗,而这种对抗性正是不断进步的唯一真正保障。因而,宗教在那里就不像它在许多其他地方那个样子———将所有一切曾经确立起来的事物的神圣化以及成为反对进一步改良的障碍。一位著名的犹太人 M. 萨尔瓦多说过,在教会和国家中,先知们和现代新闻自由具有同等的价值。此番评论,为犹太生活中的这一伟大因素在民族和世界历史中所发挥的作用提供了一个正确的但并不充分的概念。因此,关于神灵感应的教义从来不是完全的,在智力和道德情操方面最为杰出的人们,不仅可以用上帝的直接权威来抨击和谴责他们认为值得如此对待的事情,而且可以发表对民族宗教更好的和更高的解释,这些解释从此以后就成了宗教的一部分。因此,凡是那些没有把圣经当成独一无二的一本书来读的习惯的人(这种习惯直到最近在那些基督徒和非基督徒中还同样是根深蒂固的),看到摩西五书,甚至历史书(当然

(the unmistakable work of Hebrew Conservatives of the sacerdotal order), and the morality and religion of the Prophecies : a distance as wide as between these last and the Gospels. Conditions more favourable to Progress could not easily exist: accordingly, the Jews, instead of being stationary like other Asiatics, were, next to the Greeks, the most progressive people of antiquity, and, jointly with them, have been the starting-point and main propelling agency of modern cultivation.

It is, then, impossible to understand the question of the adaptation of forms of government to states of society, without taking into account not only the next step, but all the steps which society has yet to make; both those which can be foreseen, and the far wider indefinite range which is at present out of sight. It follows, that to judge of the merits of forms of government, an ideal must be constructed of the form of government most eligible in itself, that is, which, if the necessary conditions existed for giving effect to its beneficial tendencies, would, more than all others, favour and promote not some one improvement, but all forms and degrees of it. This having been done, we must consider what are the mental conditions of all sorts, necessary to enable this government to realize its tendencies, and what, therefore, are the various defects by which a people is made incapable of reaping its benefits. It would then be possible to construct a theorem of the circumstances in which that form of government may wisely be introduced; and also to judge, in cases in which it had better not be introduced, what inferior forms of polity will best carry those communities through the intermediate stages which they must traverse before they can become fit for the best form of government.

Of these inquiries, the last does not concern us here; but the first is an essential part of our subject ; for we may, without rashness, at once enunciate a proposition, the proofs and illustrations of which will present themselves in the ensuing pages ; that this ideally best form of government will be found in some one or other variety of the Representative System.

第二章

是祭司层的犹太保守主义者的著作)中的道德与宗教同预言书中的道德与宗教的巨大差距时,充满了惊叹。这种差距和预言书同福音书的之间的差距一样大。比这更有利于"进步"的条件不容易找到,因此,犹太人不像其他亚洲人那样安于现状,而是像古希腊人那样,是古代民族中最具有进取心的民族,并且和古希腊人一起,成为了现代文明的起点和主要驱动力。

所以,如果不重视下一步骤,并且不重视社会仍需采取的所有步骤,那么就不可能理解政府形式与社会状态相适应的问题:既要重视那些能够预见的,又要重视那些尚不在视野范围内的更为广阔、不确定的东西。接下来的问题是,要判断政府形式的优点,就必须建构一个最为符合条件的政府形式的理想模式,也就是说如果存在实现其有益趋向的必要条件,它就会比其他任何形式更有利和促进不仅是它的某个方面的改进,而且是所有形式和程度的改进。一旦做到了这一点,我们就必须考虑什么是能够使这种政府形式实现它趋向的各种各样的必要的智力条件,以及什么是一个民族不能受益的各种各样的缺陷。于是,我们就可能建构一条关于在什么情况下可以明智地采用那种政府形式的法则,并且也可以判断,在最好不采用这种政府形式的场合,什么样的次优政体在这些社会能适应最好政府形式之前帮助它们度过它们必须经历的中间阶段。

在上面的讨论中,后者与本书没有关系,但前者却是我们主题的基本部分,因为我们可以郑重地提出一个命题——在以下的章节中将进行这一命题的证明和阐释——就是这种理想的最好的政府形式将可以在这样或那样的代议制中找到。

CHAPTER III

That The Ideally Best Form Of Government Is Representative Government

It has long (perhaps throughout the entire duration of British freedom) been a common form of speech, that if a good despot could be ensured, despotic monarchy would be the best form of government. I look upon this as a radical and most pernicious misconception of what good government is ; which, until it can be got rid of, will fatally vitiate all our speculations on government.

The supposition is, that absolute power, in the hands of an eminent individual, would ensure a virtuous and intelligent performance of all the duties of government. Good laws would be established and enforced, bad laws would be reformed ; the best men would be placed in all situations of trust; justice would be as well administered, the public burthens would be as light and as judiciously imposed, every branch of administration would be as purely and as intelligently conducted, as the circumstances of the country, and its degree of intellectual and moral cultivation would admit. I am willing, for the sake of the argument, to concede all this ; but I must point out how great the concession is ; how much more is needed to produce even an approximation to these results, than is conveyed in the simple expression, a good despot. Their realization would in fact imply, not merely a good monarch, but an all-seeing one. He must be at all times informed correctly, in considerable detail, of the conduct and working of every branch of administration, in every district of the country,

第三章 理论上最好的政府形式是代议制政府

很长一段时间以来(或许在英国人为自由而奋斗的整个期间),有句俗语说,只要能确保有一个好的专制君主,君主专制政体将会是最理想的政府形式。依我看,这是关于什么是好的政府的一种偏激的也是最有害的误区。如果不消除这种误区,则将严重地削弱我们关于政府的一切理论。

这一俗语的预设条件是,卓越人物手中的绝对权力将确保善意地、睿智地履行好政府的所有职责。良法将被创建并加以实施,恶法将得到改革;最杰出的人将被委派到一切负责的位置上;根据这个国家的实际情形以及它的知识水平和道德教化程度所容许的条件,司法公正将得到很好的贯彻,公共赋税将规定得很轻而且恰到好处,每个行政部门将进行廉正而睿智的治理。为了便于辩论,对以上这一切,我愿意接受;但是我必须指出这种妥协是多么巨大;甚至如果要达到和这一切相接近的结果,它也要求有比好的专制君主这个简单词汇所蕴涵的意义多得多的东西。事实上,这些结果要得以实现的话,将意味着他不仅仅是一个好的君主,而且是一个全能的君主。在任何时候,他都必须非常详尽而正确地通晓国家每个地区每个行政部门的行为和工作状况,为有效地关注和监管这广阔领域的一切部分,如同赋予一个最卑微

and must be able, in the twenty-four hours per day, which are all that is granted to a king as to the humblest labourer, to give an effective share of attention and superintendence to all parts of this vast field; or he must at least be capable of discerning and choosing out, from among the mass of his subjects, not only a large abundance of honest and able men, fit to conduct every branch of public administration under supervision and control, but also the small number of men of eminent virtues and talents who can be trusted not only to do without that supervision, but to exercise it themselves over others. So extraordinary are the faculties and energies required for performing this task in any supportable manner, that the good despot whom we are supposing can hardly be imagined as consenting to undertake it, unless as a refuge from intolerable evils, and a transitional preparation for something beyond. But the argument can do without even this immense item in the account. Suppose the difficulty vanquished. What should we then have ? One man of superhuman mental activity managing the entire affairs of a mentally passive people. Their passivity is implied in the very idea of absolute power. The nation as a whole, and every individual composing it, are without any potential voice in their own destiny. They exercise no will in respect to their collective interests. All is decided for them by a will not their own, which it is legally a crime for them to disobey. What sort of human beings can be formed under such a regimen ? What development can either their thinking or their active faculties attain under it ? On matters of pure theory they might perhaps be allowed to speculate, so long as their speculations either did not approach politics, or had not the remotest connexion with its practice. On practical affairs they could at most be only suffered to suggest ; and even under the most moderate of despots, none but persons of already admitted or reputed superiority could hope that their suggestions would be known to, much less regarded by, those who had the management of affairs. A person must have a very unusual taste for intellectual exercise in and for itself, who will put himself to the trouble of thought when it is to have no outward effect, or qualify himself for functions which he has no chance of being allowed to exercise.

第三章

的劳动者的劳动时间一样,他必须能够付出他的全部时间即一天24小时;或者至少他的臣民群众中,他不仅必须识别和挑选出一大批忠诚而有才华的人,在监督和控制下,这些人适宜管理每个公共行政部门,而且必须识别和挑选出少数具有伟大美德和才华出众的人,这些人在没有监管的情形下不仅可以被委以重任,而且能对其他人行使监督。具备非凡的才华和过人的精力才能勉勉强强履行好这一职责。因此,除非为了躲避不可忍受的祸害和对将来的事情作过渡的准备,很难想象我们所假定的好的专制君主会赞同承担这种职责。但即使没有上面所提到的诸多重大责任,这一观点也站得住。倘若困难得以克服,到时候情形又如何呢?一个具有超人的精神能量的人,掌管着精神上被动消极的民众的所有事务。绝对权力这个观念,本身预示着他们的消极被动性。整个民族和构成民族的每个个体,对他们自己的命运,没有任何可能的发言权。关于他们的公共利益,他们体现不出自己的意志。不是源于他们自己意志的意志决定了他们所有的一切,而对他们来讲,不服从这种意志就是法律上的犯罪。那么,在这种制度下,能造就出什么类型的人呢?他们的思想或活动能力能得到怎样的增进呢?只要他们的理论是不牵涉到政治,或者与实践毫无关联,他们也许能被允许探究纯理论的问题。至于实际事务方面,他们充其量只能被允许提点建议。而即使在最有节制的专制君主的情况下,也只有被认为杰出或以卓越出名的人,才能指望他们的建议能被负责管理事务的人们知晓,至于受到器重就更谈不上了。一个人,当他的智力活动不会有什么外在的效果却要不辞辛苦地去思想,或者对于并无指望被允许去担任的职务,他自己却竭力去适合于它,那么,对于智力活动本身,这

The only sufficient incitement to mental exertion, in any but a few minds in a generation, is the prospect of some practical use to be made of its results. It does not follow that the nation will be wholly destitute of intellectual power. The common business of life, which must necessarily be performed by each individual or family for themselves, will call forth some amount of intelligence and practical ability, within a certain narrow range of ideas. There may be a select class of *savants*, who cultivate science with a view to its physical uses, or for the pleasure of the pursuit. There will be a bureaucracy, and persons in training for the bureaucracy, who will be taught at least some empirical maxims of government and public administration. There may be, and often has been, a systematic organization of the best mental power in the country in some special direction (commonly military) to promote the grandeur of the despot. But the public at large remain without information and without interest on all the greater matters of practice ; or, if they have any knowledge of them, it is but a *dilettante* knowledge, like that which people have of the mechanical arts who have never handled a tool. Nor is it only in their intelligence that they suffer. Their moral capacities are equally stunted. Where-ever the sphere of action of human beings is artificially circumscribed, their sentiments are narrowed and dwarfed in the same proportion. The food of feeling is action: even domestic affection lives upon voluntary good offices. Let a person have nothing to do for his country, and he will not care for it. It has been said of old, that in a despotism there is at most but one patriot, the despot himself; and the saying rests on a just appreciation of the effects of absolute subjection, even to a good and wise master. Religion remains: and here at least, it may be thought, is an agency that may be relied on for lifting men's eyes and minds above the dust at their feet. But religion, even supposing it to escape perversion for the purposes of despotism, ceases in these circumstances to be a social concern, and narrows into a personal

个人一定具有极不寻常的嗜好。智力活动的结果有被实际采纳的可能性,是智力活动的唯一充分的刺激(在一代人中,这不过是属于少数几个人的情形)。但并不由此我们就断言这个民族整体上智力水平是匮乏的。世俗生活方面的事务,它必然要由每个人或每个家庭自己料理,将激发出他们相当程度的智力和实际能力(就这些概念的一定的窄小范围而言)。或许出现过第一流的大学者,为了科学的实际用处,或者是为了在研究上得到乐趣,他们不懈地探索科学。将会有一伙官僚集团以及被教化担任官僚的人,他们将习得至少某些政府管理和公共行政的经验原则。可能有也往往有过系统化的组织,这个组织由国家的最好的智力在某个特殊方面(一般是军事方面)构成,从而增进专制君主的伟大。但一般民众依然对此一无所知,并对一切较大的实际问题缺乏兴趣;或者,如果他们对这些问题有一些了解的话,那也不过是似懂非懂,就像一个从未用过工具的人一样,尽管他了解一些机械知识。除了在知识方面他们受到妨碍外,他们的道德能力方面同样也遭受阻碍。人们的活动范围一旦受到人为的阻滞,相应地,他们的感情也就变得狭隘甚至不健全。行动是感情的滋养品:甚至家庭的感情也是由主动的照料孕育的。如果一个人不能为他的国家做任何事情,他也就不关心他的国家。一直以来,有一句谚语是这样说的,在专制国家中充其量只有一个爱国者,就是专制君主自己。这个谚语是以正确领悟绝对服从的后果为依据的,哪怕只是对善良而明智的统治者的服从。还有宗教,或许可以认为,宗教至少是一种凭借它可以用来提升人们的眼界和思想境界的种力量。但是即使假定宗教不会为了实现专制政治的意图而遭受扭曲,在这种状况下,宗教也不再是一种社会关注的事,而

affair between an individual and his Maker, in which the issue at stake is but his private salvation. Religion in this shape is quite consistent with the most selfish and contracted egoism, and identifies the votary as little in feeling with the rest of his kind as sensuality itself.

A good despotism means a government in which, so far as depends on the despot, there is no positive oppression by officers of state, but in which all the collective interests of the people are managed for them, all the thinking that has relation to collective interests done for them, and in which their minds are formed by, and consenting to, this abdication of their own energies. Leaving things to the Government, like leaving them to Providence, is synonymous with caring nothing about them, and accepting their results, when disagreeable, as visitations of Nature. With the exception, therefore, of a few studious men who take an intellectual interest in speculation for its own sake, the intelligence and sentiments of the whole people are given up to the material interests, and when these are provided for, to the amusement and ornamentation of private life. But to say this is to say, if the whole testimony of history is worth anything, that the era of national decline has arrived: that is, if the nation had ever attained anything to decline from. If it has never risen above the condition of an Oriental people, in that condition it continues to stagnate. But if, like Greece or Rome, it had realized anything higher, through the energy, patriotism, and enlargement of mind, which as national qualities are the fruits solely of freedom, it relapses in a few generations into the Oriental state. And that state does not mean stupid tranquillity, with security against change for the worse; it often means being overrun, conquered, and reduced to domestic slavery, either by a stronger despot, or by the nearest barbarous people who retain along with their savage rudeness the energies of freedom.

Such are not merely the natural tendencies, but the inherent necessities of despotic government ; from which there is no outlet, unless in so far as the despotism consents not to be despotism ; in so far as the supposed good despot abstains from exercising his power, and,

第三章

演变为个人和上帝之间的私事,他个人的救赎问题才是利益攸关的问题。这种状态的宗教和最自私自利最狭隘的利己主义是完全合拍的,和肉欲本身一样,它无法使信仰者在感情上和其同类协调起来。

好的专制政治是这样一个政府:在这个政府里,就依赖专制君主而言,不存在国家官员的实际压迫,民众的一切公共利益由政府替他们进行治理,政府会替他们考虑有关公共利益的一切,这种民众对自我的能力放弃的认同,也孕育了他们的思想。就像由上帝作主一样,一切事都由政府作主,这就意味着民众对一切事漠不关心,假使不合乎自己的意思的话,把它们的结果当作上天的惩罚来加以接受,所以,除了少数勤学的人,他们对思维本身有智力上的爱好之外,所有民众的智力和感情让位于物质的利益,并且在拥有物质利益之后进而让位于私生活的娱乐和美化。如果这样说,即意味着,如果全部历史的见证还存在价值的话,民族衰败的时代已经来临,换句话说,如果这个民族曾经实现某种文明的话。与东方民族的状况相比,如果这个民族并没有超越这种状态,在那种情况下,它将维持一种停滞的现状。但如果像希腊或罗马那样,由于这些民族具有活动能力强、爱国主义和胸襟开阔的特质,这种特质完全是自由的产物,它们曾经生成了较高的文明,在几个世代之后,它又回归到东方的状态。而那种状态并不意味着停滞不动,使情形不会变得更加糟糕,它往往意味着会遭受到更强大的专制君主,或是保持着原始和自由活力的邻近未开化民族的侵略、征服,并沦落为国内的奴隶。

这不仅是专制政府的本能倾向,而且是它的内在的必然性。除非法制体制同意本身不再足专制体制,否则就没有出路被设想为专制君主的人不执行他的权力,并且,尽管保留着这项权力,

though holding it in reserve, allows the general business of government to go on as if the people really governed themselves. However little probable it may be, we may imagine a despot observing many of the rules and restraints of constitutional government. He might allow such freedom of the press and of discussion as would enable a public opinion to form and express itself on national affairs. He might suffer local interests to be managed, without the interference of authority, by the people themselves. He might even surround himself with a council or councils of government, freely chosen by the whole or some portion of the nation ; retaining in his own hands the power of taxation, and the supreme legislative as well as executive authority. Were he to act thus, and so far abdicate as a despot, he would do away with a considerable part of the evils characteristic of despotism. Political activity and capacity for public affairs would no longer be prevented from growing up in the body of the nation ; and a public opinion would form itself, not the mere echo of the government. But such improvement would be the beginning of new difficulties. This public opinion, independent of the monarch's dictation, must be either with him or against him ; if not the one, it will be the other. All governments must displease many persons, and these having now regular organs, and being able to express their sentiments, opinions adverse to the measures of government would often be expressed. What is the monarch to do when these unfavourable opinions happen to be in the majority? Is he to alter his course ? Is he to defer to the nation ? If so, he is no longer a despot but a constitutional king; an organ or first minister of the people, distinguished only by being irremovable. If not, he must either put down opposition by his despotic power, or there will arise a permanent antagonism between the people and one man, which can have but one possible ending. Not even a religious principle of passive obedience and ' right divine' would long ward off the natural consequences of such a position. The monarch would have to succumb, and conform to the conditions of constitutional royalty, or give place to some one who would. The despotism, being thus chiefly nominal, would possess few of the advantages supposed to belong to

第三章

让政府的一般事务运转得就像是人民在真正管理自己那样,否则这是无法避免的。不管这种可能性是怎样微乎其微,我们可以想象一下有这样一个专制君主:他遵守着宪政政府的很多规则和限制,他可能允许出版和言论自由,这些使舆论得以形成,并对国家事务发表看法;他可能在地方的利益不受政府操纵的情况下允许民众自治;他甚至可能在自己周围创建一个或多个政府委员会,该政府委员会由全体或部分民众自由选出,而在自己手中保存着赋税权和最高的立法权和行政权力。假如他能如此做,并始终放弃专制君主的特权,他将消除掉专制政府独有的一大部分弊端。对公共事务的政治主动性和能力将不再受到阻碍地在人民内部得以发展,而一种公共舆论将得以自然形成,这种舆论不再是政府的附庸。不过,这样的进步将是新的障碍的开始。这种舆论,由于不受君主控制,注定是要么支持他,要么就是反对他;不是前者就是后者。全能的政府一定会招致许多人不快,而这些人现在有了能够传递他们的感情的正式的机构,因此不赞同政府措施的观点也往往会表达出来。当这些不利意见恰好是大多数人的意见时,君主该何去何从呢?他将调整他的既定方针吗?他将顺从人民的意愿吗?如果他这样做的话,他就是立宪君主,而不再是专制君主了。前者作为人民的代表机构或第一公正机构,不能罢免是这个机构的特点。如果并非如此,为了镇压反对意见,要么他就必须行使他的专制权力,要么就将出现人民和独裁者之间的持续的冲突,它的结果只能有一个。就算是消极顺从的宗教教义和"神权"也不能长期阻止这种状况的自然结果。君主将不得不妥协,并遵循立宪君主的条件,或者由愿意这样做的人取而代之。如此说来,君主专制将不再具有被认为属于绝对君主制的很多优

absolute monarchy; while it would realize in a very imperfect degree those of a free government ; since however great an amount of liberty the citizens might practically enjoy, they could never forget that they held it on sufferance, and by a concession which under the existing constitution of the state might at any moment be resumed ; that they were legally slaves, though of a prudent, or indulgent, master.

It is not much to be wondered at, if impatient or disappointed reformers, groaning under the impediments opposed to the most salutary public improvements by the ignorance, the indifference, the untractableness, the perverse obstinacy of a people, and the corrupt combinations of selfish private interests armed with the powerful weapons afforded by free institutions, should at times sigh for a strong hand to bear down all these obstacles, and compel a recalcitrant people to be better governed. But (setting aside the fact, that for one despot who now and then reforms an abuse, there are ninety-nine who do nothing but create them) those who look in any such direction for the realization of their hopes leave out of the idea of good government its principal element. , the improvement of the people themselves. One of the benefits of freedom is that under it the ruler cannot pass by the people's minds, and amend their affairs for them without amending *them*. If it were possible for a people to be well governed in spite of themselves, their good government would last no longer than the freedom of a people usually lasts who have been liberated by foreign arms without their own cooperation. It is true, a despot may educate the people ; and to do so really, would be the best apology for his despotism. But any education which aims at making human beings other than machines, in the long run makes them claim to have the control of their own actions. The leaders of French philosophy in the eighteenth century had been educated by the Jesuits. Even Jesuit education, it seems, was sufficiently real to call forth the appetite for freedom.

第三章

点,因为它基本上是名义上的;另一方面,它将在很不完全的程度上实现一个自由政府的优点。因为不管公民事实上享有的自由度可能有多大,他们绝不会忘记,他们是勉强被宽许享有这种自由的,并且在国家的现有政体下,这种自由是依赖一种随时可能被收回的让步而享有的。必须铭记他们在法律上是奴隶,尽管他们是一个审慎的或者是宽容的君主的奴隶。

如果由于人民的没有知识、漠不关心、倔强、刚愎自用,以及由于用自由制度所提供的强有力的武器武装起来的自私的个人利益的腐败,这两者的结合对最有益的公共利益的改进设置了重重障碍,而受制于这些障碍下的改革家们,他们失去了耐心,或者深感沮丧,有时居然盼望一个强权人物来摧毁所有这些障碍,以强迫不顺从的人民接受较好的治理,这是不足为奇的。但是(暂且搁下这一事实:如果出现一个不断改革弊政的专制君主,那么就会出现九十九个只会生产弊政的专制君主)朝着这一方向追求实现他们的愿望的人们,从好政府的观念中忽略了其主要的因素,即人民自身的进步。自由制度的优点之一就是在该制度下,主政者不能不去顾及人民的意愿,只是为他们改善事务,而不去提升他们。倘若不顾及人民的意愿也能将他们治理好的话,与经由外国武力解放而却没有得到与其合作的人民的自由相比,他们的理想政府的这种自由不可能比其持续得更久远。当然,专制君主可能会教化他的人民;而真正如此做的话,将是对他的专制统治的最好的辩护。但是,只要是定位于成就人而不是制作机器的教育最终都会有这样的诉求,即控制他们自己的行动。18世纪法国哲学界的先驱们就是由耶稣会会员教育出来的。看来,甚至耶稣会的教育也足以真正激发对自由的追

Whatever invigorates the faculties, in however small a measure, creates an increased desire for their more unimpeded exercise; and a popular education is a failure, if it educates the people for any state but that which it will certainly induce them to desire, and most probably to demand.

  I am far from condemning, in cases of extreme exigency, the assumption of absolute power in the form of a temporary dictatorship. Free nations have, in times of old, conferred such power by their own choice, as a necessary medicine for diseases of the body politic which could not be got rid of by less violent means. But its acceptance, even for a time strictly limited, can only be excused, if, like Solon or Pittacus, the dictator employs the whole power he assumes in removing the obstacles which debar the nation from the enjoyment of freedom. A good despotism is an altogether false ideal, which practically (except as a means to some temporary purpose) becomes the most senseless and dangerous of chimeras. Evil for evil, a good despotism, in a country at all advanced in civilization, is more noxious than a bad one; for it is far more relaxing and enervating to the thoughts, feelings, and energies of the people. The despotism of Augustus prepared the Romans for Tiberius. If the whole tone of their character had not first been prostrated by nearly two generations of that mild slavery, they would probably have had spirit enough left to rebel against the more odious one.

  There is no difficulty in showing that the ideally best form of government is that in which the sovereignty, or supreme controlling power in the last resort, is vested in the entire aggregate of the community ; every citizen not only having a voice in the exercise of that ultimate sovereignty, but being, at least occasionally, called on to take an actual part in the government, by the personal discharge of some public function, local or general.

  To test this proposition, it has to be examined in reference to the two branches into which, as pointed out in the last chapter, the inquiry into the goodness of a government conveniently divides itself,

第三章

求。不管其程度是多么小,只要是能激发人的能力,都会孕育出对顺畅地使用这种能力的更高追求;这种大众化教育,倘若达不到为了确保将激励人民去追求,并很可能会提出要求而教育人民的那一种状态,那么这样的教育就会归于失败。

在极其危急的情况下,以一时的极权形式掌管绝对的权力,对此我绝不是要谴责它。在古时候,遵从他们自己的选择,自由的民族曾经赋予了这种权力,在国家用较柔性的手段无法消除弊病的情形下,这种权力是一剂必要的猛药。但是即使是严格限定行使这种权力的时间,也只有当独裁者,像梭伦(Solon)或毕达古斯(Pittacus)那样,用他所控制的全部权力来清除妨碍民族保有自由的障碍时,对这种权力的接受才是可以宽恕的。好的专制政治完全是一种虚幻的理想,它实际上(它除了充当某种暂时性目的的手段外)是最危险的和最无意义的狂想。以毒攻毒,在一个文明程度有所提升的国家中,好的专制政治比坏的专制政治更是害人不浅,因为它尤为懈怠和钝化人民的思想、感情和活力。奥古斯都的专制政治,使罗马人为提比略创造了条件。假如不是由于近两个世代的温和奴隶制对罗马人性格的整个作风的耗损,或许,他们会有足够勇气去抗争更令人讨厌的奴隶制。

显而易见,理论上最好的政府形式就是这样一种政府:主权或作为最后手段的至高控制权力归属于社会整个集体;任何一个公民不仅对行使这种最终主权有发言的权力,而且,至少在某些时候,被要求能在政府参政议政中发挥作用,亲自履行某种地方的或一般的公共职责。

为验证该论点,就必须结合两个组成部分加以考察,这两个

namely, how far it promotes the good management of the affairs of society by means of the existing faculties, moral, intellectual, and active, of its various members, and what is its effect in improving or deteriorating those faculties.

The ideally best form of government, it is scarcely necessary to say, does not mean one which is practicable or eligible in all states of civilization, but the one which, in the circumstances in which it is practicable and eligible, is attended with the greatest amount of beneficial consequences, immediate and prospective. A completely popular government is the only polity which can make out any claim to this character. It is pre-eminent in both the departments between which the excellence of a political Constitution is divided. It is both more favourable to present good government, and promotes a better and higher form of national character, than any other polity whatsoever.

Its superiority in reference to present well-being rests upon two principles, of as universal truth and applicability as any general propositions which can be laid down respecting human affairs. The first is that the rights and interests of every or any person are only secure from being disregarded, when the person interested is himself able, and habitually disposed, to stand up for them. The second is that the general prosperity attains a greater height, and is more widely diffused in proportion to the amount and variety of the personal energies enlisted in promoting it.

Putting these two propositions into a shape more special to their present application ; human beings are only secure from evil at the hands of others, in proportion as they have the power of being, and are, self-*protecting*; and they only achieve a high degree of success in their struggle with Nature, in proportion as they are self-*dependent*, relying on what they themselves can do, either separately or in concert, rather than on what others do for them.

The former proposition—that each is the only safe guardian of his own rights and interests—is one of those elementary maxims of prudence, which every person capable of conducting his own affairs implicitly acts upon, wherever he himself is interested. Many,

部分是在上一章中为便于探究政府优势而分解出来的:前一部分就是基于社会所有成员现有道德的、智力的和积极的能力,政府增进社会公共事务的良好治理到何等程度;后一部分就是它在增进或削弱这些能力方面的效果如何。

必须明确的是,理论上最好的政府形式,并非指这种政府形式在所有的文明状态下,它都是实际可操作的或适宜的,而是指这样一种政府形式,在它是实际可操作的和适宜的条件下,它将导致有益后果的最大化,无论它是当前的还是长远的。完全的平民政府是能够宣称拥有这种特质的唯一政体。就体现政体优越性的两个部分而言,这种政体都是杰出的。它既比任何其他政体更有利于提供优质的管理,又能增进较好的和较高形式的民族性格的发展。

该政体所体现的当前福利的优势是以两个原则为基准的,像关于人类事务所能规定的任何一般论点一样,这两个定理具有同样普遍的真理性和适用性。第一个定理是,只有当每个人有能力并且自发性地保护他们的权利和利益时,他们的权利和利益才不会有被忽视的危险。第二个定理是,能促进普遍繁荣的个人能力越大,且这种能力的多样性越是丰富,就越能实现高度的普遍繁荣,并越能广泛传播。

如果将这两个命题运用到当下的情形。人们愈具有自我保护的力量并进行自我保护的话,他们就愈能避免他人的祸害;只有他们愈是自力更生,不依靠他人,遵循个别的或一致的行动,那么,在同自然的斗争中,他们才愈能取得更大的成功。

第一个命——就个人的权利和利益而言,每个人是他自己的唯一可靠的保护神——是高瞻远瞩的基本原则之一,任何一个能够应付自己事务的人,在涉及到他自己利益时,他总是本能地遵

indeed, have a great dislike to it as a political doctrine, and are fond of holding it up to obloquy as a doctrine of universal selfishness. To which we may answer, that whenever it ceases to be true that mankind, as a rule, prefer themselves to others, and those nearest to them to those more remote, from that moment Communism is not only practicable, but the only defensible form of society; and will, when that time arrives, be assuredly carried into effect. For my own part, not believing in universal selfishness, I have no difficulty in admitting that Communism would even now be practicable among the élite of mankind, and may become so among the rest. But as this opinion is anything but popular with those defenders of existing institutions who find fault with the doctrine of the general predominance of self-interest, I am inclined to think they do in reality believe, that most men consider themselves before other people. It is not, however, necessary to affirm even this much in order to support the claim of all to participate in the sovereign power. We need not suppose that when power resides in an exclusive class, that class will knowingly and deliberately sacrifice the other classes to themselves : it suffices that, in the absence of its natural defenders, the interest of the excluded is always in danger of being overlooked; and, when looked at, is seen with very different eyes from those of the persons whom it directly concerns. In this country, for example, what are called the working classes may be considered as excluded from all direct participation in the government. I do not believe that the classes who do participate in it, have in general any intention of sacrificing the working classes to themselves. They once had that intention ; witness the persevering attempts so long made to keep down wages by law. But in the present day, their ordinary disposition is the very opposite: they willingly make considerable sacrifices, especially of their pecuniary interest, for the benefit of the working classes, and err rather by too lavish and indiscriminating beneficence ; nor do I

循它而行动的。诚然,把它作为一种政治学说,许多人感到非常讨厌,并且喜欢把它公然贬抑为普遍自私自利的学说。对此我们可以这样答复,人往往总是喜欢自己胜于喜欢别人,喜欢和自己接近的人胜于喜欢较疏远的人,当这一点不再是真理的时候,从那时起,共产主义就一定不仅仅是行得通的,而且是唯一可以自我辩护的社会形式了。而且,在那时候,共产主义将注定会得以实现。在我看来,既然不相信普遍的自私自利,我倒承认甚至现在共产主义在人类的精英中就会是行得通的,在其他人中也可能变成行得通的。但是,由于现行制度的辩护者们对于这一观点很不以为然,他们不满意自私自利占有普遍优势的这一学说,我反而相信,实际上,他们的确信奉大多数人考虑自己是胜于别人的。然而,为了对所有人参与行使主权的观点表示赞同,甚至不需要做这种断言。我们不需要做这样一个假定,当一个排他性的阶级掌管着权力时,这个阶级将为了自己的利益,明知和故意地漠视其他阶级的利益。这样说已经够清楚的了:在缺失天然的捍卫者的情形下,被边缘化的阶级的利益总是有被忽视的危险。而且,即使对这种利益予以关注,他们也是用不一样的眼光去关注的,这种眼光和利益直接相关的人们的眼光是截然不同的。比如说,在我们国家,被称之为工人阶级的那个阶级,可以认为就是被排斥在对政务的直接参与之外的。我不认为组成政府的各个阶级为了自己的利益,通常都有牺牲工人阶级的任何计划。他们曾经有过那种尝试:瞧瞧那些长期以来用法律压低工资的一以贯之的努力吧!但是如今,他们通常的计划恰好相反,为了工人阶级的利益,他们愿意作出相当程度的让步,特别是金钱上的让步,而且可以说,甚至表现出极端过度的慷慨和不加区分的慈善行为。我也不

believe that any rulers in history have been actuated by a more sincere desire to do their duty towards the poorer portion of their countrymen. Yet does Parliament, or almost any of the members composing it, ever for an instant look at any question with the eyes of a working man ? When a subject arises in which the labourers as such have an interest, is it regarded from any point of view but that of the employers of labour ? I do not say that the working men's view of these questions is in general nearer to truth than the other; but it is sometimes quite as near ; and in any case it ought to be respectfully listened to, instead of being, as it is, not merely turned away from, but ignored. On the question of strikes, for instance, it is doubtful if there is so much as one among the leading members of either House, who is not firmly convinced that the reason of the matter is unqualifiedly on the side of the masters, and that the men's view of it is simply absurd. Those who have studied the question know well how far this is from being the case ; and in how different, and how infinitely less superficial a manner, the point would have to be argued, if the classes who strike were able to make themselves heard in Parliament.

It is an inherent condition of human affairs, that no intention, however sincere, of protecting the interests of others, can make it safe or salutary to tie up their own hands. Still more obviously true is it, that by their own hands only can any positive and durable improvement of their circumstances in life be worked out. Through the joint influence of these two principles, all free communities have both been more exempt from social injustice and crime, and have attained more brilliant prosperity, than any others, or than they themselves after they lost their freedom. Contrast the free states of the world, while their freedom lasted, with the contemporary subjects of monarchical or oligarchical despotism : the Greek cities with the Persian satrapies; the Italian republics, and the free towns of Flanders and Germany, with the feudal monarchies of Europe ; Switzerland, Holland, and England, with Austria or ante-revolutionary France. Their superior prosperity was too obvious ever to have been gainsayed:

第三章

认为在历史上任何统治阶级曾有过这样的想法,即发自内心的对自己的贫困潦倒的"子民"履行职责。然而议会,或者组成议会的几乎所有议员,曾有过片刻从工人的立场去考虑问题吗?当牵涉到工人自身利益的问题出现时,难道不是只是从雇主的立场去加以权衡吗?我并不是说,比起其他人的看法,工人对这种问题的见解通常更接近真理;但它有时是完全同样接近真理的。无论如何应当尊敬地征求他们的见解,而不应当像现在这样,非但不去尊重而且对其漠视。比如说,在罢工问题上,我质疑在上院或下院的主要议员中是否有一个人,能无条件地相信理由不是偏向雇主这边,而受雇者的见解仅仅是荒谬的。只要是对这个问题有研究的人,都清楚地知道情况远非如此。如果议会能够听到举行罢工的阶级的意见,将会以截然不同的、远远不是那么肤浅的方式来讨论这个问题。

与人类事务紧密联系的一种情形是,任何捍卫他人利益的愿望,不管多么发自内心,都无法用束缚他们而变得安全或带来好处。显而易见,尤为正确的情形是,只有依靠他们自身的努力,他们的生活境遇才能实现任何主动的和持续的改进。如果协作发挥出这两个原则的影响,那么,与其他的任何社会相比,或者与自由社会在剥夺自由之后相比,一切自由社会既更可能避免社会的不公和犯罪,又可实现更辉煌的繁荣。如果将世界上的自由国家(在继续维持其自由的期间)和同时代的君主专制或寡头专制国家的人民作一比较;将古希腊城市同古波斯帝国的州作一比较;将意大利的共和国和佛兰德及德意志的自由城市同欧洲的封建君主国作一比较;将瑞士、荷兰和英国同奥地利或革命前的法国作一比较的话,显而易见,自由国家的更高更强的繁荣

while their superiority in good government and social relations is proved by the prosperity, and is manifest besides in every page of history. If we compare, not one age with another, but the different governments which coexisted in the same age, no amount of disorder which exaggeration itself can pretend to have existed amidst the publicity of the free states, can be compared for a moment with the contemptuous trampling upon the mass of the people which pervaded the whole life of the monarchical countries, or the disgusting individual tyranny which was of more than daily occurrence under the systems of plunder which they called fiscal arrangements, and in the secrecy of their frightful courts of justice.

It must be acknowledged that the benefits of freedom, so far as they have hitherto been enjoyed, were obtained by the extension of its privileges to a part only of the community ; and that a government in which they are extended impartially to all is a desideratum still unrealized. But though every approach to this has an independent value, and in many cases more than an approach could not, in the existing state of general improvement, be made, the participation of all in these benefits is the ideally perfect conception of free government. In proportion as any, no matter who, are excluded from it, the interests of the excluded are left without the guarantee accorded to the rest, and they themselves have less scope and encouragement than they might otherwise have to that exertion of their energies for the good of themselves and of the community, to which the general prosperity is always proportioned.

Thus stands the case as regards present wellbeing ; the good management of the affairs of the existing generation. If we now pass to the influence of the form of government upon character, we shall find the superiority of popular government over every other to be, if possible, still more decided and indisputable.

This question really depends upon a still more fundamental one—viz. , which of two common types of character, for the general good of humanity, it is most desirable should predominate—the active,

第三章

是不容否认的,由于这种繁荣的实现它们在良好的政府和社会关系方面的优越性得以印证。此外,在历史的长河中,这一点也是显而易见的。如果我们不是把一个时代同另一时代作对比,而是将共存于同一时代的不同政府作对比的话,那么在君主制国家中,肆虐于整个生活中的对人民大众的蔑视的践踏,在他们所谓的财政安排的掠夺制度下,以及在他们的恐怖的法院暗箱操作之中,每时每刻发生的令人憎恶的个人暴政,所有这些与存在于自由国家的光明正大的混乱根本不可相提并论的。

自由的益处,应当承认,就它目前被享有的情形而言,是通过把自由的特权扩展于社会只是一部分人而得到的;而将这种特权公平地拓展到全体人民的政府,则仍旧是尚未实现的夙愿。但是尽管接近这一趋势的每一步都体现着独立的价值,并且在普遍改进的现有状态下,在许多场合也无法做到比这接近更进一步的事情,然而,全体人民都享受到自由的益处则是理想上完备的自由政府观念。无论是谁,只要有人被排除在自由之外,被排除者的利益也就无法获得其余的人所得到的保障,并且,在为他们自己以及社会的利益增进发挥能力方面,他们所拥有的活动范围,以及所得到的鼓励就比没有排斥在外的情形要少了,而国家的普遍繁荣往往是和这种能力的开发状况相协调的。

有关当前福利的情形——当代事务的良好治理就是这样。现在,如果我们转向政府形式对人的性格的影响问题,我们将发现平民政府是比其他政府形式更为优越的。这一点是毫无疑问的。

这个问题其实蕴涵着另一个更为本质的问题,这个问题就是:为了人类的普遍利益,在两种普通的性格类型中,以谁占上风

or the passive type ; that which struggles against evils, or that which endures them; that which bends to circumstances, or that which endeavours to bend circumstances to itself.

The commonplaces of moralists, and the general sympathies of mankind, are in favour of the passive type. Energetic characters may be admired, but the acquiescent and submissive are those which most men personally prefer. The passiveness of our neighbours increases our own sense of security, and plays into the hands of our wilfulness. Passive characters, if we do not happen to need their activity, seem an obstruction the less in our own path. A contented character is not a dangerous rival. Yet nothing is more certain than that improvement in human affairs is wholly the work of the uncontented characters ; and, moreover, that it is much easier for an active mind to acquire the virtues of patience than for a passive one to assume those of energy.

Of the three varieties of mental excellence, intellectual, practical, and moral, there never could be any doubt in regard to the first two, which side had the advantage. All intellectual superiority is the fruit of active effort. Enterprise, the desire to keep moving, to be trying and accomplishing new things for our own benefit or that of others, is the parent even of speculative, and much more of practical talent.

The intellectual culture compatible with the other tpye is of that feeble and vague description, which belongs to a mind that stops at amusement, or at simple contemplation. The test of real and vigorous thinking, the thinking which ascertains truths instead of dreaming dreams, is successful application to practice. Where that purpose does not exist, to give definiteness, precision, and an intelligible meaning to thought, it generates nothing better than the mystical metaphysics of the Pythagoreans or the Veds. With respect to practical improvement, the case is still more evident. The character which improves human life

更为合适——是积极的性格类型,还是消极的性格类型;同邪恶作抗争的性格类型,还是忍受邪恶的性格类型;是顺应环境的性格类型,还是努力使环境适应自己的性格类型。

根据道德学家的陈词滥调和人类的通常喜好,是喜欢消极的性格类型。充满活力的性格也许值得赞誉,但是多数个人所钟爱的则是服从的和恭顺的性格。我们邻居的保守无为平添了我们的安全感,并对我们的任性的举动能够忍受。消极性格的人——倘若不是恰好需要他们行为的话——看起来是我们自己人生道路上的较小阻碍。一个知足的人不是一个危险的敌人,但是可以明确地断言,人类事务的一切完善都是不知足的人不懈上进的结果,而且,积极的人学会忍受比消极的人变得精力过人要容易得多。

智力上的、实践上的以及道德上的这三种精神方面的优点中,就前两者而言,哪一种性格更有利于进步是再清楚不过的。一切智力上的卓越都是积极上进的必然结果。进取心是思辨的能力,更是实践的才华的根基,这种进取心是为我们自己或他人的利益而不懈努力以及反复地尝试和完成新事物的一种追求。适合于另一性格类型的智力发展是一种只凭一时兴奋,或只求简单思维的发展,这种智力发展是软弱乏力和含糊茫然的。

证明真正而有力的思维的标准——也就是探究真理而不是不切实际空想的思维的标准——就是把思维成功地运用到实践。倘若没有这种意向,赋予思想以确定性、精确性和可以领悟的意义,思想就不会产生比毕达哥拉斯学派的神秘的形而上学或是古代印度的吠陀经更好的东西。至于就现实事务的进步而言,情形就尤为明显。增进人类生活的性格是这样一种性

is that which struggles with natural powers and tendencies, not that which gives way to them. The self-benefiting qualities are all on the side of the active and energetic character; and the habits and conduct which promote the advantage of each individual member of the community, must be at least a part of those which conduce most in the end to the advancement of the community as a whole. But on the point of moral preferability, there seems at first sight to be room for doubt. I am not referring to the religious feeling which has so generally existed in favour of the inactive character, as being more in harmony with the submission due to the divine will. Christianity as well as other religions has fostered this sentiment ; but it is the prerogative of Christianity, as regards this and many other perversions, that it is able to throw them off. Abstractedly from religious considerations, a passive character, which yields to obstacles instead of striving to overcome them, may not indeed be very useful to others, no more than to itself, but it might be expected to be at least inoffensive. Contentment is always counted among the moral virtues. But it is a complete error to suppose that contentment is necessarily or naturally attendant on passivity of character; and unless it is, the moral consequences are mischievous. Where there exists a desire for advantages not possessed, the mind which does not potentially possess them by means of its own energies, is apt to look with hatred and malice on those who do. The person bestirring himself with hopeful prospects to improve his circumstances, is the one who feels goodwill towards others engaged in, or who have succeeded in, the same pursuit. And where the majority are so engaged, those who do not attain the object have had the tone given to their feelings by the general habit of the country, and ascribe their failure to want of effort or opportunity, or to their personal ill-luck. But those who, while desiring what others possess, put no energy into striving for it, are either incessantly grumbling that fortune does not do for them what they do not attempt to do for themselves, or are overflowing with envy and ill-will towards those who possess what they would like to have.

In proportion as success in life is seen or believed to be the fruit

格：它不屈从于自然力和自然倾向，而是同自然力和自然倾向作抗争。一切为自己争取利益的性格也都是积极的和有力的性格，因为增进社会每个成员的利益的习惯和行为模式，毫无疑问，至少是最终最有利于整个社会进步的习惯和行为的一部分。但是，涉及道德上是否更可取这一方面，乍看起来似乎对此有所质疑。我所提及的不是这样一种普遍存在的宗教感情，这种宗教感情赏识消极性格，并把这种性格看作更吻合对上帝的听从。和其他宗教一样，基督教孕育了这种感情；但是只有基督教能够抛却这一反常状况以及其他许多反常状况。如果抽象地对宗教进行考量，消极的性格不是去努力克服障碍，而是去屈从于障碍。的确，无论对自己或他人，这种性格可能都不是很有好处的，但至少可以知道它是没有坏处的。知足常乐总是被以为是道德上的一种美德。但是，认为知足常乐必然地或本能地依附于消极性格，这样一种看法则是完全错误的，而且是没有益处的，其道德上的后果害人不浅。当人们渴望获得自己所没有的利益时，无法用自己的力量得到这种利益的人就容易对能这样做的人充满痛恨和恶意。而满怀憧憬为改善自己的境遇而不懈上进的人，对做同一项工作或在该工作中取得成功的人却充满友善。在多数人都这样做事情时，由于受国家的一般习惯对他们的感情的深刻影响，那些无法实现目标的人会把失败归咎为努力不够或机会不多，或者归咎为他们个人的运气不佳。但那些显然渴望得到别人拥有的东西，却并不为之竭力奋斗的人，要么不断地唠叨命运没有替他们做他们自己不想去做的事情，要么对那些占有他们想要的东西的人充满忌妒和恶意。

　　如果生活中的成功越被看作或确认是命运或偶然因素的结

of fatality or accident and not of exertion, in that same ratio does envy develop itself as a point of national character. The most envious of all mankind are the Orientals. In Oriental moralists, in Oriental tales, the envious man is markedly prominent. In real life, he is the terror of all who possess anything desirable, be it a palace, a handsome child, or even good health and spirits ; the supposed effect of his mere look constitutes the all-pervading superstition of the evil eye. Next to Orientals in envy, as in activity, are some of the Southern Europeans. The Spaniards pursued all their great men with it, embittered their lives, and generally succeeded in putting an early stop to their successes. ①With the French, who are essentially a southern people, the double education of despotism and Catholicism has, in spite of their impulsive temperament, made submission and endurance the common character of the people, and their most received notion of wisdom and excellence; and if envy of one another, and of all superiority, is not more rife among them than it is, the circumstance must be ascribed to the many valuable counteracting elements in the French.

There are, no doubt, in all countries, really contented characters,

---

① I limit the expression to past time, because I would say nothing derogatory of a great, and now at last a free, people, who are entering into the general movement of European progress with a vigour which bids fair to make up apidly the ground they have lost. No one can doubt what Spanish intellect and energy are capable of; and their faults as a people are chiefly those for which freedom and industrial ardour are a real specific. character, and most of all to the great individual energy which, though less persistent and more intermittent than in the self-helping and struggling Anglo-Saxons, has nevertheless manifested itself among the French in nearly every direction in which the operation of their institutions has been favourable to it.

第三章

果而非进取的结果,嫉妒就越会发展成为民族性格的一种特性。在所有人类中,东方人的嫉妒是最厉害的。在东方的道德学家那里,在东方的传奇中,嫉妒的人是非常凸显的。在现实生活中,对一切拥有任何可以渴望的东西的人而言这是一种恐怖。不管是一座宫殿,还是一个长得漂亮的孩子,或者甚至良好的健康状况和精神状态,他只要瞄一眼就有充斥着迷信的恶毒眼光的效果。与在活动上一样,在嫉妒方面,略逊于东方人的是某些南欧人。西班牙人用嫉妒追逐着他们所有的杰出人物,使他们的生活变得艰辛,并通常使得他们的成功过早地了结。①至于法国人,他们本质上是南方民族,尽管性格易于激动,但在专制政治和罗马天主教教义的双重教育下,顺从和忍耐成为了该民族的共同特性,内化为他们一致认可的睿智和卓越的观念。如果说法国人相互之间的嫉妒,以及对一切伟大事物的嫉妒,没有实际情形突出,这种情形应该归结为以下因素:即法国人性格中许多宝贵的起消解作用的因素,特别是法国人的杰出的个人能力。这种个人能力尽管不如自助和奋斗的盎格鲁-撒克逊人那样坚忍不拔和较少中断,但是在他们制度的实施上,几乎每一个方面它都表现出对这种能力的促进。

毫无疑问,在一切国家都有着真正满足的人,他们不仅不

---

① 我将我的表述限定在过去时期,因为对于一个卓越的、现在终于是自由的民族,我不愿意说任何贬抑它的话。这个民族,以充满预期地迅猛地补偿丢失的信誉的那种旺盛精力,正投入到普遍的欧洲进步运动。没有谁会质疑西班牙人的智慧和活动力所能办到的事;而他们作为一个民族的缺陷,大体上可由那些需要用自由以及对工业的热衷——这剂真正的特效药来加以矫正。

who not merely do not seek, but do not desire, what they do not already possess, and these naturally bear no ill-will towards such as have apparently a more favoured lot. But the great mass of seeming contentment is real discontent, combined with indolence or self-indulgence which, while taking no legitimate means of raising itself, delights in bringing others down to its own level. And if we look narrowly even at the cases of innocent contentment, we perceive that they only win our admiration, when the indifference is solely to improvement in outward circumstances, and there is a striving for perpetual advancement in spiritual worth, or at least a disinterested zeal to benefit others. The contented man, or the contented family, who have no ambition to make any one else happier, to promote the good of their country or their neighbourhood, or to improve themselves in moral excellence, excite in us neither admiration nor approval. We rightly ascribe this sort of contentment to mere unmanliness and want of spirit. The content which we approve, is an ability to do cheerfully without what cannot be had, a just appreciation of the comparative value of different objects of desire, and a willing renunciation of the less when incompatible with the greater.

  These, however, are excellences more natural to the character, in proportion as it is actively engaged in the attempt to improve its own or some other lot. He who is continually measuring his energy against difficulties, learns what are the difficulties insuperable to him, and what are those which, though he might overcome, the success is not worth the cost. He whose thoughts and activities are all needed for, and habitually employed in, practicable and useful enterprises, is the person of all others least likely to let his mind dwell with brooding discontent upon things either not worth attaining, or which are not so to him. Thus the active, self-helping character is not only intrinsically the best, but is the likeliest to acquire all that is really excellent or desirable in the opposite type.

第三章

追逐,而且不渴望他们所没有的东西,自然,这些人对显然有着好运气的人是没有恶意的。但是大部分表面上的满足事实上是不知足,这种不知足是和懒惰或自我放纵混合在一块的。这种不知足的人不是使用完善自己的合法手段,而是乐于把别人贬低到他自己的水平。如果我们认真思忖一下即使是没有坏处的满足的情形,我们就会发现,只有当他们的漠不关心仅仅是对改善外部环境而言,而且力争追求精神意义上的永恒进步,或至少能受益于他人的无私热情时,我们才会赞赏这种满足的情形。一个满足的家庭,或是一个满足的人,他胸无大志,不想使任何其他人幸福,不想增进自己国家或邻居的福祉,或者不想提升自己道德方面的美德,那么,这种人或这样的家庭,既不会得到我们的赞歌,也不会获得我们的认同。理所当然,我们把这种满足归咎于一味的软弱和胸无大志。我们所认同的知足,是在无法得到的情形下快乐地工作的能力,是对不同的渴望对象的相对价值作出的正确评价,以及在无法兼顾二者时抓大放小的意愿。

然而,对积极从事增进自己或他人命运的人而言,这是必然具有的长处。不懈地依照困难程度权衡自己能力的人,明白哪些障碍是他所不能克服的,哪些障碍他虽然可能克服,但是得不偿失。这个人的全部思想和活动适应于切实可行而且有益的事业,而且他能下意识地将它们运用于该事业中,那么,相比于所有其他人而言,这个人就是最少可能让自己的思想在不值得得到,或者对他来说不值得得到的东西上滋生不满情绪的人。因此,积极的、自力更生的性格不仅就本质而言是最好的,而且得到相反的性格中一切真正好的或能渴望的东西的这种可能性是最大的。

The striving, go-ahead character of England and the United States is only a fit subject of disapproving criticism, on account of the very secondary objects on which it commonly expends its strength. In itself it is the foundation of the best hopes for the general improvement of mankind. It has been acutely remarked, that whenever anything goes amiss, the habitual impulse of French people is to say, 'Il faut de la patience'; and of English people, 'What a shame.' The people who think it a shame when anything goes wrong—who rush to the conclusion that the evil could and ought to have been prevented, are those who, in the long run, do most to make the world better. If the desires are low placed, if they extend to little beyond physical comfort and the show of riches, the immediate results of the energy will not be much more than the continual extension of man's power over material objects; but even this makes room, and prepares the mechanical appliances, for the greatest intellectual and social achievements; and while the energy is there, some persons will apply it, and it will be applied more and more, to the perfecting not of outward circumstances alone, but of man's inward nature. Inactivity, unaspiringness, absence of desire, is a more fatal hindrance to improvement than any misdirection of energy; and is that through which alone, when existing in the mass, any very formidable misdirection by an energetic few becomes possible. It is this, mainly, which retains in a savage or semi-savage state the great majority of the human race.

Now there can be no kind of doubt that the passive type of character is favoured by the government of one or a few, and the active self-helping type by that of the Many. Irresponsible rulers need the quiescence of the ruled, more than they need any activity but that which they can compel. Submissiveness to the prescriptions of men as necessities of nature, is the lesson inculcated by all governments upon those who are wholly without participation in them. The will of superiors, and the law as the will of superiors, must be passively yielded to. But no men are mere instruments or materials in the hands of their rulers, who have will or spirit or a spring of internal activity in the rest of their proceedings: and any manifestation of these qualities,

第三章

英国人和美国人奋斗的、积极上进的性格受到批评指责,只是由于他们往往把精力耗费在不怎么重要的事情上。本质上,这种性格是人类普遍进步的最值得期待的根基。人们敏锐地发现,只要事情出错,法国人的本能冲动是说"别着急",英国人则说"真丢脸"。一旦事情出错就认为是丢脸,这种急忙断言说原本能够并应该避免坏事的人,归根结底是为了使世界变得更美好而付出最大努力的人。如果把目标放在较低的位置,不外乎是追逐物质享受和炫耀财富,则精力运转的直接结果,将必然是把精力不断作用于物质对象。但即使是这种情形,也为智力上和社会上的最大成就孕育了机会和准备好了机械装备。对于旺盛的精力,有人将运用它,并越来越多地用来不仅仅改善外部环境,而且也用来提升人的内在本性。消极无为、胸无大志、缺乏意向,所有这些是比用错精力更为要命的对改进的阻碍。当这种情况出现在民众中时,才可能出现少数强有力的人的极其可怕的错误领导,主要正是基于这种情形,使人类大多数人阻滞在野蛮或半野蛮状态之中。

因而,可以深信不疑的是,独裁统治或少数几个人的统治偏多是消极被动的性格类型;而多数人的统治偏好则是积极、自力更生的性格类型。不承担职责的统治者们需要的是被统治者的顺从,即除了能做他们被迫去做的事情之外,其他的任何活动都不要去做。对完全不参加政府的人们而言,要把听从命令当做天然法则去遵循。所有政府对此都是反复灌输的。上级的意志,以及作为上级意志的法律,这是必须遵从的。但在其他的议事活动中,具备意志或精神或内心活动的动力民众,绝非统治者手中单纯工具或材料。当他们彰显出这些特质时,他们

instead of receiving encouragement from despots, has to get itself forgiven by them. Even when irresponsible rulers are not sufficiently conscious of danger from the mental activity of their subjects to be desirous of repressing it, the position itself is a repression. Endeavour is even more effectually restrained by the certainty of its impotence, than by any positive discouragement. Between subjection to the will of others, and the virtues of self-help and self-government, there is a natural incompatibility. This is more or less complete, according as the bondage is strained or relaxed. Rulers differ very much in the length to which they carry the control of the free agency of their subjects, or the supersession of it by managing their business for them. But the difference is in degree, not in principle ; and the best despots often go the greatest lengths in chaining up the free agency of their subjects. A bad despot, when his own personal indulgences have been provided for, may sometimes be willing to let the people alone; but a good despot insists on doing them good, by making them do their own business in a better way than they themselves know of. The regulations which restricted to fixed processes all the leading branches of French manufactures, were the work of the great Colbert.

Very different is the state of the human faculties where a human being feels himself under no other external restraint than the necessities of nature, or mandates of society which he has his share in imposing, and which it is open to him, if he thinks them wrong, publicly to dissent from, and exert himself actively to get altered. No doubt, under a government partially popular, this freedom may be exercised even by those who are not partakers in the full privileges of citizenship. But it is a great additional stimulus to any one's self-help and self-reliance when he starts from an even ground, and has not to feel that his success depends on the impression he can make upon the sentiments and dispositions of a body of whom he is not one. It is a great discouragement to an individual, and a still

第三章

非但得不到专制君主的赞许,反而还得为此乞求专制君主的宽恕。即使当不负责任的统治者由于尚未充分意识到来自民众的精神活动的危险性,还未对其施加压迫时,统治者的地位本身就是一种压迫。人们的努力受到更多的限制——由于它自身的明显软弱无力——比起任何积极的阻碍对它的限制。在顺从他人意志与自力更生及自治的美德之间有着天然的对立,根据束缚的大小,对立的程度也轻重不同。统治者们驾驭其民众的自由机构的程度,或取代其为民众管理其事务的程度是不一样的。但这种不同只有程度上的差异,绝非原则上的不同。通常,最好的专制君主会竭力把其民众的自由机构束缚起来。坏的专制君主,当他的个人私欲得以满足的时候,有时可能愿意让民众各尽其职;不过好的专制君主坚持为民众做善事,使民众遵照比他们自己所知晓的更好的方式自行其是。把法国制造业所有关键部门用固定工序的规则进行限制,就是由英明的科贝尔设计的。

如果一个人能体悟到他自己除自然法则或他参与规定的社会授权外不受任何其他的外在束缚,而且如果他认为这种授权是错误的,他就可以当众表达不同的看法,并积极努力谋取将它改变,这样,在这种地方人的能力的状态将截然不同。毫无疑问,在一个多少能得到民意支持的政府统治下,即使是不享有充分公民权的人也可运用这种自由。但是当任何一个人都能把平等作为根本立足点,无需觉得他的成功要取决于他在自己并非其中之一的一群人的感情和品质上所能造成的印象时,这对他的自力更生和自己依靠自己来说,就是一种巨大的格外激励因素。被排斥于政体之外,非得从门外向控制自己命运的主宰者乞求,而不是到里面去进行协商,对个人来说这是很令人沮丧的,对

greater one to a class, to be left out of the constitution ; to be reduced to plead from outside the door to the arbiters of their destiny, not taken into the consultation within. The maximum of the invigorating effect of freedom upon the character is only obtained, when the person acted on either is, or is looking forward to becoming, a citizen as fully privileged as any other. What is still more important than even this matter of feeling, is the practical discipline which the character obtains, from the occasional demand made upon the citizens to exercise, for a time and in their turn, some social function. It is not sufficiently considered how little there is in most men's ordinary life to give any largeness either to their conceptions or to their sentiments. Their work is a routine ; not a labour of love, but of self-interest in the most elementary form, the satisfaction of daily wants; neither the thing done, nor the process of doing it, introduces the mind to thoughts or feelings extending beyond individuals; if instructive books are within their reach, there is no stimulus to read them ; and in most cases the individual has no access to any person of cultivation much superior to his own. Giving him something to do for the public, supplies, in a measure, all these deficiencies. If circumstances allow the amount of public duty assigned him to be considerable, it makes him an educated man. Notwithstanding the defects of the social system and moral ideas of antiquity, the practice of the dicastery and the ecclesia raised the intellectual standard of an average Athenian citizen far beyond anything of which there is yet an example in any other mass of men, ancient or modem. The proofs of this are apparent in every page of our great historian of Greece ; but we need scarcely look further than to the high quality of the addresses which their great orators deemed best calculated to act with effect on their understanding and will. A benefit of the same kind, though far less in degree, is produced on Englishmen of the lower middle class by their liability to be placed on juries and to serve parish offices ; which, though it does not occur to so many, nor is so continuous, nor introduces them to so great a variety of elevated considerations, as to admit of comparison with the public education which every citizen of Athens obtained from her democratic institutions , must make them nevertheless very different beings ,

第三章

一个阶级来说尤其会感到垂头丧气。只有当受到影响的人成为，或者指望着成为和别人一样享有充分权利的公民时，才能得到自由对性格的最大激励效果。甚至比这个感情问题更为重要的是，它就是有时要求公民在一段时间内轮流行使某种社会职务所能得到的性格上的实际锤炼。人们还未曾充分想过，在大多数人的日常生活中，不管对他们的想法还是对他们的感情被赋予的伟大感是十分的少。他们从事的是日常工作，他们的劳作不是来源于热爱，而是来源于最基本的个人利益即满足每天的需要。无论是所做的事，还是做这事的方法，都不可能把他们的精神引导到超越于个人以外的思想或感情；即使是能接触有益的书，也没有促使他去读的刺激；而且在大多数情形下个人接触不到在教养上比自己强的人。让他们做一些有益公众的事情就可以多少补偿以上这些不足。如果情况许可，赋予他相当多的公共义务，就会使他成为有教养的人。尽管古代的社会制度和道德观念存在着缺陷，但是古代雅典的陪审员和公民会议的实践的确把普通雅典公民的智力水准提高到远远超过古代或现代任何其他群众，这是曾有过的事例。在我们杰出的希腊历史学家的记载中，相关的证据是显而易见的，但我们只要看一看杰出演说家们那些卓越的演说就够了，他们认为这最适于有效地左右民众的理解力和意志。中等阶级较低阶层的英国人，因为他们承担着出任陪审员和教区职务的职责，于是产生了性质与此相同的好处，尽管在程度上，这种好处远比不上古雅典人。这种益处，尽管不能与每个雅典公民从雅典的民主制度获得的公共教育相比，享受这种益处的人不那么多，也不是那样持续不断，也不诱导他们实现如此多样性的崇高想法，但仍然使他

in range of ideas and development of faculties, from those who have done nothing in their lives but drive a quill, or sell goods over a counter. Still more salutary is the moral part of the instruction afforded by the participation of the private citizen, if even rarely, in public functions. He is called upon, while so engaged, to weigh interests not his own ; to be guided, in case of conflicting claims, by another rule than his private partialities ; to apply, at every turn, principles and maxims which have for their reason of existence the common good: and he usually finds associated with him in the same work minds more familiarized than his own with these ideas and operations, whose study it will be to supply reasons to his understanding, and stimulation to his feeling for the general interest. He is made to feel himself one of the public, and whatever is for their benefit to be for his benefit. Where this school of public spirit does not exist, scarcely any sense is entertained that private persons, in no eminent social situation, owe any duties to society, except to obey the laws and submit to the government. There is no unselfish sentiment of identification with the public. Every thought and feeling, either of interest or of duty, is absorbed in the individual and in the family. The man never thinks of any collective interest, of any objects to be pursued jointly with others, but only in competition with them, and in some measure at their expense. A neighbour, not being an ally or an associate, since he is never engaged in any common undertaking for joint benefit, is therefore only a rival. Thus even private morality suffers, while public is actually extinct. Were this the universal and only possible state of things, the utmost aspirations of the lawgiver or the moralist could only stretch to making the bulk of the community a flock of sheep innocently nibbling the grass side by side.

From these accumulated considerations it is evident, that the only government which can fully satisfy all the exigencies of the social state, is one in which the whole people participate ; that any participation, even in the smallest public function, is useful;

第三章

们在思想的广度和能力的拓展上,和那些一生之中只是拿笔杆子或站柜台卖货的民众相比,他们成为了完全不同的人。更为有好处的是平常公民参加公共职务所接受的道德层面的教育,即使这种情况不多见。当作这种工作时,要求他考虑的不是他自己的利益;碰上彼此冲突的权利要求,应以和他个人偏好不同的原则为基准;时刻运用以公共利益为其存在理由的准则和原则;并且在同一工作中,他常看到与他共事的人们比他更熟悉这些观念以及实际运用,他们的研究将有助于他明了道理,并激发他对公共利益的感情。使他感到自己就在公众之中,只要是有益于公众的利益的事情,同样就是有益于他的利益。缺乏这种培育公共精神的学校,以及不处在显要社会地位的普通公众,除了恪守法律和顺从政府之外,几乎不会感到他们还对社会承担着义务。他们同样也不会拥有与民众一体化的无私的感情。任何一种思想或感情,不管涉及到利益还是职责,都被纳入到个人和家庭之中。个人从不顾及任何公共的利益,从不顾及与其他人一起追求的任何目标,而只是一味地和别人竞争,并在某种程度上以他们为垫脚石。邻居既不是同盟者也不是同事,因为他从来没有为共同利益做任何共同事业,所以只是一个竞争者。因此甚至私人道德也遭到削弱,而公共道德事实上已荡然无存。倘若这就是普遍和唯一可能的状态的话,立法家或道德学家的最大心愿,也就只能是使社会中大多数人成为一群不构成威胁的,紧挨着在一起啃着青草的羊而已。

经过对上述各种情形的考量,很明显,能够充分满足社会一切要求的唯一政府是全体公民参加的政府;任何参与,即使是担任最小的公共职务也是有好处的;这种参政的范围大小,应始终和社会一般进步程度所允许的范围一样;只有允许所有的人在国

that the participation should everywhere be as great as the general degree of improvement of the community will allow; and that nothing less can be ultimately desirable, than the admission of all to a share in the sovereign power of the state. But since all cannot, in a community exceeding a single small town, participate personally in any but some very minor portions of the public business, it follows that the ideal type of a perfect government must be representative.

家主权中都享有一份才是最终让人向往的。但是既然在面积和人口超过一个小城镇的社会里(除公共事务的某些极次要的部分外),所有的人亲自参与公共事务是不可能的,因而我们就可以得出结论:一个完美政府的理想类型一定是代议制政府。

CHAPTER IV
Under What Social Conditions Representative Government Is Inapplicable

We have recognized in representative government the ideal type of the most perfect polity, for which, in consequence, any portion of mankind are better adapted in proportion to their degree of general improvement. As they range lower and lower in development, that form of government will be, generally speaking, less suitable to them; though this is not true universally: for the adaptation of a people to representative government does not depend so much upon the place they occupy in the general scale of humanity, as upon the degree in which they possess certain special requisites ; requisites, however, so closely connected with their degree of general advancement, that any variation between the two is rather the exception than the rule. Let us examine at what point in the descending series representative government ceases altogether to be admissible, either through its own unfitness, or the superior fitness of some other regimen.

First, then, representative, like any other government, must be unsuitable in any case in which it cannot permanently subsist—i. e. , in which it does not fulfil the three fundamental conditions enumerated in the first chapter. These were—1. That the people should be willing to receive it. 2. That they should be willing and able to do what is necessary for its preservation. 3. That they should be willing and able to fulfil the duties and discharge the functions which it imposes on them.

The willingness of the people to accept representative government, only becomes a practical question when an enlightened ruler, or

第四章　在哪些社会条件下不适宜采用代议制政府

我们已经承认在代议制政府中最完美政体的理想类型。其结果是，人类的任何部分适用这种政体的能力是与其一般进步程度成正比的。一般说来，尽管这不是普遍正确的，但只要他们发展程度越低，这种类型的政府形式就越不适合他们。因为一个民族是否适合代议制，与其说取决于他们在人类的一般发展程度上所处的地方，不如说取决于他们拥有某些特殊的必要条件的程度。然而，必要条件跟一般进步的程度联系是如此紧密，以至于它们之间的任何变异都只是例外而不是法则。让我们考察一下在下降的序列中，代议制政府在哪个点上，要么由于它自身的不合适，要么存在着某种更为适合的政体而变得完全不可采用了。

首先，代议制，像任何其他政体一样，在任何它不能永远存在下去的场合，就一定是不合时宜的——也就是说，在它不符合第一章所列的三个条件的场合，就一定是不合时宜的。这些条件是：1.民众必须愿意采纳它；2.民众必须愿意并且能够做为了保持它所必须做的事情；3.民众必须愿意并且能够履行它赋予他们的义务和职责。

民众接受代议制的意愿，只有当一个开明的统治者，或者取

a foreign nation or nations who have gained power over the country, are disposed to offer it the boon. To individual reformers the question is almost irrelevant, since, if no other objection can be made to their enterprise than that the opinion of the nation is not yet on their side, they have the ready and proper answer, that to bring it over to their side is the very end they aim at. When opinion is really adverse, its hostility is usually to the fact of change, rather than to representative government in itself. The contrary case is not indeed unexampled ; there has sometimes been a religious repugnance to any limitation of the power of a particular line of rulers ; but in general, the doctrine of passive obedience meant only submission to the will of the powers that be, whether monarchical or popular. In any case in which the attempt to introduce representative government is at all likely to be made, indifference to it, and inability to understand its processes and requirements, rather than positive opposition, are the obstacles to be expected. These, however, are as fatal, and may be as hard to be got rid of as actual aversion ; it being easier, in most cases, to change the direction of an active feeling, than to create one in a state previously passive. When a people have no sufficient value for, and attachment to, a representative constitution, they have next to no chance of retaining it. In every country, the executive is the branch of the government which wields the immediate power, and is in direct contact with the public ; to it, principally, the hopes and fears of individuals are directed, and by it both the benefits, and the terrors and *prestige*, of government, are mainly represented to the public eye. Unless, therefore, the authorities whose office it is to check the executive are backed by an effective opinion and feeling in the country, the executive has always the means of setting them aside, or compelling them to subservience, and is sure to be well supported in doing so. Representative institutions necessarily depend for permanence upon the readiness of the people to fight for them in case of their being endangered. If too little valued for this, they seldom obtain a footing at all, and if they do, are almost sure to be overthrown, as soon as the head of the government, or any party leader who can muster force for a *coup* de *main*,

第四章

得了统治这个国家的权力的一个外来民族或多个民族,有将它作为恩惠提供这种制度的打算时,才成为一个实际问题。对单个的改革者来说,这个问题几乎是不相关的,因为,如果除了国家的舆论还不在他们这一边之外,没有其他针对他们事业的异议,那么他们就有了现成和恰当的回答,把舆论导向他们这边就是他们所设置的目标。当意见确实相左时,它通常对变化的事实是敌视的,这种敌视要胜过对代议制政府本身。相反的例子并非没有。宗教上对特定家族的统治者的权力限制表示反感的例子曾经存在过。但一般说来,消极服从的学说仅仅意味着对现有权力意志的服从,而不论它是君主的还是大众的。在任何有可能试图引进代议制政府的场合中可以预见到的障碍,对之漠不关心,无法理解它的程序和要求,而不是积极地反对。然而,这些都跟实际的反感一样是致命的,也许同样很难被清除掉。在大部分场合,改变某种积极的情感要比在先前消极的状态中产生出积极的情感容易得多。当一个民族对代议制政体缺乏足够的评价和依恋时,就几乎不会有什么机会去保留它。在每个国家中,行政机构是政府的一个分支,它拥有直接的权力,直接与民众打交道。一般说来,个人对它抱有直接的期待和恐惧,政府的好处以其恐怖和声望,也都主要通过它展现在公众的面前。因而,除非负责监督行政机关的权力机关得到了这个国家中有效的舆论和情感支持,否则行政机关总是有办法把它们晾在一边或强迫它们服从,并且很有把握做到这一点。代议制度要想持久,必然要依靠人民在它们处于危险境地时能随时上前为之斗争。如果低估了这一点,它们根本就不会有立足之地,并且如果有,只要政府首脑,或有任何有能力集中力量进行一次突袭的政党领袖,愿

is willing to run some small risk for absolute power.

These considerations relate to the first two causes of failure in a representative government. The third is, when the people want either the will or the capacity to fulfil the part which belongs to them in a representative constitution. When nobody, or only some small fraction, feels the degree of interest in the general affairs of the State necessary to the formation of a public opinion, the electors will seldom make any use of the right of suffrage but to serve their private interests, or the interest of their locality, or of some one with whom they are connected as adherents or dependents. The small class who, in this state of public feeling, gain the command of the representative body, for the most part use it solely as a means of seeking their fortune. If the executive is weak, the country is distracted by mere struggles for place; if strong, it makes itself despotic, at the cheap price of appeasing the representatives, or such of them as are capable of giving trouble, by a share of the spoil ; and the only fruit produced by national representation is, that in addition to those who really govern, there is an assembly quartered on the public, and no abuse in which a portion of the assembly are interested is at all likely to be removed. When, however, the evil stops here, the price may be worth paying, for the publicity and discussion which, though not an invariable, are a natural accompaniment of any, even nominal, representation, In the modem kingdom of Greece, for example, it can hardly be doubted, that the place-hunters who chiefly compose the representative assembly, though they contribute little or nothing directly to good government, nor even much temper the arbitrary power of the executive, yet keep up the idea of popular rights, and conduce greatly to the real liberty of the press which exists in that country. This benefit, however, is entirely dependent on the co-existence with the popular body of an hereditary king. If, instead of struggling for the favours of the chief ruler, these selfish and sordid factions struggled for the chief place itself, they would certainly, as in Spanish America, keep the country in a state of chronic revolution and civil war. A despotism, not even

第四章

意冒些小小的风险去追求绝对权力,也很快会被推翻。

这两种考虑跟代议制政府遭到失败的前两个原因有关。第三个原因是,在代议制度中,人们到何时才具有意愿或能力来实现属于他们的角色。当没有人,或者只有小部分人感觉到了国家一般事物中有形成公众舆论的必要性的那种程度的兴趣时,极少选民会不利用他们投票的权利去为他们私利的,或者是地区利益,或者是他们的追随者或依附者的利益服务的。在这样一种公众舆论下,获得控制代议团体的小阶级,大部分都只会将它作为追求自身利益的手段。如果行政权力很弱,那这个国家就会陷入争权夺利的混乱场面,如果行政权力很强,那它就通过分赃的手段,利用小小的代价来安抚代表或者他们中有能力制造麻烦的人,从而把自己变成专制政府。这样,国民议会的唯一后果就是,除了那些真正进行统治的人以外,又多了一个骑在公众头上的议会,并且凡是涉及到部分议员的弊端都无法得到根除。然而,如果罪恶到此为止,为了公开和自由的讨论——它是任何,即使是名义上的代议制,虽不是一成不变的但却是自然伴随的东西——这种代价是值得的。例如,在当今希腊王国,毫无疑问,代表大会主要是由那些谋求职位的人组成的,尽管他们对好的政府几乎没有什么直接的贡献,甚至也没怎么直接地牵制行政机关的专制权力,但却使民权观念得以保留下来,并且大大有利于存在于那个国家中的真正的新闻自由。可是,这种益处,完全是因为和这个人民团体一起还存在一个世袭的国王。如果这些自私和肮脏的派系不是竞相去讨好主要的统治者,而是由他们去角逐那个主要职位,那么他们肯定会像西属美洲那样,使国家陷入长期的革命和内战状态中去。一个专制政体,即使不

legal, but of illegal violence, would be alternately exercised by a succession of political adventurers, and the name and forms of representation would have no effect but to prevent despotism, from attaining the stability and security by which alone its evils can be mitigated or its few advantages realized.

The preceding are the cases in which representatire government cannot permanently exist. There are others in which it possibly might exist, but in which some other form of government would be preferable. These are principally when the people, in order to advance in civilization, have some lesson to learn, some habit not yet acquired, to the acquisition of which representative government is likely to be an impediment.

The most obvious of these cases is the one already considered, in which the people have still to learn the first lesson of civilization, that of obedience. A race who have been trained in energy and courage by struggles with Nature and their neighbours, but who have not yet settled down into permanent obedience to any common superior, would be little likely to acquire this habit under the collective government of their own body. A representative assembly drawn from among themselves would simply, reflect their own turbulent insubordination. It would refuse its authority to all proceedings which would impose, on their savage independence, any improving restraint. The mode in which such tribes are usually brought to submit to the primary conditions of civilized society, is through the necessities of warfare, and the despotic authority indispensable to military command. A military leader is the only superior to whom they will submit, except occasionally some prophet supposed to be inspired from above, or conjurer regarded as possessing miraculous power. These may exercise a temporary ascendancy, but as it is merely personal, it rarely effects any change in the general habits of the people, unless the prophet, like Mahomet, is also a military chief, and goes forth the armed apostle of a new religion ; or unless the military chiefs ally themselves with his influence, and turn it into a prop for their own government.

A people are no less unfitted for representative government by the contrary fault to that last specified; by extreme passiveness, and ready submission to tyranny. If a people thus prostrated by character and

第四章

是合法而是非法的暴力,也会有许多政治冒险家前赴后继交替着实行它。而代议制的名称和形式除了阻止专制取得稳定和安全外就没有其他作用了。而只有稳定和安全才能减轻代议制的弊端和实现它为数不多的好处。

前面所讲的是代议制政府不能长久存在的一些情形。还有一些情形,代议制政府也许可以存在,但别的政府形式可能更为合适。这主要是,当民众为了取得文明的进步,要汲取一些教训,有些习惯还没有养成,而要养成这些习惯,代议制政府就可能成为一种障碍。

这些事例中最明显的情形前面已经考虑过,就是人民仍需学习文明的第一课——服从。一个在和自然以及邻人作斗争中经受力量和勇气锻炼但却还未进入到永远服从任何共同领袖阶段的种族,在他们自己团体的集体政府中不太可能养成这种习惯。从他们中间产生的代表大会将只能反映它们自己的狂暴不羁。它将拒绝使用自己的权威来推行对他们野蛮的独立性加以限制的所有做法。这样的部族通常逐渐学会服从文明社会的首要条件是通过必要的战争以及军事首领的必不可少的专制权力。军事首领是他们唯一要服从的人,除非偶尔还会有某个被认为上通神意的先知,以及被认为拥有某种神奇力量的魔法师。这些人拥有暂时的支配地位,但仅仅是个人的,它很难影响人民的一般习惯上的变化,除非像穆罕默德那样的先知,他同时又是一个军事首领,并宣称自己是新宗教的武装传教士,或者除非军事首领在他的影响下形成联盟,并把这个联盟变为自己统治的依靠力量。

一个具有与前述相反的缺陷,极端消极、准备屈从于暴君的民族,也不适合采用代议制政府。如果一个被性格和环境所屈服

circumstances could obtain representative institutions, they would inevitably choose their tyrants as their representatives, and the yoke would be made heavier on them by the contrivance which *primâ facie* might be expected to lighten it. On the contrary, many a people has gradually emerged from this condition by the aid of a central authority, whose position has made it the rival, and has ended by making it the master, of the local despots, and which, above all, has been single. French history, from Hugh Capet to Richelieu and Louis XIV., is a continued example of this course of things. Even when the King was scarcely so powerful as many of his chief feudatories, the great advantage which he derived from being but one, has been recognised by French historians. To him the eyes of *all* the locally oppressed were turned; he was the object of hope and reliance throughout the kingdom; while each local potentate was only powerful within a more or less confined space. At his hands, refuge and protection were sought from every part of the country against first one, then another, of the immediate oppressors. His progress to ascendancy was slow ; but it resulted from successively taking advantage of opportunities which offered themselves only to him. It was, therefore, sure; and, in proportion as it was accomplished, it abated, in the oppressed portion of the community, the habit of submitting to oppression. The King's interest lay in encouraging all partial attempts on the part of the serfs to emancipate themselves from their masters, and place themselves in immediate subordination to himself. Under his protection numerous communities were formed which knew no one above them but the King. Obedience to a distant monarch is liberty itself, compared with the dominion of the lord of the neighbouring castle : and the monarch was long compelled by necessities of position to exert his authority as the ally, rather than the master, of the classes whom he had aided in effecting their liberation. In this manner a central power, despotic in principle though generally much restricted in practice, was mainly instrumental in carrying the people through a necessary stage of improvement, which representative government, if real, would most likely have prevented them from entering upon. There are parts of Europe

的民族能够采用代议制政府,那么他们不可避免地会选择他们的暴君作为代表,他们身上的枷锁将会因为这个表面上可能指望它得到减轻的办法而变得更加沉重。恰好相反,很多民族依靠这种中央权力的帮助,渐渐地从这种状态中摆脱出来,中央权力的地位使得它成了地方专制力量的对手,并以成为地方专制力量的主人而终结,而首要的是,中央权力变成了至高无上的权力。法国的历史,从休·卡皮特到黎塞留和路易十四,就是这一进程连续的例子。即使当国王的力量还没有许多他的封建领主大时,他从只有他一个人这一事实中得到的巨大优势是法国历史学家们所承认的。所有在地方遭受压迫的人的眼光都朝向他,他是希望所在和整个国家的依赖对象,而每个地方首领只是在多少有限的区域内拥有权力。全国各地反对接二连三的直接压迫者的人们都在他羽翼下寻求庇护。尽管他获取支配地位的进展是缓慢的,但这却是利用只有他才拥有的机会的结果。因此,那是确定的,并且,当它达到一定的比例,在这个受到压迫的群体中的屈从于压迫的习惯也就减轻了。国王的利益在于鼓励各地的农奴从他们主人那里解放出来,并使他们直接服从他本人。在他的保护之下,形成了许多团体,他们知道在他们上面只需服从国王一人。与服从邻近城堡的统治者相比,服从远处的君主本身就是一种自由。国王长期迫于其所处地位的需要,作为那些他曾经帮助过获得解放的阶级的同盟,而不是作为统治者,运用他的权威。这样一来,中央权力尽管在本质上是专制的,但在实践中却受到限制,成为帮助人民通过必要进步阶段的工具性手段。而代议制政府,如果是真的,将极有可能阻止他们进入到这一阶段。在欧洲一些

where the same work is still to be done, and no prospect of its being done by any other means. Nothing short of despotic rule, or a general massacre, could effect the emancipation of the serfs in the Russian Empire.

The same passages of history forcibly illustrate another mode in which unlimited monarchy overcomes obstacles to the progress of civilization which representative government would have had a decided tendency to aggravate. One of the strongest hindrances to improvement, up to a rather advanced stage, is an inveterate spirit of locality. Portions of mankind, in many other respects capable of, and prepared for, freedom, may be unqualified for amalgamating into even the smallest nation. Not only may jealousies and antipathies repel them from one another, and bar all possibility of voluntary union, but they may not yet have acquired any of the feelings or habits which would make the union real, supposing it to be nominally accomplished. They may, like the citizens of an ancient community, or those of an Asiatic village, have had considerable practice in exercising their faculties on village or town interests, and have even realized a tolerably effective popular government on that restricted scale, and may yet have but slender sympathies with anything beyond, and no habit or capacity of dealing with interests common to many such communities. I am not aware that history furnishes any example in which a number of these political atoms or corpuscles have coalesced into a body, and learnt to feel themselves one people, except through previous subjection to a central authority common to all. [1]It is through the habit of deferring to that authority, entering into its plans and subserving its purposes, that a people such as we have supposed, receive into their minds the conception of large interests, common to a considerable geographical extent. Such interests, on the contrary, are necessarily the predominant consideration in the mind of the central ruler, and through the relations, more

---

[1] Italy, which alone can be quoted as an exception, is only so in regard to the final stage of its transformation. The more difficult previous advance from the city isolation of Florence, Pisa, or Milan, to the provincial unity of Tuscany or Lombardy, took place in the usual manner.

第四章

地方,还有相同的工作要做,并且不存在任何其他方法去做这件事的前景。在俄罗斯帝国,只有专制统治或是一场大屠杀,农奴的解放才能得以实现。

历史的同一篇章有力地说明了无限制君主制克服障碍以促进文明进步的另一种模式。而代议制政府肯定会加重这种障碍。妨碍进步使其不能达到更高层次的最严重的障碍之一是根深蒂固的地方观念。在许多方面能够拥有自由,并且在许多方面为自由作好了准备的部分人类,也许还不能形成哪怕是最小的国家。不仅嫉妒和反感可能使他们相互排斥,并阻碍一切可能的自愿联合,而且即使假定名义上已经形成了这种联合,他们也不具备使这个联合成为真实的情感或习惯。像古代社会的公民,或亚洲村社的人民那样,他们可能在村镇利益范围内运用他们的能力方面经验丰富,并在那个有限的规模内甚至实现了相当有效的平民政府,可是他们对任何超出那个范围外的事情很少同情,并且不具备处理许多这样的团体的共同利益的习惯或能力。我不清楚是否历史提供过什么例子来说明许多这样的政治原子或微粒结合成一个团体,并逐渐感到自己是一个民族,除非来自所有人共有的以前曾服从过的中央权威。① 正是通过服从那个权威的习惯他们,参与它的计划,促进它的目的,我们所设想的民族才能在思想上接受在相当大的地理范围内共同的巨大利益的概念。相反地,这样的利益,是中央统治者必然要着重考虑的事情,并且通过他同地方逐渐建立起来的或多

---

① 意大利是唯一可以称作一个例外的例子,它也只是在它转型的最后阶段如此。其以前从孤立的城市,如佛罗伦萨,比萨或米兰的更为困难的进步,到塔斯加尼(Tuscany)或伦巴底(Lombardy)的省级联合,则是按照通常的方式完成的。

or less intimate, which he progressively establishes with the localities. they become familiar to the general mind. The most favourable concurrence of circumstances under which this step in improvement could be made, would be one which should raise up representative institutions without representative government ; a representative body, or bodies, drawn from the localities, making itself the auxiliary and instrument of the central power, but seldom attempting to thwart or control it. The people being thus taken, as it were, into council, though not sharing the supreme power, the political education given by the central authority is carried home, much more effectually than it could otherwise be, to the local chiefs and to the population generally; while, at the same time, a tradition is kept up of government by general consent, or at least, the sanction of tradition is not given to government without it, which, when consecrated by custom, has so often put a bad end to a good beginning, and is one of the most frequent cases of the sad falitity which in most countries has stopped improvement in so early a stage, because the work of some one period has been so done as to bar the needful work of the ages following. Meanwhile, it may be laid down as a political truth, that by irresponsible monarchy rather than by representaytive government can a multitude of insignificant political units be welded into a people, with common feelingsof cohesion, power enough to protect itself against conquest or foreign aggression, and affairs sufficiently various and considerable of its own to occupy worthily and expand to fit proportions the social and political intelligence of the population.

For these several reasons, kingly government, free from the control (though perhaps strengthened by the support) of representative institutions, is the most suitable form of polity for the earliest stages of any community, not excepting a citycommunity like those of ancient Greece: where, accordingly, the government of kings, under some real but no ostensible or constitutional control by public opinion, did historically precede by an unknown and probably great duration all free institutions, and gave place at last, during a considerable lapse of time, to oligarchies of a few families.

A hundred other infirmities or short-comings in a people might be pointed out, which *pro tanto* disqualify them from making the best use

第四章

或少是密切的关系,这些利益就逐渐为大众所熟悉了。最有利的情形——在这种情形下可以实现进步方面的这一步骤——可能就是在没有代议制政府的情况下培育出代议制度来的情形。来自地方的一个或多个团体,把自己当成中央权力的辅助或工具,但却很少试图去反对或控制它。人民这样,可以说,被选进议事会,尽管不分享最高权力,中央权力所给予的政治教育被他们带回到地方,更为有效地贯彻到地方首领和一般地贯彻到人民;而同时,政府普遍同意的传统被坚持了下来,或至少是对于没有普遍同意的政府不给予传统的支持。当这种普遍同意被习惯神圣化时,它常常使好的开端没有好的结局,并且,它是招致大部分国家在如此早的阶段就止步不前的那种可悲命运最常见的原因之一,因为一个时期的某项工作这样完成了,就变成了下面阶段所必须做的工作的障碍了。同时,这可以当成一条政治真理,即与其说是代议制政府,不如说是不负责任的君主政体,将大量的无足轻重的政治单位组成一个民族,具有共同的凝聚感,足以反抗征服或抵御外国入侵的权力,以及值得正当地占有并扩大以适应社会规模和人民的政治智慧发展的多种多样的大量的事务。

由于这些理由,不受代议制度的控制的王国政府(尽管可能由于它的支持而得到加强),就成了任何社会最早发展阶段的最合适的政体,城市共同体如古希腊也不例外。因此,在古希腊,国王的政府在大众舆论的某些真正而不是表面的或宪法的控制下,在历史上的确有一段很长的时期是自由制度,但最后在相当长的时间后,又让位给了几个家族的寡头统治。

一个民族也许可以从自身找出其他一百多种使其不能充分利用代议制政府的缺陷和短处,但是和这些缺点相比,

of representative government ; but in regard to these it is not equally obvious that the government of One or a Few would have any tendency to cure or alleviate the evil. Strong prejudices of any kind ; obstinate adherence to old habits ; positive defects of national character, or mere ignorance, and deficiency of mental cultivation, if prevalent in a people, will be in general faithfully reflected in their representative assemblies: and should it happen that the executive administration, the direct management of public affairs, is in the hands of persons comparatively free from these defects, more good would frequently be done by them when not hampered by the necessity of carrying with them the voluntary assent of such bodies. But the mere position of the rulers does not in these, as it does in the other cases which we have examined, of itself invest them with interests and tendencies operating in the beneficial direction. From the general weaknesses of the people or of the state of civilization, the One and his counsellors, or the Few, are not likely to be habitually exempt ; except in the case of their being foreigners, belonging to a superior people or a more advanced state of society. Then, indeed, the rulers may be, to almost any extent, superior in civilization to those over whom they rule; and subjection to a foreign government of this description, notwithstanding its inevitable evils, is often of the greatest advantage to a people, carrying them rapidly through several stages of progress, and clearing away obstacles to improvement which might have lasted indefinitely if the subject population had been left unassisted to its native tendencies and chances. In a country not under the dominion of foreigners, the only cause adequate to producing similar benefits is the rare accident of a monarch of extraordinary genius. There have been in history a few of these who, happily for humanity, have reigned long enough to render some of their improvements permanent, by leaving them under the guardianship of a generation which had grown up under their influence. Charlemagne may be cited as one instance ; Pater the Great is another. Such examples however are so unfrequent that they can only be classed with the happy accidents, which have so often decided at a critical moment whether some leading portion of humanity should

第四章

一个人或一些人的统治具有消除或减轻弊病的任何倾向则不是同样明显。任何种类的强烈偏见、顽固地坚守旧习惯、民族性格上的实际缺陷，或仅仅是无知，缺乏智力培养，这些如果在一个民族中普遍存在，则一般说来会在他们的代表大会上忠实地反映出来；并且如果恰好直接管理公众事务的行政机关掌握在那些相对没有这些缺陷的人手中，那么当他们没有被必须取得这些代表大会的自愿同意这一必要条件所阻碍时，就会做出更多的好事。但是，不像在我们已经考察其他场合那样，仅仅凭统治者的位置并不能给予他们朝有益方向发展的利益和倾向。这个统治者和他的顾问们，或少数几个统治者，不可能不会习惯性地沾上人民或文明状态的普遍弱点，除非他们是属于一个更先进的民族或一个更加高等的社会状态的外国人。因此，统治者确实可能在几乎任何程度上都要比他们所统治的人在文明方面更为优越，并且对这个类型的外国政府的服从，尽管它有不可避免的坏处，但对于一个民族来说常常是极为有利的。它可以使人民快速地经历进步的几个阶段，并扫清前进路上的障碍。如果臣属的人民对其本身的倾向和机会一筹莫展、得不到帮助的话，这些障碍可能无限期地继续存在下去。在一个不受外国控制的国家，会出现相似好处的唯一原因是具有一位非凡天才君王这样的偶然事件。在历史上有少数几个这样的君主，让人庆幸的是，他们统治的时间够长，从而使他们能通过在他们影响和保护之下成长起来的一代人将他们的一些改良持续下去。查理曼大帝是一个例子，彼得大帝是另外一个例子。然而这样的事例是如此之少，以至于可以被看作是让人高兴的巧合，这种巧合常常是一个关键时刻，决定着人类领先的某个民族应当突然崛起

make a sudden start, or sink back towards barbarism: chances like the existence of Themistocles at the time of the Persian invasion, or of the first or third William of Orange. It would be absurd to construct institutions for the mere purpose of taking advantage of such possibilities; especially as men of this calibre, in any distinguished position, do not require despotic power to enable them to exert great influence, as is evidenced by the three last mentioned. The case most requiring consideration in reference to institutions, is the not very uncommon one, in which a small but leading portion of the population, from difference of race, more civilized origin, or other peculiarities of circumstance, are markedly superior in civilization and general character to the remainder. Under these conditions, government by the representatives of the mass would stand a chance of depriving them of much of the benefit they might derive from the greater civilization of the superior ranks ; while government by the representatives of those ranks would probably rivet the degradation of the multitude, and leave them no hope of decent treatment except by ridding themselves of one of the most valuable elements of future advancement. The best prospect of improvement for a people thus composed, lies in the existence of a constitutionally unlimited, or at least a practically preponderant, authority in the chief ruler of the dominant class. He alone has by his position an interest in raising and improving the mass, of whom he is not jealous, as a counterpoise to his associates, of whom he is. And if fortunate circumstances place beside him, not as controllers but as subordinates, a body representative of the superior caste, which by its objections and questionings, and its occasional outbreaks of spirit, keeps alive habits of collective resistance, and may admit of being, in time and by degrees, expanded into a really national representation (which is in substance the history of the English Parliament), the nation has then the most favourable prospects of improvement which can well occur to a community thus circumstanced and constituted.

Among the tendencies which, without absolutely rendering a people unfit for representative government, seriously incapacitate them from reaping the full benefit of it, one deserves particular notice. There are two states of the inclinations, intrinsically very different, but which have something in common, by virtue of which they often coincide in the direction they give to the efforts of individuals and of

第四章

还是退回到野蛮状态中去。这些巧合有:波斯人入侵时期的泰米斯多克里斯,以及奥良治的威廉一世或三世。仅仅为了利用这种可能性而建立制度将会是荒唐可笑的,特别是像这种才华盖世的人,在任何突出的位置上都不会利用专制力量去使他们能发挥巨大的影响,就像上面提到的三位一样。对于制度最需要考虑的不是非常特殊的例子,即一小部分不同种族的处于领先地位的群体,因为文明的起源或其他环境特性,而是在文明和一般性格方面要比其他人显著优越。在这种条件下,由群众组成的代议制政府将可能使他们失去他们从先进阶层的更高文明中得来的大量好处。而由那些先进阶层组成的代议制政府可能会降低群众的地位,使他们除了未来进步的这种最有价值的因素外,没有任何希望得到体面的待遇。一个成分如此的民族的进步的最好前景就在于,统治阶级的主要统治者要掌握有在宪法上没有限制,或至少实际上处于优势地位的权威。由于他所处的地位,只有他才有提高和改善群众处境的兴趣,他不妒忌他们;而对他的同盟来说,他又是平衡者。并且如果他处于幸运的境地,身边有一个不是作为统治者而是作为下属的优秀阶层的代表团体,这个团体的异议和质询,它的偶尔的情绪发作,使集体反抗的习惯保持下来,并且可能逐渐地扩大成为一个真正的国民代表制(这实质上是英国议会的历史),那么,这个国家就有处在这种情况下和这样构建的社会所能有的最有利的发展前景。

在这些不绝对使一个民族不适宜代议制政府,却严重地使他们不能得到代议制的好处的趋势中,有一个值得特别重视。存在着本质上不同,但却有共同之处的两种倾向,由于这些共同点,它们在影响个人和国家的努力经常一致。一个是希望将权力

nations : one is, the desire to exercise power over others ; the other is disinclination to have power exercised over themselves. The difference between different portions of mankind in the relative strength of these two dispositions, is one of the most important elements in their history. There are nations in whom the passion for governing others is so much stronger than the desire of personal independence, that for the mere shadow of the one they are found ready to sacrifice the whole of the other. Each one of their number is willing, like the private soldier in an army, to abdicate his personal freedom of action into the hands of his general, provided the army is triumphant and victorious, and he is able to flatter himself that he is one of a conquering host, though the notion that he has himself any share in the domination exercised over the conquered is an illusion. A government strictly limited in its powers and attributions, required to hold its hands from overmeddling, and to let most things go on without its assuming the part of guardian or director, is not to the taste of such a people. In their eyes the possessors of authority can hardly take too much upon themselves, provided the authority itself is open to general competition. An average individual among them prefers the chance, however distant or improbable, of wielding some share of power over his fellow-citizens, above the certainty, to himself and others, of having no unnecessary power exercised over them. These are the elements of a people of place-hunters ; in whom the course of politics is mainly determined by place-hunting ; where equality alone is cared for, but not liberty; where the contests of political parties are but struggles to decide whether the power of meddling in everything shall belong to one class or another, perhaps merely to one knot of public men or another; where the idea entertained of democracy is merely that of opening offices to the competition of all instead of a few; where, the more popular the institutions, the more innumerable are the places created, and the more monstrous the over-government exercised by all over each, and by the executive over all. It would be as unjust as it would be ungenerous to offer this, or anything approaching to it, as an unexaggerated picture of the French people ; yet the degree in which they do participate in this type of character, has caused representative government by a limited class to break down by excess of corruption, and the attempt at representative government by the whole male population to end in giving

第四章

施加于别人,一个是厌恶他人将权力施加于自己。人类不同群体之间在这两个倾向的相对强度的不同,是它们历史上的最重要的因素。有些国家统治别的国家的热情与个人的独立的愿望相比是如此之强,以至于哪怕前者仅仅只有朦胧的征兆,他们就准备牺牲掉整个后者。他们中的每一个人都像军队中的列兵那样,把个人自由行动的权力交到他的将军手中,只要他的军队不断得胜,并且他能够将自己吹嘘为一个征服者,尽管他对自身能分享征服的胜利果实的观念不过一个幻觉。一个严格限制自己权力和职能,被要求不作过分干涉,让大部分事情在没有他充当监护人和指挥官的情况下运转的政府,不适合这样的人民。在他们的眼中,只要权力本身允许普遍的竞争,掌握权力的人是不可能负太多责任的。他们中的一般人宁愿要一种不管是多么遥远和多么不可能的一份统治他同胞的权力,而不要无人对他们行使不必要的权力的这种对自己和他人来说都是确实可靠的事情。这些是一个有追求职位偏好的民族的特性。在他们中间,政治的发展进程主要决定于他们职位的获得,在那种情况下,人们只关注平等,而不关注自由,政党之间的竞争也只是决定干涉一切事情的权力是否应当属于这个或那个阶级,或者属于这一群或那一群政治家,民主的观念也只是把公职向所有人的竞争开放而不只是向一小部分人的竞争开放,制度越普及,职位就越多,而一切人对单个人,行政对全体人民的过度统治就越恐怖。将它或任何与此接近的事情当作一幅未做夸大的法国人的图景,是既不公平也不充分的,然而他们确实具有的这种类型性格的程度,已经引起一个由有限阶级控制的代议制政府由于过度的腐败而倒台,并且使得由全体男性控制的代议制政府的尝试终结,代之以授权给一个

one man the power of consigning any number of the rest, without trial, to Lambessa or Cayenne, provided he allows all of them to think themselves not excluded from the possibility of sharing his favours. The point of character which, beyond any other, fits the people of this country for representative government, is, that they have almost universally the contrary characteristic. They are very jealous of any attempt to exercise power over them, not sanctioned by long usage and by their own opinion of right; but they in general care very little for the exercise of power over others. Not having the smallest sympathy with the passion for governing, while they are but too well acquainted with the motives of private interest from which that office is sought, they prefer that it should be performed by those to whom it comes without seeking, as a consequence of social position. If foreigners understood this, it would account to them for some of the apparent contradictions in the political feelings of Englishmen—their unhesitating readiness to let themselves be governed by the higher classes, coupled with so little personal subservience to them that no people are so fond of resisting authority when it oversteps certain prescribed limits, or so determined to make their rulers always remember they will only be governed in the way they themselves like best. Place-hunting, accordingly, is a form of ambition to which the English, considered nationally, are almost strangers. If we except the few families or connexions of whom official employment lies directly in the way, Englishmen's views of advancement in life take an altogether different direction—that of success in business, or in a profession.

They have the strongest distaste for any mere struggle for office by political parties or individuals : and there are few things to which they have a greater aversion than to the multiplication of public employments : a thing, on the contrary, always popular with the bureaucracy-ridden nations of the Continent, who would rather pay higher taxes, than diminish by the smallest fraction their individual chances of a place for themselves or their relatives, and among whom a cry for retrenchment never means abolition of offices, but the reduction of the salaries of those which are too considerable for the ordinary citizen to have any chance of being appointed to them.

第四章

人,将其余不管是多少人,都可以不经审判就被送往兰姆贝沙和卡亚,只要他让所有的人都认为有分享他恩惠的可能性就可以。一个国家人民适合采用代议制政府与别的国家相区别的性格要点在于,他们具有几乎与之相反的特征。他们对任何没有经过长期应用和没有他们权利观认可的权力施加于他们身上的企图十分嫉恨,但他们总体上对将权力施加于他人身上不太在意。尽管他们对追求职位的个人利益的动机非常了解,但他们对热衷统治的人没有丝毫同情,因此他们更喜欢权力由那些作为社会地位的结果的不经追求而得到职位的人来掌握。如果外国人理解了这点,英国人明显互相矛盾的政治情感也就可以理解了:他们毫不犹豫地让更高层次的阶级统治,但却很少有个人的屈从,以至于当权力越过了某个规定的界线时,没有哪个民族会如此喜欢反抗权威,或者是如此坚定地使他们的统治者们一直记住他们只喜欢接受他们所喜欢的统治方式。因此,对英国整个民族来说,追逐职位是野心的一种形式,英国人对它几乎是陌生的。如果我们将少数几个容易得到政府任用的家族或社会关系除外,生活中英国人对于进步的观念完全与众不同——即商业上的或专业上的成功才是进步。

他们对政党或个人仅仅为职位而争斗抱有最强烈的反感,他们对公共职位的增加再反感不过了。反之,这件事总是在欧洲大陆那些饱受官僚折磨的国家为人们所热衷,他们宁愿缴纳更为高昂的赋税,也不愿意在最小程度上减少他们或其亲戚获取职位的机会,并且,他们所谓节省的呼声绝不是要废除那些职位,而是要求减少那些对普通市民来说根本没有机会得到的那些职位的薪水,仅此而已。

CHAPTER V
Of The Proper Functions
Of Representative Bodies

In treating of representative government, it is above all necessary to keep in view the distinction between its idea or essence, and the particular forms in which the idea has been clothed by accidental historical developments, or by the notions current at some particular period.

The meaning of representative government is, that the whole people, or some numerous portion of them, exercise through deputies periodically elected by themselves, the ultimate controlling power, which, in every constitution, must reside somewhere. This ultimate power they must possess in all its completeness. They must be masters, whenever they please, of all the operations of government. There is no need that the constitutional law should itself give them this mastery. It does not, in the British Constitution. But what it does give, practically amounts to this. The power of final control is as essentially single, in a mixed and balanced government, as in a pure monarchy or democracy. This is the portion of truth in the opinion of the ancients, revived by great authorities in our own time, that a balanced constitution is impossible. There is almost always a balance, but the scales never hang exactly even. Which of them preponderates, is not always apparent on the face of the political institutions. In the British Constitution each of the three co-ordinate members of the sovereignty is invested with powers which, if fully exercised, would enable it to stop all the machinery of government. Nominally, therefore, each is invested with equal power of thwarting and obstructing the others: and if, by exerting that power, any of the three could hope to

第五章　代议机关的应有职能

在探讨代议制政体时,首先必须铭记它的概念或本质与特定形式之间的差异,在这特定形式中,偶然的历史发展或某个特定时期时尚的观念表征着这个概念。

代议制政体的内涵就是,由全体人民或大部分人民,通过他们自己定期选举的代理人行使最后的控制权。这种权力一定存在于每一种政体中的某个地方。他们必须彻底掌控这个最后的权力。无论什么时候只要他们愿意,他们必定就是驾驭政府一切运作的主人。没有必要再由宪法本身赋予他们这种控制权,尽管英国宪法没有这么做,但它实际上赋予了这种控制权。与纯粹的君主制或民主制政府一样,这种最后控制权在一个混合的和平衡的政府的条件下,实质上也是单一的。这是古代人思想中的那部分真理,即平衡的政体是不可能的,这部分真理由我们时代的杰出权威重新复兴。平衡几乎总是存在的,但天平的两头不可能保持绝对的平衡。在政治制度的表面上,哪一种力量占上风并不总是显而易见的。在英国宪法中,如果充分行使这些权力的话,主权的三个地位相同的构成部分都有权力使整个政府机器的运作停止。所以,名义上每一构成部分都保有击败和阻碍其他各部分的同等权力,并且,如果三者之中每一构成部分都能期待通过行使

better its position, the ordinary course of human affairs forbids us to doubt that the power would be exercised. There can be no question that the full powers of each would be employed defensively, if it found itself assailed by one or both of the others. What then prevents the same powers from being exerted aggressively ? The unwritten maxims of the Constitution-in other words, the positive political morality of the country: and this positive political morality is what we must look to, if we would know in whom the really supreme power in the Constitution resides.

By constitutional law, the Crown can refuse its assent to any Act of Parliament, and can appoint to office and maintain in it any Minister, in opposition to the remonstrances of Parliament. But the constitutional morality of the country nullifies these powers, preventing them from being ever used; and, by requiring that the head of the Administration should always be virtually appointed by the House of Commons, makes that body the real sovereign of the State. These unwritten rules, which limit the use of lawful powers, are, however, only effectual, and maintain themselves in existence, on condition of harmonizing with the actual distribution of real political strength. There is in every constitution a strongest power-one which would gain the victory, if the compromises by which the Constitution habitually works were suspended, and there came a trial of strength. Constitutional maxims are adhered to, and are practically operative, so long as they give the predominance in the Constitution to that one of the powers which has the preponderance of active power out of doors. This, in England, is the popular power. If, therefore, the legal provisions of the British Constitution, together with the unwritten maxims by which the conduct of the different political authorities is in fact regulated, did not give to the popular element in the Constitution that substantial supremacy over every department of the government, which corresponds to its real power in the country, the Constitution would not possess the stability which characterizes it ; either the laws or the unwritten maxims would soon have to be changed. The British government is thus a representative government in the correct sense of the term: and the powers which it leaves in hands not directly accountable to the people can only be considered as precautions which the ruling power is willing should be taken against its own errors. Such

该项权力来改善它的地位的话,那么依照人类事务的常理就肯定会动用该项权力。每个构成部分如感到自己遭受到其他一个或两个部分的攻击,就会行使其全部权力进行防御,这是确定无疑的。那么又如何才能避免这同一权力被用来进行攻击呢?如果我们要知晓宪法中真正的至高权力是属于哪一部分的话,我们必须凭借未成文的宪法原则,也就是这个国家的实际的政治道德。

按照宪法,英国国王对议会的任何决议都能够行使否决权,就算议会反对也有权任命和继续留用内阁议员。但是这些权力在这个国家的宪政道德前会变得无效,从而使这些权力从未被行使过;另外,鉴于现实中行政领导始终应由下院任命,从而使下院成为国家的真正主权拥有者。然而,这些限制行使合法权利的未成文原则,只有在和真正政治实力的实际分配相匹配的条件下才是有效的,并且才能维护它们的存在。在每一个政体中都有一个最强大的力量,这就是说,假如宪法习惯性地发挥作用的妥协办法一旦终止,而出现了力量的博弈时,那个力量将获取胜利。只要它们把宪法上的优势赋予在宪法外持有现实力量优势的那个力量,宪法的规则将得到恪守,并且实际上它也在发挥作用,这在英国就是民众的力量。因此,如果英国宪法的法律条款,以及事实上调节着各个政治权威的行为的未成文规则,没有赋予宪法中群众的因素,以适应于它在国家中的真正力量的、超越各个政府部门的实质上的至尊地位,宪法具有稳定性这一典型特点将不复存在;不管是法律还是未成文原则将很快不得不更改。因此,英国政府是在正确领悟该术语的含义上所表征的代议制政府:它保留着间接对人民负责的人手中的权力,只能被认为是统治权力愿意采取预防办法,以便修正它自己所犯的错

precautions have existed in all well-constructed democracies. The Athenian Constitution had many such provisions ; and so has that of the United States.

But while it is essential to representative government that the practical supremacy in the state should reside in the representatives of the people, it is an open question what actual functions, what precise part in the machinery of government, shall be directly and personally discharged by the representative body. Great varieties in this respect are compatible with the essence of representative government, provided the functions are such as secure to the representative body the control of everything in the last resort. There is a radical distinction between controlling the business of government, and actually doing it. The same person or body may be able to control everything, but cannot possibly do everything ; and in many cases its control over everything will be more perfect, the less it personally attempts to do. The commander of an army could not direct its movements so effectually if he himself fought in the ranks, or led an assault. It is the same with bodies of men. Some things cannot be done except by bodies ; other things cannot be well done by them. It is one question, therefore, what a popular assembly should control, another what it should itself do. It should, as we have already seen, control all the operations of government. But in order to determine through what channel this general control may most expediently be exercised, and what portion of the business of government the representative assembly should hold in its own hands, it is necessary to consider what kinds of business a numerous body is competent to perform properly. That alone which it can do well, it ought to take personally upon itself. With regard to the rest, its proper province is not to do it, but to take means for having it well done by others.

For example, the duty which is considered as belonging more peculiarly than any other to an assembly representative of the people, is that of voting the taxes. Nevertheless, in no country does the representative body undertake, by itself or its delegated officers, to prepare the estimates. Though the supplies can only be voted by the House of Commons, and though the sanction of the House is also required for the appropriation of the revenues to the different items of the public expenditure, it is the maxim and the uniform practice of the Constitution

误。这种预防办法在一切完备的民主制度都出现过。雅典宪法有过许多这种条款；美国宪法也有过。

对代议制政府而言，尽管国家中的实际最高权力应属于民众的代表这一点是根本必要的，但是代议团体应直接并亲自履行哪些实际职能，在政府机器中扮演什么角色，则是个悬而未决的问题。只要该职能能确保代议团体对一切事情的最终的控制权，那么这方面的多样性和代议制政体的本质是并不冲突的。对政府事务的控制和这些事务的实际运作之间有着根本的差异。同一个人或同一团体可能控制一切事情，但不可能做一切事情；而且，在很多情况下它企图亲自去做的事情越少，它对一切事情的控制就越完全。军队指挥官如果亲自在队伍中参加战斗或率领队伍发动攻击，就不能有效地指挥军队的行动。由人组成的团体来说，情形也是一样的。有些事情只能由团体去做；另外一些事情团体则无法做好。所以，国民议会应该控制什么是一回事，而它自己应该做什么则是另一回事。我们已经谈到过，它应该控制政府的一切行动。但为了确定通过哪些途径最易于实现这种整体上的控制，以及哪部分政府事务代议制议会应该控制在自己手中，那么考虑哪种工作是一个人数众多的团体能够适当地完成的，这一点就很有必要。只有它能干好的事情，它才应该亲自担当起来。至于其他的事情，它的应有职责不是去干这个事，而是竭力让别人把事情干好。

比如，被认为特别应该属于代表人民的议会的职责是对税收加以表决。然而，没有一个国家会让代议团体自己作出或由它委任的官员作出预算计划。尽管财政支出只能由下院表决，尽管公共费用的各个项目的支出预算也须有下院的批准，但宪法的原则

that money can be granted only on the proposition of the Crown. It has, no doubt, been felt, that moderation as to the amount, and care and judgment in the detail of its application, can only be expected when the Executive government, through whose hands it is to pass, is made responsible for the plans and calculations on which the disbursements are grounded. Parliament, accordingly, is not expected, or even permitted, to originate directly either taxation or expenditure. All it is asked for is its consent, and the sole power it possesses is that of refusal.

The principles which are involved and recognised in this constitutional doctrine, if followed as far as they will go, are a guide to the limitation and definition of the general functions of representative assemblies. In the first place, it is admitted in all countries in which the representative system is practically understood, that numerous representative bodies ought not to administer. The maxim is grounded not only on the most essential principles of good government, but on those of the successful conduct of business of any description. No body of men, unless organized and under command, is fit for action, in the proper sense. Even a select board, composed of few members, and these specially conversant with the business to be done, is always an inferior instrument to some one individual who could be found among them, and would be improved in character if that one person were made the chief, and all the others reduced to subordinates. What can be done better by a body than by any individual, is deliberation. When it is necessary, or important, to secure hearing and consideration to many conflicting opinions, a deliberative body is indispensable. Those bodies, therefore, are frequently useful, even for administrative business, but in general only as advisers; such business being, as a rule, better conducted under the responsibility of one. E yen a joint-stock company has always in practice, if not in theory, a managing director; its good or bad management depends essentially on some one person's qualifications, and the remaining directors, when of any use, are so by their suggestions to him, or by the power they possess of watching him, and restraining or removing him in ease of misconduct.

和一直以来的惯例是,只有根据国王的建议才能拨款。毫无疑问人们会感到,只有在行政机关(应经过它的手来支出)对作为支出的依据的计划和计算负责之时,才有希望做到数量上适当,对开支使用的细节有必要的关注,以及作出明智的判断。因此,不指望甚至不允许议会直接介入税收或支出,诉求于它的只是表示批准,它所保有的唯一权力就是否决权。

该宪政理论中所蕴涵和认可的各个原则,就目前情形来看,如果得以恪守,就是对限制和界定代表制议会职能的指南。首先,要承认,在代议制实际上被视为理所当然的一切国家里,人数众多的代议团体不应当管理行政事务。这个原理不仅是以好政府的最根本原则为基准,而且是以有关各种事务的良好管理的原则为基准。任何一个团体,除非对其组织化并有人领导,否则,这个团体是不适于严格意义上的行动的。甚至由少数成员组成的特别委员会,并且这些人是特别熟悉所做的业务,也总是比不上在一个人领导下那样好,如果可能的话,从他们之中选拔出一个人,使其成为领导,其他的人则听从他的指挥,那么这个委员会的性质将会有所改进。一个团体能比任何个人做得好的是对问题的辩论。当听证或权衡许多相冲突的意见成为必要的或重要的事情时,一个进行辩论的团体就是不可或缺的。因此,即使对行政事务而言,这种团体也往往是有用的,不过一般说来它只是担当咨询机关;通常这种事务最好由一个人来负责实行。甚至一个股份公司也总是在实际上——如果不是纸上谈兵的话——有一个总经理。管理的优劣主要取决于某个人的各方面的综合条件,至于其余的董事成员,如果有用,边是由于他们对他提出建议,或者由于他们享有对他监督、限制或在他管理不善时予以罢免的

That they are ostensibly equal sharers with him in the management is no advantage, but a considerable set-off against any good which they are capable of doing : it weakens greatly the sense in his own mind, and in those of other people, of that individual responsibility in which he should stand forth personally and undividedly.

But a popular assembly is still less fitted to administer, or to dictate in detail to those who have the charge of admistration. Even when honestly meant, the interference is almost always injurious. Every branch of public admistration is a skilled business, which has its own peculiar principles and traditional rules, many of them not even known in any effectual way, except to those who have at some time had a hand in carrying on the business, and none of them likely to be duly appreciated by persons not practically acquainted with the department. I do not mean that the transaction of public business has esoteric mysteries, only to be understood by the initiated. Its principles are all intelligible to any person of good sense, who has in his mind a true picture of the circumstances and conditions to be dealt with: but to have this he must know those circumstances and conditions; and the knowledge does not come by intuition. There are many rules of the greatest importance in every branch of public business (as there are in every private occupation) of which a person fresh to the subject neither knows the reason nor even suspects the existence, because they are intended to meet dangers or provide against inconveniences which never entered into his thoughts. I have known public men, ministers, of more than ordinary natural capacity, who on their first introduction to a department of business new to them, have excited the mirth of their inferiors by the air with which they announced as a truth hitherto set at naught, and brought to light by themselves, something which was probably the first thought of everybody who ever looked at the subject, given up as soon as he had got on to a second. It is true that a great statesman is he who knows when to depart from traditions, as well as when to adhere to them. But it is a great mistake to suppose that he will do this better for being ignorant of the traditions. No one who does not thoroughly know the modes of action

第五章

权力。至于他们表面上和他均等承担事务的管理绝不是什么好事,而是在相当程度上消解了他们能发挥的长处,因为这极大地削弱了在其他人的心目中以及他自己脑海中的个人责任感,那是一种应竭尽全力担负起完全职责的个人责任感。

但是国民议会更不适用于行政管理,或者事无大小对负责行政管理的人发号施令。即使用心是好的,干涉几乎总是有害的。每一个公共行政部门都是一种技能性业务,它有其自身的特殊原则和传统的规则,其中许多东西除了在某个时候参与过该业务的人以外,甚至根本上无人知晓,而且,事实上不了解该部门的人,对它们予以适当重视的这种可能性是不大的。我并非说公共事务的处理是什么内行的秘传,只有借助传授才能把握。它的原则全都是任何具有理性的人所能领悟的,只要他头脑中对所要应对的情况和条件有个真实的了解;但要达到这个要求,他必须知晓那些情况和条件,而这种知识无法从直觉之中获得。在每一个公共事务部门(正如在每一个私人职业一样)都有诸多非常重要的规则,初次碰到这个问题的人既不知道其缘由,或者甚至怀疑其存在,因为这些规则是用来应对他未曾想到过的危险或不便的。我知晓一些能力超常的官员(部长们),在他们初次进入一个他们所不熟知的业务部门时,因刚接触到这业务,他们大概会有一些想法,过一段时间之后,他们逐渐明白过来又会放弃这种最初想法,他们把这种想法的变化看作迄今被忽视并由他们自己揭示出来的真理,他们宣布这种真理时的那种神气,使他们的下级感到好笑。的确,杰出的政治家是这样一种人,他既知晓什么时候遵循传统,也知晓什么时候摒弃传统。但是认为他由于对这些传统无知就能更好地摒弃传统,则是很大的错误。只要是不彻底了

which common experience has sanctioned, is capable of judging of the circumstances which require a departure from those ordinary modes of action. The interests dependent on the acts done by a public department, the consequences liable to follow from any particular mode of conducting it, require for Weighing and estimating them a kind of knowledge, and of specially exercised judgment, almost as rarely found in those not bred to it, as the capacity to reform the law in those who have not professionally studied it. All these difficulties are sure to be ignored by a representative assembly which attempts to decide on special acts of administration. At its best, it is inexperience sitting in judgment on experience, ignorance on knowledge : ignorance which, never suspecting the existence of what it does not know, is equally careless and supercilious, making light of, if not resenting, all pretensions to have a judgment better worth attending to than its own. Thus it is when no interested motives intervene : but when they do, the result is jobbery more unblushing and audacious than the worst corruption which can well take place in a public office under a government of publicity. It is not necessary that the interested bias should extend to the majority of the assembly. In any particular case it is often enough that it affects two or three of their number. Those two or three will have a greater interest in misleading the body than other of its members are likely to have in putting it right. The bulk of the assembly may keep their hands clean, but they cannot keep their minds vigilant or their judgments discerning in masters they know nothing about : and an indolent majority, like an indolent individual, belongs to the person who takes most pains with it. The bad measures or bad appointments of a minister may be checked by Parliament; and the interest of ministers in defending, and of rival partisans in attacking, secure a tolerably equal discussion : but *quis custodiet custodes*? who shall check the Parliament ? A minister, a head of an office, feels himself under some responsibility. An assembly in such cases feels under no responsibility at all : for when did any member of Parliament lose his seat for the vote he gave on any detail of administration ? To

第五章

解通常经验所认可的行动模式的人，就不能对需要摒弃那些通常行动模式的情况作出判断。要对依靠公共部门采取行动的利益，以及管理这个部门的特定模式可能产生的后果作出权衡和评估，就需要一种知识和经过特别训练的判断力，而这些未接受过有关的教育的人中，恰如改革法律的能力在未专门研究过法律的人中一样，是很少能看到这种知识和判断力的。企图对行政的专业性行动作出决定的议会绝对会忽视所有这些困难，充其量也不过是由无经验的裁决有经验的，由无知的裁决有知的。无知的人从不相信存在有他所不知晓的事情，既心不在焉又傲慢自以为是，轻视（如果不是憎恶的话）一切比他的见解更值得听取的见解的主张。当不牵涉到利害动机时情形就是这样。但是当牵涉到利害动机时，其结果就是徇私舞弊，比在公开的政府下的一个政府部门所能发生的最坏的贪污腐化还要更厚颜无耻。这种源于个人利害的偏私，未必会渗透到议会的多数人。在任何具体场合，它影响到两三个成员往往就够了。这两三个人在使该团体犯错误方面，将比任何其他成员在修正错误方面的兴趣更大。议会的大多数人可能还清廉，但他们不能保持警惕，或在他们一无所知的问题上明辨是非。一个懒惰成性的多数，和一个懒惰成性的人一样，总是属于那个为争取它而绞尽脑汁的人。对于部长不恰当的措施或不合时宜的任命，议会可以对其予以制约；部长们关注的是辩护，反对党的人关注的是攻击，这就确保了相当平等的辩论：但是谁来看护这看守人呢？谁将监督议会呢？一个部长，一个部门的领导，感到自己承担着某种责任。议会在这种场合根本不觉得要承担什么责任，因为任何议会成员，什么时候会由于他在行政管理的细节上的投票而丢失他的席位呢？对一个部长或一个部

a minister, or the head of an office, it is of more importance what will be thought of his proceedings some time hence, than what is thought of them at the instant : but an assembly, if the cry of the moment goes with it, however hastily raised or artificially stirred up, thinks itself and is thought by everybody to be completely exculpated however disastrous may be the consequences. Besides, an assembly never personally experiences inconveniences of its bad measures, until they have reached the dimensions of national evils. Ministers and administrators see them approaching, and have to bear all the annoyance and trouble of attempting to ward them off.

The proper duty of a representative assembly in regard to matters of administration, is not to decide them by its own vote, but to take care that the persons who have to decide them shall be the proper persons. Even this they cannot advantageously do by nominating the individuals. There is no act which more imperatively requires to be performed under a strong sense of individual responsibility than the nomination to employments. The experience of every person conversant with public affairs bears out the assertion, that there is scarcely any ac trespecting which the conscience of an average man is less sensitive; scarcely any case in which less consideration is paid to qualifications, partly because men do not know, and partly because they do not care for, the difference in qualifications between one person and another. When a ministermakes what is meant to be an honest appointment, that is when he does not actually job it for his personal connexions or his party, an ignorant person might suppose that he would try to give it to the person best qualified. No such thing. An ordinary minister thinks himself a miracle of virtue if he gives it to a person of merit, or who has a claim on the public on any account, though the claim or the merit may be of the most opposite description to that required, *Ilfallit un calculateur, ce fut un danseur qui l' obtint*, is hardly more of a caricature than in the days of Figaro ; and the minister doubtless

第五章

门领导而言,一段时期以后人们将如何看待,他所采取的措施,将比起当时人们如何看待更显重要。但是只要当时的舆论是附和议会的,不管这种舆论是怎样仓促形成的,或是人为地炒作的,议会自己会以为,每个人也会认为,不管后果何等严重,它是完全清白无辜的。而且,议会绝不会亲自体会到它不合时宜的措施所带来的不便,直到这种不便成为全国性的灾难。部长们和行政官员体察到这种不便即将来临,就应该不厌其烦、地避免这种不便。

就行政事务而言,议会的应有职责不是要动用它自己的表决权来做出决定,而是要确保使那些必须做出决定的人是合适的人选。议会甚至无法通过个人的提名而便利地实现这一要求。再也没有任何行为比任命的提名更迫切需要具备强烈的个人责任感。所有洞悉公共事务的人的经验都表明,几乎没有哪种行为让普通人的良心对个人责任感是如此不敏感的;几乎没有哪种情形对综合条件权衡思虑是如此少的,部分原因是在于人们对被提名的人的背景状况一无所知,还有部分原因是在于他们不重视这个人和那个人之间资格条件的差异。当一个部长要作出一项正直的任命时,也就是说,当他实际上既不是为他个人的亲戚朋友,也不是为他的政党徇私舞弊时,一个对此不了解内情的人或许会认为他会任命最有资格的人。哪有这回事!普通的部长如果任命一个有优点的人,或是任命在公众中有不论什么样的名声的人,尽管这种名声或优点也许和所要具备的恰好相反,他就认为自己所作出的任命是多么人尽其才。一位舞蹈家所要的是一台计拍器,这只不过是费加罗时代的讽刺话;至于部长,只要他所任命的人有优点或享有名声,他就必定会认为自己不

thinks himself not only blameless but meritorious if the man dances well. Besides, the qualifications which fit special individuals for special duties can only be recognised by those who know the individuals, or who make it their business to examine and judge of persons from what they have done, or from the evidence of those who are in a position to judge. When these conscientious obligations are so little regarded by great public officers who can be made responsible for their appointments, how must it be with assemblies who cannot ? Even now, the worst appointments are those which are made for the sake of gaining support or disarming opposition in the representative body : what might we expect if they were made by the body itself ? Numerous bodies never regard special qualifications at all. Unless a man is fit for the gallows, he is thought to be about as fit as other people for almost anything for which he can offer himself as a candidate. When appointments made by a popular body are not decided, as they almost always are, by party connexion or private jobbing, a man is appointed either because he has a reputation, often quite undeserved, for general ability, or frequently for no better reason than that he is personally popular.

It has never been thought desirable that Parliament should itself nominate even the members of a Cabinet. It is enough that it virtually decides who shall be prime minister, or who shall be the two or three individuals from whom the prime minister shall be chosen. In doing this it merely recognises the fact that a certain person is the candidate of the party whose general policy commands its support. In reality, the only thing which Parliament decides is, which of two, or at most three, parties or bodies of men, shall furnish the executive government: the opinion of the party itself decides which of its members isfittest to be placed at the head. According to the existing practice of the British Constitution, these things seem to be on as good a footing as they can be. Parliament does not nominate any minister, but the Crown appoints the head of the administration in conformity to the general wishes and inclinations manifested by Parliament, and the other ministers on the recommendation of the chief ; while every minister has the undivided moral responsibility of appointing fit persons to the other offices of administration which are not permanent. In a re-

第五章

仅无可指责,而且具有伯乐相马的眼光。然而,适用于特定职责的专业人员的资格条件,要么只能得到熟悉这些人的人的认可,要么只能得到其职务就是从他们的行动,或从处于作判断的地位的人所给予的证据,对他们进行考察和判断的人的认可。当应当对任命承担责任的高级官员们不怎么重视这些源于良心的个人责任感时,不能负责的议会又应该怎么办呢?甚至目前,为了在议会中获得支持或挫败反对力量,议会作出最糟糕的任命就是这种情形。如果这种任命是由议会本身作出的,我们又能指望什么呢?包含许多人的团体一点也不重视专门资格。除非一个人罪无可赦,否则他就被以为和别人一样,适宜做一切他能申请为候选人的事情。当公共团体作出的任命不是像几乎通常情况那样,由党派关系或个人的假公济私行为所决定的时候,那么这个人的被任命,要么是因为他保有一般能力方面的声誉,尽管这往往和其职责是很不相称的,要么往往就是因为他个人享有盛誉。

由议会本身提名内阁成员的做法从来被认为是不可取的。它实际上决定内阁总理,或者决定应从哪两三个人中挑选内阁总理,这就够了。当这样做的时候,它只不过是承认某个人是议会主持其一般政策的那个政党的候选人。实际上,议会所决定的仅仅是两个或至多三个政党中,哪一个政党应组成政府。至于这个政党的成员中,谁最适于担任政府首脑则由该政党自主决定。遵循英国宪法的目前惯例,这些事似乎是名正言顺的。议会并不提名任何内阁成员,而是遵循议会所诉求的普遍愿望和意向,由国王任命内阁首脑,再由他推荐任命其他阁员。另一方面,每个阁员有连带的道义责任任命适当人员担任非常任的政府机关职务。在共和国的条件下,作某种其他的安排也是有必要的,但是在实

public, some other arrangement would be necessary : but the nearer it approached in practice to that which has long existed in England, the more likely it would be to work well. Either, as in the American republic, the head of the Executive must be elected by some agency entirely independent of the representative body; or the body must content itself with naming the prime minister and making him responsible for the choice of his associates and subordinates. To all these considerations, at least theoretically, I fully anticipate a general assent: though, practically, the tendency is strong in representative bodies to interfere more and more in the details of administration, by virtue of the general law, that whoever has the strongest power is more and more tempted to make an excessive use of it ; and this is one of the practical dangers to which the futurity of representative governments will be exposed.

But it is equally true, though only of late and slowly beginning to be acknowledged, that a numerous assembly is as little fitted for the direct business of legislation as for that of administration. There is hardly any kind of intellectual work which so much needs to be done not only by experienced and exercised minds, but by minds trained to the task through long and laborious study, as the business of making laws. This is a sufficient reason, were there no other, why they can never be well made but by a committee of very few persons. A reason no less conclusive is, that every provision of a law requires to be framed with the most accurate and long-sighted perception of its effect on all the other provisions; and the law when made should be capable of fitting into a consistent whole with the previously existing laws. It is impossible that these conditions should be in any degree fulfilled when laws are voted clause by clause in a miscellaneous assembly. The incongruity of such a mode of legislating would strike all minds, were it not that our laws are already, as to form and construction, such a chaos, that the confusion and contradiction seem incapable of being made greater by any addition to the mass. Yet even now, the utter unfitness of our legislative machinery for its purpose is making itself practically felt every year more and more. The mere time necessarily occupied in getting through Bills, renders Parliament more and more incapable of passing any, except on detached and narrow points.

第五章

际做法上,它越是接近英国一贯以来的做法,就越能进行得顺利。或者,像在美利坚合众国那样,行政首脑必须由某个机构选出,而且这个机构是完全独立于代议团体;或者,代议团体应该知足于提名内阁总理,并让他负责任命他的同僚和下级。就所有这些考虑而言,最起码在理论上,我完全可以预料会获得普遍赞同的;尽管在实际上,议会越来越干涉行政的具体事务的倾向是很强烈的,因为有谁掌控最强大力量,谁就越来越想滥用权力这一普遍定律在起作用,这就是代议制政府将来要应对的实际危险之一。

但是同样真实的是,由人数众多的人构成的议会,既不适宜于进行直接的行政事务,也不适宜于进行直接的立法事务,尽管这一观点直到最近才逐渐得到认可。几乎没有哪种智力劳动像立法事务那样,不但需要经验丰富和受过专门训练的人去做,而且需要通过长期而艰苦的研究训练有素的人去做。这就是为什么除了由极少数人组成的委员会之外,其他人很难做好立法工作的充分理由,即使没有其他理由的话。一个具有同样决定意义的理由是,法律的每个条款,必须在确切而富有远见地洞察到它对所有其他条款的影响的情况下制定,而且,凡制定的法律必须能和以往存在的法律建构成一以贯之的整体。在五方杂处的议会里,当法律逐条逐项加以表决时,要在任何程度上满足这些要求都是不可能的。倘若不是因为我们的法律已经在形式和结构上是如此混乱,以致再徒增一些混乱似乎也不能使混乱和冲突变得更厉害的话,这种立法模式中存在的不协调情形将给所有的人以深刻印象。但即使在目前,我们的立法机器一点也不合乎于它的意图的状况,实际上年复一年越来越被人们所体味到。单就使法案得以批准所要占用的时间,就使得议会越来越不能通过任何法律(除

If a Bill is prepared which even attempts to deal with the whole of any subject (and it is impossible to legislate properly on any part without having the whole present to the mind), it hangs over from session to session through sheer impossibility of time being found to dispose of it. It matters not though the Bill may have been deliberately drawn up by the authority deemed the best qualified, with all appliances and means to boot; or by a select commission, chosen for their conversancy with the subject, and having employed years in considering and digesting the particular measure: it cannot be passed, because the House of Commons will not forgo the precious privilege of tinkering it with their clumsy hands.

The custom has of late been to some extent introduced, when the principle of a Bill has been affirmed on the second reading, of referring it for consideration in detail to a Select Committee, but it has not been found that this practice causes much less time to be lost afterwards in carrying it through the Committee of the whole House: the opinions or private crotchets which have been overruled by knowledge, always insist on giving themselves a second chance before the tribunal of ignorance. Indeed, the practice itself has been adopted principally by the House of Lords, the members of which are less busy and fond of meddling, and less jealous of the importance of their individual voices, than those of the elective House. And when a Bill of many clauses does succeed in getting itself discussed in detail, what can depict the state in which it comes out of Committee! Clauses omitted, which are essential to the working of the rest; incongruous ones inserted to conciliate some private interest, or some crotchety member who threatens to delay the Bill; articles foisted in on the motion of some sciolist with a mere smattering of the subject, leading to consequences which the member who introduced or those who supported the Bill did not at the moment foresee, and which need an amending Act in the next session to correct their mischiefs. It is one of the evils of the present mode of managing these things, that the explaining and defending of a Bill, and of its various provisions, is scarcely ever performed by the person from whose mind they emanated, who probably has not a seat in the House.

一些独立而窄小的条款外)。如果准备好一个法案,试图解决一揽子问题(不通盘把握整体,只对某一部分进行适当立法,这是不可能的),却由于没有足够时间去处置,从而使得这个法案被一次又一次会议延误下去。尽管这项法案,可能是由最有资格而且具有各种设备和办法的权威审慎起草的,或者由一个特别委员会起草,这个委员会由精通该问题、多年从事于考虑和研讨特定措施的人们组成,但同样于事无补。因为下院不情愿放弃用他们的笨拙的手加以修修补补的宝贵特权,所以法案无法获得批准。

近来在某种程度上采用了这样一种惯例,即在法案的准则通过第二次研读确认之后,将法案递交一专门委员会,以便进行详细审议,但并没有搞清楚这一惯例在以后法案通过整个下院的委员会时,能少花多少时间,因为,在无知的法庭上,被知识所反驳了的那些观点或个人奇思怪想,总是坚持要得到第二次辩论的机会。其实,这一作法本身主要是上院采用的,相对于下院议员而言,上院议员不怎么迷恋于干涉太多,也不怎么看重他们个人的发言权。然而,当具有诸多条款的法案的确经过详细讨论之后,并经委员会批准时,那是一种怎样的情形呀!有些条款被遗漏掉了,尽管它对其余条款的施行是不可或缺的;为了调和某种私人利益,或为了某个扬言要延误法案的喜好争辩的议员,有些不协调的条款被硬塞了进去;在某个单纯冒充行家的一知半解的人的提议下,一些条款被塞进去了,导致提出该法案的议员或支持该法案的议员当时未曾预料到的后果,从而不得不在下次会议上提出修正案以纠正其严重后果。就目前处理这些事情的方式而言,存在这样的弊端,即对法案以及对它的各种条款的阐释和辩护,几乎从来不是由最初提出该法案的人来进行的,他大概在议会中没有席位。

Their defence rests upon some minister or member of Parliament who did not frame them, who is dependent on cramming for all his arguments but those which are perfectly obvious, who does not know the full strength of his case, nor the best reasons by which to support it, and is wholly incapable of meeting unforeseen objections. This evil, as far as Government Bills are concerned, admits of remedy, and has been remedied in some representative constitutions, by allowing the Government to be represented in either House by persons in its confidence, having a right to speak, though not to vote.

If that, as yet considerable, majority of the House of Commons who never desire to move an amendment or make a speech, would no longer leave the whole regulation of business to those who do; if they would bethink themselves that better qualifications for legislation exist, and may be found if sought for, than a fluent tongue, and the faculty of getting elected by a constituency ; it would soon be recognized, that in legislation as well as administration, the only task to which a representative assembly can possibly be competent, is not that of doing the work, but of causing it to be done ; of determining to whom or to what sort of people it shall be confided, and giving or withholding the national sanction to it when performed. Any government fit for a high state of civilization would have as one of its fundamental elements a small body, not exceeding in number the members of a Cabinet, who should act as a Commission of Legislation, having for its appointed office to make the laws. If the laws of this country were, as surely they will soon be, revised and put into a connected form, the Commission of Codification by which this is effected should remain as a permanent institution, to watch over the work, protect it from deterioration, and make further improvements as often as required. No one would wish that this body should of itself have any power of *enacting* laws; the Commission would only embody the element of intelligence in their construction ; Parliament would represent that of will. No measure would become a law until expressly sanctioned by Parliament ; and Parliament, or either House, would have the power not only of rejecting but of sending back a Bill to the Com-

第五章

　　法案和条款全部依赖某个大臣或议会议员来辩护，尽管他从来没有参与起草这些法案和条款。除了非常明显的论点以外，他都是靠临阵磨枪、不求甚解地辩护所有论点，而且他不理解他所持观点的全部分量，也不明白用以支撑其立场的最好理由，从而根本不能应对未预见到的反对意见。这种弊端，就政府法案而言，是可以根治的，并且在某些代议制政体中，已经根治了这种弊端，其做法是允许政府派信任的人代表出席两院，虽无权利表决，但有资格发言。

　　如果下院中的多数人，至今还是相当多数的那部分人，他们从不愿意作修正案动议或发言，他们不再把整个的事务调整提交那些愿作动议或发言的人，如果他们考虑到，就立法而言，除了流利的口才和获得选民选举的能力之外还有更好的条件，并且如果去寻觅就能找到的话，那么他们很快就会认识到，在立法事务上，和行政事务一样，代议制议会所能胜任的唯一职责不是从事工作，而是让人把工作做好，确定应分派谁或怎样的人去做，以及在做完工作后能否得到民众的认可。任何符合高级文明状态的政府，将会设立一个组成政府重要部分的小团体，其人数不超过内阁成员，作为一个立法委员会，这个小团体负责法律的制定。如果我国的法律能得到修正，并纳入环环相扣的形式（肯定不久就会如此），承担这一职责的法典编纂委员会应继续作为一项永久制度来监督这项工作，防止其衰退，按其要求作进一步的改进。没有谁会愿意这个团体有权自行制定法律，因为这个委员会只是反映出构建法律方面的智慧成分，议会将体现其意志因素。在没有经过议会明确批准以前，任何法案不能成为法律。而议会，或上院或下院，将不仅拥有否决法案的权力，而且有将法案发回委员会

mission for reconsideration and improvement. Either House might also exercise its initiative, by referring any subject to the Commission, with directions to prepare a law. The Commission, of course, would have no power of refusing its instrumentality to any legislation which the country desired. Instructions, concurred in by both Houses, to draw up a Bill which should effect a particular purpose, would be imperative on the Commissioners, unless they preferred to resign their office. Once framed, however, Parliament should have no power to alter the measure, but solely to pass or reject it; or, if partially disapproved of, remit it to the Commission for reconsideration. The Commissioners should be appointed by the Crown, but should hold their offices for a time certain, say five years, unless removed on an address from the two Houses of Parliament, grounded either on personal misconduct (as in the case of judges), or on refusal to draw up a Bill in obedience to the demands of Parliament. At the expiration of the five years a member should cease to hold office unless re-appointed, in order to provide a convenient mode of getting rid of those who had not been found equal to their duties, and of infusing new and younger blood into the body.

The necessity of some provision corresponding to this was felt even in the Athenian Democracy, where, in the time of its most complete ascendancy, the popular Ecclesia could pass Psephisms (mostly decrees on single matters of policy), but laws, so called, could only be made or altered by a different and less numerous body, renewed annually, called the Nomothet, whose duty it also was to revise the whole of the laws, and keep them consistent with one another. In the English Constitution there is great difficulty in introducing any arrangement which is new both in form and in substance, but comparatively little repugnance is felt to the attainment of new purposes by an adaptation of existing forms and traditions. It appears to me that the means might be devised of enriching the constitution with this great improvement through the machinery of the House of Lords. A Commission for preparing Bills would in itself be no more an innovation on the Constitution than the Board for the administration of the Poor Laws, or the Inclosure Commission. If, in consideration of the great importance and dignity of the trust, it were made a rule that every person appointed

第五章

重新考虑、或对其作进一步改进的权力。上下两院都可以发挥出主动性,把问题递交这个委员会,并指示它制定一项法律。当然,作为国家所需立法的一种工具,这个委员会没有权力拒绝发挥它的这一功能。制定一项为实现特定目的的法案的命令,经两院一致通过后,对该委员会的委员有强制力,除非他们宁愿辞去这个职位。然而,法案一旦制定,议会便没有权力加以更改,只能批准或加以否决;或者,如果不同意其中的一部,可以将该法案送回委员会重新考虑。国王任命委员会的委员,但应对任期做出规定,比如说五年,只有通过议会两院才能提议罢免,其原因要么是个人的渎职(像法官的情形那样),要么是拒绝遵照议会的要求制定法案。五年期满,这个委员会的成员即不再担任这个职位,除非经过再次任命,从而提供了一种便捷的方式来罢免那些不能胜任该职务的人,这样就给该团体注入了新鲜而年轻的血液。

甚至在雅典民主制中,也能体会到与这相当的某种规定的必要性,在那里,在民主制的鼎盛时期,公民会议能通过法令(大多是涉及单个的政策事项的法令),但所谓法律(Laws)则只能由另外一个人数较少的、称为立法团的团体制定或更改,这个团体每年都要更新,它的职能是修改全部法律,使其保持彼此的协调。就英国宪法而言,采纳任何在形式和实质上的新安排有很多障碍因素,但相对来说,对于使现有形式和传统合乎实现新的目的,则不会抱有多大的反感。依我看,可能设计出方法,借助上院的机构用这一巨大改进来完善宪法。与扶贫法管理局或圈地委员会相比,在宪法上,一个准备法案的委员会本质上不是更大的创新。如果考虑到这种委托的极端重要性和尊严,要规定所有被任命为立法委员会成员的人,除

a member of the Legislative Commission, unless removed from office on an address from Parliament, should be a Peer for life, it is probable that the same good sense and taste which leave the judicial functions of the Peerage practically to the exclusive care of the Law Lords, would leave the business of legislation, except on questions involving political principles and interests, to the professional legislators; that Bills originating in the Upper House would always be drawn up by them ; that the Government would devolve on them the framing of all its Bills ; and that private members of the House of Commons would gradually find it convenient, and likely to facilitate the passing of their measures through the two Houses, if instead of bringing in a Bill and submitting it directly to the House, they obtained leave to introduce it and have it referred to the Legislative Commission. For it would, of course, be open to the House to refer for the consideration of that body not a subject merely, but any specific proposal, or a Draft of a Bill *in extenso*, when any member thought himself capable of preparing one such as ought to pass ; and the House would doubtless refer every such draft to the Commission, if only as materials, and for the benefit of the suggestions it might contain: as they would, in like manner, refer every amendment or objection, which might be proposed in writing by any member of the House after a measure had left the Commissioners' hands. The alteration of Bills by a Committee of the whole House would cease, not by formal abolition, but by desuetude ; the right not being abandoned, but laid up in the same armoury with the royal veto, the right of withholding the supplies, and other ancient instruments of political warfare, which no one desires to see used, but no one likes to part with, lest they should at any time be found to be still needed in an extraordinary emergency. By such arrangements as these, legislation would assume its proper place as a work of skilled labour and special study and experience; while the most important liberty of the nation, that of being governed only by laws assented to by its elected representatives, would be fully preserved, and made more valuable by being detached from the serious, but by no means unavoidable, drawbacks which now accompany it in the form of ignorant and ill-considered legislation.

非通过议会提议罢免,按惯例应成为上院终身贵族议员,那么将司法职能完全委托给上院掌管司法的议员的那种理性和经验,就很可能会把立法事务(除涉及政治原则和利益的议题之外)委托给专业的立法者。由上院提议的法案将会总是由他们起草。政府就会委托他们制定所有法案了。而且上院中非阁员的议员如果不把法案直接提交下院,而是被准许由下院提出来,并经由下院把它送达给立法委员会,逐渐地他们就会觉得方便,并可能有利于使他们的法案在上下两院得以批准。因为毫无疑问,下院不仅可以把问题交付给这个团体考虑,而且可以把特别建议甚至法案全文的草案交付给这个团体考虑,如果任何议员认为自己能够准备这样一个应该会被批准的法案的话。无疑,下院一定会把每个这样的草案提交该委员会,即使这样的草案只是作为材料,或者为了其中可能提出的建议,就好比在一次议案离开委员会的手之后,下院同样会把议员可能会提出的书面的修正案或反对意见提交委员会。如果这样的话,由整个议会的委员会更改法案的做法虽然没有正式废除,但会废而不用。这项权力不是被否决了,而是同国王否决权、扣发国库开支拨款权以及其他的政治斗争的古老手段一起被扔在军械库中搁置。没有人期待看到它们被行使,但也没有人愿意放弃这种权力,以免随时在非常紧急状态下仍然需要这种权力。经过这样一些安排,立法就会拥有这样一种正当地位:即作为技术性劳动和需要特殊研究和经验的工作的一种恰当地位;另一方面,国民最重要的自由——只受他们选出的代表所认可的法律统治的自由——将会完全予以保持,这种自由,由于克服了目前在无知和考虑不周的立法形式上带有的严重但并非不可避免的缺点,从而变得更有价值。

代议制政府

Instead of the function of governing, for which it is radically unfit, the proper office of a representative assembly is to watch and control the government ; to throw the light of publicity on its acts ; to compel a full exposition and justification of all of them which any one considers questionable ; to censure them if found condemnable, and, if the men who compose the government abuse their trust, or fulfil it in a manner which conflicts with the deliberate sense of the nation, to expel them from office, and either expressly or virtually appoint their successors. This is surely ample power, and security enough for the liberty of the nation. In addition to this, the Parliament has an office not inferior even to this in importance ; to be at once the nation's Committee of Grievances, and its Congress of Opinions: an arena in which not only the general opinion of the nation, but that of every section of it, and as far as possible of every eminent individual whom it contains, can produce itself in full light and challenge discussion ; where every person in the country may count upon finding some body who speaks his mind, as well as or better than he could speak it himself-not to friends and partisans exclusively, but in the face of opponents, to be tested by adverse controversy; where those whose opinion is overruled, feel satisfied that it is heard, and set aside not by a mere act of will, but for what are thought superior reasons, and commend themselves as such to the representatives of the majority of the nation ; where every party or opinion in the country can muster its strength, and be cured of any illusion concerning the number or power of its adherents ; where the opinion which prevails in the nation makes itself manifest as prevailing, and marshals its hosts in the presence of the government, which is thus enabled and compelled to give way to it on the mere manifestation, without the actual employment, of its strength ; where statesmen can assure themselves, far more certainly than by any other signs, what elements of opinion and power are growing, and what declining, and are enabled to shape their measures with some regard not solely to present exigencies, but to tendencies in progress. Representative assemblies are often taunted bytheir enemies

第五章

代议制议会的职能不是管理（这是完全不适合的），而是制衡和控制政府：把政府的行为透明化，促使其对公众认为存在问题的一切行为作出完整的解释和辩护；对那些应受指责的行为进行谴责，此外，如果组成政府的官员滥用职权，或者履行职责的做法与这个国家经过认真思考的理性相抵触，就把他们免职，并明确地或事实上委任其继任者。代议制议会的确拥有广泛的权力，它足以确保民众的自由。此外，议会还有一项职能，其重要性不亚于上述职能：它既是民众的诉苦委员会，又是民众表达诉求的大会。它是这样一个舞台：在这舞台上，不仅民众的一般诉求，而且每个部分民众的诉求，以及尽可能地使民众中每个伟大个人的诉求，都能得以充分表达并要求讨论；在这舞台上，这个国家的每个人都可以希望有某个人把他想要表达的意思说出来，和他自己说得一样好，甚至比他自己说得还要好，这不是只对亲朋好友和同党的人说，而是当着反对者的面，接受相反争论的挑战。在这舞台上，自己观点被别人驳倒的那些人会觉得满足，因为已经把观点作了表述，这个观点没有被听取，不是由于一味随意的行为，而是由于被认为是更好的观点而得到大多数人民代表赞同；在这舞台上，每个政党或每种观点都能估量自己的力量，也都能更正有关它的支持者的人数或力量的任何错觉；在这舞台上，民众中占上风的观点明确表明它的优势，并当着政府的面集聚队伍，这样，在它只是展示力量而没有实际使用力量的情况下，从而就使得政府能够并被迫向它妥协；在这舞台上，与依靠任何其他信号相比，政治家可以更稳妥地搞清楚哪些观点和力量成份正在上升，哪些正在下降，这样在拟定措施时，不仅能够关注当前紧急事务而且关注到发展中的倾向。它的对手往往讥笑代议制议会是一个纯粹清谈和空谈的

with being places of mere talk and *bavardage*. There has seldom been more displaced derision. I know not how a representative assembly can more usefully employ itself than in talk, when the subject of talk is the great public interests of the country, and every sentence of it represents the opinion either of some important body of persons in the nation, or of an individual in whom some such body have reposed their confidence. A place where every interest and shade of opinion in the country can have its cause even passionately pleaded, in the face of the government and of all other interests and opinions, can compel them to listen, and either comply, or state clearly why they do not, is in itself, if it answered no other purpose, one of the most important political institutions that can exist anywhere, and one of the foremost benefits of free government. Such 'talking' would never be looked upon with disparagement if it were not allowed to stop 'doing' ; which it never would, if assemblies knew and acknowledged that talking and discussion are their proper business, while *doing*, as the result of discussion, is the task not of a miscellaneous body, but of individuals specially trained to it ; that the fit office of an assembly is to see that those individuals are honestly and intelligently chosen, and to interfere no further with them, except by unlimited latitude of suggestion and criticism, and by applying or withholding the final seal of national assent. It is for want of this judicious reserve, that popular assemblies attempt to do what they cannot do well-to govern and legislate-and provide no machinery but their own for much of it, when of course every hour spent in talk is an hour withdrawn from actual business. But the very fact which most unfits such bodies for a Council of Legislation, qualifies them the more for their other office-namely, that they are not a selection of the greatest political minds in the country, from whose opinions little could with certainty be inferred concerning those of the nation, but are. when properly constituted, a fair sample of every grade of intellect among the people which is at all entitled to a voice in public affairs. Their part is to indicate wants, to be an organ

第五章

地方。很少有比这更大的误会。当谈论的议题事关国家巨大公共利益的时候，我不认为除了在谈论中工作外，代议制议会还有比这更合适的方式，因为谈论中的每一句话，要么代表着某个重要团体的观点，要么代表着某个重要团体所信赖的某个人的观点；在这舞台上，在政府面前以及其他一切利益和观点面前，这个国家的每一种利益和每一个观点都能对自身的理由进行甚至激烈的辩护，并能使它们必定被人们听到，要么赞同，要么清楚表述不赞同的理由，这样一个地方实质上就是（如果它不是为了其他目的的话）任何地方所能有的最重要的一种政治制度之一，它也是自由政府的最重要的好处之一。这种"谈论"，如果不会阻碍"行动"，就绝不应该低估它。谈论绝不会阻碍行动，如果议会明了并接纳谈论和讨论是它的题中之意，而作为讨论结果的行动则不是一个五方杂处的团体的职责，而是特别经过所需训练的人们的职责；明了并认可议会的应有职能是竭力使那些人被诚实地和明智地挑选出来，并不再干涉他们，除了接受广泛范围的建议和批评，以及是否给予民众同意的最后批准之外。正是因为缺乏这种明智的保留，导致民主议会试图做它不可能做好的事情——行政管理和立法事务——并除了它自己的机构不去设立其他机构，这时当然在谈论中所用的时间就是不从事实际事务的时间。但正是使这种团体最不适合充当立法会议的这一事实，却使它们更适于它们的另一种职能——即它们不是这个国家最杰出的政治人物的选拔，因为关于民众的观点很少能从这种人物的观点中可靠地进行推导，而是当这个机关适当地组成时，毕竟它是有资格在公共事务上发表议论的，民众中的智力程度不等的一个相当好的标本。它们的职能就是反映出各种需要，成为表达民众需求的机

for popular demands, and a place of adverse discussion for all opinions relating to public matters, both great and small ; and, along with this, to check by criticism, and eventually by withdrawing their support, those high public officers who really conduct the public business, or who appoint those by whom it is conducted. Nothing but the restriction of the function of representative bodies within these rational limits, will enable the benefits of popular control to be enjoyed in conjunction with the no less important requisites (growing ever more important as human affairs increase in scale and in complexity) of skilled legislation and administration. There are no means of combining these benefits, except by separating the functions which guarantee the one from those which essentially require the other ; by disjoining the office of control and criticism from the actual conduct of affairs, and devolving the former on the representatives of the Many, while securing for the latter, under strict responsibility to the nation, the acquired knowledge and practised intelligence of a specially trained and experienced Few.

The preceding discussion of the functions which ought to devolve on the sovereign representative assembly of the nation, would require to be followed by an inquiry into those properly vested in the minor representative bodies, which ought to exist for pur- poses that regard only localities. And such an inquiry forms an essential part of the present treatise; but many reasons require its postponement, until we have considered the most proper composition of the great representative body, destined to control as sovereign the enactment of laws and the administration of the general affairs of the nation.

第五章

关,以及成为一个有关大小公共事务的所有观点进行激烈辩论的场所。此外,就是予以批评,最终并决定不给予其支持,从而对事实上管理公共事务的高级官员或任命他们的高级官员进行监督。只有把代议团体的职能限制在这些合理的界限内,才能既获得对民众实行控制的好处,又满足同等重要的对娴熟的立法和行政的要求(随着人类事务在规模上和复杂程度上的增大而愈来愈重要)。要实现这些好处的结合,除了确保前者的职能从要求后者的职能中分开之外,没有其他办法。通过把控制和批评的职能与对事务的实际管理分离,从而把前者委托给多数人的代表,同时在对民众承担严格责任下,为后者确保得到通过特别培训又有经验的少数人所具备的知识和熟练的智慧。

以上对必须赋予主权国家的代议制议会的职能所作的探讨,将要求紧接着对适当地赋予小的代议制团体的职能作一些研究,这些团体应该只是作为有关地方的目的而存在。对它的探讨是这本专著的一个不可或缺的部分;但是由于诸多原因,必须在探讨了作为主权者对立法和国家行政进行控制的大代议制团体的最合适的构成以后,我们再进行这种探讨。

CHAPTER VI
Of The Infirmities And Dangers To Which Representative Government Is Liable

The defects of any form of government may be either negative or positive. It is negatively defective if it does not concentrate in the hands of the authorities, power sufficient to fulfil the necessary offices of a government ; or if it does not sufficiently develop by exercise the active capacities and social feelings of the individual citizens. On neither of these points is it necessary that much should be said at this stage of our inquiry.

The want of an amount of power in the govern ment, adequate to preserve order and allow of progress in the people, is incident rather to a wild and rude state of society generally, than to any particular form of political union. When the people are too much attached to savage independence, to be tolerant of the amount of power to which it is for their good that they should be subject, the state of society (as already observed) is not yet ripe for representative government. When the time for that government has arrived, sufficient power for all needful purposes is sure to reside in the sovereign assembly ; and if enough of it is not entrusted to the executive, this can only arise from a jealous feeling on the part of the assembly towards the administration, never likely to exist but where the constitutional power of the assembly to turn them out of office has not yet sufficiently established itself. Wherever that constitutional right is admitted in principle and fully operative in practice, there is no fear that the assembly will not be willing to trust its own ministers with any amount of power really desirable; the danger is, on the contrary, lest they should grant it too ungrudgingly, and too indefinite in extent, since the power of the

第六章　代议制政府容易有的薄弱环节和危险

政府形式的缺陷可以说是积极的,也可以说是消极的。如果它不将权力集中在权力部门,使之有足够的力量去履行政府必要的职能,或者如果它不能依靠发挥单个公民的积极能力和社会情感来求得充分的发展,那它就是消极的。在目前的研究阶段,这两点都没有必要做过多的论述。

政府缺乏足够的用以维持秩序和允许人民进步的权力,与其说是一个在野蛮和残暴的社会状态中常见的事件,不如说是任何特定的政治联合形式的常见事件。当人民过于依恋那种未开化的独立,而不能容忍那种为了他们的利益就必须臣服的一定权力时,这种社会状态(如我们早已注意到的那样)仍然不适合采用代议制政府。当适合那种政府形式的时机到来时,各方面都需要的足够权力必需来自于至高无上的议会;如果行政部门没有被赋予足够的权力,这只能是议会对行政权力的嫉妒心使然,而这种情况只有在议会罢免官员的宪法权力本身还没有充分建立起来时才会存在。当宪法权利在原则上被确立,而在实践中又得到施行,就不用担心议会不把部长们真正想要的权力赋予他们。反过来,危险的是,权力的赋予会过分慷慨,在范围上过于模糊,

minister is the power of the body who make and who keep him so. It is, however, very likely, and is one of the dangers of a controlling assembly, that it may be lavish of powers, but afterwards interfere with their exercise; may give power by wholesale and take it back in detail, by multiplied single acts of interference in the business of administration. The evils arising from this assumption of the actual function of governing, in lieu of that of criticising and checking those who govern, have been sufficiently dwelt upon in the preceding chapter. No safeguard can in the nature of things be provided against this improper meddling, except a strong and general conviction of its injurious character.

The other negative defect which may reside in a government, that of not bringing into sufficient exercise the individual faculties, moral, intellectual, and active, of the people, has been exhibited generally in setting forth the distinctive mischiefs of despotism. As between one form of popular government and another, the advantage in this respect lies with that which most widely diffuses the exercise of public functions ; on the one hand, by excluding fewest from the suffrage;on the other, by opening to all classes of private citizens, so far as is consistent with other equally important objects, the widest participation in the details of judicial and administrative business; as by jury trial, admission to municipal offices, and above all by the utmost possible publicity and liberty of discussion, whereby not merely a few individuals in succession, but the whole public, are made, to a certain extent, participants in the government, and sharers in the instruction and mental exercise derived from it. The further illustration of these benefits, as well as of the limitations under which they must be aimed at, will be better deferred until we come to speak of the details of administration.

The *positive* evils and dangers of the representative, as of every other form of government, may be reduced to two heads: first, general ignorance and incapacity, or, to speak more moderately, insufficient mental qualifications, in the controlling body ; secondly, the danger of its being under the influence of interests not identical with the general welfare of the community.

第六章

因为部长们的权力就是使他具有并保持权力的那个团体的权力。然而,很可能会出现这种情形,并且这是一个支配性的议会所具有的危险之一,就是议会在赋予权力时很慷慨,但后来却对他们行使权力进行干涉;可能整批整批地授予权力,但却通过对行政事务的多次单独的干涉行为将之悉数收回。这种以实际的管理代替批评和督促那些管理者的设想所产生的害处,在前面一章就作了充分的详细研究。对这种不恰当的干涉,除了对它的有害的本质进行深刻而普遍的认识外,理所当然是没有什么可以用来防止的。

政府另外一个消极缺陷,即不能使个人的能力,即道德的、智力的和行动上的才能得到充分的发挥的缺陷,在阐述专制政治的明显的危害时就大概地揭示出来了。就一种形式的平民政府与另一种形式相比较来说,这方面的优势属于那种最广泛地分散行使权力的政府,一方面,它把最少数的人排除在选举权之外;另一方面,只要与别的同等重要的目标一致,它使所有的阶级和单个的公民都能最广泛地参与具体的司法和行政事务;如通过参与司法审判,谋求市政职务,最重要的是通过最大可能的公开和自由的讨论,不仅仅是少数人相继参加政府,而是整个大众,在某种程度上,都是政府的参与者,并分享从政府管理中得到的教育和智力的锻炼。我们在详细谈到行政管理的时候,会对这些好处和他们指望得到这些好处时所受的限制,作进一步的说明。

如同其他政府形式一样,代议制的积极方面的弊端和危险可以简化为两个方面:第一,普遍的无知和无能,或者换种更温和的说法,就是统治集团的智力水平不够高;第二,易受与社会普遍福利不相同的利益影响的危险。

The former of these evils, deficiency in high mental qualifications, is one to which it is generally supposed that popular government is liable in a greater degree than any other. The energy of a monarch, the steadiness and prudence of an aristocracy, are thought to contrast most favourably with the vacillation and short-sightedness of even the most qualified democracy. These propositions, however, are not by any means so well founded as they at first sight appear.

Compared with simple monarchy, representative government is in these respects at no disadvantage. Except in a rude age, hereditary monarchy, when it is really such, and not aristocracy in disguise, much surpasses democracy in all the forms of incapacity supposed to be characteristic of the last. I say, except in a rude age, because in a really rude state of society there is a considerable guarantee for the intellectual and active capacities of the sovereign. His personal will is constantly encountering obstacles from the wilfulness of his subjects, and of powerful individuals among their number. The circumstances of society do not afford him much temptation to mere luxurious self-indulgence; mental and bodily activity, especially political and military, are his principal excitements; and among turbulent chiefs and lawless followers he has little authority, and is seldom long secure even of his throne, unless he possesses a considerable amount of personal daring, dexterity, and energy. The reason why the average of talent is so high among the Henrys and Edwards of our history, may be read in the tragical fate of the second Edward and the second Richard, and the civil wars and disturbances of the reigns of John and his incapable successor. The troubled period of the Reformation also produced several eminent hereditary monarchs, Elizabeth, Henri Quatre, Gustavus Adolphus ; but they were mostly bred up in adversity, succeeded to the throne by the unexpected failure of nearer heirs, or had to contend with great difficulties in the commencement of their reign. Since European life assumed a settled aspect, anything above mediocrity in a hereditary king has become extremely rare, while the general average has been even below mediocrity, both in talent and in vigour of character.

第六章

前一种弊端,即高级智力水平的缺乏,是一个一般认为平民政府比任何形式的政府都容易有的更大程度上的缺陷。君主的旺盛精力,贵族统治的坚定和审慎,是人们最喜欢拿来与哪怕是最合格的民主政治的优柔寡断和短视相比的地方。然而,这些命题决不像它们在初看之下显得那么站得住脚。

同简单的君主制相比,代议制政府在这些方面不是没有优势。除了野蛮时代外,当世袭君主制是真正的而不是以贵族政治为掩饰的政体时,其通常被认为是各种形式的民主制特点的无能方面要超越民主制。我得说,这要除开野蛮时代,因为在一个真正野蛮的社会状态中,君主在智力和积极能力方面是有相当保障的。他的个人意志常常要面对来自他的臣民以及他臣民当中强势人物的存心阻挠。社会环境没有给他太多纯粹奢豪放纵的机会,身心的活动,特别是政治和军事活动是令他兴奋的主要活动。他在他那些放荡不羁的首领们和无法无天的随从们当中并没有太多的权威,并且除非拥有相当大的个人勇气、机智和精力,否则他甚至很难长久保持他的王位。历史上每个亨利和爱德华的平均才能都那么高的原因,也许可以从爱德华二世和理查德二世的悲惨命运和约翰王与他的无能的后继者的统治时期的内战和动乱中找到。宗教改革的动乱时期也出现过几位杰出的世袭君主,如伊利莎白、亨利·卡特、古斯塔夫斯·阿道尔弗斯等;但他们几乎都在艰难环境中长大,由于继承顺位较多的王位继承人的出乎意料的失败而承继大统,或者他们刚登王位时就不得不与各种巨大困难作斗争。自从欧洲的生活呈现出安定的局面以来,在才能和性格魅力方面,世袭君主中的任何非凡的地方都变得极为罕见,

A monarchy constitutionally absolute now only maintains itself in existence (except temporarily in the hands of some active-minded usurper) through the mental qualifications of a permanent bureaucracy. The Russian and Austrian Governments, and even the French Government in its normal condition, are oligarchies of officials, of whom the head of the State does little more than select the chiefs. I am speaking of the regular course of their administration; for the will of the master of course determines many of their particular acts.

The governments which have been remarkable in history for sustained mental ability and vigour in the conduct of affairs, have generally been aristocracies. But they have been, without any exception, aristocracies of public functionaries. The ruling bodies have been so narrow, that each member, or at least each influential member, of the body, was able to make, and did make, public business an active profession, and the principal occupation of his life. The only aristocracies which have manifested high governing capacities, and acted on steady maxims of policy, through many generations, are those of Rome and Venice. But, at Venice, though the privileged order was numerous, the actual management of affairs was rigidly concentrated in a small oligarchy within the oligarchy, whose whole lives were devoted to the study and conduct of the affairs of state. The Roman government partook more of the character of an open aristocracy like our own. But the really governing body, the Senate, was in general exclusively composed of persons who had exercised public functions, and had either already filled or were looking forward to fill the higher offices of the state, at the peril of a severe responsibility in case of incapacity and failure. When once members of the Senate, their lives were pledged to the conduct of public affairs ; they were not permitted even to leave Italy except in the discharge of some public trust ; and unless turned out of the Senate by the censors for character or conduct deemed disgraceful, they retained their powers and responsibilities to the end of life. In an aristocracy thus constituted, every member felt his personal importance entirely bound up with the dignity and estimation of the commonwealth which he administered, and with the part he

第六章

而其平均水平甚至低于常人。在宪法上绝对的君主制现在只能通过一个长久存在的官僚机构的智力条件来维持其自身的存在(除非它暂时被控制在某个思维活跃的篡位者手中)。俄罗斯与奥地利政府,甚至处于正常情况下的法国政府,都是官员的寡头政治,国家首脑除了选择官员之外别无他事。我所谈的是他们政府的常规行动,因为掌权者的意志决定着政府的许多特定行为。

那些在历史上为了维持它们处理事务的智力水平和精力的政府,一般来说是贵族政府。但毫无例外,它们都是公共官员的贵族政府。统治集团是那样的有限,以至于每个成员,或至少集团的每个有影响的成员,能够使而且确实使公共事务变成一项积极的职业和他生活中的主要职业。那些罗马和威尼斯的贵族政府,是唯一显示出高超的管理能力、好几代都按照稳健的政策原则行事的政府。但在威尼斯,尽管特权等级不计其数,但管理事务的真正权力被高度集中在寡头集团中的一小部分寡头手中,他们毕其一生,研究和管理国家事务。罗马政府则更加带有像我们自己的开放的贵族政府所具有的特征。但是真正的统治集团,即元老院,一般只是由那些曾经担任过公职,以及早已在担任或正在谋求更高的国家职位的人——他们冒着万一无能或失败就要承担严重后果的危险——组成。一旦成为元老院的一员,他们就必须保证终生从事公共事务;他们除非执行某项公务,否则不能离开意大利;除非检察官由于他们品行不端而将他们逐出元老院,否则他们可以一辈子行使他们的权力和履行他们的责任。在一个如此构成的贵族政府里,每个成员都感到个人的重要性完全与他所管理的国家的尊严和威望,以及他在政府中所能起的作用联系在一起。这种尊严和威望与普通市民团体的繁

was able to play in its councils. This dignity and estimation were quite different things from the prosperity or happiness of the general body of the citizens, and were often wholly incompatible with it. But they were closely linked with the external success and aggrandizement of the State: and it was, consequently, in the pursuit of that object almost exclusively, that either the Roman or the Venetian aristocracies manifested the systematically wise collective policy, and the great individual capacities for government, for which history has deservedly given them credit.

It thus appears that the only governments, not representative, in which high political skill and ability have been other than exceptional, whether under monarchical or aristocratic forms, have been essentially bureaucracies. The work or government has been in the hands of governors by profession; which is the essence and meaning of bureaucracy. Whether the work is done by them because they have been trained to it, or they are trained to it because it is to be done by them, makes a great difference in many respects, but none at all as to the essential character of the rule. Aristocracies, on the other hand, like that of England, in which the class who possessed the power derived it merely from their social position, without being specially trained or devoting themselves exclusively to it (and in which, therefore, the power was not exercised directly, but through representative institutions oligarchically constituted) have been, in respect to intellectual endowments, much on a par with democracies; that is, they have manifested such qualities in any considerable degree only during the temporary ascendancy which great and popular talents, united with a distinguished position, have given to some one man. Themistocles and Pericles, Washington and Jefferson, were not more completely exceptions in their several democracies, and were assuredly much more splendid exceptions, than the Chathams and Peels of the representative aristocracy of Great Britain, or even the Sullys and Colberts of the aristocratic monarchy of France.

A great minister, in the aristocratic governments of modern Europe, is almost as rare a phenomenon as a great king.

第六章

荣和幸福是完全不同的事情,并且往往不能和它相互调和。但两者都与国家的外在成功与扩张紧密联系在一起。因此,就是在几乎只为追求那个目标的过程中,不管是罗马还是威尼斯的贵族政府都表现出了明智的集体政策,以及对政府管理的个人非凡才能,对此历史给了它们应得的荣誉。

因此,看来只有一贯具备高度政治技巧和能力,但又不是代议制的政府,不管是君主制还是贵族制,都曾经在本质上是官僚政治。政府的工作由专业的管理人员来做——这是官僚政治的本质和内涵。工作要由他们来做是因为他们受过这方面的训练,还是他们受这方面的训练是因为工作要由他们来做,在很多方面是有很大不同的,但就这规律的本质来说没有任何不同。另一方面,贵族统治——比如英格兰,在那里,掌权的阶级的权力仅仅来自其社会地位,他们没有受过专门训练,或者不专门从事那种工作(因此,在这种政体中,权力不是直接行使的,而是通过按寡头政治的原则构成的代表机构行使的)——从智力禀赋方面来说与民主政治大体上是相同的。也就是说,它们只是在伟大的和广受欢迎的天才和显著地位结合在一起,使某个人被置于暂时的支配地位时,才在某种较大程度上显示出这种性质。泰米斯托克里斯和伯利克里,华盛顿和杰弗逊,在他们各自的民主政体里,都不是比英国贵族代表政体中的查塔姆与皮尔斯、或甚至是法国贵族君主政体中的萨利和科尔伯特更彻底的例外,但肯定是更为杰出的例外。现代欧洲贵族政府的一个伟大的大臣,几乎像一个伟大的国王那样是罕见的现象。

因此,人们必须就代议制民主政体与官僚机构在政府的智力

The comparison, therefore, as to the intellectual attributes of a government, has to be made between a representative democracy and a bureaucracy : all other governments may be left out of the account. And here it must be acknowledged that a bureaucratic government has, in some important respects, greatly the advantage. It accumulates experience, acquires well-tried and well-considered traditional maxims, and makes provision for appropriate practical knowledge in those who have the actual conduct of affairs. But it is not equally favourable to individual energy of mind. The disease which afflicts bureaucratic governments, and which they usually die of, is routine. They perish by the immutability of their maxims ; and, still more, by the universal law that whatever becomes a routine loses its vital principle, and having no longer a mind acting within it, goes on revolving mechanically though the work it is intended to do remains undone. A bureaucracy always tends to become a pedantocracy. When the bureaucracy is the real government, the spirit of the corps (as with the Jesuits) bears down the individuality of its more distinguished members. In the profession of government, as in other professions, the sole idea of the majority is to do what they have been taught; and it requires a popular government to enable the conceptions of the man of original genius among them, to prevail over the obstructive spirit of trained mediocrity. Only in a popular government (setting apart the accident of a highly intelligent despot) could Sir Rowland Hill have been victorious over the Post Office. A popular government installed him in the Post Office, and made the body, in spite of itself, obey the impulse given by the man who united special knowledge with individual vigour and originality. That the Roman aristocracy escaped this characteristic disease of a bureaucracy, was evidently owing to its popular element. All special offices, both those which gave a seat in the Senate and those which were sought by senators, were conferred by popular election. The Russian government is a characteristic exemplification of both the good and bad side of bureaucracy: its fixed maxims, directed with Roman perseverance to the same unflinchingly-pursued ends from age to age; the remarkable skill with which those ends are generally pursued;

第六章

属性方面加以比较,而所有其他形式的政府就不必加以考虑。在这里,我们必须承认官僚政治的政府在某些重要方面具有很大的优势:它可以积累经验,获得经过试验证明效果良好的和考虑周全的传统原则,为那些实际管理事务的人准备适当的实践知识。但它对个人的思想活力来说却不是同样有利的。折磨官僚政治政府并通常使它们衰亡的弊病就是墨守成规。它们由于一成不变的原则而招致死亡;并且更多的是由于这样一条普遍法则而遭致死亡,即凡是墨守成规时就失去了它至关重要的原则,其内部也没有起作用的活力了,只是机械地转动着,它要做的工作却仍然未做。官僚政治总是趋向于变成腐儒政治。当官僚政治大行其道时,团体的精神(像耶稣会那样的情形)压抑着团体中更为出色的成员的个性。在政府的职业中,如同其他的职业一样,多数人的唯一想法就是做别人教他们做的事情;需要一个平民政府来使他们中具有独创天才的人的想法能战胜那些训练有素的平庸之才形成的阻碍性氛围。只有在平民政府(具有高超才能的专制君主的偶然事件暂且不论)才能使罗兰德·希尔爵士赢得对邮局的胜利。平民政府使他在邮局任职,使得这个团体,不由自主地服从这个具备专门知识,具有个人魅力和创造性的人所带来的推动。而罗马贵族政治摆脱官僚政治所具有的弊病的原因显然是它的平民因素。一切专门职位,如那些给予元老院职位和那些元老们谋求的职位,都由普选授予。俄罗斯政府是官僚政治优点和缺点并存的典范:它有固定的原则,以罗马人坚定不移的精神世世代代坚持不懈地追求同一个目标;有高超的技巧,使得那些目标一般能够达到;但也有可怕的内部腐败,以及来自外部的对进步的持续的有组织的仇视,甚至精力旺盛思维活跃的皇帝的专制权

the frightful internal corruption, and the permanent organized hostility to improvements from without, which even the autocratic power of a vigorousminded Emperor is seldom or never sufficient to overcome ; the patient obstructiveness of the body being in the long run more than a match for the fitful energy of one man. The Chinese Government, a bureaucracy of Mandarins, is, as far as known to us, another apparent example of the same qualities and defects.

In all human affairs, conflicting influences are required to keep one another alive and efficient even for their own proper uses ; and the exclusive pursuit of one good object, apart from some other which should accompany it, ends not in excess of one and defect of the other, but in the decay and loss even of that which has been exclusively cared for. Government by trained officials cannot do, for a country, the things which can be done by a free government ; but it might be supposed capable of doing some things which free government, of itself, cannot do. We find, however, that an outside element of freedom is necessary to enable it to do effectually or permanently even its own business. And so, also, freedom cannot produce its best effects, and often breaks down altogether, unless means can be found of combining it with trained and skilled administration. There could not be a moment's hesitation between representative government, among a people in any degree ripe for it, and the most perfect imaginable bureaucracy. But it is, at the same time, one of the most important ends of political institutions, to attain as many of the qualities of the one as are consistent with the other; to secure, as far as they can be made compatible, the great advantage of the conduct of affairs by skilled persons, bred to it as an intellectual profession, along with that of a general control vested in, and seriously exercised by, bodies representative of the entire people. Much would be done towards this end by recognizing the line of separation, discussed in the preceding chapter, between the work of government properly so called, which can only be well performed after special cultivation, and that of selecting, watching, and, when needful, controlling the governors, which in this case, as in others, properly devolves, not on those who do the work, but on those for whose benefit it ought to be done.

第六章

力也很少能或决不足以克服它;长远看来,官僚集团持续的阻力要比个人断断续续的精力大得多。我们所知的中国政府,一个满清官僚集团,就是另一个具有相同品质和缺陷的明显的例子。

在一切人类事务中,相互冲突的影响,就算是为了保持它们适当的效用,也必须;保持相互之间的活力和效率专门追求一个好的目标,不管某些应当伴随它的其他目标,结果不是一个过多而另一个不足,而是连所追求的目标也达不到。由训练有素的官员掌控的政府不能为国家做自由政府能为国家做的事情;但可以认为它能够做到自由政府本身不能做到的事情。然而,我们看到在自由因素之外还有必要使它有效地或持久地做甚至是它自身的事情。因此,自由不但不能产生出它最好的效果,而且常常完全地垮掉,除非能找到将自由与训练有素、技巧娴熟的行政结合起来的办法。我们可能会在代议制政府(时机已经成熟到那个民族在任何程度上都适合采用它)与最完美的可以想象得到的官僚制政府之间毫不犹豫地选择前者,但同时,尽可能地获得后者好的特质来与前者协调一致,是政治制度最主要的目的之一;只要能做到和谐一致,除了要确保在由整个人民代表机关授予并认真执行的一般控制的好处,还要有作为专业技术人员的熟练的官员管理事务所带来的好处。方法在前一章所讨论过的分界线,即分清只有在经过特别训练之后才能很好地执行被恰如其分地称作行政的工作,以及选择、监督、对官员必要时的控制的工作之间的界线,那么就很有利于达到这一目的。后一种工作在这种场合与其他场合一样,不是交给那些做行政工作的人去做,而是完全交给那些享受那种工作所带来的利益的人去做。要得到一个熟练的民主制是不可能的,除非这种民主制愿意让那种需

No progress at all can be made towards obtaining a skilled democracy, unless the democracy are willing that the work which requires skill should be done by those who possess it. A democracy has enough to do in providing itself with an amount of mental competency sufficient for its own proper work, that of superintendence and check.

How to obtain and secure this amount, is one of the questions to be taken into consideration in judging of the proper constitution of a representative body. In proportion as its composition fails to secure this amount, the assembly will encroach, by special acts, on the province of the executive ; it will expel a good, or elevate and uphold a bad, ministry ; it will connive at, or overlook, in them, abuses of trust, will be deluded by their false pretences, or will withhold support from those who endeavour to fulfil their trust conscientiously; it will countenance, or impose, a selfish, a capricious and impulsive, a short-sighted, ignorant, and prejudiced general policy, foreign and domestic ; it will abrogate good laws, or enact bad ones, let in new evils, or cling with perverse obstinacy to old; it will even, perhaps, under misleading impulses, momentary or permanent, emanating from itself or from its constituents, tolerate or connive at proceedings which set law aside altogether, in cases where equal justice would not be agreeable to popular feeling. Such are among the dangers of representative government, arising from a constitution of the representation which does not secure an adequate amount of intelligence and knowledge in the representative assembly.

We next proceed to the evils arising from the prevalence of modes of action in the representative body dictated by sinister interests (to employ the useful phrase introduced by Bentham) ; that is, interests conflicting more or less with the general good of the community.

It is universally admitted, that. of the evils incident to monarchical and aristocratic governments, a large proportion arise from this cause. The interest of the monarch, or the interest of the aristocracy, either collective or that of its individual members, is promoted, or they themselves think that it will be promoted, by conduct opposed to that which the general interest of the community requires. The interest, for example, of the government is to tax heavily : that of the

第六章

要技巧的工作由拥有技术的人去做。民主在为其固有的工作即监督与制约工作提供充分的智力资格方面有足够多的事情要做。

如何获得和保障这种智力条件,是在判断一个代议团体的适当构成时应当考虑的问题之一。当它的组成不能保障这个智力条件时,代表机关会通过特殊的方式侵蚀行政权力范围;它将驱逐好的官员或者提拔和吹捧一个坏的官员;它将纵容或忽视他们的滥用职权,被他们的虚假伪善所迷惑,或者不支持那些凭良心恪尽职守的人;它将支持或施行自私、反复无常、冲动、短视、无知以及充满偏见的国内国外的一般政策;它将取消良法,或者实行恶法,引发新的弊病,或顽固坚持旧的弊病;也许,在盲目的冲动下,不管这种冲动是暂时的还是持久的,源自自身的还是宪法的,它甚至将容忍或默许完全无视法律存在的行为,在这种场合,公正的司法与公众感情格格不入。这些都是代议制政体中所存在的危险,它们源于代议制的那不能在代表大会中拥有足够的智力和知识条件的结构。

我们下面将进一步讨论在由有害利益(采用边沁的说法)控制的代议制团体中,由行为方式的流行而引起的弊病。这种有害利益,也就是同社会普遍利益或多或少存在冲突的利益。

人们普遍承认,君主制和贵族制政体中易出现的弊病,有很大部分是由这个原因引起的。君主的利益或贵族的利益——不管是集体利益还是成员个人利益——是因为与社会共同利益要求相反的行动而得到促进的,或者他们自己认为将得到促进。例如,政府的利益是课以重税,而社会的利益则是好政府允许征收尽可能少的税来维持其必要的开支。国王的利益以及进行管理

community is, to be as little taxed as the necessary expenses of good government permit. The interest of the king, and of the governing aristocracy, is to possess, and exercise, unlimited power over the people; to enforce, on their part, complete conformity to the will and preferences of the rulers. The interest of the people is, to have as little control exercised over them in any respect, as is consistent with attaining the legitimate ends of government. The interest, or apparent and supposed interest, of the king or aristocracy is to permit no censure of themselves, at least in any form which they may consider either to threaten their power, or seriously to interfere with their free agency. The interest of the people is that them should be full liberty of censure on every public officer, and on every public act or measure. The interest of a ruling class, whether in an aristocracy or an aristocratic monarchy, is to assume to themselves an endless variety of unjust privileges, sometimes benefiting their pockets at the expense of the people, sometimes merely tending to exalt them above others, or, what is the same thing in different words, to degrade others below themselves. If the people are disaffected, which under such a government they are very likely to be, it is the interest of the king or aristocracy to keep them at a low level of intelligence and education, foment dissensions among them, and even prevent them from being too well off, lest they should ' wax fat, and kick ' ; agreeably to the maxim of Cardinal Richelieu in his celebrated Testament Politique. ' All these things are for the interest of a king or aristocracy, in a purely selfish point of view, unless a sufficiently strong counter-interest is created by the fear of provoking resistance. All these evils have been, and many of them still are, produced by the sinister interests Of kings and aristocracies, where their power is sufficient to raise them above the opinion of the rest of the community ; nor is it rational to expect, as the consequence of such a position, any other conduct.

These things are superabundantly evident in the case of a monarchy or an aristocracy ; but it is sometimes rather gratuitously assumed, that the same kind of injurious influences do not operate in a democracy. Looking at democracy in the way in which it is commonly conceived, as the rule of the numerical majority, it is surely

第六章

的贵族的利益,则是拥有、行使对人民的无限权力,在他们看来,就是要使统治者的意志和偏好完全一致。人民的利益却政府和在任何方面对他们实行尽可能少的控制,都要与达到政府合法目的相一致。国王或贵族的利益,或表面的以及假定的利益,就是不允许自己受到责难,至少不能有他们认为要么威胁到他们的权力,要么严重干涉他们自由行事的任何方式的责难。人民的利益是对每个官员、每个公共行为或措施都能有完全批评的自由。不管是贵族统治还是贵族式君主制中的统治阶级,他们的利益就是要保障他们能拥有无穷无尽、各式各样的不当特权,有时能以人民的利益为代价中饱私囊,有时仅仅是为了爬到别人上面去,或者说,让别人处于比自己更低的位置。如果人民不服(被这样的政权统治他们很可能不服),国王或贵族的利益就是使他们的智力和教育水平处于很低的状态,离间他们,甚至不让他们过分富裕,以免他们会"盛而骄";这很符合红衣主教黎塞留在他著名的《政治遗嘱》中所提出的原则。从纯粹自私的角度看,所有这些事情都符合国王或贵族的利益,除非因为害怕激起人民反抗而形成足够强大的相反的利益。在他们权力能使他们足够超脱于其余社会意见之外的地方,国王或贵族的有害利益就产生出了所有这些弊端,其中许多仍然在产生着。由于这样的地位的结果,期望任何其他的行为是不理性的。

这些事情在君主制或贵族制中实在是太明显了,但认为在民主制中具有相同的有害影响从而不起作用是相当没有道理的推测。按通常构想的方式去看看民主制吧,作为多数人的统治,统治权力完全有可能处于地方或阶级利益的支配之下,不按对

possible that the ruling power may be under the dominion of sectional or class interests, pointing to conduct different from that which would be dictated by impartial regard for the interest of all. Suppose the majority to be whites, the minority negroes, or *vice versâ*: is it likely that the majority would allow equal justice to the minority ? Suppose the majority Catholics, the minority Protestants, or the reverse: will there not be the same danger ? Or let the majority be English, the minority Irish, or the contrary: is there not a great probability of similar evil ? In all countries there is a majority of poor, a minority who, in contradistinction, may be called rich. Between these two classes, on many questions, there is complete opposition of apparent interest. We will suppose the majority sufficiently intelligent to be aware that it is not for their advantage to weaken the security of property, and that it would be weakened by any act of arbitrary spoliation. But is there not a considerable danger lest they should throw upon the possessors of what is called realized property, and upon the larger incomes, an unfair share, or even the whole, of the burden of taxation, and having done so, add to the amount without scruple, expending the proceeds in modes supposed to conduce to the profit and advantage of the labouring class ? Suppose, again, a minority of skilled labourers, a majority of unskilled: the experience of many Trade Unions, unless they are greatly calumniated, justifies the apprehension, that equality of earnings might be imposed as an obligation, and that piecework, payment by the hour, and all practices which enable superior industry or abilities to gain a superior reward, might be put down. Legislative attempts to raise wages, limitation of competition in the labour market, taxes or restrictions on machinery, and on improvements of all kinds tending to dispense with any of the existing labour--even, perhaps, protection of the home producer against foreign industry--are very natural (I do not venture to say whether probable) results of a feeling of class interest in a governing majority of manual labourers.

It will be said that none of these things are for the *real* interest of the most numerous class : to which I answer, that if the conduct of human beings was determined by no other interested considerations

第六章

人民利益不偏不倚的关怀所要求的原则来行事。假设多数人是白人,少数人是黑人,或相反;多数可能允许少数得到公平的审判吗?假设天主教徒是多数,新教徒是少数,或相反,不会有同样的危险吗?或者把英国人当成多数,爱尔兰人当作少数,或相反;不会有出现相似的弊端的可能性吗?在所有国家穷人都是多数,而与之相对的被称为少数的是富人。这两个阶级,在很多问题上都有全然不同的利益。我们将假定这个多数有足够的智力知道削弱财产的安全是不符合他们的利益的,而任何恣意的掠夺都会削弱财产的安全。但是他们将不公平的赋税分担,甚至将整个赋税分担,都加到所谓的实际财产拥有者以及拥有较大收入的人的头上,并且一旦这么做了,就毫不顾忌地增加支出数额,以被认为有助于劳动阶级的利益与好处的方式耗费这笔收益,这难道就不会有相当大的危险吗?再假设一下,熟练的劳动者是少数,不熟练的劳动者是多数:许多工会的经验(除非它们受到极大的歪曲)证明了这种担心,即收入平等会作为义务强加于人,计件工资,计时工资,以及所有能使更勤奋或能力更强的人得到更高收入的做法,都可能被搁置。增加工资的立法尝试,限制劳动市场的竞争,对机械进行征税和限制,以及倾向于免除现有劳动的一切改进——甚至还可能反对外国企业以保护国内工业——是一个由体力劳动者组成的多数所具有的情感和阶级利益的极为自然的(我不敢说是否是可能的)结果。

人们会说,所有这些事情都不符合人数最多的阶级的真正的利益,对此我的回答是,如果人类行为不是由其他有利害关系的考虑事项,而是由那些构成他们"真正的"利益来决定的话,那么君主制或是寡头制都不会是像它们现在所表现的那样的坏政府。

than those which constitute their 'real' interest, neither monarchy nor oligarchy would be such bad governments as they are ; for assuredly very strong arguments may be, and often have been, adduced to show that either a king or a governing senate are in much the most enviable position when ruling justly and vigilantly over an active, wealthy, enlightened, and high-minded people. But a king only now and then, and an oligarchy in no known instance, have taken this exalted view of their self-interest : and why should we expect a loftier mode of thinking from the labouring classes ? It is not what their interest is, but what they suppose it to be, that is the important consideration with respect to their conduct : and it is quite conclusive against any theory of government, that it assumes the numerical majority to do habitually what is never done, or expected to be done, save in very exceptional cases, by any other depositaries of power—namely, to direct their conduct by their real ultimate interest, in opposition to their immediate and apparent interest. No one, surely, can doubt that the pernicious measures above enumerated, and many others as bad, would be for the immediate interest of the general body of unskilled labourers. It is quite possible that they would be for the selfish interest of the whole existing generation of the class. The relaxation of industry and activity, and diminished encouragement to saving, which would be their ultimate consequence, might perhaps be little felt by the class of unskilled labourers in the space of a single lifetime. Some of the most fatal changes in human affairs have been, as to their more manifest immediate effects, beneficial. The establishment of the despotism of the Cæsars was a great benefit to the entire generation in which it took place. It put a stop to civil war, abated a vast amount of malversation and tyranny by prætors and proconsuls ; it fostered many of the graces of life and intellectual cultivation in all departments not political; it produced monuments of literary genius dazzling to the imaginations of shallow readers of history, who do not reflect that the men to whom the despotism of Augustus (as well as of Lorenzo de' Medici and of Louis XIV.) owes its brilliancy, were all formed in the generation preceding. The accumulated riches, and the mental energy and

第六章

因为人们可以确切地举出证据来表明,不管是国王还是一个正在进行统治的参议院,当他们公正且审慎地统治着那积极、富裕、开明和高尚的人民时,所处的地位是最令人羡慕的。但是国王只是时而采取这种有关他们私利的高尚观点,而寡头统治则从来没有采取过,那么为什么我们应该期待劳动阶级那里会有更高尚的思想模式呢?不是他们的利益是什么,而是他们认为什么是他们的利益,才是针对他们行动的重要的考虑。假定人数上占多数的集团习惯去做任何其他当权者没有做过的事情,或除在极其例外的情况外也没有被期望去做的事情——也就是说,按照他们真正的最终利益来指导其行为,反对他们直接的和显而易见的利益——的确是不符合任何政府理论的。的确,没有人能怀疑上面列举的有害的措施以及其他许多同样不好的东西,会符合不熟练劳动者一般团体的眼前利益的。很可能它们是为了这个阶级整个一代人的自私利益的。勤奋和活力的松弛,以及由此导致的最终后果的不鼓励节约,也许在仅仅一生的时间里很难为非熟练劳动者所觉察到。人类事务中一些最重大的变化,就它们更加明显直接的效果来说,曾经是有益的。恺撒专制政体的建立,对那时的整整一代人来说,是很有益处的。它平息了内战,减少了执政官和地方总督的数量巨大的腐败行为和暴政;它在非政治领域外的所有部门培育了许多生活情趣和学识素养;它产生了使那些浅薄的历史读者——他们不会细想那些使奥古斯都(还有洛伦佐·德梅第奇和路易十四的专制)的专制大放光芒的人,全都是在前一代形成的——为之眼花缭乱的天才的不朽作品。由好几个世纪的自由所产生的积聚起来的自由和智力能量与智力活动,对第一代奴隶仍有好

activity, produced by centuries of freedom, remained for the benefit of the first generation of slaves. Yet this was the commencement of a *régime* by whose gradual operation all the civilization which had been gained, insensibly faded away, until the Empire which had conquered and embraced the world in its grasp, so completely lost even its military efficiency, that invaders whom three or four legions had always sufficed to coerce, were able to overrun and occupy nearly the whole of its vast territory. The fresh impulse given by Christianity came but just in time to save arts and letters from perishing, and the human race from sinking back into perhaps endless night.

When we talk of the interest of a body of men, or even of an individual man, as a principle determining their actions, the question what would be considered their interest by an unprejudiced observer, is one of the least important parts of the whole matter. As Coleridge observes, the man makes the motive, not the motive the man. What it is the man's interest to do or refrain from, depends less on any outward circumstances, than upon what sort of man he is. If you wish to know what is practically a man's interest, you must know the cast of his habitual feelings and thoughts. Everybody has two kinds of interests, interests which he cares for, and interests which he does not care for. Everybody has selfish and unselfish interests, and a selfish man has cultivated the habit of caring for the former, and not caring for the latter. Every one has present and distant interests, and the improvident man is he who cares for the present interests and does not care for the distant. It matters little that on any correct calculation the latter may be the more considerable, if the habits of his mind lead him to fix his thoughts and wishes solely on the former. It would be vain to attempt to persuade a man who beats his wife and illtreats his children, that he would be happier if he lived in love and kindness with them. He would be happier if he were the kind of person who *could* so live; but he is not, and it is probably too late for him to become, that kind of person. Being as he is, the gratification of his love of domineering, and the indulgence of his ferocious temper,

第六章

处。然而,这就是一个政权的开始,通过这个政权的逐渐运作,一切已经获得的文明又慢慢地消失了,直到那个征服并将世界控制在手中的帝国彻底地丧失了其军事能力,致使只要三至四个罗马军团就足以控制的侵略者能够蹂躏和侵占它的几乎整个庞大的领土。基督教带来的新鲜动力及时地拯救了艺术和文化,使之免于毁灭,也拯救了人类,使之免于重新回到也许是漫无边际的长夜。

当我们把人类团体的利益或者甚至是单个人的利益当成决定他们行为的一条原则来谈时,什么是公正的观察者所认为的他们的利益呢?这个问题是整个问题中最不重要的部分。正如科尔里奇观察到的,人决定动机,而不是动机决定人。什么是人感兴趣和不感兴趣的不太取决于任何外部的环境,而更取决于他是哪类人。如果你想知道什么是一个人实际上的利益,你必须了解他惯常的感情和思想所投向的地方。每个人都有两种利益,即他所关心的利益和他不关心的利益。每个人都有自私和不自私的利益,而一个自私的人养成的习惯是关注前者,对后者却漠不关心。每个人都有当前利益和长远利益,目光短浅的人关心的是当前利益而无视长远利益。如果一个人的思维习惯使他把自己的思维和愿望都集中在了前者,那么依据任何正确计算认为后者更加重要的看法就显得无关紧要。试图劝说一个打老婆和虐待儿女的男人,对他说如果他们相亲相爱地生活在一起就会更加快乐将是徒劳的。如果他是那种能与家人那样生活的人,他会更加快乐,可惜他不是,对他来说,成为那种人也许为时过晚。由于他是那种人,所以他满足于作威作福,脾气暴躁放任,在他看来,这些要比他从家属的快乐和亲情中得到的益处大得

are to his perceptions a greater good to himself than he would be capable of deriving from the pleasure and affection of those dependent on him. He has no pleasure in their pleasure, and does not care for their affection. His neighbour, who does, is probably a happier man than he; but could he be persuaded of this, the persuasion would, most likely, only still further exasperate his malignity or his irritability. On the average, a person who cares for other people, for his country, or for mankind, is a happier man than one who does not; but of what use is it to preach this doctrine to a man who cares for nothing but his own ease, or his own pocket ? He cannot care for other people if he would. It is like preaching to the worm who crawls on the ground: how much better it would be for him if he were an eagle.

Now it is an universally observed fact, that the two evil dispositions in question, the disposition to prefer a man's selfish interests to those which he shares with other people, and his immediate and direct interests to those which are indirect and remote, are characteristics most especially called forth and fostered by the possession of power. The moment a man, or a class of men, find themselves with power in their hands, the man's individual interest, or the class's separate interest, acquires an entirely new degree of importance in their eyes. Finding themselves worshipped by others, they become worshippers of themselves, and think themselves entitled to be counted at a hundred times the value of other people; while the facility they acquire of doing as they like without regard to consequences, insensibly weakens the habits which make men look forward even to such consequences as affect themselves. This is the meaning of the universal tradition, grounded on universal experience, of men's being corrupted by power. Every one knows how absurd it would be to infer from what a man is or does when in a private station, that he will be and do exactly the like when a despot on a throne; where the bad parts of his human nature, instead of being restrained and kept in subordination by every circumstance of his life and by every person surrounding him, are courted by all persons, and ministered to by all circumstances. It would be quite as absurd to entertain a similar expectation in regard to a class of men ; the Demos, or any other. Let them be ever so modest

第六章

多。他不以他们的快乐为快乐,也不在乎他们的亲情。他那与亲人相亲相爱的邻居可能要比他快乐得多;但假如人们拿这个来劝他,那么就可能只是使他更加暴躁狠毒、敏感易怒。一般说来,一个关心他人、关心国家、甚至关心人类的人要比不关心这些的人要幸福。但对一个只关心他自己的舒适或者钱袋子的人来讲,鼓吹这些教条又有什么用呢?假使他能够关心他人也不会这样去做。这就像对一条在地上爬行的虫子说,如果它是一只雄鹰那将会要好得多一样。

如今人们普遍看到,这两种正在讨论的坏倾向——即个人的私利要比他与别人分享的利益更为优先,现实和直接的利益要比间接的和遥远的利益更为优先——是权力的占有最容易产生和助长起来的特征。当一个人或一个阶级发现权力掌握在他们自己手中的时候,单个人的利益在他们眼中或阶级的单独利益就更加重要了。当发觉自己被别人所崇拜时,他们就变成了自己的崇拜者,认为自己要比别人重要一百倍;然而当他们获得了可以随心所欲、不计后果的便利之时,便渐渐地削弱了令人期盼甚至影响到他们自己下场的习惯。这就是基于普遍经验的,为权力所腐蚀的人类普遍传统。每个人都明白,要从一个处在普通地位的人的所作所为来推导出他处于专制君主的地位时会变得怎样以及怎样行事,是多么地荒唐啊。处于后者地位时,他本性中的坏的成分不但没有被他生活的环境和他周围的每个人所约束和压制,反而被所有的人所吹捧,并且各种环境对他都有利。就一个阶级而言,抱相似的期待也将会是完全可笑的,平民阶级或任何其他阶级都一样。如果在他们之上有比他们更强大的力量时,他们思考问题时就会表现出是非常的谦逊和服从的人,但当他们自己变成了最强大的力量

and amenable to reason while there is a power over them stronger than they, we ought to expect a total change in this respect when they themselves become the strongest power.

Governments must be made for human beings as they are, or as they are capable of speedily becoming: and in any state of cultivation which mankind, or any class among them, have yet attained, or are likely soon to attain, the interests by which they will be led, when they are thinking only of self-interest, will be almost exclusively those which are obvious at first sight, and which operate on their present condition. It is only a disinterested regard for others, and especially for what comes after them, for the idea of posterity, of their country, or of mankind, whether grounded on sympathy or on a conscientious feeling, which ever directs the minds and purposes of classes or bodies of men towards distant or unobvious interests. Andit cannot be maintained that any form of government would be rational, which required as a condition that these exalted principles of action should be the guiding and master motives in the conduct of average human beings. A certain amount of conscience, and of disinterested public spirit, may fairly be calculated on in the citizens of any community ripe for representative government. But it would be ridiculous to expect such a degree of it, combined with such intellectual discernment as would be proof against any plausible fallacy tending to make that which was for their class interest appear the dictate of justice and of the general good. We all know what specious fallacies may be urged in defence of every act of injustice yet proposed for the imaginary benefit of the mass. We know how many, not otherwise fools or bad men, have thought it justifiable to repudiate the national debt. We know how many, not destitute of ability, and of considerable popular influence, think it fair to throw the whole burthen of taxation upon savings, under the name of realized property, allowing those whose progenitors and themselves have always spent all they received, to remain, as a reward for such exemplary conduct, wholly untaxed. We know what powerful arguments, the more dangerous because there is a portion of truth in them, may be brought against all inheritance, against the power of bequest, againstevery advantage which one person seems to

第六章

时,我们也应当预想到这方面的完全变化。

政府必须按照人类现实情况或他们能够迅速组成的情形来组成。在人类或他们中的任何阶级已经达到或很快要达到的文明状态下,当他们考虑自我利益时,引导他们的利益几乎毫无例外就是那些一望而知的明显利益或在他们当前条件下起作用的利益。只有对他人,特别是对他们身后的事情的无私关怀,对子孙后代,对国家,对人类的关怀,不管这种关怀是基于同情还是基于责任心,才能将阶级或人类团体的思想和目的引向遥远的或不明显的利益。任何把这些高尚的行动原则作一般人们行为的主导动机这一点作为条件来要求的政府形式,都不能被认为是理性的。在任何达到实行代议制政府条件的社会中,可以指望其人民具有一定程度的良知和无私的公共精神。但是期望这种程度的良知和无私的公共精神,并有这样一种洞察力,可作为证明来反对把他们的阶级利益说成是合乎正义和普遍利益的似是而非的谬论,将是可笑的。我们都知道在为想象中的大众利益所列举的每一项不公正作辩护时,什么样的似是而非的谬论都可能出现。我们知道有许多人,他们在其他方面不是傻子或坏蛋,却认为拒付国债是合理的。我们知道有许多人,并不缺乏能力,并且具有相当的群众影响,却认为将整个税收都放在被冠以实际财产名义的储蓄上,而让那些其先人和自己总是将收入全部花完的人完全不纳税,作为对这样可以作为模范的行为的奖赏是公平的。我们知道哪些强有力的论据(由于它们具有部分的合理性所以更加危险),可以用来反对一切遗产继承,反对遗赠权力,反对一个人似乎对另一人所具有的每一种优势。我们知道要证明几乎每个学科没有用处是多么容易的一件事,这对那些不拥有这些知识的人

have over another. We know how easily the uselessness of almost every branch of knowledge may be proved, to the complete satisfaction of those who do not possess it. How many, not altogether stupid men, think the scientific study of languages useless, think ancient literature useless, all erudition useless, logic and metaphysics useless, poetry and the fine arts idle and frivolous, political economy purely mischievous ? Even history has been pronounced useless and mischievous by able men. Nothing but that acquaintance with external nature, empirically acquired, which serves directly for the production of objects necessary to existence or agreeable to the senses, would get its utility recognised if people had the least encouragement to disbelieve it. Is it reasonable to think that even much more cultivated minds than those of the numerical majority can be expected to be, will have so delicate a conscience, and so just an appreciation of what is against their own apparent interest, that they will reject these and the innumerable other fallacies which will press in upon them from all quarters as soon as they come into power, to induce them to follow their own selfish inclinations and short-sighted notions of their own good, in opposition to justice, at the expense of all other classes and of posterity ?

One of the greatest dangers, therefore, of democracy, as of all other forms of government, lies in the sinister interest of the holders of power : it is the danger of class legislation : of government intended for (whether really effecting it or not) the immediate benefit of the dominant class, to the lasting detriment of the whole. And one of the most important questions demanding consideration, in determining the best constitution of a representative government, is how to provide efficacious securities against this evil.

If we consider as a class, politically speaking, any number of persons who have the same sinister interest-that is, whose direct and apparent interest points towards the same description of bad measures-the desirable object would be that no class, and no combination of classes likely to combine, should be able to exercise a preponderant influence in the government. A modern community, not divided within itself by strong antipathies of race, language, or nationality, may be considered as in the main divisible into two sections, which,

第六章

来说是多么惬意的事情啊。有多少并非完全愚蠢的人,会认为对语言的科学研究是无用的,古代文学是无用的,一切博学是无用的,逻辑与形而上学是无用的,诗歌与美术是没有价值和意义的,政治经济学纯粹就是有害的呢?甚至那些能人已经断言历史是无用的和有害的。只有由经验而得的外部自然知识——它直接为生产生存必需品或为感官服务时,它的有用之处才会得到承认,如果几乎没有人受到鼓励去怀疑它的话。认为那些更具修养的人与那些所能预期的多数相比,将拥有那么美好的良知,对于与他们自己的明显利益相悖的东西具有如此正确的评价,以至于他们将拒绝这些和其他无数的谬误——一旦他们掌握权力,这些谬误将从四面八方对他们形成压力,诱使他们遵循着他们自私的倾向以及他们对自身利益的浅短的观念,反对正义,并牺牲掉其他阶级和子孙后代的利益——是合乎情理的吗?

因此,民主制与一切其他政府形式一样,其最大的危险之一就在于当权者恶意的利益;这是阶级立法的危险,即为统治阶级的当前利益服务(不管是否真正实现)而损害整个社会利益的政府的危险。在决定代议制政府最好的构成时需要加以考虑的最重要的问题之一就是如何提供有效的措施来防止这种危害。

从政治上说,如果我们把阶级当成任何具有同样恶意的利益的人群的话,也即是说,这些人的直接明显的利益指向同样的糟糕的措施,那么称心如意的目标就是在政府中,不要有阶级,以及不要有可能联合起来的阶级联合能够起主导的影响作用。一个内部没有为种族、语言或民族的强烈憎恶所分裂的现代社会,大体上可以分为两个部分。不考虑局部变化,这两个部分整体上与表面利益的两个互相背离的方向相当。让我们把一方

in spite of partial variations, correspond on the whole with two divergent directions of apparent interest. Let us call them (in brief general terms) labourers on the one hand, employers of labour on the other: including however along with employers of labour, not only retired capitalists, and the possessors of inherited wealth, but all that highly paid description of labourers (such as the professions) whose education and way of life assimilate them with the rich, and whose prospect and ambition it is to raise themselves into that class. With the labourers, on the other hand, may be ranked those smaller employers of labour, who by interests, habits, and educational impressions, are assimilated in wishes, tastes, and objects to the labouring classes ; comprehending a large proportion of petty tradesmen. In a state of society thus composed, if the representative system could be made ideally perfect`, and if it were possible to maintain it in that state, its organization must be such, that these two classes, manual labourers and their affinities on one aide, employers of labour and their affinities on the other, should be, in the arrangement of the representative system, equally balanced, each influencing about an equal number of votes in Parliament: since, assuming that the majority of each class, in any difference between them, would be mainly governed by their class interests, there would be a minority of each in whom that consideration would be subordinate to reason, justice, and the good of the whole; and this minority of either, joining with the whole of the other, would turn the scale against any demands of their own majority which were not such as ought to prevail. The reason why, in any tolerably constituted society, justice and the general interest mostly in the end carry their point, is that the separate and selfish interests of mankind are almost always divided ; some are interested in what is wrong, but some, also, have their private interest on the side of what is right: and those who are governed by higher considerations, though too few and weak to prevail against the whole of the others, usually after sufficient discussion and agitation become strong enough to turn the balance in favour of the body of private interests which is on the same side with them. The representative system ought to be so constituted as to maintain this state of things: it ought not to allow any of the various sectional interests to be so powerful as to be capable of prevailing against truth and justice and the other sectional interests combined.

第六章

称作(用简明的一般术语)劳动者,另一方称作劳动力的雇佣者;可是雇主这边包括的不仅有退休资本家,遗产继承人,而且还有所有的高收入的劳动者(例如专业人员),这些人的教育背景和生活方式与富人相似,他们的愿望与期望也是使自己跻身于富人阶级。另一方面,劳动者也可以包括那些小雇佣主,他们的兴趣、习惯、和受教育程度在愿望、品味与目标方面都与劳动阶级相似;这里还包括大部分小商人。在一个这样组成的社会状态中,如果代议体系能够完美无缺,如果它在那种状态中可能存在下去,那么它的组织就必须是这样的:即以体力劳动者及其同类为一边,以劳动力雇佣者及其同类为一边,这两大阶级在代议体系的安排中应当保持平衡,每一边在议会中持有相等的票数。因为假定每一个阶级的多数在他们之间的分歧将主要受他们的阶级利益支配,那么每一方都会有一个少数,他们的考虑从属于理智、正义和整个阶级的利益;而任何一个阶级的少数与另一个阶级的多数联合起来,将会扭转局面,来反对自己阶级中多数的那些不这样(联合)就会得逞的要求。在任何组织得还过得去的社会,正义与普遍利益大部分最终得以达到目的的原因就是人类个别的和自私的利益总是分裂的,有些人对错误的东西感兴趣,但有些人的私人利益却与好的东西联系在一起,那些被更高的考虑所支配的人,尽管因人少且力量薄弱而不能胜过全部其他的人,通常在经过充分的讨论和鼓动之后,能够强大到足以改变平衡,使之转向有利于和他们同在一方的那个团体的私人利益。代议制体系应当如此构成,以保持这一事态:它不应当允许任何各种各样的部门利益强大到能够压倒真理和正义以及其他所有部门

There ought always to be such a balance preserved among personal interests, as may render any one of them dependent for its successes on carrying with it at least a large proportion of those who act on higher motives, and more comprehensive and distant views.

利益的总和。在个人利益中总是应当保持一种平衡,使任何一种个人利益要获得成功有赖于得到那些按更高动机和更全面、更长远的观点行事的人中的至少一大部分人的支持。

CHAPTER VII
Of True And False Democracy; Representation Of All, And Representation Of The Majority Only

It has been seen that the dangers incident to a representative democracy are of two kinds : danger of a low grade of intelligence in the representative body, and in the popular opinion which controls it ; and danger of class legislation on the part of the numerical majority, these being all composed of the same class. We have next to consider, how far it is possible so to organize the democracy, as, without interfering materially with the characteristic benefits of democratic government, to do away with these two great evils, or at least to abate them, in the utmost degree attainable by human contrivance.

The common mode of attempting this is by limiting the democratic character of the representation, through a more or less restricted suffrage. But there is a previous consideration which, duly kept in view, considerably modifies the circumstances which are supposed to render such a restriction necessary. A completely equal democracy, in a nation in which a single class composes the numerical majority, cannot be divested of certain evils; but those evils are greatly aggravated by the fact, that the democracies which at present exist are not equal, but systematically unequal in favour of the predominant class. Two very different ideas are usually confounded under the name democracy. The pure idea of democracy, according to its definition, is the government of the whole people by the whole people, equally represented. Democracy as commonly conceived and hitherto practised, is the government of the whole people by a mere majority of the people

第七章　真民主与假民主；代表全体和仅仅代表多数

我们已经谈到,代议制民主容易产生两种危险:代议团体成员的智力水平偏低以及控制代议团体的公众舆论的智力水平偏低的危险;由构成同一阶级的多数人口实行阶级立法的危险。我们接下来就得考虑,在多大的程度上可以在本质上不妨碍民主政体特有好处的情况下,通过人为设计能最大程度消除,或者至少能够减轻这两大弊病。

试图达到这一目的的通常模式就是通过或多或少受到限制的选举权来限制代议制的民主特性。但是人们头脑中存在着一种成见的考虑,这种成见在相当程度上改变了应当实施这种必要限制的环境。在一个由单一阶级组成了人口上占多数的国家里,一个完全平等的民主政体是无法根除某些弊病的,但是由于存在现有的民主政体是不平等的这一事实,而一贯的不平等则有利于支配性的阶级,因此这些弊病就更严重了。在民主的名义下,两种全然不同的观念常常混淆在一起。纯粹的民主观念,根据其定义,就是全体人民的政府由全体人民平等地代表着。通常人们设想的、迄今仍在运转的民主观,就是全体人民的政府由人民的多数排他地代表着;前者即是全体公民

exclusively represented. The former is synonymous with the equality of all citizens; the latter, strangely confounded with it, is a government of privilege, in favour of the numerical majority, who alone possess practically any voice in the State.

This is the inevitable consequence of the manner in which the votes are now taken, to the complete disfranchisement of minorities. The confusion of ideas here is great, but it is so easily cleared up, that one would suppose the slightest indication would be sufficient to place the matter in its true light before any mind of average intelligence. It would be so, but for the power of habit ; owing to which the simplest idea, if unfamiliar, has as great difficulty in making its way to the mind as a far more complicated one. That the minority must yield to the majority, the smaller number to the greater, is a familiar idea; and accordingly men think there is no necessity for using their minds any further, and it does not occur to them that there is any medium between allowing the smaller number to be equally powerful with the greater, and blotting out the smaller number altogether. In a representative body actually deliberating, the minority must of course be o-verruled; and in an equal democracy (since the opinions of the constituents, when they insist on them, determine those of the representative body) the majority of the people, through their representatives, will outvote and prevail over the minority and their representatives. But does it follow that the minority should have no representatives at all ? Because the majority ought to prevail over the minority, must the majority have all the votes, the minority none ? Is it necessary that the minority should not even be heard? Nothing but habit and old association can reconcile any reasonable being to the needless injustice. In a really equal democracy, every or any section would be represented, not disproportionately, but proportionately. A majority of the electors would always have a majority of the representatives; but a minority of the electors would always have a minority of the representatives. Man for man, they would be as fully represented as the majority. Unless they are, there is not equal government, but a government

第七章

平等的同义词,而后者——相当奇怪地与前者混在一起——则是一个特权政府,有利于多数人,而只有这个多数人实际上拥有这个国家的所有话语权。

这是目前采用的投票方式所不可避免的结果,完全将少数人的权利剥夺掉了。在这里,两种观念非常混乱,但是要澄清它们却是如此简单,人们最微小的暗示就足以向任何具备一般智力水平的人说清楚。事情的本来面目如果不是因为惯性使然,也许可以做得到,但由于惯性,最简单的观念,如果不熟悉的话,就会跟复杂得多的观念一样很难融入人的头脑中去。少数服从多数,就是为人们所熟悉的一个观念,因此,人们认为没有必要再去多想,他们也就想不到在允许让少数同多数一样强大与将少数完全抹杀掉之间,还会有什么回旋的余地。在一个进行实际协商的代表团体里,少数必须理所当然地被多数所压倒;在一个平等的民主政体里(由于选民的意见,当他们坚持这些意见时,就决定了代表团体的意见),民众的多数通过他们的代表,将在票数上超过并且战胜少数及其他们的代表。但是难道因此少数就不应当有他们的代表吗?因为多数应当会胜过少数,所以多数就应该得到全部的票,而少数就一张都不应该有吗?少数的意见甚至没有必要听取吗?只有习惯以及陈旧的联系能使一个理智的人认为这种毫无必要的不公正是合理的。在一个真正平等的民主政体里,每个部分或者任何部分都会有其代表,这些代表与他们的人数不是不成比例的,而是成一定比例的。选民的多数总会有多数的代表,但是选民的少数也总会有少数的代表。就人对人来讲,少数应当和多数一样得到充分的代表,除非不存在一个平等的政府,而是存在一个不平等的、拥有特权的政府,在那里,一部

of inequality and privilege : one part of the people rule over the rest: there is a part whose fair and equal share of influence in the representation is withheld from them ; contrary to all just government, but above all, contrary to the principle of democracy, which professes equality as its very root and foundation.

The injustice and violation of principle are not less flagrant because those who suffer by them are a minority; for there is not equal suffrage where every single individual does not count for as much as any other single individual in the community. But it is not only a minority who suffer. Democracy thus constituted does not even attain its ostensible object, that of giving the powers of government in all cases to the numerical majority. It does something very different: it gives them to a majority of the majority; who may be, and often are, but a minority of the whole. All principles are most effectually tested by extreme cases. Suppose then that, in a country governed by equal and universal suffrage, there is a contested election in every constituency, and every election is carried by a small majority. The Parliament thus brought together represents little more than a bare majority of the people. This Parliament proceeds to legislate, and adopts important measures by a bare majority of itself. What guarantee is there that these measures accord with the wishes of a majority of the people ? Nearly half the electors, having been outvoted at the hustings, have had no influence at all in the decision ; and the whole of these may be, a majority of them probably are, hostile to the measures, having voted against those by whom they have been carried. Of the remaining electors nearly half have chosen representatives who, by supposition, have voted against the measures. It is possible, therefore, and not at all improbable, that the opinion which has prevailed was agreeable only to a minority of the nation, though a majority of that portion of it, whom the institutions of the country have erected into a ruling class. If democracy means the certain ascendancy of the majority, there are no means of insuring that, but by allowing every individual figure to tell equally in the summing up . Any minority left out either

分人统治着另一部分的人,一部分人在代议制中所拥有的公平和对影响的平等分享被剥夺了,这与一切公正的统治相悖,而且最重要的是违反了民主的原则,因为民主将平等作为它真正的根源和基础。

这种不公正以及对原则的违反并非因为受害的是少数就不那么臭名昭著,因为如果社会上每一个个体不能像其他个体一样重要,那么就不存在平等的选举权。但是受害的不仅仅是少数。这样的民主甚至达不到它表面的目标,即在所有情况下将政府的权力给予在人数上占多数的群体。它所做的是完全不同的事情,即它将权力交给多数人中的多数,而这些人可能,而且经常是全体人民中的少数。所有的原则都能够通过极端的例子得到有效的检验。因此假设在一个平等的、实现了普选权的国家里,有着一批相互竞争的选民,每次选举都是由刚超过半数的多数来操纵,这样选出的议会所代表的也只不过是勉勉强强的多数,而这个议会又通过它本身的勉强的多数来进行立法和采取重大的措施,那么又用什么来保证这些措施与多数人的愿望相一致呢?将近一半的选民在选举过程中被击败了,因而对决策起不到什么影响,而这些选民的大多数,由于曾经投票反对过那些通过这些措施的人,因而可能会反对这些措施。在其余的选民当中,根据假设,有将近一半人投过那些反对通过这些措施的议员的票,因此,就完全有可能,通过的意见仅仅为少数的国民所同意,尽管它是国家机器提升为统治阶级的那部分人中的多数。如果民主政治就意味着多数人占支配地位,那么除了允许每一个个体在陈述中平等地表达自己的观点外,就没有什么办法可以保证这种支配地位。任何受到冷落的少数,不管是出于故意还是

purposely or by the play of the machinery, gives the power not to a majority, but to a minority in some other part of the scale.

　　The only answer which can possibly be made to this reasoning is, that as different opinions predominate in different localities, the opinion which is in a minority in some places has a majority in others, and on the whole every opinion which exists in the constituencies obtains its fair share of voices in the representation. And this is roughly true in the present state of the constituency ; if it were not, the discordance of the House with the general sentiment of the country would soon become evident. But it would be no longer true if the present constituency were much enlarged; still less, if made co-extensive with the whole population ; for in that case the majority in every locality would consist of manual labourers; and when there was any question pending, on which these classes were at issue with the rest of the community, no other class could succeed in getting represented anywhere. Even now, is it not a great grievance, that in every Parliament a very numerous portion of the electors, willing and anxious to be represented, have no member in the House for whom they have voted? Is it just that every elector of Marylebone is obliged to be represented by two nominees of the vestries, every elector of Finsbury or Lambeth by those (as is generally believed) of the publicans ? The constituencies to which most of the highly educated and public spirited persons in the country belong, those of the large towns, are now, in great part, either unrepresented or misrepresented. The electors who are on a different side in party politics from the local majority, are unrepresented. Of those who are on the same side, a large proportion are misrepresented ; having been obliged to accept the man who had the greatest number of supporters in their political party, though his opinions may differ from theirs , on every other point . The state of things is , in

第七章

机制的问题,将权力给了意义在其他上处于少数的人,而不是将权力给予多数。

对上述推论或许可以作出的唯一解答就是,由于不同的意见在不同的地方的支配地位不同,在某些地方是少数的意见在其他地方却居于多数,并且在总体上存在于选民中的每一种意见都在代议制中得到公平的发言权,并且这点就选民的当前情况而言大体上是正确的,如果不是这样的话,议会与整个国家舆论之间的不协调状况很快就会变得明显。但是如果把当前的选民范围扩大,那就不再是正确的了;如果把选民范围扩大到全部的人口,那就会更加不正确了,因为在那种情况下,每个地区的多数就将由体力劳动者构成,并且当存在着任何悬而未决的问题时,如果这些阶级与社会上的其他阶级意见不一致,那么其他阶级就不可能在任何地方赢得代表权。即使现在每个议会中,相当多的选民希望甚至渴望得到出席权,但在议会中却没有他们所选的代表,这难道不是一件令人悲哀的事情吗?马里立本的所有选民不得不由教区的两名被提名人来代表,每个芬斯伯里教区或兰贝斯教区的选民不得不由酒馆老板的被提名人来代表(就像人们通常所认为的那样),这样是公正的吗?这个国家大部分受过良好教育的人和具有公益精神的人所属的选区,那些大城市的选区,目前大部分要么没有代表,要么就得不到合适的代表。在政党政治中,凡是不站在地方多数一边就得不到代表。而那些站在同一阵营的人们,有相当一部分得不到适当的代表,因为他们不得不接受在党内拥有最多支持者的那个人,尽管那个人的意见可能在其他的每个方面都与他们的意见不一致。在某些方面,事态甚至要比不让少

some respects, even worse than if the minority were not allowed to vote at all ; for then, at least the majority might have a member who would represent their own mind best: while now, the necessity of not dividing the party, for fear of letting in its opponents, induces all to vote either for the person who first presents himself wearing their colours, or for the one brought forward by their local leaders ; and these, if we pay them the compliment, which they very seldom deserve, of supposing their choice to be unbiassed by their personal interests, are compelled, that they may be sure of mustering their whole strength, to bring forward a candidate whom none of the party will strongly object to-that is, a man without any distinctive peculiarity, any known opinions except the shibboleth of the party. This is strikingly exemplified in the United States; where, at the election of President, the strongest party never dares put forward any of its strongest men, because every one of these, from the mere fact that he has been long in the public eye, has made himself objectionable to some portion or other of the party, and is therefore not so sure a card for rallying all their votes, as a person who has never been heard of by the public at all until he is produced as the candidate. Thus, the man who is chosen, even by the strongest party, represents perhaps the real wishes only of the narrow margin by which that party outnumbers the other. Any section whose support is necessary to success, possesses a veto on the candidate. Any section which holds out more obstinately than the rest, can compel all the others to adopt its nominee ; and this superior pertinacity is unhappily more likely to be found among those who are holding out for their own interest, than for that of the public. The choice of the majority is therefore very likely to be determined by that portion of the body who are the most timid, the most narrow-minded and prejudiced, or who cling most tenaciously to the exclusive classinterest ; in which case the electoral rights of the minority, while useless for the purposes for which votes are given, serve only for compelling the majority to accept the candidate of the weakest or worst portion of themselves.

　　That while recognising these evils, many should consider them as

第七章

数人投票要糟糕得多,因为如果那样做的话,至少多数人还能有一个能够最好地代表他们意见的人,而现在,为了不使党发生分裂,防止反对党的人当选,迫使所有的人要么选举他们中第一个站出来竞选的人,要么选举由地方领导人提名的人,而这些地方领导人,如果我们说句恭维他们的话(他们极少值得这样的恭维),假设他们的选择不是出自个人的私利,那么他们为了确保能够集中全党的力量,他们不得不提名一个党内没有人会强烈加以反对的人,也就是说,提名一个没有任何与众不同的个性,除了会说该党的陈词滥调之外就提不出任何为人所知的意见的人。这样的情况在美国得到突出的反映:在那个国家,当进行总统选举时,最强大的政党从来不敢提名它最厉害的人作候选人,因为这些人中的每一个人都长期处于公众的眼皮底下,使得他受到党内的这部分或那部分的人的反对,因此,同那些直到被提名为候选人时才为公众所知的那些人相比,在集中党内所有选票方面,他们就不是那么可靠的一张牌。因此,即使是最强大政党提出的候选人,代表的可能也只是这个党在数量上胜出另一政党的微小差数的那部分人的真正愿望。党内任何比其他群体更为坚决的群体能够强迫其余所有人去接受它提名的人;但不幸的是,这种顽强的坚持更可能在那些维护自己利益的人而不是在维护公共利益的人当中发现。因此,多数人的选择极可能由团体中最胆小怕事、最思维狭隘和最有偏见的那部分人,或者是最顽固地坚持排他性阶级利益的人来决定,在这种情况下,尽管对于投票意图来说是无用的,少数的投票权只起到强迫多数去接受他们当中最弱或最差的那部分人提出的候选人。

尽管很多人会认为承认这些弊病是自由政府所必需付出

the necessary price paid for a free government, is in no way surprising : it was the opinion of all the friends of freedeom, up to a recent period. But the habit of passing them over as irremediable has become so inveterate, that many persons seem to have lost the capacity of looking at them as things which they would be glad to remedy if they could. From despairing of a cure, there is too often but one step to denying the disease ; and from this follows dislike to having a remedy proposed, as if the proposer were creating a mischief instead of offering relief from one. People are so inured to the evils, that they feel as if it were unreasonable, if not wrong, to complain of them. Yet, avoidable or not, he must be a purblind lover of liberty on whose mind they do not weigh ; who would not rejoice at the discovery that they could be dispensed with? Now, nothing is more certain, than that the virtual blotting out of the minority is no necessary or natural consequence of freedom ; that, far from having any connexion with democracy, it is diametrically opposed to the first principle of democracy, representation in proportion to numbers. It is an essential part of democracy that minorities should be adequately represented. No real democracy, nothing but a false show of democracy, is possible without it.

Those who have seen and felt, in some degree, the force of these considerations, have proposed various expedients by which the evil may be, in a greater or less degree, mitigated. Lord John Russell, in one of his Reform Bills, introduced a provision, that certain constituencies should return three members, and that in these each elector should be allowed to vote only for two ; and Mr. Disraeli, in the recent debates, revived the memory of the fact by reproaching him for it; being of opinion apparently, that it befits a Conservative statesman to regard only means, and to disown scornfully all fellow-feeling with any one who is betrayed, even once, into thinking of

第七章

的代价,但也就没有必要感到奇怪。这是近来所有赞同自由的朋友们的观点。但是将这些弊病当成不可治疗的东西轻轻放过的习惯变得如此根深蒂固,以至于很多人似乎丧失了将它们看成是如果他们能够的话,就会很乐意去加以矫正的事情的能力。对医治的失望常常离否认疾病只有一步之遥,而且随之而来的就是不喜欢提出的治疗方案,好像提出方案的人是在制造悲伤而不是在提供从疾病中解脱出来的方法似的。人们对这些弊病是如此习惯,以至于,就算抱怨是对人他们觉得抱怨它们也是不合理的。然而,不管是否能够避免,他必定是个迟钝的自由的爱好者,在他看来这些弊病是无足轻重的;谁会因为发现了这些弊病可以根除而不欢欣鼓舞呢?现在,实质上将少数加以忽略既没有必要,也不是自由的结果;将少数加以忽略与民主毫不相干,而且直接违反民主的第一原则,即违反按人数比例的代表制,这是再确定不过的事情了。少数人必须充分地得到代表,这是民主政治的关键部分。没有它就没有真正的民主政治,有的也只不过是虚假的民主政治罢了。

　　那些在某种程度上认识到或感觉到以上考虑的影响的人,提出了各种不同的,也许可以或多或少减轻这些弊病的权宜之计。约翰·拉塞尔勋爵在他的一份改革议案中提出了一种方案,规定某些选区应选出三个议员,而这些地区的选民只允许投两个人的票。迪斯雷利先生在最近的辩论中就此方案谴责拉塞尔时使人想起了这事。迪斯雷利的意见显然是,一个保守的政治家应关心的只是手段,并且轻蔑地表示,对于任何一个忽视手段而去关心结果的人,也没有丝毫

ends. ①Others have proposed that each elector should be allowed to vote only for one. By either of these plans, a minority equalling or exceeding a third of the local constituency, would be able, if it attempted no more, to return one out of three members. The same result might be attained in a still better way, if, as proposed in an able pamphlet by Mr. James Garth Marshall, the elector retained his three votes, but was at liberty to bestow them all upon the same candidate. These schemes, though infinitely better than none at all, are yet but makeshifts, and attain the end in a very imperfect manner ; since all local minorities of less than a third, and all minorities however numerous, which are made up from several constituencies, would remain unrepresented. It is much to be lamented, however, that none of these plans have been carried into effect, as any of them would have recognised the right principle, and prepared the way for its more complete application. But real equality of representation is not obtained unless any set of electors amounting to the average number of a constituency, wherever in the country they happen to reside, have the power of combining with one another to return a representative. This degree of perfection in representation appeared impracticable, until a man of

---

① This blunder of Mr. Disraeli (from which, greatly to his credit, Sir John Pakington took an opportunity, soon after, of separating himself) is a speaking instance, among many, how little the Conservative leaders under. stand Conservative principles. Without presuming to require from political parties such an amount of virtue and discernment as that they should comprehend, and know when to apply, the principles of their opponents, we may yet say that it would be a great improvement if each party understood and acted upon its own. Well would it be for England if Conservatives voted consistently for everything conservative, and Liberals for everything liberal. We should not then have to wait long for things which, like the present and many other great measures, are eminently both the one and the other. The Conservatives, as being by the law of their existence the stupidest party, have much the greatest sins of this description to answer for: and it is a melancholy truth, that if any measure were proposed, on any subject, truly, largely, and far-sightedly conservative, even if Liberals were willing to vote for it, the great bulk of the Conservative party would rush blindly in and prevent it from being carried.

第七章

认同感①。其他人则提议每个选民应该只能投一个人的票,通过这些方案中的任何一个方案,一个占地方选民三分之一或多于三分之一的少数群体,将能够从三个议员中选出其中的一个,如果它不想拥有更多的议员的话。如果像詹姆斯·加思·马歇尔先生在他所写的一本极富才华小册子中所提议的那样,选民保留他的三票,但是可以自由地将三票投给同一个候选人,那么同样的结果可以通过更好的方法获得。这些方案,尽管比没有好,却只是一些权宜之计,只能以极不完善的手段达到目的,因为所有人数上少于三分之一的少数群体,以及由几个选区组成的不管人数上怎样的多的少数群体,仍然不会有代表。然而,令人遗憾的是,这些方案都没有付诸实行过,因为它们中的任何一个都会承认正确的原则是在为更加完善的应用方案铺平道路。但是真正平等的代表制是不可能的,除非任何一批达到选区平均数的选民,不管他们住在哪儿,都有能力彼此联合起来获得代表。这种完美程度的代表制,在托马斯·黑尔先

---

① 迪斯雷利的这一重大错误(值得赞扬的是,约翰·帕金顿爵士在不久之后,就找了个机会摆脱了这种错误)许多能说明问题的例子中的一个,用以说明保守党的领袖们对保守党的原则理解程度之低。不需要冒昧地要求政党具有理解并且知道何时去运用对手的原则那样的优点和辨别力,但我们还是可以说,如果每个政党理解并按照自己的原则来行事,那就会是一个重大的进步。就英国而言,如果保守党人始终投票赞同保守的主张,而自由党人始终投票赞同自由主义的主张,那么英国就会很好了。那么,我们就不必为了那些明显地既是前者又是后者(就像现在的和其他的许多重大措施)那样的事情去等待很长的时间了。保守党由于按照其生存法则是最愚蠢的政党,所以保守党人要对许多这样描述的最大罪过承担责任。而令人悲哀的事实是,如果在任何议程上有人提出了某种方案,的的确确,在很大程度上,有远见的保守党人,甚至是自由党人都愿意投票赞成它,那么保守党人的多数就会盲目地加以干预,阻止方案的通过。

great capacity, fitted alike for large general views and for the contrivance of practical details—Mr. Thomas Hare-had proved its possibility by drawing up a scheme for its accomplishment, embodied in a Draft of an Act of Parliament : a scheme which has the almost unparalleled merit, of carrying out a great principle of government in a manner approaching to ideal perfection as regards the special object in view, while it attains incidentally several other ends, of scarcely inferior importance.

According to this plan, the unit of representation, the quota of electors who would be entitled to have a member to themselves, would be ascertained by the ordinary process of taking averages, the number of voters being divided by the number of seats in the House: and every candidate who obtained that quota would be returned, from however great a number of local constituencies it might be gathered. The votes would, as at present, be given locally, but any elector would be at liberty to vote for any candidate, in what ever part of the country he might offer himself. Those electors, therefore, who did not wish to be represented by any of the local candidates, might aid by their vote in the return of the person they liked best among all those throughout the country who had expressed a willingness to be chosen. This would, so far, give reality to the electoral rights of the otherwise virtually disfranchised minority. But it is important that not those alone who refuse to vote for any of the local candidates, but those also who vote for one of them and are defeated, should be enabled to find elsewhere the representation which they have not succeeded in obtaining in their own district. It is therefore provided that an elector may deliver a voting paper, containing other names in addition to the one which stands foremost in his preference. His vote would only be counted for one candidate ; but if the object of his first choice failed to be returned, from not having obtained the quota, his second perhaps might be more fortunate. He may extend his list to a greater number, in the order of his preference, so that if the names which stand near the top of the

第七章

生——一个极富能力、善于提出一般见解,又擅长作实践方面的具体设计的人——起草的《议会决议草案》中的某个方案得到通过、实现其设计,在证明它是可能做到的之前,似乎是不可能实现的。这个方案具有无可比拟的优点,在有关我们考虑的特殊目的方面,以接近完美的方式贯彻了政府的一条重要原则,而且它还顺便达到了其他几个并不那么重要的目的。

根据这个方案,代表制的单位,即那些有资格拥有自己的议员的选民的配额,将由取平均数的普通方式来确定,即用选民的数目除以下院中议席的数目。每个获得那个配额的候选人将当选,而不管这个配额是由多少地方的选民集中起来的。就像当前所做的那样,在地方进行投票,但是所有选民都可以自由地投任何一个候选人的票,不管这个候选人来自全国的什么地方。因此,那些不愿意由地方候选人来代表的选民,将通过他们的投票在全国那些愿意竞选的人当中选择他们最喜欢的候选人。这样一来,就能使那些否则就被剥夺了选举权的少数群体实现其选举权利,但重要的是,不仅那些拒绝投本地区候选人票的人,而且那些投了本地区其中一个候选人的票但却遭到了失败的人,都能够在其他地方找到在他们选区没有顺利地得到的代表。因此,方案作了这样的规定,即选民可以提交一份选举纸,这张纸上除了有他最愿意选择的人之外,还有其他候选人的名字,他的选票只能按一个候选人来计算,但是如果他最先选择的没有当选,没有获得必要的配额,则他第二个选择的人可能会比前一个更走运而当选。他可以按照他优先选择的顺序来将他选举纸上的名单扩展到一个较大的数目,这样的话,如果他名单上靠前的名字没有获得必要的配额,或者不

list either cannot make up the quota, or are able to make it up without his vote, the vote may still be used for some one whom it may assist in returning. To obtain the full number of members required to complete the House, as well as to prevent very popular candidates from engrossing nearly all the suffrages, it is necessary, however many votes a candidate may obtains that no more of them than the quota should be counted for his return: the remainder of those who voted for him would have their vote counted for the next person on their respective lists who needed them, and could by their aid complete the quota. To determine which of a candidate's votes should be used for his return, and which set free for others, several methods are proposed, into which we shall not here enter. He would of course retain the votes of all those who would not otherwise be represented; and for the remainder, drawing lots, in default of better, would be an unobjectionable expedient. The voting papers would be conveyed to a central office, where the votes would be counted, the number of first, second, third, and other votes given for each candidate ascertained, and the quota would be allotted to every one who could make it up, until the number of the House was complete; first votes being preferred to second, second to third, and so forth. The voting papers, and all the elements of the calculation, would be placed in public repositories, accessible to all whom they concerned ; and if any one who had obtained the quota was not duly returned, it would be in his power easily to prove it.

These are the main provisions of the scheme. For a more minute knowledge of its very simple machinery, I must refer to Mr. Hate's 'Treatise on the Election of Representatives' (a small volume published in 1859), [1]and to a pamphlet by Mr. Henry Fawcett, published

---

[1] In a second edition, published very recently, Mr. Hare has made important improvements in some of the detailed provisions.

第七章

需要他那张选票也可以当选,他的选票仍然可以用来帮助它可以帮助的人当选。为了选出下院所需的足够数目的议员,同时也为了防止十分出名的候选人独占几乎所有的选票,就有必要规定,不管一个候选人得到多少票,他的选票也应按照能够使他当选的配额来计算,而投给他的那些剩余的票则应该计入各自选民的选举纸上的第二个需要选票的人,并且这个候选人应该通过他们的帮助达到规定的配额。要决定一个候选人的选票哪些可以用来帮助他当选,哪些可以释放出来让与别人,有好几种方法,在这里我们就不加以讨论了。他当然可以保留所有那些非他不选的选民的投票,而剩余的票,因为没有更好的办法而采取抽签的方式,将是不会引起大家反对的权宜的办法。选举纸将被送到一个计票中心,在那里,将进行计票工作,投给每个候选人的第一、第二、第三及其他的选票数目将得到确认,配额将分配给那些能够凑足票数的候选人,直到下院的议员满额为止。第一选票比第二选票要优先,第二则比第三优先,依此类推。选举纸和所有的统计资料都将存放在公共的保管场所,供任何人查阅,而且如果任何人得到了配额却没有及时当选,依靠他自己的力量很容易就可以证明。

这就是这个方案的主要规定。想要知道这一简单方法更为详细的知识,则必须提及黑尔先生的《论代表的选举》(发表于1859年的一本小册子)①以及亨利·福西特(Henry Fawcett)在1860年出版的名为《对黑尔先生改革法案的简化和说明》一本小

---

① 在最近出版的第二版中,黑尔先生对一些详细的规定做了重要的修正。

in 1860, and entitled 'Mr. Hare's Reform Bill simplified and explained.' This last is a very clear and concise exposition of the plan, reduced to its simplest elements, by the omission of some of Mr. Hare's original provisions, which, though in themselves beneficial, were thought to take more from the simplicity of the scheme than they added to its practical advantages. The more these works are studied, the stronger, I venture to predict, will be the impression of the perfect feasibility of the scheme, and its transcendent advantages. Such and so numerous are these, that, in my conviction, they place Mr. Hare's plan among the very greatest improvements yet made in the theory and practice of government.

In the first place, it secures a representation, in proportion to numbers, of every division of the electoral body: not two great parties alone, with perhaps a few large sectional minorities in particular places, but every minority in the whole nation, consisting of a sufficiently large number to be, on principles of equal justice, entitled to a representative. Secondly, no elector would, as at present, be nominally represented by some one whom he had not chosen. Every member of the House would be the representative of an unanimous constituency. He would represent a thousand electors, or two thousand, or five thousand, or ten thousand, as the quota might be, every one of whom would have not only voted for him, but selected him from the whole country; not merely from the assortment of two or three perhaps rotten oranges, which may be the only choice offered to him in his local market. Under this relation the tie between the elector and the representative would be of a strength, and a value, of which at present we have no experience. Every one of the electors would be personally identified with his representative, and the representative with his constituents. Every elector who voted for him would have done so either because he is the person in the whole list of candidates for Parliament who best expresses the voter's own opinion, or because he is one of those whose abilities and character the voter most respects, and whom he most willingly trusts to think for him. The member would represent persons, not the mere bricks and mortar of the town-the voters themselves, not a few vestrymen or parish notabilities merely. All, however, that is worth preserving in the representation of places would be preserved. Though the Parliament of the nation ought to have as little as possible to do with purely local affairs, yet, while it has to do with

册子。后者是对这一方案的清晰、简练的说明,通过删去黑尔先生原来的一些规定(尽管这些规定,本身是有益的,却被认为增加了实际的好处而丧失了方案的简明性),将方案简化为最简单的原理。我敢预言,对这些著作的研究越深入,我们对该方案的可行性以及它卓越的优势印象就越为强烈。这些优势如此之多,使我深信,这些卓越的优势将使得黑尔先生的方案成为迄今政府在理论和实践方面所取得的最伟大的改进之一。

首先,它保证每个选举团体能够按照其人口的一定比例得到一个代表:不仅仅是两大政党,以及某些特殊地区的几个较大的区域性少数群体,而且是全国的每一个少数群体,只要有足够的人口,就能按照平等公正的原则选出代表。其次,选民不会像现在这样,在名义上由不是他选举的人代表着。每个下院的议员将是意见一致的选民群体的代表,他可能依照配额所规定的人数,代表一千或两千,或五千选民,每个选民不仅选了他,而且是在全国的范围上选了他,不是从当地市场提供给他的唯一可供选择的两个或三个也许是烂橘子的货色中挑选出来的。有了这种关系,选民与代表之间的关系将会很紧密,也很有价值,这是我们当前还没有体验到的。每个选民都将认同他的代表,而代表也认同他的选民。要么每个投他的票的选民是因为他是参加竞选的候选人中最好地表达选民意见的人,要么是因为选民极为敬重他的能力和性格,最愿意委托其作为自己的代表。议员代表的是人群而不仅仅是城市的砖瓦;代表的是选民自身,而不仅仅是几个教区委员或教区的头面人物。可是,地方代表制一切值得保留的东西将被保留下来,尽管国家议会应当尽可能不插手纯属地方的事务,但是一旦它和地方事务

them, there ought to be members specially commissioned to look after the interests of every important locality: and these there would still be. In every locality which could make up the quota within itself, the majority would generally prefer to be represented by one of themselves ; by a person of local knowledge, and residing in the locality, if there is any such person to be *found* among the candidates, who is otherwise well qualified to be their representative. It would be the minorities chiefly, who being unable to return the local member, would look out elsewhere for a candidate likely to obtain other votes in addition to their own.

Of all modes in which a national representation can possibly be constituted, this one affords the best security for the intellectual qualifications desirable in the representatives. At present, by universal admission, it is becoming more and more difficult for any one, who has only talents and character, to gain admission into the House of Commons. The only persons who can get elected are those who possess local influence, or make their way by lavish expenditure, or who, on the invitation of three or four tradesmen or attorneys, are sent down by one of the two great parties from their London clubs, as men whose votes the party can depend on under all circumstances. On Mr. Hare's system, those who did not like the local candidates, would have the power to fill up their voting papers by a selection from all the persons of national reputation, on the list of candidates, with whose general political principles they were in sympathy. Almost every person, therefore, who had made himself in any way honourably distinguished, though devoid of local influence, and having sworn allegiance to no political party, would have a fair chance of making up the quota ; and with this encouragement such persons might be expected to offer themselves, in numbers hitherto undreamt of. Hundreds of able men of independent thought, who would have no chance whatever of being chosen by the majority of any existing constituency, have by their writings, or their exertions in some field of public usefulness, made themselves known and approved by a few persons in almost every district of the kingdom ; and if every vote that would be given for them in every place could be counted for their election, they might be able

第七章

发生关系的时候,就应该专门任命议员来关注每个重要地区的利益,并且这些利益仍然存在。在每个能够在其范围内达到配额要求的地区,一般说来,多数将倾向于选举他们中的某个人来做代表,选举一个具有地方知识,并且居住在当地的人做代表,如果在正式候选人当中有这样的人,而他在其他方面又很适于做他们的代表的话。问题主要在于少数群体,由于他们不能选举本地区的人作代表,所以指望在其他地方找到一个除他们的选票外还能得到其他选票的候选人作他们的代表。

在有可能形成全国性代表制度的所有方法中,这种方法最能保证能达到人们希望的议员智力水平。目前,那些只有才华和个性的人越来越难通过普选当选为下院的议员了。那些能够当选的人只能是具有地区影响的人,或者是用金钱开路的人,或者是受了三四个商人或商业代理人邀请、由两大政党中的一个从它们的伦敦总部派下去的人,他们的选票是其政党在任何情况下都可以指望的。按照黑尔先生的体系,那些不喜欢地区候选人的选民,将有权力从候选人名单中所列的具有全国声望的人当中,选择其观点能与他们发生共鸣的人填入选举纸。因此,几乎每个以任何方式体面地出名的人,就算他缺乏地方影响,也没有宣誓效忠过什么政党,也将会有公平的机会得到所需的配额。有了这样的激励,我们可以期待这样的人会以至今难以想象的数目涌现出来。成百上千具有独立思维能力的能人志士,他们无论如何都没有机会被任何现有选民中的多数所选中,他们通过他们所写的书籍,或者在公益方面的一些事务中发挥他们的作用,使他们几乎在王国的每个角落都会有了解和赞同他们的人,并且如果每个地方投给他们的选票能够算到他们头上的话,他们就可能达到选举

to complete the number of the quota. In no other way which it seems possible to suggest, would Parliament be so certain of containing the very *élite of* the country.

And it is not solely through the votes of minorities that this system of election would raise the intellectual standard of the House of Commons. Majorities would be compelled to look out for members of a much higher calibre. When the individuals composing the majority would no longer be reduced to Hobson's choice, of either voting for the person brought forward by their local leaders, or not voting at all; when the nominee of the leaders would have to encounter the competition not solely of the candidate of the minority, but of all the men of established reputation in the country who were willing to serve; it would be impossible any longer to foist upon the electors the first person who presents himself with the catchwords of the party in his mouth, and three or four thousand pounds in his pocket. The majority would insist on having a candidate worthy of their choice, or they would carry their votes somewhere else, and the minority would prevail. The slavery of the majority to the least estimable portion of their number would be at an end : the very best and most capable of the local notabilities would be put forward by preference; if possible, such as were known in some advantageous way beyond the locality, that their local strength might have a chance of being fortified by stray votes from elsewhere. Constituencies would become competitors for the best candidates, and would vie with one another in selecting from among the men of local knowledge and connexions those who were most distinguished in every other respect.

The natural tendency of representative government, as of modern civilization, is towards collective mediocrity: and this tendency is increased by all reductions and extensions of the franchise, their effect being to place the principal power in the hands of classes more and more below the highest level of instruction in the community. But though the superior intellects and characters will necessarily be outnumbered, it makes a great difference whether or not they are heard. In the false democracy which, instead of giving representation to all, gives it only to the local majorities, the voice of the instructed minority

所要求的配额数。除此之外,似乎没有什么别的办法可以使议会网罗到这个国家真正的精英了。

并不只是通过少数群体的投票,这套选举体系才能提升下院议员的智力水平。多数人将不得不物色更具才能的人。当构成多数的个人不再是别无选择的时候,即不再是要么选举由地方领袖提出的候选人,要么就根本不选的时候,当这些地方领袖提名的候选人不得不面临着不仅是少数群体的候选人,而且是所有在全国早就有了名望、并热心公益的人的竞争时,就不再可能把嘴里喊着口号、兜里装着三四千英镑的人当成第一候选人硬塞给选民了。多数群体会坚持他们的候选人应当值得他们去选,否则的话他们就会把票投往别处,这样的话,少数群体就会获胜。多数群体被他们当中极小部分人奴役的状态将走向终结:最优秀且最有能力的地方知名人士首先被推举出来,如果可能的话,因为这些人在地区之外也有些名气,所以他们有机会得到地区以外一些零散的选票,从而加强他们在当地的力量。选民将为得到最好的候选人而竞争,他们将会为选择具有地方知识并有地方关系,而且在其他方面也最为出色的人而展开激烈的竞争。

代议制政府的自然倾向,就像现代文明的自然倾向那样,是倾向于选择平庸之才,而这种倾向由于选举权的不断下放和扩大而有所增强,而选举权的不断下放和扩大产生的后果就是主要权力落入到越来越低于社会的最高教养水平的阶级手中。尽管具有出色智力水平和优良品质的人的数目很少,但是,他们的意见能否让人听到却有很大的不同。在虚假的民主政治中(在这种政治中,选举代表的权力只给了当地的多数群体而不是给了全体人民),有教养的少数群体可能在代议团体中根本没有代表。

may have no organs at all in the representative body. It is an admitted fact that in the American democracy, which is constructed on this faulty model, the highly-cultivated members of the community, except such of them as are willing to sacrifice their own opinions and modes of judgment, and become the servile mouthpieces of their inferiors in knowledge, do not even offer themselves for Congress or the State Legislatures, so certain is it that they would have no chance of being returned. Had a plan like Mr. Hare's by good fortune suggested itself to the enlightened and patriotic founders of the American Republic, the Federal and State Assemblies would have contained many of these distinguished men, and democracy would have been spared its greatest reproach and one of its most formidable evils. Against this evil the system of personal representation, proposed by Mr. Hare, is almost a specific. The minority of instructed minds scattered through the local constituencies, would unite to return a number, proportioned to their own numbers of the very ablest men the country contains. They would be under the strongest inducement to choose such man, since in no other mode could they make their small numerical strength tell for anything considerable. The representatives of the majority, besides that they would themselves be improved in quality by the operation of the system, would no longer have the whole field to themselves. They would indeed outnumber the others, as much as the one class of electors outnumbers the other in the country: they could always outvote them, but they would speak and vote in their presence, and subject to their criticism. When any difference arose, they would have to meet the arguments of the instructed few, by reasons, at least apparently, as cogent ; and since they could not, as those do who are speaking to persons already unanimous, simply assume that they are in the right, it would occasionally happen to them to become convinced that they were in the wrong. As they would in general be well-meaning (for thus much may reasonably be expected from a fairly-chosen national representation), their own minds would be insensibly raised by the influence of the minds with which they were in contact, or even in conflict. The champions of unpopular doctrines would not put forth their arguments merely in books and periodicals, read only by their own side; the

第七章

确凿的事实就是,在美国构建得并不很完善的民主政治的模式中,社会中受过高等教育的人,除非愿意放弃自己的观点及其判断是非的方法,并且卑躬屈膝成为在学问方面比他差的人的代言人,否则的话,是不愿意成为国会议员或州议员的,而且同样可以肯定的是,他们也不会有当选的机会。如果类似黑尔先生的方案的计划有幸被美国那些开明、爱国的开国元勋们想到的话,联邦以及州议会将会有许多杰出的人物,而民主政治也不会受到最大的诟病,也不会有最可怕的弊病了。要消除这个弊病,黑尔先生提议的个人代表制几乎就是一副特效药。分散于地方选区的受过教育的人将联合起来选出一定数目这个国家最有能力的人,他们有着强烈的动机选择这样的人,因为没有其他办法可以使他们那小小人数对任何值得考虑的事情产生影响。多数群体的代表除了通过这个制度的运转使自身素质得到提高之外,将不再把整个地盘都占为己有。他们确实将在人数上超过其他代表,就像在一个国家里,一个阶级的选民超过另外一个阶级一样。他们在票数上总是要胜过其他代表,但是他们将在有其他代表的面前发言和表决,并受到他们的批评。当出现任何分歧时,他们将不得不同受过教育的少数争辩,而理由至少在表面上应该有说服力。既然他们不能像跟意见早已一致的人说话那样简单地假定自己是对的,他们偶尔也会承认自己是错的。由于一般说来他们是善意的(因为这样就可以理所当然地对公平选出来的代表有所期待),因此他们自己的觉悟可以通过与他们接触、甚至发生冲突的人的思想的影响而不知不觉得到提高。不受欢迎的主张的拥护者将不仅在只有他们才看的书籍和杂志上发表自己的意见,而且互相对立的阶级

opposing ranks would meet face to face and hand to hand, and there would be a fair comparison of their intellectual strength, in the presence of the country. It would then be found out whether the opinion which prevailed by counting votes would also pervail if the votes were weighed as well as counted. The multitude have often a true instinct for distinguishing an able man when he has the means of displaying his ability in a fair field before them. If such a man fails to obtain any portion whatever of his just weight, it is through institutions or usages which keep him out of sight. In the old democracies there were no means of keeping out of sight any able man: the bema was open to him: he needed nobody's consent to become a public adviser. It is not so in a representative government; and the best friends of representative democracy can hardly be without misgivings, that the Themistocles or Demosthenes whose counsels would have saved the nation, might be unable during his whole life ever to obtain a seat. But if the presence in the representative assembly can be insured, or even a few of the first minds in the country, though the remainder consist only of average minds, the influence of these leading spirits is sure to make itself sensibly felt in the general deliberations, even though they be known to be, in many respects, opposed to the tone of popular opinion and feeling. I am unable to conceive any mode by which the presence of such minds can be so positively insured, as by that proposed by Mr. Hare.

This portion of the Assembly would also be the appropriate organ of a great social function, for which there is no provision in any existing democracy, but which in no government can remain permanently unfulfilled without condemning that government to infallible degeneracy and decay. This may be called the function of Antagonism. In every government there is some power stronger than all the rest ; and the power which is strongest tends perpetually to become the sole power. Partly by intention, and partly unconsciously, it is ever striving to make all other things bend to itself ; and is not content while there is anything which makes permanent head against it, any influence not in

将面对面地短兵相接,这样他们的智力水平就可以在全国面前进行充分的比较。那么,就可以发现,按照计算票数而胜出的观点,在计算票数的同时也掂量它的分量的话,是否也能同样胜出。当一个具有真才实学的人在一个公平的场合向人们展示他的能力时,群众总是有识别他的本能。如果这样的人不能得到按其实力所应有的地位时,那是因为制度或习惯使他远离公众的视野。在古代的民主政治中,没有什么方法可以使任何有能力的人不进入公众的视野的,讲坛是开放的,他不需要经过任何人的同意就可以为公众出谋划策。而在代议制政府中情况却不是这样,像泰米斯多克里斯或德莫西尼那样,其意见可以拯救整个国家,可是一辈子却得不到一个议席,这是代议制民主的最好的朋友也不能不为之感到不安的。但是如果代表大会能够保证有甚至是几个全国一流的人物出席,那么尽管其余的人只具有一般的智力水平,在进行协商时,这些主要灵魂人物的影响肯定会使其本身变得突出,即使在很多方面,他们是以反对流行的观点和情绪而出名的。我无法设想有什么办法能像黑尔先生提议的那样,更能保证这样的人物能够参加到议会中来。

议会的这部分人同样可以是具有重大社会职能的适当的机关,现有的民主政治中并没有规定这样的社会职能,但是政府不实行这项社会职能就注定要走向堕落和腐化。这项职能可以被称之为对抗职能。在每个政府,都会有某种力量要比其余的力量更加强大,而最强大的力量总是倾向于成为唯一的力量。它总是自觉不自觉地努力使其他事物服从自己,而当存在任何持续跟它作对的事物、任何与其精神不相一致

agreement with its spirit. Yet if it succeeds in suppressing all rival influences and moulding everything after its own model, improvement, in that country, is at an end, and decline commences. Human improvement is a product of many factors, and no power ever yet constituted among mankind includes them all: even the most beneficent power only contains in itself some of the requisites of good, and the remainder, if progress is to continue, must be derived from some other source. No community has ever long continued progressive but while a conflict was going on between the strongest power in the community and some rival power: between the spiritual and temporal authorities; the military or territorial and the industrious classes; the king and the people; the orthodox, and religious reformers. When the victory on either side was so complete as to put an end to the strife, and no other conflict took its place, first stagnation followed, and then decay. The ascendancy of the numerical majority is less unjust, and on the whole less mischievous, than many others, but it is attended with the very same kind of dangers, and even more certainly ; for when the government is in the hands of One or a Few, the Many are always existent as a rival power, which may not be strong enough ever to control the other, but whose opinion and sentiment are a moral, and even a social, support to all who, either from conviction or contrariety of interest, are opposed to any of the tendencies of the ruling authority. But when the Democracy is supreme, there is no One or Few strong enough for dissentient opinions and injured or menaced interests to lean upon. The great difficulty of democratic government has hitherto seemed to be, how to provide in a democratic society, what circumstances have provided hitherto in all the societies which have maintained themselves ahead of others-a social support, *a point d' appui*, for individual resistance to the tendencies of the ruling power ; a protection, a rallying point, for opinions and interests which the ascendant public opinion views with disfavour. For want of such a *point d' appui'* the older societies, and all but a few modern ones, either fell

第七章

势力时,它就不会满足。然而,如果它成功地压制了所有的势力并按照自己的模式来塑造一切的时候,那个国家就不会有什么进步,而衰退就开始了。人类的进步是多种因素的产物,而人类中迄今有过的力量都不能包括这一切因素,甚至最仁慈的力量也只包含了某些好的要素,而其他要素,如果进步在继续的话,就必须来自其他方面。当冲突持续存在于社会最强大的力量与某个对抗力量之间,存在于精神权威与世俗权威之间,军人或领主与劳动阶级之间,国王与人民之间,正统教会与宗教改革者之间时,社会才会取得持续的进步。当胜利的任何一方如此完全地终结了斗争,并且没有其他冲突发生时,最初的停滞发生了,接着就是衰退。让人数上占多数的群体处于支配地位要比其他群体处于支配地位更加公平些,且总体上不会有那么多害处,但它伴随着同样性质的危险,甚至是更为确定的危险,因为当政府被一个或少数几个群体控制时,许多群体一直作为对立力量存在,他们也许不会强大到控制前者的地步,但他们的观念及情感是所有出于坚定信仰或利益矛盾而为统治阶级的任何趋向所反对的人一种道义的甚至是社会的声援。但是当民主至上的时候,就不存在一个或少数几个群体强大到可以压制意见和依靠损害或威胁别人的利益过活了。迄今为止民主政府的最大困难似乎在于,在一个民主社会里,如何提供某种社会支持,即一个支撑点;在迄今为止的一切保持先进的社会里又提供了什么环境,使个人得以反抗统治权威;提供某种保护,某个聚集点,使不被主流舆论所赞成的观点得以聚集。在较古老的社会以及绝大部分现代社会,由于缺乏这样的支撑点,让只有少数享受社会和精神福利的那部分人独揽大权,结果要么陷于解体,要么

into dissolution or became stationary (which means slow deterioration) through the exclusive predominance of a part only of the conditions of social and mental well-being.

Now, this great want the system of Personal Representation is fitted to supply, in the most perfect manner which the circumstances of modern society admit of. The only quarter in which to look for a supplement, or completing corrective, to the instincts of a democratic majority, is the instructed minority: but, in the ordinary mode of constituting democracy, this minority has no organ: Mr. Hare's system provides one. The representatives who would be returned to Parliament by the aggregate of minorities, would afford that organ in its greatest perfection. A separate organization of the instructed classes, even if practicable, would be in vidious, and could only escape from being offensive by being totally without influence. But if the *élite* of these classes formed part of the Parliament, by the same title as any other of its members-by representing the same number of citizens, the same numerical fraction of the national will-their presence could give umbrage to nobody, while they would be in the position of highest vantage, both for making their opinions and counsels heard on all important subjects, and for taking an active part in public business. Their abilities would probably draw to them more than their numerical share of the actual administration of government ; as the Athenians did not confide responsible public functions to Cleon or Hyperbolus (the employment of Cleon at Pylus and Amphipolis was purely exceptional), but Nicias, and Theramenes, and Alcibiades were in constant employment both at home and abroad, though known to sympathize more with oligarchy than with democracy. The instructed minority would, in the actual voting, count only for their numbers, but as a moral they would count for much more, in virtue of their knowledge, and of the influence it would give them over the rest. An arrangement better adapted to keep popular opinion within reason and justice, and to guard it from the various deteriorating influences which assail the weak side of democracy, could scarcely by human ingenuity be devised.

第七章

开始停滞不前,也即是说,开始慢慢地衰落了。

现在,个人代表制以现代社会容许有的最完美的方式满足了这一巨大的需要。只有从有教养的少数群体中才能为民主制的多数的本能倾向找到某种补充,或进行彻底的矫正。但是,一般说来,在构建的民主政治的普遍模式中,少数群体没有发言机构,而黑尔先生的政治设计提供了这样的机构。那些通过积攒少数人的投票而进入议会的代表,提供了一个最完善的机关。一个专属于有教养的阶级的组织,即使是可行的,也会招人妒忌,最后只能是毫无影响才不会招人讨厌。但是如果这些阶级的精英成为了议会的一部分,有了跟其他群体一样的头衔——代表同样数量的公民,同样多的一部分国民意志——那么他们的存在就不会引起任何人的不快,而他们则处于最有利的地位,使他们在各个重要议题方面发表的意见和建议都有人倾听,使他们能在公共事务方面发挥积极的作用。他们的才能也许能够使他们担任按其所代表的人数所得份额更多的政府行政工作,正如雅典人不曾让克莱昂或海帕波拉斯担任负责的公职(而在派洛斯和安菲波利斯雇佣克莱昂则纯属例外),但是尼西阿斯、特拉米尼斯和阿尔西巴德则长期担任国内外的各种职务,尽管人们知道他们更赞同的是寡头政治而不是民主政治。在实际投票中,虽然有教养的少数群体只能按照他们的人数计算,但借助于他们的知识,以及他们具有的对其他人的影响,他们作为一种道义的力量就重要得多。人类的聪明才智很难设想出比这更加合适的安排,能将舆论保持在理性和公正的范围内,并使之不受那些攻击民主的 弱环节的各种堕落的势力的影响。这样,民主的人民

A democratic people would in this way be provided with what in any other way it would almost certainly miss-leaders of a higher grade of intellect and character than itself. Modern democracy would have its occasional Pericles, and its habitual group of superior and guiding minds.

With all this array of reasons, of the most fundamental character, on the affirmative side of the question, what is there on the negative ? Nothing that will sustain examination, when people can once be induced to bestow any real examination upon a now thing. Those indeed, if any such there be, who under pretence of equal justice, aim only at substituting the class ascendancy of the poor for that of the rich, will of course be unfavourable to a scheme which places both on a level. But I do not believe that any such wish exists at present among the working classes of this country, though I would not answer for the effect which opportunity and demagogic artifices may hereafter have in exciting it. In the United States, where the numerical majority have long been in full possession of collective despotism, they would probably be as unwilling to part with it as a single despot, or an aristocracy. But I believe that the English democracy would as yet be content with protection against the class legislation of others, without claiming the power to exercise it in their turn.

Among the ostensible objectors to Mr. Hare's scheme, some profess to think the plan unworkable ; but these, it will be found, are generally people who have barely heard of it, or have given it a very slight and cursory examination. Others are unable to reconcile themselves to the loss of what they term the local character of the representation. A nation does not seem to them to consist of persons, but of artificial units, the creation of geography and statistics. Parliament must represent towns and counties, not human beings. But no one seeks to annihilate towns and counties. Towns and counties, it may be presumed, are represented, when the human beings who inhabit them are represented. Local feelings cannot exist without somebody who feels them; nor local interests without somebody interested in them.

第七章

将拥有在其他任何情况下肯定得不到的东西,即比他们自己在智慧和品质方面更高一级的领袖。现代民主政治将偶尔会拥有自己的伯利克里,以及经常会有一批出众的、起引导作用的人物。

在所有这一系列有关这问题的、最具根本性质的正面理由之外,会有什么反面的理由呢?当人们一旦对某个新事物进行真正的考察时,是没有什么东西能够经得住这样的考察的。那些披着平等公正的外衣,而真正的目标只是要使穷人阶级取得支配地位,以替代富人阶级的人——假如有这样的人的话——当然不会赞成将两者置于平等地位的方案。但是我不相信在我国工人阶级当中存在着任何这种愿望,尽管我无法保证时机和煽动人心的手段会在今后煽起这种愿望方面产生怎样的结果。在美国,人数上占多数的群体长期以来完全就是集体的专制,他们也许与一个专制君主或贵族政体一样不愿把它丢掉。但是我相信英国的民主政治对防范其他阶级进行阶级立法会表示满意,也不会要求他们自己拥有进行阶级立法的权力。

在那些表面上反对黑尔先生方案的人当中,有些人声称这个方案没法实行。可是我们会发现,这些人就是那些几乎没有听过这个方案的人,或者是对该方案只进行过肤浅草率的考察的人。还有些是不甘心失去他们称之为代表权的地方特性的人。在他们眼中,国家不是由人组成的,而是由人为的单元组成的,是地理区划和统计学的产物。议会必须代表市镇和郡县,而不是代表人,但是并没有人试图取消市镇和郡县。当居住在市镇和郡县的人民得到代表时,就可以假定,这些地方也就被代表了。如果地方情结没有人去感觉它,它是不可能存在的,同样,如果

If the human beings whose feelings and interests these are have their proper share of representation, these feelings and interests are represented, in common with all other feelings and interests of those persons. But I cannot see why the feelings and interests, which arrange mankind according to localities, should be the only ones thought worthy of being represented; or why people who have other feelings and interests, which they value more than they do their geographical ones, should be restricted to these as the sole principle of their political classification. The notion that Yorkshire and Middlesex have rights apart from those of their inhabitants, or that Liverpool and Exeter are the proper objects of the legislator's care, in contradistinction to the population of those places, is a curious specimen of delusion produced by words.

In general, however, objectors cut the matter short by affirming that the people of England will never consent to such a system. What the people of England are likely to think of those who pass such a summary sentence on their capacity of understanding and judgment, deeming it superfluous to consider whether a thing is right or wrong before affirming that they are certain to reject it, I will not undertake to say. For my own part, I do not think that the people of England have deserved to be, without trial, stigmatized as insurmountably prejudiced against anything which can be proved to be good either for themselves or for others. It also appears to me that when prejudices persist obstinately, it is the fault of nobody so much as of those who make a point of proclaiming them insuperable, as an excuse to themselves for never joining in an attempt to remove them. Any prejudice whatever will be insurmountable, if those who do not share it themselves, truckle to it, and flatter it, and accept it as a law of nature. I believe, however, that in this case there is in general, among those who have yet heard of the proposition, no other hostility to it, than the natural and healthy distrust attaching to all novelties which have not been sufficiently canvassed to make generally manifest all the pros

第七章

没有人对地方利益发生兴趣,地方利益也不可能存在。如果具有这种情结和利益的人得到适当的代表,那么这种情结和利益就和那些人的所有情感和利益一样被代表了。可是我不明白,为什么人类根据地区安排的地方情结和利益,应该是唯一被认为值得去代表的情感和利益,或者说,为什么拥有其他情感和利益——人们把这些情感和利益看得比地理上的情感和利益要更重些——的人们,应当只讲地方感情和利益,并以此作为他们政治区分的唯一原则。认为约克郡和米德尔塞克斯郡拥有不同于其居民所拥有权利的权利,或者认为利物浦和埃克塞特才是立法者应加以关注的适当对象,而不是住在那里的人民,这样的观念,是话语产生的错觉而导致的一个奇怪的例子。

然而,大体上,反对者是将问题简单化,断言英国人民决不会同意这样的制度。英国人民会怎样看待那些人,即对他们的理解和判断能力下如此简单的判断、认为在断言他们必定会加以反对之前没有必要考虑一件事情正确与否的那些人,我不想作什么评论。就我自己而言,我不认为不加检验就污蔑英国人民,说他们对任何能够证明对他们自己或别人有好处的事情都抱有难以克服的偏见的看法,是合适的。我还觉得,当偏见顽固不化时,过错在于那些宣称这些偏见难以克服,并以此作为他们从不试图去消除这些偏见的借口的人。如果不怀偏见的人自己对偏见抱着讨好奉承的态度,并将之作为自然法则的话,不管是什么偏见,都将是难以克服的。然而,我相信在这种情况下,在那些从来没有听说过这种方案的人当中,由于他们没有经过充分的讨论把问题的所有赞成和反对的理由弄清楚,所以他们对一切新事物都抱有自然而健康的不信任态

and cons of the question. The only serious obstacle is the unfamiliarity: this indeed is a formidable one, for the imagination much more easily reconciles itself to a great alteration in substance, than to a very. small one in names and forms. But unfamiliarity is a disadvantage which, when there is any real value in an idea, it only requires time to remove. And in these days of discussion, and generally awakened interest in improvement, what formerly was the work of centuries, often requires only years.

Since the first publication of this Treatise, several adverse criticisms have been made on Mr. Hare's plan, which indicate at least a careful examination of it, and a more intelligent consideration than had previously been given to its pretensions. This is the natural progress of the discussion of great improvements. They are at first met by a blind prejudice, and by arguments to which only blind prejudice could attach any value. As the prejudice weakens, the arguments it employs for some time increase in strength; since, the plan being better understood, its inevitable inconveniences, and the circumstances which militate against it at once producing all the benefits it is intrinsically capable of, come to light along with its merits. But, of all the objections, having any semblance of reason, which have come under my notice, there is not one which had not been foreseen, considered and canvassed by the supporters of the plan, and found either unreal or easily surmountable.

The most serious, in appearance, of the objections, may be the most briefly answered, the assumed impossibility of guarding against fraud, or suspicion of fraud, in the operations of the Central Office Publicity, and complete liberty of inspecting the voting papers after the election, were the securities provided; but these, it is maintained, would be unavailing ; because to check the returns a voter would have to go over all the work that had been done by the staff of clerks. This would be a very weighty objection if there were any necessity that the returns should be verified individually by every voter.

度,除此之外,并不存在其他的敌对。唯一严重的障碍就是对它不熟悉,这才是真正可怕的,因为人的想象力更容易接受在本质上发生了巨大变化的事物,而不容易接受在名称和形式方面的微小变化。但是当一个观念中包含着真正价值时,不熟悉便是一个需要时间去加以消除的不利条件。而经过这些天的讨论,以及对进步的兴趣的广泛的觉醒,以前需要花几个世纪完成的事情,往往只需要短短的几年时间。

本文初次发表以来,人们对黑尔先生的方案就作了一些批评,这些批评至少表明对这个方案进行了详细的考察,并且跟以往反对的理由相比,这些思考也更为睿智。这是在对伟大改进进行讨论时的自然进程。这些改进首先招致的是无知和偏见,以及只有无知和偏见才会加以重视的论据的攻击。当偏见减少时,它所持的论据过一段时间就会增强,因为方案一旦得到更好的理解,它不可避免的不便利,以及妨碍它立即发挥其固有优势的客观形势,与它的优点一起显露出来。但是,我所注意到的似乎合理的一切反对意见,没有哪种意见不曾被方案的支持者们所预见、考虑和讨论过,并且发现这些意见要么是不符合事实的,要么就很容易克服。

表面上看来最为严重的反对意见却可以简要地进行回答。这种意见就是假定在有关选举的中央办公室的运转过程中,不可能防止欺诈或有欺诈的嫌疑。选举公开,以及在选举之后可以完全自由地检查选举纸,就是方案提供的用以防止欺诈的措施。但是反对者说这些措施是没有什么用的,因为要对选举结果进行检查,选民就必须把职员们所做过的所有工作都核实一遍。如果每个选民真的有必要亲自把选举结果核实一遍的话,这的确是一条很

All that a simple voter could be expected to do in the way of verification would be to check the use made of his own voting paper; for which purpose every paper would be returned after a proper interval to the place from whence it came But what he could not do would be done for him by the unsuccessful candidates and their agents. Those among the defeated who thought that they ought to have been returned, would, singly or a number together, employ an agency for verifying the entire process of the election; and if they detected an error, the documents would be referred to a Committee of the House of Commons, by whom the entire electoral operations of the nation would be examined and verified, with a tenth part the time and expense necessary for the scrutiny of a single return before an Election Committee, under the system now in force.

Assuming the plan to be workable, two modes have been alleged, in which its benefits might be frustrated, and injurious consequences superinduced in lieu of them. First, it is said that undue power would be given to knots or cliques ; sectarian combinations; associations for special objects, such as the Maine Law League, the Ballot or Liberation Society; or bodies united by class interests or community of religious persuasion. It is in the second place objected, that the system would admit of being worked for party purposes. A central organ of each political party would send its list of 658 candidates all through the country, to be voted for by the whole of its supporters in every constituency. Their votes would far outnumber those which could ever be obtained by any independent candidate. The 'ticket' system, it is contended, would, as it does in America, operate solely in favour of the great organized parties whose tickets would be accepted blindly, and voted for in their integrity ; and would hardly ever be outvoted except occasionally by the sectarian groups, or knots of men bound together by a common crotchet, who have been already spoken of.

The answer to this appears to me conclusive. No one pretends

第七章

有分量的反对意见。在检查方面我们能期待单个的选民去做的一切,就是核查一下他自己的那张选举纸的使用情况,为了这一目的,每张选举纸在间隔一段时间之后退回到它的来源之处。至于选民所不能做到的可以由落选的候选人及其经纪人去完成。那些失利的候选人中认为自己应该当选的人,将会单独或联合在一起,聘用一个机构来核查选举的整个过程,而如果他们发现了错误,这些文件将被提交到下院的一个委员会,由这个委员会来检查和核对全国的整个选举过程,其所需时间和花费仅仅是现行制度下选举委员会对每个当选议员进行详细审查的所需时间和费用的十分之一。

还有些反对者假定方案是可行的,但宣称方案实行之后可能会产生两种情况,在这两种情况下,方案的好处无从发挥,反而产生了有害的结果。首先,据说过多的的权力将会落入到小团体或派系、宗派联合体、像缅因法律同盟、国教废除促进会等具有特殊目的的社团、或由阶级利益或宗教信仰联合起来的团体手中。其次,他们认为这种制度可能会为政党目的服务。每个政党的中央机关将把它那列有658名候选人的名单送到全国各地,让每个选区的支持者来投票选举。这些候选人所得的选票将远远超出那些独立候选人所得的票数。他们争辩道,"候选人名单"制度,就像在美国那样,将只对有组织的政党有利,这些政党所开出的候选人名单将盲目地被选民全盘接受并投票赞同,并且除非偶尔被宗派团体或者因为某种共同的奇怪念头而联合在一起的一些群体(这些人前面已经提到过)在票数上超过之外,几乎不会有失利的时候。

在我看来,对上述的回答是确定无疑的。没有人会自称按照

that under Mr. Hare's or any other plan, organization would cease to be an advantage. Scattered elements are always at a disadvantage, compared with organized bodies. As Mr. Hare's plan cannot alter the nature of things, we must expect that all parties or sections, great or small, which possess organization, would avail themselves of it to the utmost to strengthen their influence. But under the existing system those influences are everything. The scattered elements are absolutely nothing. The voters who are neither bound to the great political nor to any of the little sectarian divisions, have no means of making their votes available. Mr. Hare's plan gives them the means. They might be more, or less, dexterous in using it. They might obtain their share of influence, or much less than their share. But whatever they did acquire would be clear gain. And when it is asssumed that every petty interest, or combination for a petty object, would give itself an organization, why should we suppose that the great interest of national intellect and character would alone remain unorganized ? If there would be Temperance tickets, and Ragged School tickets, and the like, would not one public-spirited person in a constituency be sufficient to put forth a 'personal merit' ticket, and circulate it through a whole neighbourhood ? And might not a few such persons, meeting in London, select from the list of candidates the most distinguished names, without regard to technical divisions of opinion, and publish them at a trifling expense through all the constituencies ? It must be remembered that the influence of the two great parties, under the present mode of election, is unlimited : in Mr. Hare's scheme it would be great, but confined within bounds. Neither they, nor any of the smaller knots, would be able to elect more members than in proportion to the relative number of their adherents. The ticket system in America operates under conditions the reverse of this. In America electors vote for the party ticket, because the election goes by a mere majority, and a vote for any one who is certain not to obtain the majority is thrown away. But, on Mr. Hare's system, a vote given to a person of known worth has almost as much chance of obtaining its object as one given to a party candidate. It might be hoped, therefore, that every Liberal

第七章

黑尔先生的或其他人的方案,组织将不再是一种优势。同组织起来的团体相比,分散的个人总是处于不利的地位。正如黑尔先生的方案也不能改变事物的本质一样,我们应该期望一切组织起来的政党或部门,不管是大是小,都将最大程度地利用组织来加强它们的影响。但是在现在的制度下面,那些影响就是一切,而分散的个人则完全什么都不是。那些既不属于大的政党也不属于任何小的宗派团体的选民,将没法使他们的选票变得有用。黑尔先生的方案为他们提供了办法,他们可以或多或少地加以巧妙应用。他们可以发挥他们应有的影响,也许比他们应有的影响要小得多。而且当我们假定每一个小小的利益或为一个小小的目标的联合本身就会产生一个组织时,为什么我们要认为国民的智力和品质这一巨大的利益就仍然要停留在无组织的状态呢?如果存在禁酒候选人名单,以及贫民儿童免费学校候选人名单等诸如此类的名单,难道某个选区的热心公益的人士就没有资格提出一张"个人美德"候选人名单,并将之在整个地区散发吗?难道这样一些热心公益的人士,就不能到伦敦碰个头,从候选人名单中把那些最杰出的人物挑出来,不将他们的观点作技术上的区分,然后花一点钱在所有选区内将这些内容刊印出来吗?在现有的选举模式下,必须记住两大政党的影响是无穷的,而在黑尔先生的方案中,虽然它们的影响仍然会很大,但将被限制在一定范围内。在美国,候选人名单制度运转的情况与此刚好相反。在美国,选民们按政党候选人名单投票,因为选举是按简单多数进行的,而投给任何肯定不能获得多数票的候选人的票就白白地被浪费掉了。可是,按照黑尔先生的方案,投给知名人物的票与投给政党候选人的票有同样的机会达到它的目的。因此,人们希望,每个

or Conservative, who as anything besides a Liberal or a Conservative—who had any preferences of his own in addition to those of his party—would scratch through the names of the more obscure and insignificant party candidates, and inscribe in their stead some of the men who are an honour to the nation. And the probability of this fact would operate as a strong inducement with those who drew up the party lists, not to confine themselves to pledged party men, but to include along with these, in their respective tickets, such of the national notabilities as were more in sympathy with their side than with the opposite.

The real difficulty, for it is not to be dissembled that there is a difficulty, is that the independent voters, those who are desirous of voting for unpatronized persons of merit, would be apt to put down the names of a few such persons, and to fill up theremainder of their list with mere party candidates, thus helping to swell the numbers against those by whom they would prefer to be represented. There would be an easy remedy for this, should it be necessary to resort to it, namely, to impose a limit to the number of secondary or contingent votes. No voter is likely to have an independent preference, grounded on knowledge, for 658, or even for 100 candidates. There would be little objection to his being limited to twenty, fifty, or whatever might be the number in the selection of whom there was some probability that his own choice would be exercised—that he would vote as an individual, and not as one of the mere rank and file of a party. But even without this restriction, the evil would be likely to cure itself as soon as the system came to be well understood. To counteract it would become a paramount object with all the knots and cliques whose influence is so much deprecated. From these, each in itself, a small minority, the word would go forth, ' Vote for your *special* candidates only ; or at least put their names foremost, so as to give them the full chance which your numerical strength warrants, of obtaining the quota by means of first votes, or without descending low in the scale. ' And

第七章

自由党人或保守党人,每个不单纯属于自由党或保守党的人,即除了有自己党内候选人可选之外还有自己喜欢的候选人的那些人,将从政党候选人名单中把那些不出名、不重要的候选人划掉,并代之以某些让国家感到骄傲的人。有了这种可能,那些制定政党候选人名单的人就有一种强烈的动机,他们将不仅仅局限于选择那些宣誓效忠本党的人,而且还会在他们各自的候选人名单中,将那些相比较起来更加倾向于同情他们立场的全国知名人士包括进去。

我们不能掩饰我们所面临的困难,而真正的困难是,独立的选民,那些渴望选举那些无人赞助的优秀人士的选民,将倾向于选上几个这样的人士,而将名单中剩下的空位填上政党候选人的名字,这样一来,就增大了一部分的人数,而这部分人对他们愿意选作代表的那些人来说是不利的。如果有必要采取措施的话,简单的补救措施就是,对第二位的或附带的投票加以限制。面对658个候选人,甚至面对100个候选人,选民不大可能全部对他们有所了解,从而进行独立的选择。把候选人名单的人数限制在20个、50个,或者限制在任何一个有利于选民独立进行选择的数目,是不大会有人反对的,这样他就可以作为个人进行投票,而不是仅仅作为政党的一个普通成员进行投票。但即使没有这样的限制,只要这种制度能被很好地理解,这种弊端就可能会自行消除。抵制这种弊端将成为所有其势力受到极大轻视的派系的一个极为重要的目标。这些派系本身都是小小的少数,它们会提出这样的口号:"只投你特定候选人的票,或者至少把他们名字放在第一的位置上,这样你们的人数就可以保证他有充分的机会通过第一选票获得当选所需配额,或者不至于得票过少。"那些不

those voters who did not belong to any clique, would profit by the lesson.

The minor groups would have precisely the amount of power which they ought to have. The influence they could exercise would be exactly that which their number of voters entitled them to ; not a particle more: while, to ensure even that, they would have a motive to put up, as representatives of their special objects, candidates whose other recommendations would enable them to obtain the suffrages of voters not of the sect or clique. It is curious to observe how the popular line of argument in defence of existing systems veers round, according to the nature of the attack made upon them. Not many years ago it was the favourite argument in support of the then existing system of representation, that under it all 'interests' or 'classes' were represented. And certainly, all interests or classes of any importance ought to be represented, that is, ought to have spokesmen, or advocates, in Parliament. But from thence it was argued that a system ought to be supported, which gave to the partial interests not advocates merely, but the tribunal itself. Now behold the change. Mr. Hare's system makes it impossible for partial interests to have the command of the tribunal, but it ensures them advocates, and for doing even this it is reproached. Because it unites the good points of class representation and the good points of numerical representation, it is attacked from both sides at once.

But it is not such objections as these that are the real difficulty in getting the system accepted ; it is the exaggerated notion entertained of its complexity and the consequent doubt whether it is capable of being carried into effect. The only complete answer to this objection would be actual trial. When the merits of the plan shall have become more generally known, and shall have gained for it a wider support among impartial thinkers, an effort should be made to obtain its introduction experimentally in some limited field, such as the municipal

第七章

属于任何派系的选民,也可以从这个口号中学到一些东西。

各个小集团将正好具有它们应当拥有的力量。他们能够发挥的影响将恰好是那些选民在人数上赋予他们的影响,一点也不会多。要保证做到这一点,他们将有意提出一些能够得到这个派系以外选民的投票的候选人,作为他们特定目的的代表。奇怪的是,为现行制度辩护的流行观点会根据对这个制度的攻击的性质而改变。就在几年前,支持现行的代议制度的流行论点是,在这种制度下,一切"利益"或"阶级"都得到了代表。所有具有任何重要意义的利益或阶级都应当被代表,也就是说,他们应当在议会里有代言人或辩护人,这是理所当然的事情。但是从那时起,人们又争论说,不仅能为部分利益进行辩护,而且给它提供自己裁决能力的制度应当得到支持。现在我们来看这种变化,黑尔先生的方案不可能让部分利益团体拥有自己裁决的能力,但却保证这些利益拥有自己的辩护人,而甚至这样做也受到责备。因为它把阶级代表制的好的方面与多数代表制的好的方面统一起来了,所以立即遭到来自两个方面的攻击。

但是,要使这一制度得到人们的接受,像这样的反对意见还不是真正的困难。真正的困难在于夸大了这种制度的复杂性,从而怀疑它是否能够付诸实施。对这种反对意见的唯一彻底的回答就是进行实际的试验。当这个方案的优点慢慢地为人们所知,并且赢得那些秉持公心的思想家们的更为广泛的支持的时候,在某个限定的范围内就可以做些推广性的试验,如在某个大城市的选举中加以试行。当人们决定将约克郡西区划分开来,以便给它四名议员,而不是试用一下新规则,即不把这个选区分开,且允许候选人在无论是第一位还

election of some great town. An opportunity was lost, when the decision was taken to divide the West Riding of Yorkshire for the purpose of giving it four members ; instead of trying the new principle, by leaving the constituency undivided, and allowing a candidate to be returned on obtaining either in first or secondary votes a fourth part of the whole number of votes given. Such experiments would be a very imperfect test of the worth of the plan; but they would be an exemplification of its mode of working ; they would enable people to convince themselves that it is not impracticable ; would familiarize them with its machinery, and afford some materials for judging whether the difficulties which are thought to be so formidable, are real or only imaginary. The day when such a partial trial shall be sanctioned by Parliament, will, I believe, inaugurate a new era of Parliamentary Reform; destined to give to Representative Government a shape fitted to its mature and triumphant period, when it shall have passed through the militant stage in which alone the world has yet seen it.

第七章

是第二位选票中得到选票总数的四分之一就能当选时,就失去了对这一方案进行试验的一次机会。这种实验并不是对这个方案的一次完美的检验,但它们将会向人们演示它的工作模式,它们可以使人们相信这个方案并不是不能实行的,使他们熟悉它的运作机制,向人们提供一些材料来判断这些被认为很可怕的困难究竟是真实的还是只是一种想象。当有一天,议会批准进行这样的局部试验时,我相信,这将开辟一个议会改革的新时代,它必定要给代议制政府以适合于它的成熟和胜利时期的形式,到那时,代议制政府应当已经度过了它那当今世界所能看到的、战斗的阶段。

CHAPTER VIII
Of The Extension Of The Suffrage

Such a representative democracy as has now been sketched, representative of all, and not solely of the majority-in which the interests, the opinions, the grades of intellect which are outnumbered would nevertheless be heard, and would have a chance of obtaining by weight of character and strength of argument an influence which would not belong to their numerical force-this democracy, which is alone equal, alone impartial, alone the government of all by all, the only true type of democracy-would be free from the greatest evils of the falsely-called democracies which now prevail, and from which the current idea of democracy is exclusively derived. But even in this democracy absolute power, if they chose to exercise it, would rest with the numerical majority ; and these would be composed exclusively of a single class, alike in biasses, prepossessions, and general modes of thinking, and a class, to say no more, not the most highly cultivated. The constitution would therefore still be liable to the characteristic evils of class government: in a far less degree, assuredly, than that exclusive government by a class, which now usurps the name of democracy ; but still, under no effective restraint, except what might be found in the good sense, moderation, and forbearance, of the class itself. If checks of this description are sufficient, the philosophy of constitutional government is but solemn trifling. All trust in constitutions is grounded on the assurance they may afford, not that the depositaries of power will not, but that they cannot, misemploy it. Democracy is

第八章　关于扩大选举权

　　这样的代议制民主政体现在已经被描述为代表所有人,而不仅仅代表大多数人的民主政体。在这样的政体中,各种睿智的人的利益、意见虽然居少数,但仍然会为人们所听见,并且有机会依靠其品质的力量和论据的有力来获得影响,而这种影响按其人数来说是得不到的。这种民主政体,是唯一平等的,唯一公正的,唯一由全体管理的属于全体的政府,唯一真正的民主政体。它将免于当下流行的被不实地称作民主政体所具有的最大的害处,而时下的关于民主政治的观念就是源自这种流行的民主政体。但即使在这种民主政体中,绝对权力,假使他们会选择用它的话,将取决于人数上的多数,并且这些人将组成一个具有相似的偏见、偏好和一般的思维模式。这样的一个阶级,不消多说,不是具有最高素养的。因此,这样的构造仍然容易受到阶级政府特有缺陷的侵害,尽管确实要比现在仍然打着民主政治旗号的阶级的排他政府在程度上要小得多。除了这个阶级自身的善意、节制和自制之外,仍然处于没有有效约束的状态。如果这种约束是足够的话,那么有关宪政学说就只不过是一件仪式隆重的微小之事而已。所有宪法上的信任都基于他们可能提供的保证,不是以权力的受托人不愿滥用权力,而是以它可以提供他们不

not the ideally best form of government unless this weak side of it can be strengthened; unless it can be so organized that noclass, not even the most numerous, shall be able to reduce all but itself to political insignificance, and direct the course of legislation and administration by its exclusive class interest. The problem is, to find the means of preventing this abuse, without sacrificing the characteristic advantages of popular government.

These twofold requisites are not fulfilled by the expedient of a limitation of the suffrage, involving the compulsory exclusion of any portion of the citizens from a voice in the representation. Among the foremost benefits of free government is that education of the intelligence and of the sentiments, which is carried down to the very lowest ranks of the people when they are called to take a part in acts which directly affect the great interests of their country. On this topic I have already dwelt so emphatically, that I only return to it, because there are few who seem to attach to this effect of popular institutions all the importance to which it is entitled. People think it fanciful to expect so much from what seems so slight a cause-to recognise a potent instrument of mental improvement in the exercise of political franchises by manual labourers. Yet unless substantial mental cultivation in the mass of mankind is to be a mere vision, this is the road by which it must come. If any one supposes that this road will not bring it, I call to witness the entire contents of M. de Tocqueville's great work;and especially his estimate of the Americans. Almost all travellers are struck by the fact that every American is in some sense both a patriot, and a person of cultivated intelligence; and M. de Tocqueville has shown how close the connexion is between these qualities and their democratic institutions. No such wide diffusion of the ideas, tastes, and sentiments of educated minds, has ever been seen elsewhere, or even conceived of as attainable. Yet this is nothing to what we might look for in a government equally democratic in its unexclusiveness, but better organized in other important points . For political life is indeed

第八章

能滥用权力的保证为根据的。除非民主政体这个薄弱之处可以得到加强,除非它能如此组织,使得没有一个阶级,甚至是人数最多的阶级,能够将除它之外的所有人都降低到政治上无足轻重的地位上去,并以它排他的阶级利益来指导立法和行政工作,否则民主政体不是最理想的政府形式,。问题是要找到可以防止这种权力滥用的方法,同时不牺牲掉平民政府所特有的优势。

这些双重的要求是不能通过限制选举权——包括强制性地将任意一部分公民排除在代表制之外,不让其有发言权——的权宜办法来达到。自由政府的主要好处之一就是当人民被要求参加可以直接影响其国家重大利益的行动时,即使是处于最底层的人民也能享受到智力训练和情操教育。这个话题我早已经如此强调过了,因此我只是重新提到它,因为很少人将平民政府有资格拥有的一切重要性与它的这个效果联系起来。人们认为从看上去如此微小的动机中去期待这么多——从体力劳动者行使公民权利中看到精神进步的有力工具,是离奇古怪的。然而除非人类大众中的实质性的智力培养只是一个幻觉,这就是必须走的道路。如果有人推断这条路行不通,我就用托克维尔(M. de Tocqueville)伟大著作中的全部内容来证明,特别是他对美国所作的评论。几乎所有的旅行者都会为这样一个事实,即每个美国人在某种意义上都既是爱国者,又是有教养的人这个事实所震惊。托克维尔揭示了这些品质与他们的民主制度有着紧密的联系。在其他地方从来看不到,甚至从来没有被认为可以达到如此广泛普及的受过教育的人们的思想、品味和情感。然而,对于我们这样一个在非排他性方面具有同样民主,而在其他更重要的方面却组织得更好的政府中可能要找的东西来说,这算不了什么。因为,

in America a most valuable school, but it is a School from which the ablest teachers are excluded; the first minds in the country being as effectually shut out from the national representation, and from public functions generally, as if they were under a formal disqualification, The Demos, too, being in America the one source of power, all the selfish ambition of the country gravitates towards it, as it does in despotic countries towards the monarch: the People, like the despot, is pursued with adulation and sycophancy, and the corrupting effects of power fully keep pace with its improving and ennobling influences.

If even with this alloy, democratic institutions produce so marked a superiority of mental development in the lowest class of Americans, compared with the corresponding classes in England and elsewhere, what would it be if the good portion of the influence could be retained without the bad ? And this, to a certain extent, may be done; but not by excluding that portion of the people, who have fewest, intellectual stimuli of other kinds, from so inestimable an introduction to large, distant, and complicated interests as is afforded by the attention they may be induced to bestow on political affairs. It is by political discussion that the manual labourer, whose employment is a routine, and whose way of life brings him in contact with no variety of impressions, circumstances, or ideas, is taught that remote causes, and events which take place far off, have a most sensible effect even on his personal interests ; and it is from political discussion, and collective political action, that. one whose daily occupations concentrate his interests in a small circle round himself, learns to feel for and with his fellow-citizens, and becomes consciously a member of a great community. But political discussions fly over the heads of those who have no votes, and are not endeavouring to acquire them. Their position, in comparison with the electors, is that of the audience in a court of justice, compared with the twelve men in the jury-box. It is not *their* suffrages that are asked, it is not their opinion that is sought to be influenced ; the appeals are made, the arguments addressed, to others than them; nothing depends on the decision they may arrive at, and

第八章

在美国,政治生活虽然是一所最有价值的学校,但这是一所将最有才能的老师拒之门外的学校;由于国内一流的人才完全没有机会获取代表权以及公共职务,好像他们被正式剥夺了资格,在美国,民众也是权力的唯一来源,这个国家所有自私的抱负都被吸引到它那里,就像在专制国家中,一切都被吸引到君主那里一样:民众就像专制君主一样,为阿谀奉承所包围,权力的腐化效应与它的改善和提高的影响齐头并进。如果,即使有这样好坏作用参半的情况,和英国以及其他地方相应的阶级比较起来,民主制度在美国的最下层阶级中产生出如此明显的智力发展上的优越性,那么,如果我们保留这种好的影响而去掉它坏的成分,又会是怎么个样子呢?这在某种程度上是可以做到的;但不是通过将那部分人民排除在外,他们除了因为可能被诱使对政治事务加以注意而产生对远大而复杂的利益的难能可贵的关心外,是很少有其他方面的智力刺激的。只有通过政治讨论,才能使那些工作按部就班,生活方式又接触不到各种感慨、环境或观念的体力劳动者认识到,遥远的原因和发生在很远的地方的事件,甚至也会对他们个人的利益也会有最深远的影响。并且只有通过政治讨论,以及集体的政治行动,才能使一个其日常工作就是将他的利益局限在他周围的小圈子的人学会同情和支持他的同胞,并且自觉变成一个伟大社会的成员。但是政治讨论对那些没有投票权并且也不积极争取投票权的人来说是没有关系的。他们的地位与选民相比,就如法庭中的听众与坐在陪审席上的12个陪审员一样。需要的不是他们的投票,力求加以影响的也不是他们的观点。提出的呼吁,陈述的观点,是针对别人而不是他们的。没有什么需要依赖他们可能作出的决定,既没有必要也没有什么诱因使他们作

there is no necessity and very little inducement to them to come to any. Whoever, in an otherwise popular government, has no vote, and no prospect of obtaining it, will either be a permanent malcontent, or will feel as one whom the general affairs of society do not concern; for whom they are to be managed by others; who 'has no business with the laws except to obey them,' nor with public interests and concerns except as a looker-on. What he will know or care about them from this position, may partly be measured by what an average woman of the middle class knows and cares about politics, compared with her husband or brothers.

Independently of all these considerations, it is a personal injustice to withhold from any one unless for the prevention of greater evils, the ordinary privilege of having his voice reckoned in the disposal of affairs in which he has the same interest as other people. If he is compelled to pay, if he may be compelled to fight, if he is required implicitly to obey, he should be legally entitled to be told what for; to have his consent asked, and his opinion counted at its worth, though not at more than its worth. There ought to be no pariahs in a full-grown and civilized nation: no persons disqualified, except through their own default. Every one is degraded, whether aware of it or not, when other people, without consulting him, take upon themselves unlimited power to regulate his destiny. And even in a much more improved state than the human mind has ever yet reached, it is not in nature that they who are thus disposed of should meet with as fair play as those who have a voice. Rulers and ruling classes are under a necessity of considering the interests and wishes of those who have the suffrage; but of those who are excluded, it is in their option whether they will do so or not; and however honestly disposed, they are in general too fully occupied with things which they *must* attend to, to have much room in their thoughts for anything which they can with impunity disregard. No

第八章

出任何决定。在一个就其他方面来讲是平民的政府中,那些没有投票权,也没有期望去获取投票权的人,要么就是永远对之不满的人,要么就是觉得一般的社会事务与自己无关的人。对他们来说,社会事务是由别人来管理的;他"除了遵守法律之外与法律没有关系",除了作为一个看客之外,公共利益和对之的关注也与他们没有关系。处于这个地位,关于政治,他所愿意了解的或关心的,可以部分地用一个中等阶级普通妇女(与她的丈夫或兄弟相比较而言)对政治的了解和关心程度来衡量。

暂且撇开所有的这些考虑不说,除非为了防止更大的恶,将任何一个人拥有的在与其他人一样的相同利益的事件的处理上发表意见的普通的权利加以剥夺,是对他个人的不公。如果他被迫交税,如果他被迫去打仗,如果他被要求绝对服从,在法律上他应当有权利要求被告知原因,有权要求征询他的意见,有权要求按照其价值(尽管不是超过其价值)来对待他的意见。在一个充分发展和文明开化的国家里,不应该有贱民,除了他们自己的过错,没有人会被取消资格。当其他人不与他协商就使他们拥有无限的权力去控制他的命运时,他的地位就降低了,不管他知不知晓。即使在一个人类思想还没有想到过的更为进步的国家里,遭到这样处置的人会拥有与那些拥有发言机会的人同样公平的待遇,也是不可能的。统治者和统治阶级必须考虑那些有选举权的人的利益和愿望;但对那些没有选举权的人来说,他们的利益和愿望有没有得到考虑,就要看统治者的脸色了。不管本性如何诚实,一般来讲,他们满脑子都是他们必须加以考虑的事情,以至于没有多少余地来思考他们可以将其忽视而又没有什么后果的事情。因此,将任何个人或阶级专横地排除在外的选举

arrangement of the suffrage, therefore, can be permanently satisfactory, in which any person or class is peremptorily excluded ; in which the electoral privilege is not open to all persons of full age who desire to obtain it.

There are, however, certain exclusions, required by positive reasons, which do not conflict with this principle, and which, though an evil in themselves, are only to be got rid of by the cessation of the state of things which requires them. I regard it as wholly inadmissible that any person should participate in the suffrage, without being able to read, write, and, I will add, perform the common operations of arithmetic. Justice demands, even when the suffrage does not depend on it, that the means of attaining these elementary acquirementsshould be within the reach of every person, either gratuitously, or at an expense not exceeding what the poorest, who earn their own living, can afford. If this were really the case, people would no more think of giving the suffrage to a man who could not read, than of giving it to a child who could not speak; and it would not be society that would exclude him, but his own laziness. When society has not performed its duty, by rendering this amount of instruction accessible to all, there is some hardship in the case, but it is a hardship that ought to be borne. If society has neglected to discharge two solemn obligations, the more important and more fundamental of the two must be fulfilled first: universal teaching must precede universal enfranchisement. No one but those in whom an ápriori theory has silenced common sense, will maintain, that power over others, over the whole community, should be imparted to people who have not acquired the commonest and most essential requisites for taking care of themselves ; for pursuing intelligently their own interests, and those of the persons most nearly allied to them. This argument, doubtless, might be pressed further, and made to prove much more. It would be eminently desirable that other things besides reading, writing, and arithmetic, could be made necessary to the suffrage ; that some knowledge of the conformation of the earth, its natural and political divisions, the elements of general history, and of the history and institutions of their own country,

第八章

权安排不可能永远地令人满意;不将选举权给予那些渴望获得这种权利的所有适龄选民的安排也不可能永远令人满意。

然而,作出某些排除确实有一定的理由,这些理由与这个原则并不冲突,并且尽管它们本身就有害处,但只有在需要它们的事态消失了之后才能摆脱它们。我认为一个人如果没有读写能力,我还要加上一点,没有算术能力,那么他参加选举是完全不允许的。即使当投票不依赖于公正,公正也要求获得这些基本需要的手段应该是每个人都能有的,要么是免费的,要么不超出那些自谋生路的最贫穷的人所能承担得起的范围。如果真的是这样的话,人们就不会再想要把选举权给予一个不会读写的人,正如不会把这种权利给予一个不会说话的孩子一样。那么将他排除在选举之外的就不是社会,而是他本人的懒惰了。当社会没有承担它的责任,让所有的人都能获得这种程度的教育时,在这种情形下就有些难处,但这是必然会有的难处。假如社会没能履行它两大义务,那么这两者中更重要更基本的义务必须得到履行:普遍的教育必须先于普遍的选举权。只有常识受到一种先验理论压制过的那些人会坚持说,支配别人以及支配整个社会的权力应当给予那些尚不具备照顾自己所必需的最普通、最基本的条件的人,给予那些不能明智地追求自己利益的人,以及那些情况跟他们最紧密结合在一起的人。毫无疑问,这种论点可以更进一步,可以说明更多的问题。尤其值得期待的是,除了读写与算术之外,其他事情也能作为选举权的必要条件;关于地球构造的知识,它的自然的与政治的分区,一般历史的要素,以及他们自己国家的历史和制度,能够作为一切选民的条件。但这些知识,不管

could be required from all electors. But these kinds of knowledge, however indispensable to an intelligent use of the suffrage, are not, in this country, nor probably anywhere save in the Northern United States, accessible to the whole people ; nor does there exist any trustworthy machinery for ascertaining whether they have been acquired or not. The attempt, at present, would lead to partiality, chicanery, and every kind of fraud. It is better that the suffrage should be conferred indiscriminately, or even withheld indiscriminately, than that it should be given to one and withheld from another at the discretion of a public officer. In regard, however, to reading, writing, and culculating, there need be no difficulty. It would be easy to require from every one who presented himself for registry, that he should, in the presence of the registrar, copy a sentence from an English book, and perform a sum in the rule of three ; and to secure, by fixed rules and complete publicity, the honest application of so very simple a test. This condition, therefore, should in all cases accompany universal suffrage; and it would, after a few years, exclude none but those who cared so little for the privilege, that their vote, if given, would not in general be an indication of any real political opinion.

It is also important, that the assembly which votes the taxes, either general or local, should be elected exclusively by those who pay something towards the taxes imposed. Those who pay no taxes, disposing by their votes of other people's money, have every motive to be lavish, and none to economize. As far as money matters are concerned, any power of voting possessed by them is a violation of the fundamental principle of free government; a severance of the power of control, from the interest in its beneficial exercise. It amounts to allowing them to put their hands into other people's pockets, for any purpose which they think fit to call a public one ; which in some of the great towns of the United States is known to have produced a scale of local taxation onerous beyond example, and wholly borne by the wealthier classes. That representation should be co-extensive with taxation, not stopping short of it, but also not going beyond it, is in accordance with the theory of British institutions. But to reconcile this, as a condition annexed to the representation with universality, it is essential, as it is on many other accounts desirable, that taxation, in a visible shape, should descend to the poorest class. In this country

第八章

它们是在合理应用选举权时是如何不可或缺,在这个国家或除美国之外的任何国家都不容易为整个人民所接触到,也不存在确证这些知识获取与否的可靠机制。眼下试图这样做会导致偏私、欺骗和各种欺诈行为。一律给予选举权或一律不给予选举权,要比由一个公务员来决定将它分配给这个,不分配给那个要强得多。可是,关于读写与算术,就不存在什么问题。要求每个登记的选民做到当着登记官的面从一本书中抄写一个句子,以及按比例法运算一则数学题并不是什么难事。通过确定的规则和绝对的公开,保证这样如此简单的测试也是很容易做到的。因此,这种条件应当在所有场合都与普选联系在一起,并且经过几年后,选举只是将那些对这种特权漠不关心,以至于如果让他们投票一般也不能表明任何政治见解的人加以排除。

同样重要的是,对税收进行表决的议会,不管是全国性的还是地方性的,都应当专门由那些交纳税款的人组成。那些不交纳税款却通过他们的投票处置别人钱财的人,常常有浪费的动机,并且根本不会考虑到节省。把钱的因素考虑进来,那么只要由他们拥有投票权,就是对自由政府基本原则的违背,就是将控制权力与权力的有益行使断然分割开来的做法。这简直就是让这些人以任何他们认为适合称之为公共目的的名义来将手伸进他人的口袋。据了解,这在美国的一些大城市已经产生出空前繁重的地方赋税,并且完全由更为富有的阶级来承担。代表权的范围应当与纳税的范围相一致,无过无不及,这与英国的制度理论是相符合的。但是为了使这一点作为具有普遍性的代表制的一个附属条件,向最贫穷的阶级征收看得见的税是必要的,正如它在其他考虑上是人们想要的。在这个国家和其他大部分国家,或许没有哪

and in most others, there is probablyno labouring family which does not contribute to the indirect taxes, by the purchase of tea, coffee, sugar, not to mention narcotics or stimulants. But this mode of defraying a share of the public expenses is hardly felt: the payer, unless a person of education and reflection, does not identify his interest with a low scale of public expenditure, as closely as when money for its support is demanded directly from himself ; and even supposing him to do so, he would doubtless take care that, however lavish an expenditure he might, by his vote, assist in imposing upon the government, it should not be defrayed by any additional taxes on the articles which he himself consumes. It would be better that a direct tax, in the simple form of a capitation, should be levied on every grown person in the community ; or that every such person should be admitted an elector, on allowing himself to be rated *extra ordinem* to the assessed taxes, or that a small annual payment, rising and falling with the gross expenditure of the country, should be required from every registered elector ; that so every one might feel that the money which he assisted in voting was partly his own, and that he was interested in keeping down its amount.

However this may be, I regard it as required by first principles, that the receipt of parish relief should be a peremptory disqualification for the franchise. He who cannot by his labour suffice for his own support has no claim to the privilege of helping himself to the money of others. By becoming dependent on the remaining members of the community for actual subsistence, he abdicates his claim to equal rights with them in other respects. Those to whom he is indebted for the continuance of his very existence, may justly claim the exclusive management of those common concerns, to which he now brings nothing, or less than he takes away. As a condition of the franchise, a term should be fixed, say five years previous to the registry, during which the applicant's name has not been on the parish books as a recipient of relief. To be an uncertificated bankrupt, or to have taken the benefit of the Insolvent Act, should disqualify for the franchise until the person has paid his debts, or at least proved that he is not now, and has not for some long period, been dependent on eleemosynary support. Non-payment of taxes, when so long persisted in that it cannot have risen from inadvertence, should disqualify while it lasts.

第八章

个劳动阶级家族没有通过购买茶叶、咖啡和糖来间接纳税的,更不用说通过买麻醉品或兴奋剂来纳税了。但这种承担公共开支的方式很难被察觉到:付款人,除非他是受过教育或善于反思的人,不会像直接要求他出钱来支持公共开支那样密切地将他的利益与低水平的公共开支联系起来,并且假使他那样做了,毫无疑问会防范不管他的投票强加给政府的开支有多么浪费,这种开支不会由他所消费物品上的附加税来支付。更好的方法就是以人头税的简单方式向社会中的每个成年人征收直接税;或者每个成年人都应被承认为选举人,让他们缴纳一笔额外的税;或者每个登记的选民都应当根据国家每年的大致开支交纳一小笔年金;这样每个人就会觉得他投票表决的钱数部分地就是他自己的钱,并且他愿意将之缩减。

不管怎样,我认为正如基本原则所要求的那样,应当强行取消那些接受教区救济的人的选举权资格。一个不能通过自身的劳动来维持自己生活的人没有资格得到使用他人金钱的特权。由于他变成了依赖其他社会成员生活的人,他就放弃了在其他方面与他们具有同等权利的要求。那些使他能继续生存下来的人,可以正当地要求由他们专门对那些共同关心的事情进行管理,而他对这些事情无所贡献,或贡献的比不上他拿走的多。作为选举权的一项条件应该规定一个期限,也如说在登记前5年这个其间之内,申请人的名字没有出现在教区领取救济的名册里。一个没有保证的破产者,或是从《破产法》中得到过好处的人,应当取消他的选举权,直到他偿还了他的债务,或至少要证明他现在没有,或某段较长时期没有依赖救济金过日子。不是因为出于疏忽而长期不交税时,就应在继续不交税期间取消他的选举

These exclusions are not in theirnaturepermanent. They exact such conditions only as all are able, or ought to be able, to fufil if they choose. They leave the suffrage accessible to all who are in the normal condition of a human being : and if any one has to forgo it, he either does not care sufficiently for it to do for its sake what he is already bound to do, or he is in a general condition of depression and degradation in which this slight addition, necessary for the security of others, would be unfelt, and on emerging from which, this mark of inferiority would disappear with the rest. In the long run, therefore (supposing no restrictions to exist but those of which we have now treated), we might expect that all, except that (it is to be hoped) progressively diminishing class, the recipients of parish relief, would be in possession of votes, so that the suffrage would be, with that slight abatement, universal. That it should be thus widely expanded is, as we have seen, absolutely necessary to an enlarged and elevated conception of good government. Yet in this state of things, the great majority of voters, in most countries, and emphatically in this, would be manual labourers; and the twofold danger, that of too low a standard of political intelligence, and that of class legislation, would still exist, in a very perilous degree. It remains to be seen whether any means exist by which these evils can be obviated.

They are capable of being obviated, if men sincerely wish it, not by any artificial contrivance, but by carrying out the natural order of human life, which recommends itself to every one in things in which he has no interest or traditional opinion running counter to it. In all human affairs, every person directly interested, and not under positive tutelage, has an admitted claim to a voice, and when his exercise of it is not inconsistent with the safety of the whole, cannot justly be excluded.from it. But (though every one ought to have a voice) that every one should have an equal voice is a totally different proposition. When two persons who have a joint interest in any business, differ in opinion, does justice require that both opinions should be held of

第八章

权资格。这些排除在其本质上并不是长久的。它们要求的只是所有人如果去做的话,都能够或者应该能够履行的条件。它们将选举权给予那些处于正常状态中的人,如果有人不得不放弃它的话,他要么是不关心去做为了它必须去做的事情,要么就是大体上处于一种消沉与落魄的状态,在这种状态下,增加一点这种对他人安全来说是必要的微小限制,他将不会察觉,而他从这种状态中摆脱出来后,这种卑贱的标志将随之消失。因此,长远看来——不妨设想除了我们刚才讲到的限制外就不存在其他的限制——我们可以期望除了(希望如此)日渐减少的阶级,靠教区救济金度日的人之外,所有人都能拥有投票权,这样的话,除了少数例外,选举权是普遍的。正如我们所看到的那样,选举权应该作如此一般地扩大,这对一个扩大了的和提高了的政府来说是必要的。然而,在这种情形中,大部分国家特别是我国的大多数选民是体力劳动者,那么,就在很可怕的程度上存在着双重危险,即政治智力水平低下和阶级立法的危险。是否存在避免这些危险的方法则有待观察。

如果人们真心希望避免这些危险的话是能够做到的。这不是通过任何人为的设计,而是通过实现人类生活的自然秩序来达到的。这种自然秩序在并无利害关系或与之相对的传统看法的事情上是每个人都满意的。在人类一切事务中,每个有直接利益关系而又不在别人的保护之下的人都有公认的发言权,并且当他对发言权的行使与全体的安全不矛盾时,就不能正当地加以排除。但是(尽管每个人都应当有发言权),要使每个人都有平等的发言权是一个完全不同的命题。当两个有共同利益的人发生意见分歧时,要保持公平就需要两种意见都被看作具有完全

exactly equal value ? If with equal virtue one is superior to the other in knowledge and intelligence-or if with equal intelligence, one excels the other in virtue-the opinion, the judgment, of the higher moral or intellectual being, is worth more than that of the inferior ; and if the institutions of the country virtually assert that they are of the same value, they assert a thing which is not. One of the two, as a wiser or better man, has a claim to superior weight : his difficulty is in ascertaining which of the two it is; a thing impossible as between individuals, but taking men in bodies and in numbers, it can be done with a certain approach to accuracy. There would be no pretence for applying this doctrine to any case which could with reason be considered as one of individual and private right. In an affair which concerns only one of two persons, that one is entitled to follow his own opinion, however much wiser the other may be than himself. But we are speaking of things which equally concern them both ; where, if the more ignorant does not yield his share of the matter to the guidance of the wiser man, the wiser man must resign his to that of the more ignorant. Which of these modes of getting over the difficulty is most for the interest of both and most conformable to the general fitness of things? If it be deemed unjust that either should have to give way, which injustice is greatest? that the better judgment should give way to the worse, or the worse to the better ?

Now, national affairs are exactly such a joint concern, with the difference, that no one needs ever be called upon for a complete sacrifice of his own opinion. It can always be taken into the calculation, and counted at a certain figure, a higher figure being assigned to the suffrages of those whose opinion is entitled to greater weight. There is not, in this arrangement, anything necessarily invidious to those to whom it assigns the lower degrees of influence. Entire exclusion from a voice in the common concerns, is one thing : the concession to others of a more potential voi ce , on the ground of greater capacity for the

第八章

同等的价值吗?如果两者道德价值相同而其中一人比另一个在知识与智力水平上更优越,或者两者智力水平相同而一者比另一者在道德价值上更优越,那么具有更高道德价值或更高智力水平的意见或判断,就要比道德价值或智力水平更低的意见或判断更有价值;如果国家制度实际上声称它们具有同样的价值,那么它就不是实事求是。两人中更聪明或更有道德的人,有权主张拥有更优越的分量。困难在于确定哪一个是更有道德的人或更聪明的人。这件事情在个人之间是不可能得到解决的,但是如果把人们看成团体或集体,则能做到某种程度上的精确。并没有人要求把这个原则应用于任何有理由被认为是个人或私人权利的场合。在仅仅关系到两者中的一个的事情上,一个人就有权遵循他自己的意见,而不管另一个人和他比起来是如何明智得多。但我们现在谈的事情关系到两者,在这种场合中,如果那个较愚笨的人不服从较为聪明的人的领导,那这个较为聪明的人必须使自己听从于较愚笨的人。这些克服困难的方法哪一个最符合两者利益并且最符合事情的一般道理呢?如果任何一方让步都被认为是不公正的,那么哪一种不公正是最大的呢?是较好的意见给更为糟糕的意见让步,还是相反?

如今,国家事务就是这样一件共同关心的事情,不同的是,没有人需要完全牺牲他自己的意见。意见总是可以被计算进去,并且以某个确定的数字来计算,较大的数字就被用来表示那些意见具有较大分量的人的投票。在这样的安排下,就没有什么事情必定会招致那些具有较低程度影响的人们的嫉妒。完全排除对共同关心的事情的发言权是一回事;出于为了更有能力管理好共同关心的事情而将发言权让渡给其他更具潜力的人,则是另

management of the joint interests, is another. The two things are not merely different, they are incommensurable. Every one has a right to feel insulted by being made a nobody, and stamped as of no account at all. No one but a fool, and only a fool of a peculiar description, feels offended by the acknowledgment that there are others whose opinion, and even whose wish, is entitled to a greater amount of consideration than his. To have no voice in what are partly his own concerns, is a thing which nobody willingly submits to ; but when what is partly his concern is also partly another's, and he feels the other to understand the subject better than himself, that the other's opinion should be counted for more than his own, accords with his expectations, and with the course of things which in all other affairs of life he is accustomed to acquiesce in. It is only necessary that this superior influence should be assigned on grounds which he can comprehend, and of which, he is able to perceive the justice.

I hasten to say, that I consider it entirely inadmissible, unless as a temporary makeshift, that the superiority of influence should be conferred in consideration of property. I do not deny that property is a kind of test: education in most countries, though anything but proportional to riches, is on the average better in the richer half of society than in the poorer. But the criterion is so imperfect; accident has so much more to do than merit with enabling men to rise in the world ; and it is so impossible for any one, by acquiring any amount of instruction, to make sure of the corresponding rise in station, that this foundation of electoral privilege is always, and will continue to be, supremely odious. To connect plurality of votes with any pecuniary, qualification would be not only objectionable in itself, but a sure mode of discrediting the principle, and making its permanent maintenance impracticable. The Democracy, at least of this country, are not at present jealous of personal superiority, but they are naturally, and most justly so, of that which is grounded on mere pecuniary circumstances. The only thing which can justify reckoning on person's opinion as equivalent to morethan one, is individual mental superiority; and what is wanted is some approximate means of ascertaining that.

第八章

一回事。这两者不仅是不同的,而且是不能比较的。如果被小看了、被打上了毫无价值的记号的话,每个人都有权认为受到了污辱。除了傻瓜,并且只有某些种类的傻瓜,才会因为承认有些人的意见,甚至他们的愿望,被认为有资格比他们的意见或愿望更值得考虑而感到不高兴。对部分属于他自己的事情没有发言权,是一件任何人都不愿意接受的事情;但是当跟他有关的事情跟别人也有关系并且他觉得别人对这事情的理解要比他理解得更透彻时,别人的意见要比他自己的意见更加受到重视这是符合他的期望的,并且是符合在所有其他的生活事务中他习惯默许的事物的发展过程的。唯一必要的是,应该根据他所能理解的理由给予这种更大的影响,并且他能够认识到这种理由的公正性。

我得赶紧说,我认为除非作为权宜之计,否则将财产上升到优越的地位是完全不能允许的。我不否认财产是一种评价标准:在大部分国家中,教育尽管绝不是按财富的比例,但平均来讲,在社会中富人所受的教育要比穷人所受的教育更好。但是这个标准却很不完善。使人飞黄腾达的更多的是偶然事件而不是某种优点。任何人都不可能通过获得一定的教育就能保证在职位上得到相应的提升,因此这种以财产作为选举特权基础的做法总是,并且将来也是非常令人讨厌的。将多重投票权与金钱联系起来,选举资格不仅本身会遭到反对,而且也是贬损该原则的灵验方法,并使得这条原则无法长久地保持下去。民主政治,至少我国的民主政治,当前并不妒忌个人的优越性,但它们很自然地,并且很正当地要妒忌仅仅基于金钱的优越性。唯一能证明将个人的意见视作与多个人的意见等同为正当的做法,就是个人智力上的优越性,而所缺少的就是大致确定它的方法。如果存

If there existed such a thing as a really national education, or a trustworthy system of general examination, education might be tested directly. In the absence of these, the nature of a person's occupation is some test. An employer of labour is on the average more intelligent than a labourer ; for he must labour with his head, and not solely with his hands. A foreman is generally more intelligent than an ordinary labourer, and a labourer in the skilled trades than in the unskilled. A banker, merchant, or manufacturer, is likely to be more intelligent than a tradesman, because he has larger and more complicated interests to manage. In all these cases it is not the having merely undertaken the superior function, but the successful performance of it, that tests the qualifications ; for which reason, as well as to prevent persons from engaging nominally in an occupation for the sake of the vote, it would be proper to require that the occupation should have been persevered in for some length of time (say three years). Subject to some such condition, two or more votes might be allowed to every person who exercises any of these superior functions. The liberal professions, when really and not nominally practised, imply, of course, a still higher degree of instruction ; and wherever a sufficient examination, or any serious conditions of education, are required before entering on a profession, its members could be admitted at once to a plurality of votes. The same rule might be applied to graduates of universities; and even to those who bring satisfactory certificates of having passed through the course of study required by any school at which the higher branches of knowledge are taught, under proper securities that the teaching is real, and not a mere pretence. The ' local ' or ' middle class ' examinations for the degree of Associate, so laudably and public-spiritedly established by the University of Oxford, and any similar ones which may be instituted by other competent bodies (provided they are fairly open to all comers), afford a ground on which plurality of votes might with great advantage be accorded to those who have passed the test. All these suggestions are open to much discussion in the detail, and to objections which it is of no use to anticipate. The time is not come for giving to such plans a practical shape, nor should I wish to be bound by the particular proposals which I have

第八章

在真正的国民教育,或可以信赖的综合考试系统,那么也许可以直接对教育进行检验。而没有这些检验手段,那个人的职业性质就是某种检验标准。雇主一般来说要比工人更加聪明,因为他必须进行脑力劳动,而不仅仅用手劳动。工头一般要比普通工人聪明,技术行业的工人要比非技术行业的工人聪明。银行家、商人或企业主可能要比零售商更聪明,因为他有更大、更复杂的利益要去经营。在所有这些例子中,检验其是否合格的不仅仅是是否担任了更高级的职务,而是是否成功地履行了这些职务。因为这个缘故,同时为了防止人们为了投票而在名义上从事某项职业,有必要规定人们从事某项职业必须达到一定年限(比如说3年)。在满足这样的条件的情况下,对从事更高级职业的人应当允许他们每人拥有两张或两张以上的投票权。自由职业,当人们真正地而不是名义上从事这些职业时,当然意味着受过更高程度的教育。有些职业,人们在进入这些职业之前要经过充分的考试,或者接受严格的教育,那么从事这些职业的人应该马上得到多重投票权。同样的规则也适用于大学毕业生,甚至适用于那些在讲授各种高级学科知识的学校(在适当保证这个学校进行的是真正的教学而不是敷衍了事的情况下)里获得合格证书的那些人。牛津大学令人称赞地、热心公益地建立的授予大专生学位的"地方"或"中等"考试,以及其他有资格的团体(只要它们对一切人开放)举行的任何相似的做法,提供了可以很方便地给予那些通过了这种考试的人以多重投票权的依据。所有这些建议都可以公开详细地加以讨论,并且容易受到不用加以预测的反对。将这些谋划加以实施尚待时日,我也不想被我所提的建议所束缚。但对我来说明显的是,这一方向代表着代议制政府的真正理想,并且通

made. But it is to me evident, that in this direction lies the true ideal of representative government ; and that to work towards it, by the best practical contrivance which can be found, is the path of real political improvement.

If it be asked, to what length the principle admits of being carried, or how many votes might be accorded to an individual on the ground of superior qualifications, I answer, that this is not in itself very material, provided the distinctions and gradations are not made arbitrarily, but are such as can be understood and accepted by the general conscience and understanding. But it is an absolute condition, not to overpass the limit prescribed by the fundamental principle laid down in a former chapter as the condition of excellence in the constitution of a representative system. The plurality of votes must on no account be carried so far, that those who are privileged by it, or the class (if stay) to which they mainly belong, shall outweigh by means of it all the rest of the community. The distinction in favour of education, right in itself, is further and strongly recommended by its preserving the educated from the class legislation of the uneducated; but it must stop short of enabling them to practise class legislation on their own account. Let me add, that I consider it an absolutely necessary part of the plurality scheme, that it be open to the poorest individual in the community to claim its privileges, if he can prove that, in spite of all difficulties and obstacles, he is, in point of intelligence, entitled to them. There ought to be voluntary examinations at which any person whatever might present himself, might prove that he came up to the standard of knowledge and ability laid down as sufficient, and be admitted, in consequence, to the plurality of votes. A privilege which is not refused to any one who can show that he has realized the conditions on which in theory and principle it is dependent, would not necessarily be repugnant to any one's sentiment of justice: but it would certainly be so, if, while conferred on general presumptions not always infallible, it were denied to direct proof.

Plural voting, though practised in vestry elections and those of poor-law guardians, is so unfamiliar in elections to parliament, that it

第八章

过能够找到的最好的实践办法朝这个方向努力,就是真正的政治进步的道路。

如果有人问,这项原则可以执行到什么程度,或者说个人基于他的优秀品质应该给予多少投票权,我的回答是,这在本质上并不很重要,重要的是区别和等级不是任意划分的,而是能被一般的良知和理解力所理解和接受的。但是,绝对必要的是,不超出在前一章中作为代议制体系构成上的优越条件所规定下来的基本原则所设的界限。相对多重投票决不能被弄到这种地步,以至于那些拥有这种特权的人,或者他们所属的阶级(如果有的话)会通过它来压倒社会中一切其余的人。这个有利于教育的区别本质上是正确的,它由于能保护受过教育的人免遭没有受过教育的人的阶级立法的侵害而大受推举;但这种区别必须不会导致使他们为了自己的利益而进行阶级立法。我要加一点,我认为对多重投票方案来说绝对重要的一点是,这种特权应当向社会中最穷的人开放,让他们有机会得到这种特权,只要他们证明,不管有多么艰难与险阻,他们就智力而言,有资格拥有这种特权。应当有自愿的考试,在这种考试中,任何人不管他用什么来表现自己,都可以证明他充分达到了知识与能力的标准,从而被允许给予多重投票权。一项特权,如果它不拒绝任何能表明他已经实现了他在理论和原则上所依赖的条件的人,就不一定会与任何人的正义感相抵触,但是假如当特权的给予是基于并不总是没有错误的一般推测时,它就得不到直接的证明,因此肯定会与人们的正义感相抵触。

尽管多重投票权实行于教区选举和济贫法监护人的选举,但它在议会选举中却不为人们所熟悉,因此不可能被很快或欣

is not likely to be soon or willingly adopted; but as the time will certainly arrive when the only choice will be between this and equal universal suffrage, whoever does not desire the last, cannot too soon begin to reconcile himself to the former. In the meantime, though the suggestion, for the present, may not be a practical one, it will serve to mark what is best in principle, and enable us to judge of the eligibility of any indirect means, either existing or capable of being adopted, which may promote in a less perfect manner the same end. A person may have a double vote by other means than that of tendering two votes at the same hustings ; he may have a vote in each of two different constituencies: and though this exceptional privilege at present belongs rather to superiority of means than of intelligence, I would not abolish it where it exists, since until a truer test of education is adopted, it would be unwise to dispense with even so imperfect a one as is afforded by pecuniary circumstances. Means might be found of giving a further extension to the privilege, which would connect it in a more direct manner with superior education. In any future Reform Bill which lowers greatly the pecuniary conditions of the suffrage, it might be a wise provision to allow all graduates of universities, all persons who had passed creditably through the higher schools, all members of the liberal professions, and perhaps some others, to be registered specifically in those characters, and to give their votes as such in any constituency in which they chose to register: retaining, in addition, their votes as simple citizens in the localities in which they reside.

Until there shall have been devised, and until opinion is willing to accept, some mode of plural voting which may assign to education as such the degree of superior influence due to it, and sufficient as a counterpoise to the numerical weight of the least educated class ; for so long, the benefits of completely universal suffrage cannot be obtained without bringing with them, as it appears to me, more than equivalent evils. It is possible, indeed (and this is perhaps one of the transitions through which we may have to pass in our progress to a really good representative system), that the barriers which restrict the suffrage might be entirely levelled in some particular constituencies ,

第八章

然接受。但是由于这样一个时刻终究要到来,到那时将在它与普选权之间作出唯一的选择,凡是那些不期待后者的人也不可能很快地倒向前者。同时,尽管这条建议暂时还不可以实行,它可以用来表示在原则上什么是最好的,使我们能够对任何现有的或可被采用的、可能以不完善方式促进同一目的的间接方法是否适宜作出判断。一个人可能按照在同一选举活动中投两票之外的方法行使双倍投票权;他可以在两个不同的选区各投一票。尽管目前这种例外的特权与其说属于智力上的优越不如说属于财产上的优越,我不主张废除现有的这种办法,因为在采取确切的教育检验标准之前,将它作为由金钱状况提供的哪怕是极不完善的标准加以废除也是不完善的。人们也许可以找到进一步扩展这个特权的方法,这种方法将以更直接的方式把它同更高等的教育联系起来。在任何将来大大降低选举权的财产条件的改革法案中,让所有的大学毕业生,所有顺利通过了更高等学校的考试的人,所有自由职业者,也许还有另外一些人,以这些资格进行特别登记,在他们选择登记的选区按这样的资格给予他们选票,另外,保留他们在其居住地作为普通公民拥有的选票,可能是一项明智的措施。

在某种可能给教育本来就应当有的这种程度的优越影响,并且足够平衡受最少教育的阶级人数上的优势的多重投票权被设计出来,并且舆论愿意接受它之前,在我看来,长久以来,在完全普选权带来的好处的同时不可能不带来更多的坏处。的确,有可能出现这样的情形(这也许是在向真正的好的代议制体系迈进时不得不经历的过渡之一),即限制选举权的障碍在某些特殊选区可能被完全铲平了,因而其成员主

whose members, consequently, would be returned principally by manual labourers ; the existing electoral qualification being maintained elsewhere, or any alteration in it being accompanied by such a grouping of the constituencies as to prevent the labouring class from becoming preponderant in Parliament. By such a compromise, the anomalies in the representation would not only be retained, but augmented: this however is not a conclusive objection; for if the country does not choose to pursue the right ends by a regular system directly leading to them, it must be content with an irregular makeshift, as being greatly preferable to a system free from irregularities, but regularly adapted to wrong ends, or in which some ends equally necessary with the others have been left out. It is a far graver objection, that this adjustment is incompatible with the intercommunity of local constituencies which Mr. Hare's plan requires ; that under it every voter would remain imprisoned within the one or more constituencies in which his name is registered, and unless willing to be represented by one of the candidates for those localities, would not be represented at all.

So much importance do I attach to the emancipation of those who already have votes, but whose votes are useless, because always outnumbered ; so much should I hope from the natural influence of truth and reason, if only secured a hearing and a competent advocacy-that I should not despair of the operation even of equal and universal suffrage, if made real by the proportional representation of all minorities, on Mr. Hare's principle. But if the best hopes which can be formed on this subject were certainties, I should still contend for the principle of plural voting. I do not propose the plurality as a thing in itself undesirable, which, like the exclusion of part of the community from the suffrage, may be temporarily tolerated while necessary to prevent greater evils. I do not look upon equal voting as among the things which are good in themselves, provided they can be guarded against inconveniences. I look upon it as only relatively good ; less objectionable than inequality of privilege grounded on irrelevant or adventitious circumstances, but in principle wrong, because recognising a wrong standard, and exercising a bad influence on the voter's mind.

要由劳动者选出,而在其他地方现存的选举资格将得以维持,或者选举资格的任何变更都伴随着选区中的这样一种分组,以防止劳动阶级在议会中占据优势地位。通过此番妥协,代议制度中的异常情况不仅被保留了下来,还被扩大了。然而,这不是一个致命的缺陷,因为如果国家不选择通过直接通向正确目的的正规体系去实现它们,那么它必定满足于不正规的权宜之计,作为一个不存在不规则性,但却常常适用于错误的目的的体系,或忽视了其他一些同等必要的目的的体系的更为可取的办法。更为严重的反对意见是,这种调整办法与黑尔先生的设想所要求的地方选区之间的互通有无相互矛盾;在这种情况下每个选民都会限制在他所登记过的一个或一个以上的选区里,并且除非愿意选举那些地区的一个候选人为代表,否则就根本不可能被代表。

我对那些早已有了选举权,但因为总是在数量上被超过而使其选举权变得无用的人的解放非常重视;我对真理和理性的自然影响寄予厚望,要是能保证它们被听到并得到有力的辩护就好了。如果按黑尔先生的原则,通过所有少数派的按比例代表制来使平等和普遍的选举权得以实施,我也将不会感到失望。但是假如能在这个问题上形成的最好希望只是确凿的事情,那么我依然主张多重投票权的原则。我并不打算将复数票看作是本身就不受欢迎的一件事情,这件事情,就如将社会的一部分排除在选举之外一样,当有必要防止更大的恶时,可以暂时容忍。我并不把平等投票权看作只要能避免不便就是本质上好的事情,我只是将这看作相对好的事物。它比基于无关或偶然场合产生的特权的不平等要好些,但它在原则上是错误的,因为它承认一个错误的标准,在投票人头脑中留下不好的影响。国家的宪法宣布无知应

It is not useful, but hurtful, that the constitution of the country should declare ignorance to be entitled to as much political power as knowledge. The national institutions should place all things that they are concerned with, before the mind of the citizen in the light in which it is for his good that he should regard them : and as it is for his good that he should think that every one is entitled to some influence, but the better and wiser to more than others, it is important that this conviction should be professed by the State, and embodied in the national institutions. Such things constitute the *spirit* of the institutions of a country : that portion of their influence which is least regarded by common, and especially by English, thinkers; though the institutions of every country, not under great positive oppression, produce more effect by their spirit than by any of their direct provisions, since by it they shape the national character. The American institutions have imprinted strongly on the American mind, that any one man (with a white skin) is as good as any other ; and it is felt that this false creed is nearly connected with some of the more unfavourable points in . American character. It is not a small mischief that the constitution of any country should sanction this creed ; for the belief in it, whether express or tacit, is almost as detrimental to moral and intellectual excellence, as any effect which most forms of government can produce.

It may, perhaps, be said, that a constitution which gives equal influence, man for man, to the most and to the least instructed, is nevertheless conducive to progress, because the appeals constantly made to the less instructed classes, the exercise given to their mental powers, and the exertions which the more instructed are obliged to make for enlightening their judgment and ridding them of errors and prejudices, are powerful stimulants to their advance in intelligence. That this most desirable effect really attends the admission of the less educated classes to some, and even to a large share of power, I admit, and have already strenuously maintained. But theory and experience alike prove that a counter current sets in when they are made the possessors of all power. Those who are supreme over everything, whether they be One, or Few, or Many, have no longer need of

第八章

该与知识一样有同等的政治权利,这不仅无益而且有害。国家机构应当把它们所关心一切事情都摆在公民眼前,关心这些事情是为了他自己的利益。并且为了他自己的利益,他应当认为每个人都具有某种影响,但更优秀和更聪明的人的影响要比别人的大,因此,这种信念应当由国家公开宣称,并体现在国家制度中,这显得非常重要。这些事情是一国制度的精神所在,而制度的这部分影响很少为一般思想家,特别是英国思想家所关心,尽管每个国家的制度,无不处于巨大的实际压迫之下,制度的精神产生的作用要比任何制度的直接规定所产生的作用要大得多,因为正是通过它来形成国民的性格的。美国的制度在美国人心中打下了这样一条深深的烙印,即每个(有白色皮肤的)人和别人都一样好,并且人们感觉到,这一错误信条与美国人的性格中某些更为不利的地方密切联系在一起。任何国家的宪法要是认可这样的信条,就不能算是小小的危害了;因为抱有这样的信条,不管是明示的还是默许的,对道德和智力上的卓越性的影响几乎和大多数政府形式所产生的作用一样有害。

也许人们会说,给予最有教养和最没有教养的人以同等影响(就一个人对另一个人来讲)的宪法仍然有助于进步,因为不断向受较少教育的人发出的呼吁,给予他们脑力的锻炼,以及更有教养的人为了启发他们的判断与摆脱错误和偏见所做的努力,都是激励他们在智力上发展的强大刺激。至于这种最让人想要的效果会真的使受较少教育的阶级有资格得到某种、甚至取得一大部分权力,我是承认的,并且早就在极力主张了。但是理论和经验证明,当他们拥有所有权力的时候就会发生一股逆流。那些凌驾于一切事物之上的人,不管是一个人还是几个人,还是许多人,不再需要

the arms of reason; they can make their mere will prevail ; and those who cannot be resisted are usually far too well satisfied with their own opinions to be willing to change them, or listen without impatience to any one who tells them that they are in the wrong. The position which gives the strongest stimulus to the growth of intelligence is that of rising into power, not that of having achieved it; and of all resting-points, temporary or permanent, in the way to ascendancy, the one which develops the best and highest qualities is the position of those who are strong enough to make reason prevail, but not strong enough to prevail against reason. This is the position in which, according to the principles we have laid down, the rich and the poor, the much and the little educated, and all the other classes and denominations which divide society between them, ought as far as practicable to be placed. And by combining this principle with the otherwise just one of allowing superiority of weight to superiority of mental qualities, a political constitution would realize that kind of relative perfection, which is alone comparable with the complicated nature of human affairs.

In the preceding argument for universal, but graduated suffrage, I have taken no account of difference of sex. I consider it to be as entirely irrelevant to political rights, as difference in height, or in the colour of the hair. All human beings have the same interest in good government ; the welfare of all is alike affected by it, and they have equal need of a voice in it to secure their share of its benefits. If there be any difference, women require it more than men, since, being physically weaker, they are more dependent on law and society for protection. Mankind have long since abandoned the only premisses which will support the conclusion that women ought not to have votes. No one now holds that women should be in personal servitude; that they should have no thought, wish, or occupation, but to be the domestic drudges of husbands, fathers, or brothers. It is allowed to unmarried, and wants but little of being conceded to married women, to hold property, and have pecuniary and business interests, in the same manner as men . It is considered suitable and proper that women

第八章

理性的武器了,他们可以使自己单纯的意志成为流行的意志。那些没人能反抗得了的人通常对自己的观点很满意,不愿意改变它们,或者不愿意耐心地倾听任何人告诉他们说这些观点是错误的。给予智力的发展以最强烈刺激的地位是正在崛起的地位,而不是已经获得权力的地位;在通向支配道路的所有阶段中,不管是暂时的还是永久的,发展最好和具有最高品质的人是处于强大到能使理性盛行,而不是强大到与理性抗衡的地位的人。根据我们已经设下的原则,这就是在可实行的范围内,富人和穷人,受过教育和没受过教育的人,以及将社会划分开来的所有其他阶级与宗派等所应处的位置。并且通过把这条原则与另一条允许智力上的优越性具备分量上的优越性的正当原则结合起来,政治组织就会实现那种相对的完美,而这种完美是唯一与人类事务的复杂性相符合的。

在前面针对普遍的但区分等级的选举权的讨论中,我没有考虑过性别的差异。我把它当成与政治权利完全无关的事,就像身高的差别或头发的颜色差别那样。所有人都对好的政府具有同样的兴趣;所有人的福利都毫无例外要受到它的影响,并且为了保证分享它的福利,他们需要在政府中有同等的发言权。如果说有什么差别的话,就是妇女要比男人更需要政府,因为由于体能上要弱些,她们更需要依赖法律和社会来保护。人类早已摒弃了用来支持妇女不应有投票权这一结论的唯一前提。如今没人坚持认为妇女应该处于个人奴隶的状态,认为她们不应该有思想、愿望或职业,而只是丈夫、父亲或兄弟的家庭苦力。应当允许未婚女子(与允许给已婚妇女的差不多)同男人一样拥有财产、金钱和商业利益。妇女应该思考、写作和担任教师,这被认为是合理和恰当的。只要

should think, and write, and be teachers. As soon as these things are admitted, the political disqualification has no principle to rest on. The whole mode of thought of the modem world is, with increasing emphasis, pronouncing against the claim of society to decide for individuals what they are and are not fit for, and what they shall and shall not be allowed to attempt. If the principles of modem politics and political economy are good for anything, it is for proving that these points can only be rightly judged of by the individuals themselves: and that, under complete freedom of choice, wherever there are real diversities of aptitude, the great number will apply themselves to the things for which they are on the average fittest, and the exceptional course will only be taken by the exceptions. Either the whole tendency of modem social improvements has been wrong, or it ought to be carried out to the total abolition of all exclusions and disabilities which close any honest employment to a human being.

But it is not even necessary to maintain so much in order to prove that women should have the suffrage. Were it as right, as it is wrong, that they should be a subordinate class, confined to domestic occupations and subject to domestic authority, they would not the less require the protection of the suffrage to secure them from the abuse of that authority. Men; as well as women, do not need political rights in order that they may govern, but in order that they may not be misgoverned. The majority of the male sex are, and will be all their lives, nothing else than labourers in corn-fields or manufactories ; but this does not render the suffrage less desirable for them, nor their claim to it less irresistible, when not likely to make a bad use of it. Nobody pretends to think that women would make a bad use of the suffrage. The worst that is said is, that they would vote as mere dependants, at the bidding of their male relations. If it be so, so let it be. If they think for themselves, great good will be done, and if they do not, no harm. It is a benefit to human beings to take off their fetters, even if they do not desire to walk. It would already be a great improvement in the moral position of women, to be no longer declared by law incapable of an opinion, and not entitled to a preference, respecting the most important concerns of humanity. There would be some benefit to them individually in having something to bestow which their male rela-

第八章

人们承认这些东西,那么政治上取消资格就无据可依了。现代世界的整个思维模式是越来越强调反对社会有权决定个人适合做什么和不适合做什么,以及允许做什么和不允许做什么的主张。如果现代政治和政治经济的原则是有效的话,就是证明这些问题只能由个人自己来进行恰当的判断,并证明在完全自由选择的情况下,不管有没有才智的差异,大部分人都会选择他们一般来说最合适做的事情,而例外的做法只能被当成是例外了。要么现代社会进步的整个趋势是错误的,要么它应当被贯彻到完全废除一切排他行为,以及废除使一个人没有任何诚实工作的机会的那种无能。

但是为了证明妇女应当有选举权,甚至没有必要提出这么多的主张。即使这种说法是对的,即说妇女应当是一个附属的阶级,从事家庭劳动,从属于家庭权威,这和这种说法是错误的一样,她们依然需要选举权的保护,以使她们不受家庭权威滥用的伤害。男人和女人一样,不是为了统治,而是为了使他们不受统治不当的祸害才需要政治权利的。男性的大多数人在他们一生中,都只不过是玉米地里或工厂里的劳力罢了,但这并不致使他们不想要选举权,或者就可以对他们对选举权的要求加以反对。没有人会故意认为妇女会不恰当地使用选举权。据说最糟糕的是,她们会仅仅作为一个附属者根据她们男性亲属的命令来投票。如果是这样的话,那就让它这样吧。如果她们为自己着想就会有很大的好处,但如果她们不这样,也不会有什么害处。人类脱去他们的枷锁是件好事,即使他们不愿意走路也好。在涉及人类最重要的事情上,妇女不再被法律宣布为没有能力发表意见,没有资格进行优先选择的人,这对于她们来说就是道德地位的一东西,对她们个人来说会有某种好处。同样,丈夫必须跟他的

tives cannot exact, and are yet desirous to have. It would also be no small matter that the husband would necessarily discuss the matter with his wife, and, that the vote would not be his exclusive affair, but a joint concern. People do not sufficiently consider how markedly the fact, that she is able to have some action on the outward world independently of him, raises her dignity and value in a vulgar man's eyes, and makes her the object of a respect which no personal qualities would ever obtain for one whose social existence he can entirely appropriate. The vote itself, too, would be improved in quality. The man would often be obliged to find honest reasons for his vote, such as might induce a more upright and impartial character to serve with him under the same banner. The wife's influence would often keep him true to his own sincere opinion. Often, indeed, it would be used, not on the side of public principle, but of the personal interest or worldly vanity of the family. But wherever this would be the tendency of the wife's influence, it is exerted to the full already, in that bad direction; and with the more certainty, since under the present law and custom she is generally too utter a stranger to politics in any sense in which they involve principle, to be able to realize to herself that there is a point of honour in them ; and most people have as little sympathy in the point of honour of others, when their own is not placed in the same thing, as they have in the religious feelings of those whose religion differs from theirs. Give the woman a vote, and she comes under the operation of the political point of honour. She learns to look on politics as a thing on which she is allowed to have an opinion, and in which if one has an opinion it ought to be acted upon; she acquires a sense of personal accountability in the matter, and will no longer feel, as she does at present, that whatever amount of bad influence she may exercise, if the man can but be persuaded, all is right, and his responsibility covers all. It is only by being herself encouraged to form an opinion, and obtain an intelligent comprehension of the reasons which ought to prevail with the conscience against the temptations of personal or family interest, that she can ever cease to act as a disturbing force on the political conscience of the man. Her indirect agency can only be prevented from being politically mischie-

第八章

妻子讨论,并且,投票不是他一个人的事,而是共同关心的事情,这也是一大好处。人们不会充分考虑这个事实,即她能独立于男人进行某种活动这个事实,多么明显地提高了她在普通男人眼中的尊严和价值,使她受到尊重,这种尊重对于一个其社会存在完全依赖男人的妇女来说,不是她个人品质曾经得到过的。投票本身也会在质的方面有所改进。男人不得不为他的投票寻找诚实的理由,例如可以促使一个更正直更公正的人与他一起在同一阵营里服务。妻子的影响常常会使他忠于自己真实的意见。当然,这种影响经常不是用在公共原则方面,而是用在个人利益或家庭的世俗虚荣方面。但是凡是妻子的影响具有这方面倾向的地方,这种影响在错误的方向早就被发挥殆尽了。还可以更加确定,由于在现行的法律和习惯下,一般说来,她在任何涉及原则方面对政治是完全陌生的,不能认识到政治中包含有荣誉问题,大部分人,当他们自己的荣誉问题都不能被当成一回事时,也很少对别人的荣誉问题加以同情,这有点像他们对那些宗教信仰与他们不同的人所具有的宗教情感少有同情一样。给妇女以投票权,她就会感受到政治活动中的荣誉问题。她学会将政治看作一件她被允许发表意见,并且如果一个人有了意见,他就必须有所行动的事情;她在这件事情上得到一种个人责任感,并且不再像她现在认为那样,觉得不管她施加多大的坏影响,如果男人可以被说服,一切就很好,而且他的责任掩盖了一切。只有通过鼓励她自己去形成个人观点,并获得了理解应该和良知一起战胜个人或家庭利益诱惑的那些理由的能力,她才不会是一种对男人的政治良知起干扰作用的力量。她间接的力量只有通过把选举权变成直接的力量才能防止选举权在

vous by being exchanged for direct.

I have supposed the right of suffrage to depend, as in a good state of things it would, on personal conditions. Where it depends, as in this and most other countries, on conditions of property, the contradiction is even more flagrant. There is something more than ordinarily irrational in the fact, that when a woman can give all the guarantees required from a male elector, independent circumstances, the position of a householder and head of a family, payment of taxes, or whatever may be the conditions imposed, the very principle and system of a representation based on property is set aside, and an exceptionally personal disqualification is created for the mere purpose of excluding her. When it is added that in the country where this is done, a woman[①] now reigns, and that the most glorious ruler whom that country ever had was a woman, the picture of unreason, and scarcely disguised injustice, is complete. Let us hope that as the work proceeds of pulling down, one after another, the remains of the mouldering fabric of monopoly and tyranny, this one will not be the last to disappear ; that the opinion of Bentham, of Mr. Samuel Bailey, of Mr. Hare, and many other of the most powerful political thinkers of this age and country (not to speak of others), will make its way to all minds not rendered obdurate by selfishness or inveterate prejudice ; and that, before the lapse of another generation, the accident of sex, no more than the accident of skin, will be deemed a sufficient justification for depriving its possessor of the equal protection and just privileges of a citizen.

---

① Queen Victoria.

第八章

政治上的祸害。

我曾经设想过选举权依赖于个人条件,正如在好的事态下它会呈现的那样。正如在我国与大多数国家那样,选举权依赖于财产的地方,矛盾就更加突出。当妇女能提供男性选民必需的一切保证时,却规定独立的身份,处于户主或家长的地位,纳税以及其他条件,且不说基于财产的代表制和它的原则本身,以及仅仅为了排除妇女而设计格外的限制资格等,这种情况比普通的不理智更为不合理。如果补充一点,即在这个已经做到了这一点的国家,一个妇女①现在统治着,并且这个国家曾经有过的最显赫的统治者是个女人,那么非理性的画面,以及不加掩饰的不公,就是完整的了。让我们企盼,随着将垄断与专制的模具结构之残余一个接一个地加以摧毁的工作的不断深入,这一点将不是最后消失的;希望边沁的观点,萨缪尔·贝利先生的观点,黑尔先生的观点,以及我国的其他这个时代的许多杰出的政治思想家(这里不说其他思想家)的观点,将渗入那些还没有由于自私或根深蒂固的偏见而变得顽固不化的人的头脑里面;还企盼,在另一代人的消失之前,性别的偶然因素,不再像肤色的偶然因素那样,成为剥夺公民平等保护和应有权利的一条充足的理由。

---

① 维多利亚女王。

CHAPTER IX
Should There Be Two Stages Of Election ?

In some representative constitutions the plan has been adopted of choosing the members of the representative body by a double process, the primary electors only choosing other electors, and these electing the member of parliament. This contrivance was probably intended as a slight impediment to the full sweep of popular feeling; giving the suffrage, and with it the complete ultimate power, to the Many, but compelling them to exercise it through the agency of a comparatively few, who, it was supposed, would be less moved than the Demos by the gusts of popular passion ; and as the electors, being already a select body, might be expected to exceed in intellect and character the common level of their constituents, the choice made by them was thought likely to be more careful and enlightened, and would in any case be made under the greater feeling of responsibility, than election by the masses themselves. This plan of filtering, as it were, the popular suffrage through an intermediate body, admits of a very plausible defence ; since it may be said, with great appearance of reason, that less intellect and instruction are required for judging who among our neighbours ean be most safely trusted to choose a member of parliament, than who is himself fittest to be one.

In the first place, however, if the dangers incident to popular power may be thought to be in some degree lessened by this indirect arrangement, so also are its benefits ; and the latter effect is much more certain than the former. To enable the system to work as desired, it must be carried into effect in the spirit in which it is planned;

第九章 选举应该分为两个阶段吗？

在一些代议制政体中，人们通过双重程序来选择代议团体的成员，即初选时，基层选举一些人为选举人，然后由这些选举人选出议会的议员。这种设计可能是要给民众情感的冲击设置一个小小的障碍。给予多数人以选举权，并赋予他们以最终的权力，但是强迫他们通过由相对少数人组成的机构来行使这种权力。人们认为，这些少数人与民众比较起来，将不太会被舆论所左右。而由于这些选举人是经过挑选而组成的团体，人们全期望他们在智力和性格等方面都能够比他们的委托人要强些，人们认为他们所作出的决定与大众亲自作出的决定相比，将是更加谨慎和明智的，在任何情况下都能体现更大的责任感。这种过滤方案，即通过一个中介团体来行使投票权的方案，有着一个貌似有理的辩解，因为人们可以在表面上颇为理性地说，判断我们的邻居中谁最适合作议员，比判断谁本人最适合当议员所要求的智力水平和受教育程度要少得多。

然而，首先，如果公众权力容易发生的危险在某种程度上可以由这种间接的安排减轻的话，民众权力所带来的好处也会相应地减少，而且后者的结果要比前者的结果肯定得多。要使这种制度按照人们所期望的方式运转，它就必须按照所设计的精神来

the electors must use the suffrage in the manner supposed by the theory, that is, each of them must not ask himself who the member of parliament should be, but only whom he would best like to choose one for him. It is evident, that the advantages which indirect is supposed to have over direct election, require this disposition of mind in the voter ; and will only be realized by his taking the doctrine *au sérieux*, that his sole business is to choose the choosers, not the member himself. The supposition must be, that he will not occupy his thoughts with political opinions and measures, or political men, but will be guided by his personal respect for some private individual, to whom he will give a general power of attorney to act for him. Now if the primary electors adopt this view of their position, one of the principal uses of giving them a vote at all is defeated : the political function to which they are called fails of developing public spirit and political intelligence ; of making public affairs an object of interest to their feelings and of exercise to their faculties. The supposition, moreover, involves inconsistent conditions; for if the voter feels no interest in the final result, how or why can he be expected to feel any in the process which leads to it ? To wish to have a particular individual for his representative in parliament is possible to a person of a very moderate degree of virtue and intelligence ; and to wish to choose an elector who will elect that individual, is a natural consequence : but for a person who does not care who is elected, or feels bound to put that consideration in abeyance, to take any interest whatever in merely naming the worthiest person to elect another according to his own judgment, implies a zeal for what is right in the abstract, an habitual principle of duty for the sake of duty, which is possible only to persons of a rather high grade of cultivation, who, by the very possession of it, show that they may be, and deserve to be, trusted with political power in a more direct shape. Of all public functions which it is possible to confer on the poorer members of the community, this surely is the least cal-

第九章

实行,选民们就必须按照理论所假定的方式来行使投票权,也就是说,每个人都不能去问自己,议会议员应当是谁,而只能问他最喜欢让谁来替他选择议员。很明显,间接选举被认为胜过直接选举的优点要求选民具有这样的心理倾向,而且只有靠他认真接受这样的学说才能实现,那就是,他唯一要做的就是选择选举人,而不是选举议员。由此产生的推论就必定是,他不需要有什么政治观点或政治方法,也不需要记住什么政治人物,他只需要按照他个人对某个人物的尊敬程度,将选择的权力委托给他,让他替自己选举。既然这样,那么如果最初的选民对他们的地位采取这种看法,给予他们选举权的一个主要目的就达不到了。人们要求他们发挥的政治职能不能发展成为公共精神与政治才能,不能把公共事务变成他们感情上关心的一个利益目标以及锻炼他们能力的一次机会。此外,这种推论包含着相互矛盾的情形,因为如果选民对最终结果缺乏兴趣,又怎样或者说何以能期望他关心导致最后结果的过程呢?期望有个特定的人物在议会作他的代表,对一个具有中等程度道德修养以及智力水平的人来说是可能做到的,并且他自然地就会期望选择一个将会选举那个人的选举人。但是对一个并不怎么关心哪个人当选、或者感到不得不暂时搁置这种考虑的人来说,要使他对仅仅提名一个最具价值的人来根据自己的判断去选举另一个人发生兴趣,就意味着对理论上正确的事情有某种热情,即对为了义务而尽义务的习惯原则抱有某种热情,这只有具备了相当高教养的人才能做到。而这样的人由于具有高度的素养,表明他们可以,也应当可以委以更为直接的选举权力了。在所有可能给予社会中较为贫穷成员的公共职能中,除了能够激发人们诚实履行一切义务的善良决心之外,这肯定是最不适于激发他们的情感的,并且最

culated to kindle their feelings, and holds out least natural inducement to care for it, other than a virtuous determination to discharge conscientiously whatever duty one has to perform: and if the mass of electors cared enough about political affairs to set any value on so limited a participation in them, they would not be likely to be satisfied without one much more extensive.

In the next place, admitting that a person who, from his narrow range of cultivation, cannot judge well of the qualifications of a candidate for parliament, may be a sufficient judge of the honesty and general capacity of somebody whom he may depute to choose a member of parliament for him ; I may remark, that if the voter acquiesces in this estimate of his capabilities, and really wishes to have the choice made for him by a person in whom he places reliance, there is no need of any constitutional provision for the purpose, he has only to ask this confidential person privately what candidate he had better vote for. In that case the two modes of election coincide in their result, and every advantage of indirect election is obtained under direct. The systems only diverge in their operation, if we suppose that the voter would prefer to use his own judgment in the choice of a representative, and only lets another choose for him because the law does not allow him a more direct mode of action. But if this be his state of mind ; if his will does not go along with the limitation which the law imposes, and he desires to make a direct choice, he can do so notwithstanding the law. He has only to choose as elector a known partisan of the candidate he prefers, or some one who will pledge himself to vote for that candidate. And this is so much the natural working of election by two stages, that, except in a condition of complete political indifference, it can scarcely be expected to act otherwise. It is in this way that the election of the President of the United States practically takes place. Nominally, the election is indirect: the population at large does not vote for the President ; it votes for electors who choose the President. But the electors are always chosen under an express engagement to vote for a particular candidate: nor does a citizen ever vote for an elector because of any preference for the man ; he votes for the Lin-

第九章

不能提供自然的诱发因素来关心这种权力。如果选民对政治事务很关心,对如此有限的政治参与也加以关注的话,那么他们对缺乏更加广泛的政治参与是不会感到满意的。

其次,即使承认一个文化水平不高、不能很好地判断议会候选人资质的人,具有能够很好地判断某个他可以委以替他选择议会议员重任的人,这样一种诚实与一般能力,对此我也会说,假使选民承认这种对他能力的评估,并且真心希望能够有一个他可以信赖的人来替他进行选择,也没有必要在宪法上作出这种规定,他只需私下问一下他的这位好友他最好选哪一个候选人就可以了。这样的话,两种选举模式的结果是一致的,而间接选举的每一种好处在直接选举的情况下也能够得到。如果我们假定选民在选举代表的时候更喜欢依靠自己的判断,而只是因为法律不允许他进行更为直接的选举的情况下他才会让别人替他选择的话,那么这两种制度只是在做法上有所不同罢了。但是,假如这是他的心理状态,假如他的意志不受法律施加的限制,并且他希望进行直接选举,那么尽管有法律的限制,他仍然会那样去做。他只需选择一个他所喜欢的知名的候选人,或者某个保证会投这个候选人票的人作为选举人就行了。并且这就是通过两阶段选举的自然结果,也就是说,除了对政治完全不关心的情况之外,很难指望它能起到什么作用。美国的总统选举就是按照这种方式来进行的。名义上,选举是间接的:民众并不直接选举总统,他们投票选举那些选择总统的选举人。但是这些选举人总是在明确承诺选举某个特定总统候选人的情况下才被选出的,公民投选举人的票绝不是因为他个人喜欢这个选举人,他投的是林肯(Lincoln)候选人名

coln ticket, or the Breckenridge ticket. It must be remembered, that the electors are not chosen in order that they may search the country and find the fittest person in it to be President, or to be a member of parliament. There would be something to be said for the practice if this were so : but it is not so ; nor ever will be, until mankind in general are of opinion, with Plato, that the proper person to be entrusted with power is the person most unwilling to accept it. The electors are to make choice of one of those who have offered themselves as candidates: and those who choose the electors, already know who these are. If there is any political activity in the country, all electors, who care to vote at all, have made up their minds which of these candidates they would like to have ; and will make that the sole consideration in giving their vote. The partisans of each candidate will have their list of electors ready, all pledged to vote for that individual ; and the only question practically asked of the primary elector will be, which of these lists he will support.

The case in which election by two stages answers well in practice, is when the electors are not chosen solely as electors, but have other important functions to discharge, which precludes their being selected solely as delegates to give a particular vote. This combination of circumstances exemplifies itself in another American institution, the Senate of the United States. That assembly, the Upper House, as it were, of Congress, is considered to represent not the people directly, but the States as such, and to be the guardian of that portion of their sovereign rights which they have not alienated. As the internal sovereignty of each State is, by the nature of an equal federation, equally sacred whatever be the size or importance of the State, each returns to the Senate the same number of members (two), whether it be little Delaware, or the 'Empire State' of New York. These members are not chosen by the population, but by the State Legislatures, themselves elected by the people of each State; but as the whole ordinary business of a legislative assembly, internal legislation and the control

第九章

单的票,或是布雷肯里奇候选人名单的票。需要记住的是,选举人的选择并不是为了使这些选举人能够在全国范围内去寻找并且发现最合适的总统人选,或者议员人选。如果情况果真是这样,这种作法还说得过去,但情况并不是这样,而且将来情况也不会是这样,除非人们普遍同意柏拉图的观点,即能够委以权力的合适人选就是最不愿意接受权力的那个人。选举人将从那些作为候选人的人士中选择一个,而那些选择选举人的人对这些候选人是早已知晓的。如果在这个国家里有某项政治运动,那么,所有愿意投票的选民就已经决定好了在这些候选人当中选择哪一个,并将在投票时作为自己唯一的考虑。每个候选人的支持者都将有一份准备好了的选举人名单,这些选举人都作出了投该候选人的票的保证,而实际上要求选民回答的唯一问题就是他将支持哪一张选举人名单。

两阶段选举在实践上可行的情况是,选举人并不只是单纯作为选举人被推选出来,而是能够履行其他重要的职能,这样他们就不只是作为某次特定的投票代表而被选举出来了。这种情况可以再举另外一种美国制度即美国参议院作为例子加以说明。国会的那个院,类似于我们的上院,被认为不是直接代表人民,而是代表每个州,是各个州没有让渡的那部分权力的护卫者。根据平等联邦的性质,每个州的内部主权是神圣不可侵犯的,不论州的大小和重要与否,不论是小小的特拉华,还是纽约"帝国州",每个州在参议院的议员数是相同的(即为两个)。这些议员不是由民众所选出的,而是由州立法机关选出的,而州立法机关本身是由各州人民选举成立的。但是由于这些立法机关的整个日常事务,如内部立法和行政监督,都由这些团体负责,因此

of the executive, devolves upon these bodies, they are elected with a view to those objects more than to the other ; and in naming two persons to represent the State in the Federal Senate, they for the most part exercise their own judgment, with only that general reference to public opinion necessary in all acts of the government of a democracy. The elections, thus made, have proved eminently successful, and are conspicuously the best of all the elections in the United States, the Senate invariably consisting of the most distinguished men among those who have made themselves sufficiently known in public life. After such an example, it cannot be said that indirect popular election is never advantageous. Under certain conditions, it is the very best system that can be adopted. But those conditions are hardly to be obtained in practice, except in a federal government like that of the United States, where the election can be entrusted to local bodies whose other functions extend to the most important concerns of the nation. The only bodies in any analogous position which exist or are likely to exist in this country, are the municipalities, or any other boards which have been or may be created for similar local purposes. Few persons, however, would think it any improvement in our Parliamentary constitution, if the members for the City of London were chosen by the Aldermen and Common Council, and those for the borough of Marylebone avowedly, as they already are virtually, by the vestries of the component parishes. Even if those bodies, considered merely as local boards, were far less objectionable than they are, the qualities that would fit them for the limited and peculiar duties of muncipal or parochialæ dileship, are no guarantee of any special fitness to judge of the comparative qualifications of candidates for a seat in Parliament. They probably would not fulfil this duty any better than it is fulfilled by the inhabitants voting directly; while, on the other hand, if fitness for electing members of parliament had to be taken into consideration in selecting persons for the office of vestrymen or town councillors, many of those who are fittest for that more limited duty would inevitably be excluded from it, if only by the necessity there would be of choosing persons whose sentiments in general politics agreed with those of the voters who elected them. The mere indirect political influ-

第九章

他们更多的是为了上述目的而不是别的什么目的被选举出来的；而在任命两个联邦参议院代表方面，他们在很大的程度上运用自己的判断力，只是一般地参考舆论的意见，而这种对舆论意见的参考在一个民主政府的一切行为中是必不可少的。这样进行的选举证明是极其成功的，并且显然是美国所有的选举中最好的，参议员总是由那些在公共生活中为公众所知的人之中最杰出的人士组成。有了这样一个例子，我们就不能说间接选举就一点好处都没有。在某些条件下，它是所能采用的最好的制度，但是在实践中，很难得到那样的条件，除非在像美国这样的一个联邦制政府中，选举能委托给地方团体，而这些地方团体的其他职能延伸到了最重要的国家事务方面。在我国存在的或可能存在的具有类似地位的唯一团体就是市政府，或者是为了类似的地方目的已经创立的或者可能创立的其他任何管理委员会。然而，如果伦敦市的议会议员由高级市政官和市议员选出，马里立本自治市的议会议员则公开宣布（而事实上已经是）是由各教区的教区委员会选出，那么几乎没有人会认为这在我们议会制度中有任何进步。即使这些团体仅仅作为地方委员会加以考虑，不值得像实际上那样遭到反对，但是使它们适于市政或教区的有限和特殊职能的性质，不能保证能特别恰当地对议会候选人的有关资质作出判断。他们可能不能比居民的直接投票更好地完成这一职责，而在另一方面，如果在选择教区委员或镇议员时必须对适合议会议员的选举加以考虑的话，那么，只要有选择那些在一般政治上其感情和选举他们的选民的情感相一致的人的必要，许多能够充任有限职务的人就不可避免地要被排除在外。镇议会的那点小小的间接政治影响，由于把市选举

ence of town-councils has already led to a considerable perversion of muncipal elections from their intended purpose, by making them a matter of party politics. If it were part of the duty of a man's bookkeeper or steward to choose his physician, he would not be likely to have a better medical attendant than if he chose one for himself. While he would be restricted in his choice of a steward or book-keeper to such as might without too great danger to his health be entrusted with the other office.

It appears, therefore, that every benefit of indirect election which is attainable at all, is attainable under direct; that such of the benefits expected from it, as would not be obtained under direct election, will just as much fail to be obtained under indirect; while the latter has considerable disadvantages peculiar to itself. The mere fact that it is an additional and superfluous wheel in the machinery, is no trifling objection. Its decided inferiority as a means of cultivating public spirit and political intelligence, has already been dwelt upon: and if it had any effective operation at all—that is, if the primary electors did to any extent leave to their nominees the selection of their Parliamentary representative—the voter would be prevented from identifying himself with his member of Parliament, and the member, would feel a much less active sense of responsibility to his constituents. In addition to all this, the comparatively small number of persons in whose hands, at last, the election of a member of Parliament would reside, could not but afford great additional facilities to intrigue, and to every form of corruption compatible with the station in life of the electors. The constituencies would universally be reduced, in point of conveniences for bribery, to the condition of the small boroughs at present. It would be sufficient to gain over a small number of persons, to be certain of being returned. If it be said that the electors would be responsible to those who elected them, the answer is obvious, that, holding no permanent office, or position in the public eye, they would risk nothing by a corrupt vote except what they would care little for, not to be appointed electors again; and the main reliance must still be on the penalties for bribery, the insufficiency of which reliance, in small constituencies, experience has made notorious to all the world. The evil would be exactly proportional to the amount of discretion left to the chosen electors. The only case in which they would probably be

第九章

变成一场政党政治,早就导致了市选举在相当程度上偏离了它原来的目标。如果挑选医生是一个人所雇佣的账房先生或管家的分内之事,那么这个人就不大可能得到比他亲自挑选的更好的医生,另一方面,他在挑选管家或账房先生时又会受到限制,即他必须挑选在不十分危及他的健康的情况下又能够委托以其他职务的人。

因此,显然间接选举所能得到的每一种好处在直接选举中都能够得到;在间接选举的情况下,期望得到在直接选举条件下得不到的好处,同样是不可能的,而间接选举还有其自身特有的相当大的缺陷。单就它画蛇添足这一事实,就不是什么小毛病。它在培养公共精神和政治智慧方面的明显劣势早已经论述过了,如果说它还有什么有效的作用的话,那就是,如果基层在任何程度上将让他们所提名的人去选择议会代表的话,那么投票者就无法使自己被议会议员知道,而议员对他的委托人的责任感也会小得多。除了这一切之外,相对少数的人手中握有选择议会议员的权力,势必就会为各种阴谋诡计以及符合选举人身份的各种形式的腐败打开了方便之门。就方便贿赂而言,将选民减少到目前小小的市镇规模级别就行了。要确保当选,只要说服为数不多的人就足够了。如果有人说,选举人将对选择他们的人负责,那么回答是很明显的,也就是说,由于没有固定的职务,在公众眼中没有什么地位,选举人进行贿选是没有什么风险的,除非不能再次当选为选举人,而他们对这一点是不怎么在乎的。杜绝贿赂主要还是要靠惩罚,而在小的选区,这种惩罚力度是不够的,这一点已经为经验所证明,是众所周知的事情。弊端的大小和给予被选出的选举人的自由裁量权是恰好成比例的。他们可能不敢利用他

afraid to employ their vote for the promotion of their personal interest, would be when they were elected under an express pledge, as mere delegates, to carry as it were the votes of their constituents to the hustings. The moment the double stage of election began to have any effect, it would begin to have a bad effect. And this we shall find true of the principle of indirect election however applied, except in circumstances similar to those of the election of Senators in the United States.

It is unnecessary, as far as England is concerned, to say more in opposition to a scheme which has no foundation in any of the national traditions. An apology may even be expected for saying so much, against a political expedient which perhaps could not, in this country, muster a single adherent. But a conception so plausible at the first glance, and for which there are so many precedents in history, might perhaps, in the general chaos of political opinions, rise again to the surface, and be brought forward on occasions when it might be seductive to some minds ; and it could not, therefore, even if English readers were alone to be considered, be passed altogether in silence.

们的投票权来谋取私利的唯一情形就是，他们在当选时作出明确保证，仅作为他们选民的代表在选举活动中进行投票。一旦两阶段选举开始出现效果，坏的结果也就开始出现了。我们将发现这就是间接选举原则无论怎么运用都将发生的实际情况，除了类似于美国参议员选举的情况之外。

就英国而言，没有必要就反对一个缺乏任何国家传统基石的方案多说些什么。但要反对这样一个或许在我国连一个信徒也无处可寻的政治上的权宜之计，我们还是期望能进行这样的解释。但是，这样一个看似可行的、在历史上也有许多先例的方案，在政治观点的普遍性的争论之中，又一次起死回生，并因其为某些思想家所着迷而不时地被提出来。因此，即使英国读者单独对这个方案去加以考虑，该方案也不会在公众的沉默之中被通过。

CHAPTER X
Of The Mode Of Voting

The question of greatest moment in regard to modes of voting, is that of secrecy or publicity; and to this we will at once address ourselves.

It would be a great mistake to make the discussion turn on sentimentalities about skulking or cowardice. Secrecy is justifiable in many cases, imperative in some, and it is not cowardice to seek protection against evils which are honestly avoidable. Nor can it be reasonably maintained that no cases are conceivable, in which secret voting is preferable to public. But I must contend that these cases, in affairs of a political character, are the exception, not the rule.

The present is one of the many instances in which, as I have already had occasion to remark, the *spirit of* an institution, the impression it makes on the mind of the citizen, is one of the most important parts of its operation. The spirit of vote by ballot-the interpretation likely to be put on it in the mind of an elector—is that the suffrage is given to him for himself ; for his particular use and benefit, and not as a trust for the public. For if it is indeed a trust, if the public are entitled to his vote, are not they entitled to know his vote ? This false and pernicious impression may well be made on the generality, since it has been made on most of those who of late years have been conspicuous advocates of the ballot. The doctrine was not so understood by its earlier promoters ; but the effect of a doctrine on the mind is

第十章 投票的模式

关于投票模式最重要的问题就是秘密或公开的问题。我们将立即着手探讨这个问题。

认为由于民众存在躲避或怯懦的心理而导致对这个问题的讨论，是非常错误的。在许多情形下，秘密是有理由的，在有些情形下是必须的，而且，谋求不遭受原本可以避免的邪恶的侵犯，并非是胆小怕事。也没有理由认为，无记名投票在所有情形下都不如公开投票那样优越。但是我必须申明，在政治性质的事务上，这些情形不是惯例只是例外。

正如我已经有机会谈及的，在许多事例中，制度的精神，它在公民心中留下的印象，是该制度所能发挥的作用的一个最重要部分，目前所要谈及的就是这种事例之一。无记名投票制度的精神——选举人心中对它可能作的解释——是，选举权是他自己享有的权利；是为了他的特定用处和利益，而不是担负对公众的一种责任。因为假如它的确是一种责任，假如公众对投票享有某种权利，他们不是就有权利知道他的投票吗？很可能，多数人心中已深深地留下了这种错误而有害的印象，因为近年来惹人注意的提倡无记名投票的多数人都给人这种印象。这个学说的早期提倡者们并非是这样理解的，但是一种学说作用在公众心中出现的效

best shown, not in those who form it, but in those who are formed by it. Mr. Bright and his school of democrats think themselves greatly concerned in maintaining that the franchise is what they term a right, not a trust. Now this one idea, taking root in the general mind, does a moral mischief outweighing all the good that the ballot could do, at the highest possible estimate of it. In whatever way we define or understand the idea of a right, no person can have a right (except in the purely legal sense) to power over others: every such power, which he is allowed to possess, is morally, in the fullest force of the term, a trust. But the exercise of any political function, either as an elector or as a representative, is power over others. Those who say that the suffrage is not a trust but a right, can scarcely have considered the consequences to which their doctrine leads. If it is a right, if it belongs to the voter for his own sake, on what ground can we blame him for selling it, or using it to recommend himself to any one whom it is his interest to please ? A person is not expected to consult exclusively the public benefit in the use he makes of his house, or his three per cent. stock, or anything to which he really has a right. The suffrage is indeed due to him, among other reasons, as a means to his own protection, but only against treatment from which he is equally bound, so far as depends on his vote, to protect every one of his fellow-citizens. His vote is not a thing in which he has an option ; it has no more to do with his personal wishes than the verdict of a juryman. It is strictly a matter of duty; he is bound to give it according to his best and most conscientious opinion of the public good. Whoever has any other idea of it is unfit to have the suffrage ; its effect on him is to pervert, not to elevate his mind. Instead of opening his heart to an exalted patriotism and the obligation of public duty, it awakens and nourishes in him the disposition to use a public function for his own interest,

第十章

果,不是表现在倡导该学说的人当中,而是在信奉该学说的人中表现得尤为突出。布赖特先生和他的民主主义学派对倡导选举权是他们所称谓的一种权利而并非一种责任的学说感到十分关切。目前这一确立在普通人心中的观念所产生的道德上的危害,超过了无记名投票哪怕是在最高的评估上可能出现的一切好处。无论我们如何界定或阐释这个权利观念,任何人都无权享有一种支配他人权力的权利(除了在纯粹法律的意义上),因此,在该术语的最完整的含义上,一个人被允许拥有的任何这样一种权力,同时也是在道义上的一种责任。但是行使任何政治职能,不论是作为选举人,还是作为代表,都是控制他人的权力。认为选举权不是责任而是权利的民众,绝不会认可他们的学说所导致的这种结论。假如它是权利,假如它是为了选民自己而属于选民的话,我们又凭什么去责备他把选票卖掉,或者利用选票来获取与他利益相关的人的欢心呢? 在一个人使用他的住宅,或者他的百分之三的股票,或者他真正享有权利的任何其他东西的时候,不要期待他会专门去考虑公众的利益。除了其他的理由之外,作为保护自己的一种手段,选举权的确是他应当享有的,但只是为了使他不受到那样的待遇,即在依靠行使选举权的范围内,他同样有义务保护他的同胞不受到的那种待遇。他的投票,不是一件他可以随意选择的事情;和陪审员的判决一样,他的投票与他的个人意愿是没有关联的。严格地说,投票是个责任问题;遵照他对公共利益的最好的和出自良心的见解,他要有责任地去投票。只要是有其他想法的人,都不适于享有选举权;对这种人来说,选举权非但不能提升他的思想,反而会使他思想败坏。不是激发起他的高尚爱国心以及对公职的职责,而是唤起和滋生他为自己的利益、享乐或任

pleasure, or caprice ; the same feelings and purposes, on a humbler scale which actuate a despot and an oppressor. Now, an ordinary citizen in any public position, or on whom there devolves any social function, is certain to think and feel, respecting the obligations it imposes on him, exactly what society appears to think and feel in conferring it. What seems to be expected from him by society forms a standard which he may fall below, but which he certainly will not rise above. And the interpretation which he is almost sure to put upon secret voting, is that he is not bound to give his vote with any reference to those who are not allowed to know how he gives it ; but may bestow it simply as he feels inclined.

This is the decisive reason why the argument does not hold, from the use of the ballot in clubs and private societies, to its adoption in parliamentary elections. A member of a club is really, what the elector falsely believes himself to be, under no obligation to consider the wishes or interests of any one else. He declares nothing by his vote, but that he is or is not willing to associate, in a manner more or less close, with a particular person. This is a matter on which, by universal admission, his own pleasure or inclination is entitled to decide: and that he should be able so to decide it without risking a quarrel, is best for everybody, the rejected person included. An additional reason rendering the ballot unobjectionable in these cases, is that it does not necessarily or naturally lead to lying. The persons concerned are of the same class or rank, and it would be considered improper in one of them to press the other with questions as to how he had voted. It is far otherwise in parliamentary elections, and is likely to remain so, as long as the social relations exist which produce the demand for the ballot; as long as one person is sufficiently the superior of another, to think himself entitled to dictate his vote. And while this is the case, silence or an evasive answer is certain to be construed as proof that the vote given has not been that which was desired.

In any political election, even by universal suffrage (and still more obviously in the case of a restricted suffrage), the voter is under

性而行使公共职能的倾向;在较低的等级上,这与驱使着专制君主和压迫者的感情和意志是相同的东西。本来,担任某种公共职位,或者负责某种社会职能的普通公民的想法——对这种职能所赋予他的职责的想法——肯定和社会赋予这种职能时的想法是完全合拍的。社会对他的期望形成一个标准,这个标准,他或许无法达到,但他很少会超出这个标准。对于无记名投票,他几乎肯定会作出这样的解释:他没有义务遵照那些不被允许知道他怎样投票的人的意愿来投票,而完全可以根据自己的意愿投票。

　　从上述论点中,我们可以看出之所以不能对俱乐部、私人团体以及议会选举一律适用无记名投票的决定性的原因。像选举人错误地设想的那样,俱乐部的成员确实是没有考虑他人意愿和利益的义务。他通过投票所宣告的,不过是他愿意还是不愿意在较密切的方式上和某个特定的人发生联系,这是一件他有权依照自己的希望或意向去决定的事情,这一点已得到普遍的认可。而且让他能这样作出决定,并且没有造成争吵,将对每一个人,包括他所反对的人在内,都能带来好处。无记名投票不会必然地或自然地导致说谎,是它在这些场合不会引起民众反对的另一个原因。这些相关的人的阶级和社会地位是一样的,让其中一人迫使另一人就有关他投票的情况作出回答,将被认为是不合适的。议会选举的情形就截然不同了,而且只要存在需要无记名投票的社会关系,只要一个人比另一个人的地位高,高到足以使他认为自己有权命令另一个人的投票,这种情形将极有可能持续下去。在这种情形下,肯定会把沉默或模棱两可的回答看作是没有根据所希望的那样投票的证据。

　　在任何政治选举中,甚至遵循普遍选举制(在受限制选举制

an absolute moral obligation to consider the interest of the public, not his private advantage, and give his vote to the best of his judgment, exactly as he would be bound to do if he were the sole voter, and the election depended upon him alone. This being admitted, it is at least a *primâ facie* consequence, that the duty of voting, like any other public duty, should be performed under the eye and criticism of the public ; every one of whom has not only an interest in its performance, but good title to consider himself wronged if it is performed otherwise than honestly and carefully. Undoubtedly neither this nor any other maxim of political morality is absolutely inviolable; it may be overruled by still more cogent considerations. But its weight is such that the cases which admit of a departure from it must be of a strikingly exceptional character.

It may, unquestionably, be the fact, that if we attempt, by publicity, to make the voter responsible to the public for his vote, he will practically be made responsible for it to some powerful individual, whose interest is more opposed to the general interest of the community than that of the voter himself would be, if, by the shield of secresy, he were released from responsibility altogether. When this is the condition, in a high degree, of a large proportion of the voters, the ballot may be the smaller evil. When the voters are slaves, anything may be tolerated which enables them to throw off the yoke. The strongest case for the ballot is when the mischievous power of the Few over the Many is increasing. In the decline of the Roman republic, the reasons for the ballot were irresistible. The oligarchy was yearly becoming richer and more tyrannical, the people poorer and more dependent, and it was necessary to erect stronger and stronger barriers against such abuse of the franchise as rendered it but an instrument the more in the hands of unprincipled persons of consequence. As little can it be doubted that the ballot, so far as it existed, had a beneficial

的场合中特别突出),选民有绝对的道义上的责任考虑公众的利益,而不只是他的个人利益,进行投票时要以他所能作出的最好判断为根据,就好比只有他一个选举人,而且选举完全取决于他的情况下所要做的那样。这一点得到认可之后,显而易见的结果,至少是和任何其他的公共职务一样,投票的责任,应当着公众的面行使并接受公众的批评;履行这种职责,不仅对公众的每一个人存在利害关系,并且,假如他的职责没有诚实而谨慎地得以履行的话,他有合法的权利认为自己受到了侵犯。毋庸置疑,不管是这个准则,还是任何其他的政治道德准则,都并非绝对不可侵犯的;它可以被更令人信服的考虑驳回。但是这个准则的分量是如此之重,以致只要允许偏离该准则的情形都应当被视为是明显的例外。

  毋庸置疑,事实上,基于公开的原则,假如我们尝试使选举人的投票对公众负责,他实际上将变成对某个强有力的个人负责,相对于其在秘密原则的遮盖下完全免除责任时选举人自己的利益,这个强有力的个人的利益更加违背社会的公共利益。假如这种情形在很大程度上是一大部分选民的情形,无记名投票或许就具有较小的危害。假如选举人是奴隶,那么,他们可以容忍任何能使他们摆脱枷锁的事情。在少数支配多数的有害权力正在滋长的时候,无记名投票是最令人信服的。在罗马共和国的衰落时期,支持无记名投票的理由是无法抗拒的。少数寡头年复一年地变得愈来愈富、愈来愈残暴,人民则变得愈来愈穷困、愈来愈丧失独立性,为了反抗把选举日益蜕变为没有道德顾忌的重要人物手中的单纯工具的滥用,设置越来越坚固的障碍就很有必要。同样不容置疑的是,对于无记名投票曾经出现过的情形来说,它在雅典的政体中

operation in the Athenian constitution. Even in the least unstable of the Grecian commonwealths, freedom might be for the time destroyed by a single unfairly obtained popular vote: and though the Athenian voter was not sufficiently dependent to be habitually coerced, he might have been bribed, or intimidated by the lawless outrages of some knot of individuals, such as were not uncommon even at Athens among the youth of rank and fortune. The ballot was in these cases a valuable instrument of order, and conduced to the Eunomia by which Athens was distinguished among the ancient commonwealths.

But in the more advanced states of modern Europe, and especially in this country, the power of coercing voters has declined and is declining ; and bad voting is now less to be apprehended from the influences to which the voter is subject at the hands of others, than from the sinister interests and discreditable feelings which belong to himself, either individually or as a member of a class. To secure him against the first, at the cost of removing all restraint from the last, would be to exchange a smaller and a diminishing evil for a greater and increasing one. On this topic, and on the question generally, as applicable to England at the present date, I have, in a pamphlet on Parliamentary Reform, expressed myself in terms which, as I do not feel that I can improve upon, I will venture here to transcribe.

'Thirty years ago, it was still true that in the election of members of Parliament, the main evil to be guarded against was that which the ballot would exclude—coercion by landlords, employers, and customers. At present, I conceive, a much greater source of evil is the selfishness, or the selfish partialities, of the voter himself. A base and mischievous vote is now, I am convinced, much oftener given from the voter's personal interest, or class interest, or some mean feeling in his own mind, than from any fear of consequences at the hands of others: and to these influences the ballot would enable him to yield himself up, free from all sense of shame or responsibility.

第十章

曾发挥过有益的作用。甚至在最稳定的希腊共和国里,自由可能一时被仅仅一次使用非法手段所获得的民众选举毁掉。雅典的选民虽然没有陷入习惯性被强制的地步,但他可能被贿买,甚至受到一帮人的非法暴行的胁迫,譬如即使在雅典的有钱有势的青年人中,这种人也是很常见的。在这种情形下,无记名投票就成为维护秩序的重要手段,并对于欧诺弥亚是有益的——在雅典古代共和国中享有盛誉的那个维护秩序的女神。

但是在现代欧洲比较发达的国家,尤其是在我们国家,强制选举人的权力已经被削弱和正在被削弱;现在对不合法投票的顾虑,并非来自于其他人对选举人的影响,而是来自于选举人自身的邪恶的利益和羞耻的感情——不管选举人是作为个人还是作为阶级成员。以解除对选举人的邪恶利益和羞耻感情的一切限制为代价,来保证其他人不对选举人施加影响将会是因小失大,得不偿失。关于这个议题以及关于这个的一般问题,在当前英国的适用方面,我在探讨议会改革的一本小册子中,已经表达了我的观点,对于其中的见解,我觉得不能进一步改进?因此我冒昧地将其抄录在下文之中。

"在议会议员的选举中,应当防止的主要弊端即地主、雇主和顾客三者所施加的强制影响,是要由无记名投票进行排除的,在30年前这样认为依然是正确的。而现在我则认为,选举人自己的自私自利或利己的偏心,是生成弊端的一个更大的根源。我深信,卑鄙无耻而有害的投票,现在更往往是来源于个人利益,或者是阶级利益,或者是选举人自己心中某种可耻的感情,而不是由于担心受他人操纵,在这些东西的影响下,他完全屈服于无记名投票,而没有一点羞愧感和责任感。

'In times not long gone by, the higher and richer classes were in complete possession of the government. Their power was the master grievance of the country. The habit of voting at the bidding of an employer, or of a landlord, was so firmly established, that hardly anything was capable of shaking it but a strong popular enthusiasm, seldom known to exist but in a good cause. A vote given in opposition to these influences was therefore, in general, an honest, a public-spirited vote; but in any case, and by whatever motive dictated, it was almost sure to be a good vote, for it was a vote against the monster evil, the overrulling influence of oligarchy. Could the voter at that time have been enabled, with safety to himself, to exercise his privilege freely, even though neither honestly nor intelligently, it would have been a great gain to reform ; for it would have broken the yoke of the then ruling power in the country—the power which had created and which maintained all that was bad in the institutions and the administration of the State—the power of landlords and boroughmongers.

'The ballot was not adopted; but the progress of circumstances has done and is doing more and more, in this respect, the work of the ballot. Both the political and the social state of the country, as they affect this question, have greatly changed, and are changing every day. The higher classes are not now masters of the country. A person must be blind to all the signs of the times, who could think that the middle classes are as subservient to the higher, or the working classes dependent on the higher and middle, as they were a quarter of a century ago. The events of that quarter of a century have not only taught each class to know its own collective strength, but have put the individuals of a lower class in a condition to show a much bolder front to those of a higher. In a majority of cases, the vote of the electors, whether in opposition to or in accordance with the wishes of their superiors, is not now the effect of coercion, which there are no longer the same means of applying, but the expression of their own personal or political partialities. The very vices of the present electoral system are a proof of this. The growth of bribery, so loudly complained of,

第十章

"在不久以前的时代,政府完全是由上等阶级和富裕阶级所控制的。它们的权力是这个国家主要的不平等。遵循雇主或地主的命令投票的习惯已经如此牢固地确立,从而导致除了在正义事业中才会出现的强大的民众热情,几乎没有什么东西能够撼动它。因此,为抵制这种影响投的票,通常来说就是正直的、忠心公益的票。但无论如何,也不管动机到底如何,它几乎肯定是有益的投票,因为投票的目的,是反对寡头政府的统治势力这一巨大祸害。倘若选举人能在确保自己安全的情况下自由地行使他的特权,即使既不正直也不睿智,也会是改革层面的一大改进,因为它将挣脱当时的国家统治权力的奴役,这种权力是形成并维护国家制度和行政中一切坏事的权力,即地主和市镇商人的权力。

"无记名投票没有被采用,不过在这方面,情况的发展已经并正在使无记名投票的工作越来越多。无论是国家的政治状态还是社会状态,由于它们影响着这个问题,已经极大地改变了,并且每时每刻都在改变着。现在上等阶级已不是国家的主人。如果一个人还有着这样一种看法,即中产阶级还像 25 年以前那样对上等阶级阿谀奉承,或者劳动阶级还像以前那样受上等和中产阶级的荫庇,那么他必定是对时代发展的一切信号视而不见。那二十五年中发生的种种事件,不仅使每个阶级学会知道它自己的集体力量,而且使地位较低阶级的人在面对地位较高的阶级时表现出更大胆得多的态度。在多数情形下,选举人的投票,不论是违背还是符合其上级的意愿,现在都不是被强制的结果,因为已不再有行使强制的手段了,而是选举人自己个人的或政治上所表现出来的偏好。当前选举制度的弊端本身就揭示了这一点。导致民众

and the spread of the contagion to places formerly free from it, are evidence that the local influences are no longer paramount; that the electors now vote to please themselves, and not other people. There is, no doubt, in counties and in the smaller boroughs, a large amount of servile dependence still remaining; but the temper of the times is adverse to it, and the force of events is constantly tending to diminish it. A good tenant can now feel that he is as valuable to his landlord as his landlord is to him ; a prosperous tradesman can afford to feel independent of any particular customer. At every election the votes are more and more the voters' own. It is their minds, far more than their personal circumstances, that now require to be emancipated. They are no longer passive instruments of other men's will—mere organs for putting power into the hands of a controlling oligarchy. The electors themselves are becoming the oligarchy.

'Exactly in proportion as the vote of the elector is determined by his own will, and not by that of somebody who is his master, his positions is similar to that of a member of Parliament, and publicity is indispensable. So long as any portion of the community are unrepresented, the argument of the Chartists, against ballot in conjunction with a restricted suffrage, is unassailable. The present electors, and the bulk of those whom any probable Reform Bill would add to the number, are the middle class; and have as much a class interest, distinct from the working classes; as landlords or great manufacturers. Were the suffrage extended to all skilled labourers, even these would, or might, still have a class interest distinct from the unskilled. Suppose it extended to all men—suppose that what was formerly called by the misapplied name of universal suffrage, and now by the silly title of manhood suffrage, became the law; the voters would still have a class interest, as distinguished from women. Suppose that there were a question before the Legislature specially affecting women; as whether women should be allowed to graduate at Universities; whether the mild

第十章

愤懑的贿赂大行其道,而且蔓延到原本没有这种恶习的地方,印证了地方势力已不再是至高无上;印证了选举人现在投票是为了自己高兴,而并非是取悦别人。毋庸讳言,在郡县和小市镇里,仍然保有大量奴役性的依赖关系;但是,时代的趋势是和这相反的,而且不断发生的事件正有助于使这种关系不断地减少。一个正直的佃户现在能感到他和他的地主一样有价值,就像他的地主和他一样有价值一样;一个生意兴隆的小商人完全可以感到不依靠于任何特定主顾。每次选举中,所投的票愈来愈成为选举人自己的票。现在需要解放的远远不是选举人的个人境况,而是他们的思想。他们已经不再是其他人意志的消极工具——把权力演化为处于控制地位的寡头政府手中的单纯工具。选举人自己正在变为寡头政府。

"选举人对投票所作的决定,越是遵循他自己的意愿而不是遵循他的主人的意愿,他的地位就越是和议会议员的地位相类似,因而投票就应当是公开的。只要社会的某一部分是没有代表的,宪章运动派反对与受限制的选举权相联系的无记名投票的论点就是无可争辩的。目前的选举人,以及任何可能提出的改革法案所要增加的选举人中的大多数,是中产阶级,他们和地主或大制造商一样,存在和工人阶级不同的阶级利益。倘若把选举权普及到所有的熟练工人,就是这些人也仍然将具有或可能具有不同于非熟练工人的阶级利益。倘若把选举权普及到所有的男人——假定将以前被误称为普遍选举权,而现在用成年男人选举权这一可笑名称称呼的东西变为法律,选举人仍旧会存在和妇女不一样的阶级利益。假定在议会中有特别牵涉妇女的问题,如:妇女是否应当允许大学毕业,对每天都把妻子打得几乎死去活来的

penalties inflicted on ruffians who beat their wives daily almost to death's door, should be exchanged for something more effectual ; or suppose that any one should propose in the British Parliament, what one State after another in America is enacting not by a mere law, but by a provision of their revised Constitutions—that married women should have a right to their own property. Are not a man's wife and daughters entitled to know whether he votes for or against a candidate who will support these propositions?

'It will of course be objected, that these arguments derive all their weight from the supposition of an unjust state of the suffrage: That if the opinion of the non-electors is likely to make the elector vote more honestly, or more beneficially, than he would vote if left to himself, they are more fit to be electors than he is, and ought to have the franchise: That whoever is fit to influence electors, is fit to be an elector: That those to whom voters ought to be responsible, should be themselves voters ; and being such, should have the safeguard of the ballot, to shield them from the undue influence of powerful individuals or classes to whom they ought not to be responsible.

'This argument is specious, and I once thought it conclusive. It now appears to me fallacious. All who are fit to influence electors are not, for that reason, fit to be themselves electors. This last is a much greater power than the former, and those may be ripe for the minor political function, who could not as yet be safely trusted with the superior. The opinions and wishes of the poorest and rudest class of labourers may be very useful as one influence among others on the minds of the voters, as well as on those of the Legislature ; and yet it might be highly mischievous to give them the preponderant influence, by admitting them, in their present state of morals and intelligence, to the full exercise of the suffrage. It is precisely this indirect influence of those who have not the suffrage over those who have, which, by its progressive growth, softens the transition to every fresh extension of the franchise, and is the means by which, when the time is ripe,

恶棍所施加的轻微的惩罚是否需更改为某种更奏效的惩罚；或者假定有人在英国议会提出建议，即实施美国各州相继不再采用单纯的法律，而是用州宪法的修正条款来制定决定——已婚妇女应当享有保有她们自己财产的权利，那么，对于这个人究竟是投票赞成还是投票反对支持这些建议的候选人，难道这个人的妻子和女儿没有权利知道吗？

"当然有人会反对说，这些论点所具有的分量是来源于选举权的不平等状态这种假设；并且还说，如果和让他自己去投票相比较，非选举人的主张可能使选举人的投票更公正、更有好处的话，那么，这些非选举人就比他更适合担任选举人；只要是适于对选举人产生影响的人就是适合担任选举人的人；选举人必须对其负责的那些人，他们本人应当是选举人；以及作为选举人就应当受到无记名投票的保护，这样才不会受到他们不应该对其负责的强有力的个人或阶级的不适当影响。

"这一论点是似是而非的，我一度曾以为它是无可辩驳的。但现在在我看来，这一论点是一种谬论。凡适于对选举人产生影响的人，并不能因此说明他们自己就适合做选举人。后一种权力比起前一种权力要大得多，而那些尚不能稳妥地委托以高级政治职责的民众，在履行低级政治职责方面，他们或许是称职的。最贫穷和最粗野的劳动阶级的看法和愿望，从这些对选举人以及立法机关意见的一种影响来说，或许是很有好处的。但是从他们目前的道德和智力状态来看，允许他们充分行使选举权，从而给他们以占优势的影响，就可能是非常有害的。正是没有选举权的人对享有选举权的人的这种间接的影响，通过渐进性的发展，使得向每一次新的扩大选举权的过渡变得更为顺畅，并且，在时机成熟

the extension is peacefully brought about. But there is another and a still deeper consideration which should never be left out of the account in political speculations. The notion is itself unfounded, that publicity, and the sense of being answerable to the public, are of no use unless the pubic are qualified to form a sound judgment. It is a very superficial view of the utility of public opinion to suppose that it does good, only when it succeeds in enforcing a servile conformity to itself. To be under the eyes of others—to have to defend oneself to others—is never more important than to those who act in opposition to the opinion of others, for it obliges them to have sure ground of their own. Nothing has so steadying an influence as working against pressure. Unless when under the temporary sway of passionate excitement, no one will do that which he expects to be greatly blamed for, unless from a preconceived and fixed purpose of his own; which is always evidence of a thoughtful and deliberate character, and, except in radically bad men, generally proceeds from sincere and strong personal convictions. Even the bare fact of having to give an account of their conduct, is a powerful inducement to adhere to conduct of which at least some decent account can be given. If any one thinks that the mere obligation of preserving decency is not a very considerable check on the abuse of power, he has never had his attention called to the conduct of those who do not feel under the necessity of observing that restraint. Publicity is inappreciable, even when it does no more than prevent that which can by no possibility be plausibly defended—than compel deliberation, and force every one to determine, before he acts, what he shall say if called to account for his actions.

' But, if not now (it may be said), at least here after, when all are fit to have votes, and when all men and women are admitted to vote in virtue of their fitness ; *then* there can no longer be danger of class legislation; then the electors, being the nation, can have no interest apart from the general interest: even if individuals still vote ac-

第十章

时,成为和平地实现这种扩大的手段。但是在政治推论中,存在着不能不去考虑的另外一层,而且是更深入一层的考虑。下面的看法本身是没有事实根据的:除非公众有能力作出正确的判断,否则,公诸于众和对公众的责任感都是没有用处的。认为公众舆论只有在它能强求一致时才是有效用的,这是对公众舆论的效用的极浅薄的看法。对那些行动违反别人看法的人来说,没有什么比必须当着别人的面为自己进行辩护更重要的了,因为这使他们必须具备他们自己的有把握的理由。没有什么事情比得上顶着压力做事更具有那样坚定不移的力量。倘若不是在一时感情冲动的情况下,没有谁会去做他预料到将受到很大指责的事情,除非是源于他事先预想好的和确定的目的。这种目的常常是一种慎重、深思熟虑性格的证明,并且,除了在极坏的人身上之外,通常都是源于真挚的和强烈的个人信念。甚至单单是应当对他们的行为作出解释这一事实,就是遵守至少能提出某种适当理由的行为的强有力的诱因。假如有人认为单纯保持适当的责任不能对权力的滥用起到多大的规制作用,他就一点都没有注意到那些觉得没有必要遵从那种限制的人的行为。甚至当公开性只不过是防止不可能作出好像有理的辩护的事情——即只不过是迫使人不得不考虑,使每个人在他行动之前不得不决定如被要求解释其行为他应当说些什么时——公开性是毫无价值的。

"但是,或许有人会说,如果不是现在,至少在今后,当所有的人都适于有投票权,并且当由于所有的男人和妇女都适合有投票权,因而他们(或她们)都被允许投票的时候,那时,就不再存在阶级立法的危险了;那时选民是整个民族,他们的任何利益也就不会和公共利益相对立了,因为即使个人仍旧遵循个人的或阶级的

cording to private or class inducements, the majority will have no such inducement ; and as there will then be no non-electors to whom they ought to be responsible, the effect of the ballot, excluding none but the sinister influences, will be wholly beneficial.

'Even in this I do not agree. I cannot think that even if the people were fit for, and had obtained, universal suffrage, the ballot would be desirable. First, because it could not, in such circumstances, be supposed to be needful. Let us only conceive the state of things which the hypothesis implies ; a people universally educated, and every grown-up human being possessed of a vote. If, even when only a small proportion are electors, and the majority of the populations almost uneducated, public opinion is already, as every one now sees that it is, the ruling power in the last resort ; it is a chimera to suppose that over a community who all read, and who all have votes, any power could be exercised by landlords and rich people against their own inclination, which it would be at all difficult for them to throw off. But though the protection of secrecy would then be needless, the control of publicity would be as needful as ever. The universal observation of mankind has been very fallacious, if the mere fact of being one of the community, and not being in a position of pronounced contrariety of interest to the public at large, is enough to ensure the performance of a public duty, without either the stimulus or the restraint derived from the opinion of our fellow-creatures. A man's own particular share of the public interest, even though he may have no private interest drawing him in the opposite direction, is not, as a general rule, found sufficient to make him do his duty to the public without other external inducements. Neither can it be admitted that even if all had votes, they would give their votes as honestly in secret as in public. The proposition that the electors, when they compose the whole of the community, cannot have an interest in voting against the interest of the community, will be found on examination to have more sound than meaning in it. Though the community as a whole can have (as the terms imply) no other interest than its collective interest,

第十章

动机去投票,大多数人将不存在这种动机;而且,由于那时没有他们应当对之负责的非选民,在把不良的影响排斥之后,无记名投票的效果将是完全有益的。

"甚至在这一点上我也不赞同。我不能认为,即使人民已适于并获取普遍选举权,无记名投票就会成为值得期待的。首先,因为在这种情形下,它不能被认为是必要的。我们只要想一下这种假设所蕴含的情形:民众普遍接受教育,每个成年人都享有投票权。假如,甚至当只有一小部分是选民,民众的大多数几乎是没有受到教育的时候,那么,正如每个人现在所看到的那样,公众舆论就已经是作为最后诉诸的统治力量,倘若在一个所有的人都能阅读并都享有投票权的社会,地主和富有的人能违背行使权力的倾向——一种民众毕竟难以割舍的倾向,那么,这真是一种奇谈怪论。但是尽管这样一来,不需要对秘密性作保护,但对公开性作调控则仍然是必要的。如果说,作为社会的一分子,并且出于其利益不会与一般公众利益明显对立这一单纯事实,就以为即使在没有受到公众舆论的激励或制约的情况下,也足以保证其能履行公共职务,那么我们对人类的普遍观察就一直是非常错误的。即使一个人,或许没有私人利益把他拖到对立的方向,他在公共利益中的特定的一份,在没有其他外部刺激物的情况下,常常不足以使他履行他对公众的职责。同样不能接受的是,即使所有的人都享有选举权,他们会一样公正地投票,无论是在秘密的情况下还是在公开的情况下。这样一种说法,即当选民组成社会全体时,他们在选举中就不会有和社会的利益相对立的利益,在经过对其仔细推敲之后,会发现它只是听起来像一回事而在实际上是没什么意义的。尽管社会作为一个整体不可能存在(如该术语

any or every individual in it may. A man's interest consists of whatever he takes interest *in*. Everybody has as many different interests as he has feelings; likings or dislikings, either of a selfish or of a better kind. It cannot be said that any of these, taken by itself, constitutes "his interest": he is a good man or a bad, according as he prefers one class of his interests or another. A man who is a tyrant at home will be apt to sympathise with tyranny (when not exercised over himself): he will be almost certain not to sympathise with resistance to tyranny. An envious man will vote against Aristides because he is called the Just. A selfish man will prefer even a trifling individual benefit, to his share of the advantage which his country would derive from a good law ; because interests peculiar to himself are those which the habits of his mind both dispose him to dwell on, and make him best able to estimate. A great number of the electors will have two sets of preferences—those on private, and those on public grounds. The last are the only ones which the elector would like to avow. The best side of their character is that which people are anxious to show, even to those who are no better than themselves. People will give dishonest or mean votes from lucre, from malice, from pique, from personal rivalry, even from the interests or prejudices of class or sect, more readily in secret than in public. And cases exist—they may come to be more frequent—in which almost the only restraint upon a majority of knaves consists in their involuntary respect for the opinion of an honest minority. In such a case as that of the repudiating States of North America, is there not some check to the unprincipled voter in the shame of looking an honest man in the face ? Since all this good would be sacrificed by the ballot, even in the circumstances most favourable to it, a much stronger case is requisite than can now be made out for its necessity (and the case is continually becoming

第十章

所暗示的)社会的集体利益之外的利益,但社会中的任何一个人或每一个人都可以有其他的利益。一个人的利益是由他所感兴趣的一切事物构成的。每一个人有许多不一样的兴趣,就好比他有许多不同的感情一样。有各种各样的爱好或厌恶,无论是源于自私自利的或是用心良好的,不能说任何一种兴趣单独构成'他的利益'。他是一个好人还是一个坏人,是由他选择这一种兴趣还是那一种兴趣来决定的。在家里是暴君的人常常同情暴政(在没有对他本人实行的时候),因此他几乎肯定不会对反抗暴政表示同情。一个嫉妒的人将投票反对阿里斯蒂德斯,因为他被称之为公正的人。一个自私自利的人宁愿选择甚至是极小的个人利益,而不选择他的国家会从好的法律中获取的他应得的那一份好处。因为他自己特有的利益,也就是他的思想习惯是他无法割舍也最容易作出评估的利益。很多选民有两种选择,一种是基于个人理由的选择,另一种是基于公共理由的选择。而对于后者,选民才愿意坦率承认。人们迫切想展示的是他们性格的最好方面,即使是对比不上他们自己的人展示也好。与在公开的情况下投票相比而言,由于贪婪、怨恨、不满、个人的敌对,甚至由于阶级或党派的利益或偏见,民众在秘密的情况下将更容易作出不公正的或不正当的投票。有着这样的情形——这种情形或许变得更时常发生——那就是:对坏人的大多数所能作出的几乎唯一的限制,是他们对正直的少数的观点的不知不觉的尊重。在像拒绝清付债务的美国一些州的情形,在正视正直人所体验到的羞耻中,难道没有对毫无道德顾忌的选民的某种节制吗?由于无记名投票会毁掉所有这一切好处,所以即使在对它最有利的情形下,也需要有比现在所能列举出的更强有力的事例(而这种

still weaker) to make its adoption desirable.' ①

On the other debateable points connected with the mode of voting, it is not necessary to expend so many words. The system of personal representation, as organized by Mr. Hare, renders necessary the employment of voting papers. But it appears to me indispensable that the signature of the elector should be affixed to the paper at a public polling place, or if there be no such place conveniently accessible, at some office open to all the world, and in the presence of a responsible public officer. The proposal which has been thrown out of allowing the voting papers to be filled up at the voter's own residence, and sent by the post, or called for by a public officer, I should regard as fatal. The act would be done in the absence of the salutary, and the presence of all the pernicious, influences. The briber might, in the shelter of privacy, behold with his own eyes his bargain fulfilled, and the intimidator could see the extorted obedience rendered irrevocably on the spot ; while the beneficent counter-influence of the presence of those who knew the voter's real sentiments, and the inspiring effect of the sympathy of those of his own party or opinion, would be shut out. ②The polling places should be so numerous as to be within easy reach of every voter ; and no expenses of conveyance, at the cost of the candidate, should be tolerated under any pretext. The infirm, and they only on medical certificate, should have the right of claiming suitable carriage conveyance, at the cost of the State, or of the locality. Hustings, poll-clerks, and all the necessary machinery of elections, should be at the public charge.

---

① *Thoughts on Parliamentary Reform*, 2nd ed. pp. 32-36.

② 'This expedient has been recommended, both on the score of saving expense, and on that of obtaining the votes of many electors who otherwise would not vote, and who are regarded by the advocates of the plan as a particularly desirable class of voters. The scheme has Been carried into practice in the election of poorlaw guardians, and its success in that instance, is appealed to in favour of adopting it in the more important case of voting for a member of the Legislature. But the two cases appear to me to differ in the point on which the benefits of the expedient depend. In a local election for a special kind of administrative business, which consists mainly in the dispensation of a public fund, it is an object to prevent the choice from being exclusively in the hands of those who actively concern themselves about it ; for the public interest which

事例正不断变得越加软弱无力)来使无记名投票的采用成为值得期待的。"①

其他与投票方法有关的可探讨之处,没有必要再浪费更多的篇幅。依照黑尔先生所提出的个人代表制,应当使用选举纸。但是,在我看来最重要的是,选举人的签名应当附在公共投票处的纸上,或者,如果附近没有这种方便场所,则在任何人都可以进出的办公室,并当着一个负责的公务员的面在选举纸上签名。有人提出允许选举人在自己的住所填写选举纸,并且通过邮寄送达,或者通过公务员收取的建议,我不得不认为这一建议是毁灭性的。这样,一切将以缺乏有益影响并面对一切有害影响的方式进行。在秘密性的庇护下,行贿者可以亲眼目睹他的交易得以成功,胁迫者能够看到强迫下的服从当场变得不可更改;而另一方面,了解选举人真实情感的民众的在场所能引发的有益的反影响,以及他的同党或舆论的同情所产生的鼓舞作用,就都被排斥在外了。② 应当多增设投票处使得每个选民能就近投票;不允许以任何借口向候选人收取交通费用。体弱有病的由医生证明,应当享有要求适当的车费的权利,通过国家或地方负担。议会议员竞选场、投票处办事处,以及所有必要的选举机构,都应当从公费中支

---

① 《关于议会改革的思考》,第 2 版,第 32 页至 36 页。
② "这一权宜之计被推荐出来,既是为了节约开支,又是为了获得许多否则就不会投票的选举人的票,而这些人是被该方案的支持者认为特别值得期待的一类选民。济贫监护人的选举就执行了这个方案,在这种情况下获得的成功,被用来支持在更重要的议会议员的选举中采纳它。但是在我看来,这两种情况在作为该权宜之计的益处所依靠的要点上是不一样的。在为了特种行政事务的地方选举中,这种行政事务主要职能就是分配公共基金,目的之一就是防止人选完全落入对它表示积极关心的那些人手中;

Not only the candidate should not be required, he should not be permitted, to incur any but a limited and trifling expense for his election. Mr. Hare thinks it desirable that a sum of 50*l*. should be required from every one who places his name on the list of candidates, to prevent persons who have no chance of success, and no real intention of attempting it, from becoming candidates in wantonness or from mere love of notoriety, and perhaps carrying off a few votes which are needed for the return of more serious aspirants. There is one expense which a candidate or his supporters cannot help incurring, and which it can hardly be expected that the public should defray for every one who may choose to demand it ; that of making his claims known to the electors, by advertisements, placards, and circulars. For all necessary expenses of this kind the 50*l* proposed by Mr. Hare, if allowed to be drawn upon for these purposes (it might be made 100*l* if requisite), ought to be sufficient. If the friends of the candidate choose to go to expense on committees and canvassing, there are no means of preventing them; but such expenses out of the candidate's own pocket, or any expenses whatever beyond the deposit of 50*l*. (or 100*l*.) should be illegal and punishable. If there appeared any likelihood that opinion would refuse to connive at falsehood, a

---

attaches to the election being of a limited kind, and in most cases not very great in degree, the disposition to make themselves busy in the matter is apt to be in a great measure confined to persons who hope to turn their activity to their own private advantage ; and it may be very desirable to render the intervention of other people as little onerous to them as possible, if only for the purpose of swamping these private interests. But when the matter in hand is the great business of national government, in which every one must take an interest who cares for anything out of himself, or who cares even for himself intelligently, it is much rather an object to prevent those from voting who are indifferent to the subject, than to induce them to vote by any other means than that of awakening their dormant minds. The voter who does not care enough about the election to go to the poll, is the very man who, if he can vote without that small trouble, will give his vote to the first person who asks for it, or on the most trifling or frivolous inducemerit. A man who does not care whether he votes, is not likely to care much which way he votes; and he who is in that state of mind has no moral right to vote at all ; since, if he does so, a vote which is not the expression of a conviction, counts for as much, and goes as far in determining the result, as one which represents the thoughts and purposes of a life. ' —Thoughts, etc. , p. 39.

第十章

出。不仅不应要求,而且除了有限的少数选举费用之外,不能允许候选人负担其他任何的费用。黑尔先生认为合适的做法是,让每一个把自己的名字放上候选人名单的人交纳 50 镑金额,以防范那些没有胜出可能、也并不是真正有意要取得成功的人防止恶作剧的候选人或只是爱出风头的人,却可能挤占比较严肃认真的积极参加者当选所需的少数选票。候选人或其支持者不能不负担的,也是难以期望公众会为想提出要求的人支付的一项费用,就是通过广告、招贴和传单等方式让选民熟悉候选人的主张所需的费用。为了支付所有这些必要的开支,黑尔先生所提议的 50 镑,如果许可为这些目的花费的话(必要时可定为 100 镑),应当是足够的。假如候选人的赞同者想为委员会和拉选票支付费用,对此没有办法进行制止;但是,从候选人自己口袋里支付这种费用,或者超过 50 镑(或 100 镑)押金的任何费用,都是非法的并应当受到惩处的。假如出现舆论不许可虚报费用的情况,那么,每个

因为和这种选举有关的公共利益种类有限,而且在多数情形下为数也不很多,常常只有期望获取他们自己的私人利益而活动的人才愿意忙于这种事情。对于他们来说,或许他人的干涉越少麻烦越少,只要实现把这些私人利益排斥在外的目的就足够了。但是当目前的问题是一国政府的大事的时候,只要是关心自己以外的事情的人,或甚至能理智地关心自己事情的人,都必定会对它产生兴趣的,这时的目的毋宁是防止对这问题漠不关心的人投票,而不是用唤醒他们沉睡的思想之外的方法促使他们投票。对选举关心的程度还不足以促使他去投票处的选民,就正是那种如果能在省掉那小小的麻烦的情况下投票,就会把选票投给最先问他要选票的人,或者因最无关紧要的诱因从而投给他的选票的人。对投票与否漠不关心的人,大概不会很关心用什么方法投票。带有这种心理状态的人完全没有投票的道德权利。因为,假如他去投票,这张并不表达信念的选票,却在决定选举结果方面,和传达着一个人的思想和意愿的选票一样有价值,一样发挥作用。"——《关于议会改革的意见》,第 2 版,第 39 页。

declaration on oath or honour should be required from every member on taking his seat, that he had not expended, nor would expend, money or money's worth, beyond the 50*l*, directly or indirectly, for the purposes of his election; and if the assertion were proved to be false or the pledge to have been broken, he should be liable to the penalties of perjury. It is probable that those penalties, by showing that the Legislature was in earnest, would turn the course of opinion in the same direction, and would hinder it from regarding, as it has hitherto done, this most serious crime against society as a venial peccadillo. When once this effect had been produced, there need be no doubt that the declaration on oath or honour would be considered binding. ①' Opinion

---

① Several of the witnesses before the Committee of the House of Commons in 1860, on the operation of the Corrupt Practices Prevention Act, some of them of great practical experience in election matters, were favourable (either absolutely or as a last resort) to the principle of requiring a declaration from members of Parliament ; and were of opinion that, if supported by penalties, it would be, to a great degree, effectual. —(*Evidence*, pp. 46, 54-7, 67, 123, 198-202, 208.) The Chief Commissioner of the Wakefield Inquiry said (in reference certainly to a different proposal) , ' If they see that the Legislature is earnest upon the subject, the machinery will work.... I am quite sure that if some personal stigma were applied upon conviction of bribery, it would change the current of public opinion. ' (pp. 26and 32.) A distinguished member of the Committee (and of the present Cabinet) seemed to think it very objectionable to attach the penalties of perjury to a merely promissory as distinguished from an assertory oath: but he was reminded, that the oath taken by a witness in a court of justice is a promissory oath : and the rejoinder (that the witness's promise relates to an act to be done at once, while the member's would be a promise for all future time) would only be to the purpose, if it could be supposed that the swearer might forget the obligation he had entered into, or could possibly violate it unawares : contingencies which, in a case like the present, are out of the question.

A more substantial difficulty is, that one of the forms most frequently assumed by election expenditure, is that of subscriptions to local charities, or other local objects ; and it would be a strong measure to enact that money should not be given in charity, within a place, by the member for it, When such subscriptions are *bonâ* fide, the popularity which may be derived from them is an advantage which it seems hardly possible to deny to superior riches. But the greatest part of the mischief consists in the fact that money so contributed is employed in bribery, under the euphonious name of keeping up the member's interest. To guard against this, it should be part of the member's promissory declaration, that all sums expended by him in the place, or for any purpose connected with it or with any of its inhabitants, (with the exception perhaps of his own hotel expenses,) should pass through the hands of the election auditor, and be by him (and not by the member himself or his friends) applied to its declared purpose. The principle of making all lawful expenses of elections a charge not upon the candidate, but upon the locality, was upheld by two of the best witnesses. (pp. 20, 65-70, 277.)

第十章

议员在就职时,就应当宣誓保证他没有也不会为了他的选举的目的直接或间接支出超过 50 镑钱或相当的价值;假如所声明的被证明是虚假的或者所作出的保证已被违反,他便要以伪证罪而受到处罚。极有可能的是,由于这些惩罚反映出议会是严肃认真的,它们将使舆论偏向同一方向,使它不会像迄今那样把这一最严重的反社会罪行视为一种可宽恕的过失。这种效果一旦出现,宣誓就毋庸置疑地被认为是具有约束力的。① "只有当舆论已经容忍被

---

① 1860 年对贪污行为防止法加以实施时在出席下院委员会作证的一些人当中,有些是在选举事项方面具有相当丰富的实际经验,他们支持(绝对地或者作为最后的诉诸手段)要求议会议员宣誓的原则,并且认为如设置处罚规定,在很大程度上,它将是奏效的。(《证据》,第 46 页,第 54 至 57 页,第 67 页,第 123 页,第 198 页至 202 页,第 208 页。)韦克菲尔德调查(Wakefield Inquiry)的主任委员说(肯定是就另一建议说的),"假如他们知道议会在这问题上是严肃认真的,这一措施就会起作用。……我敢保证地说,如果某个人污名适用于贿赂的定罪,公众舆论的趋势就会改变"(第 26 和 32 页)。上述委员会(也是现内阁)的一个杰出成员似乎认为,对迥异于肯定誓言的单纯有约束力的誓言附加伪证罪的惩罚是应当反对的。但是他应当记住,证人在法庭上作的誓言就是有约束力的誓言,而且提出的反驳(说证人的保证涉及立即要做的行为,而议员的保证则是针对将来的)不过是表达这样一层意思:宣誓者或许会忘记他曾许诺的义务,或者可能在无意之中违反了这种义务。但在现在这种场合,意外的事是根本不可能发生的。

更为实质性的困难是,选举支出最常采取的形式之一,是对地方慈善事业或其他地方事业的捐款,而规定议员不能在选出他的地区内提供慈善款项将是一种强有力的措施。假如这种捐款是诚实的,由此衍生的声望,则是巨额财富几乎一定会获得的一种好处。但是,最大的害处则在于,这样捐赠的款项,事实上是在保持该议员的利益的美名下被运用于贿赂。为防止这一点,议员应当作出这样的有约束力的誓言:他在当地,或为了和当地或当地居民有关的目的所支付的全部金额(也许除了他自己的旅馆费用之外),须经过选举审计员之手,并且由他(而不是由议员本人或他的支持者)运用到公然宣布的目的。两位最好的证人都赞同这一原则:使一切合法的选举开支由地方而不是由候选人承担。(第 20 页,第 65 至 70 页,第 277 页)。

tolerates a false disclaimer, only when it already tolerates the thing disclaimed. ' This is notoriously the case with regard to electoral corruption. There has never been among political men, any real and serious attempt to prevent bribery, because there has been no real desire that elections should not be costly. Their costliness is an advantage to those who can afford the expense, by excluding a multitude of competitors; and anything, however noxious, is cherished as having a conservative tendency, if it limits the access to Parliament to rich men. This is a rooted feeling among our legislators of both political parties, and is almost the only point on which I believe them to be really ill-intentioned. They care comparatively little who votes, as long as they feel assured that none but persons of their own class can be voted for. They know that they can rely on the fellow-feeling of one of their class with another, while the subservience of *nouveaux enrichis* who are knocking at the door of the class, is a still surer reliance ; and that nothing very hostile to the class interests or feelings of the rich need be apprehended under the most democratic suffrage, as long as democratic persons can be prevented from being elected to Parliament. But, even from their own point of view, this balancing of evil by evil, insteading of combining good with good, is a wretched policy. The object should be to bring together the best members of both classes, under such a tenure as shall induce them to lay aside their class preferences, and pursue jointly the path traced by the common interest ; instead of allowing the class feelings of the Many to have full swing in the constituencies subject to the impediment of having to act through persons imbued with the class feelings of the Few.

There is scarcely any mode in which political institutions are more morally mischievous—work greater evil through their spirit—than by representing political functions as a favour to be conferred, a thing which the depositary is to ask for as desiring it for himself, and even pay for as if it were designed for his pecuniary benefit. Men are not fond of paying large sums for leave to perform a laborious duty.

第十章

否认的事情时,它才容忍作虚伪的否认的人。"这就是声名狼藉的有关选举舞弊的情况。在政界人士圈内,任何真正的和认真的防止行贿的努力仍然尚未作出过,因为一直还未曾有希望选举的开销不是太大的真诚愿望。对于支付得起这笔费用的人来说,选举所需费用大是有好处的,可以把为数众多的竞争者排斥在外;任何事情,不管是如何有害处,只要把进入议会限定在富有的人当中,就被视为有保守倾向而受到重视。这就是我们两党的立法者们的一种根深蒂固的感情,并且几乎是我认为他们唯一真正心怀叵测之处。比较而言,只要他们觉得对此有把握,即只有他们自己阶级的人能获得选票,他们不怎么在乎谁投票。他们知道,他们能依赖他们阶级的人彼此之间的同情,而正敲着这个阶级之门的新贵们的卑躬屈节则尤其是一种有把握的依靠。他们还知道,只要能阻挠民主主义者们被选入议会,在最民主的选举制下,就不需要担心有什么和富有阶级的利益或感情极其敌对的事情。但是,即使从他们自己的观点来看,以恶制恶,而不是与人为善的这样一种做法也是恶劣的。目标应当是,在将使得他们抛开阶级偏好的状况下,把两个阶级最好的议员聚集在一起,共同沿着一致的利益所开拓出来的道路努力,而不是在必须通过受少数阶级感情左右的人去行动这种限制下,允许让多数的阶级感情在选民当中为所欲为。

政治制度在道德上最为有害,并且由它们的精神所滋生的最有害的方式,就是把政治职能视为一种恩赐,受委托人应当把它看作是自己所想拥有的东西而去要求这种职能,甚至为了获得这种职能而去付出代价,似乎它是一种有利于他的金钱利益的东西。人们不喜欢为了同意他去做艰辛的工作而支付一大笔钱。

Plato had a much juster view of the conditions of good government, when he asserted that the persons who should be sought out to be invested with political power are those who are personally most averse to it, and that the only motive which can be relied on for inducing the fittest men to take upon themselves the toils of government, is the fear of being governed by worse men. What must an elector think, when he sees three or four gentlemen, none of them previously observed to be lavish of their money on projects of disinterested beneficence, vying with one another in the sums they expend to be enabled to write M. P. after their names ? Is it likely he will suppose that it is for *his* interest they incur all this cost ? And if he forms an uncomplimentary opinion of their part in the affair, what moral obligation is he likely to feel as to his own ? Politicians are fond of treating it as the dream of enthusiasts, that the electoral body will ever be uncorrupt: truly enough, until they are willing to become so themselves: for the electors, assuredly, will take their moral tone from the candidates. So long as the elected member, in any shape or manner, pays for his seat, all endeavours will fail to make the business of election anything but a selfish bargain on all sides. ' So long as the candidate himself, and the customs of the world, seem to regard the function of a member of Parliament less as a duty to be discharged, than a personal favour to be solicited, no effort will avail to implant in an ordinary voter the feeling that the election of a member of Parliament is also a matter of duty and that he is not at liberty to bestow his vote on any other consideration than that of personal fitness.

The same principle which demands that no payment of money, for election purposes, should be either required or tolerated on the partof the person elected, dictates another conclusion, apparently of contrary tendency, but really directed to the same object. It negatives what has often been proposed as a means of rendering Parliament accessible to persons of all ranks and circumstances ; the payment of members of parliament. If, as in some of our colonies, there are

第十章

对于好政府的条件,柏拉图(Plato)持有一种非常精确的观点,他声称,应当赋予政治权力的人是那些自己对政治权力极有反感的人。又主张,可以拿来说服最适当的人承担起治理国家的诸多事务的唯一动机,是担心被更坏的人来治理国家。当一个选民发现三四个先生们以前从来没有对无私的慈善事业慷慨解囊,现在却抢着花钱以便能在他们的名字后面写上下院议会议员的职务,这个选民将会有什么想法呢?他可能会假定他们是为了他的利益而付出这些代价吗?假如他对他们的作为作出贬抑的评价,他又可能觉得他自己又有什么道德义务呢?对于选举团体永远不会腐败的这一看法,政客们喜欢把它看作是狂热者的梦想,在政客们自己愿意变得不腐败之前,情况的确如此。因为选民的道德品格必定将受候选人的影响。只要被选议员在任何形式或任何方式上为获得他的席位而花费金钱,一切努力都将不能阻止选举事务蜕变为彻头彻尾利己的交易。"只要候选人自己以及众人的习惯不是把议会议员的职能视为一种必须的责任,而是视为一种应当追逐的个人利益的话,要在一个普通选民中树立这样一种看法——选举议会议员也是一种责任问题,他除了考虑候选人是否适当以外不能根据任何其他的考虑自由地投票——任何努力都将是无济于事的。"

在被选人这方面,既不应当要求,也不应当允许存在为选举目的作任何金钱支付的同一原则产生出另一个结论,这个结论表面上是与目标相左的,但实际上是趋向同一目标。这个结论对议会议员的报酬做出了否定的回答,对议会议员的报酬,常常被提议作为使议会能为各种阶级地位和各种不同情况的民众所接近的手段。假如,像在我们有些殖民地那样,几乎没有任何合适

scarcely any fit persons who can afford to attend to an unpaid occupation, the payment should be an indemnity for loss of time or money, not a salary. The greater latitude of choice which a salary would give, is an illusory advantage. No remuneration which any one would think of attaching to the post would attract to it those who were seriously engaged in other lucrative professions, with a prospect of succeeding in them. The business of a member of parliament would therefore become an occupation in itself; carried on like other professions, with a view chiefly to its pecuniary returns, and under the demoralizing influences of an occupation essentially precarious. It would become an object of desire to adventurers of a low class ; and 658 persons in possession, with ten or twenty times as many in expectancy, would be incessantly bidding to attract or retain the suffrages of the electors, by promising all things, honest or dishonest, possible or impossible, and rivalling each other in pandering to the meanest feelings and most ignorant prejudices of the vulgarest part of the crowd. The auction between Cleon and the sausage-seller in Aristophanes is a fair caricature of what would be always going on. Such an institution would be a perpetual blister applied to the most peccant parts of human nature. It amounts to offering 658 prizes for the most successful flatterer, the most adroit misleader of a body of his fellow-countrymen. Under no despotism has there been such an organized system of tillage for raising a rich crop of vicious courtiership. ①When, by reason of pre-eminent qualifications (as may at any time happen to be the case), it is desirable that a person entirely without independent means, either derived from property or from a trade or profession, should be brought into Parliament to render services whichno noother person accessible can render as well, there is the resource of a public subscription; he may be supported while in Parliament, like Andrew Marvel, by the contributions

---

① 'As Mr. Lorimer remarks, by creating a pecuniary inducement to persons of the lowest class to devote themselves to public affairs, the calling of the dema-

第十章

的人能担负得起从事没有报酬的职业,那么报酬就应该是对时间或金钱损失的一种补偿,而不是薪水。以为薪水能给予较大范围的选择,是一种错觉。人们所能想到的提供给这职位的任何报酬,都不能把那些带着成功的希望认真做其他赚钱行业的人吸引过来。因此,议会议员的职务本质上将成为一种职业,和其他职业一样,担任这一职务的人主要想实现金钱上的获利,而且受到一种本质上不稳定的职业的令人泄气的影响。这一职务将成为低等阶级的冒险家们所期待的目标。658人占有着议会席位,而其他十倍或二十倍的人则指望着这种席位,通过对选民作一切承诺,真实的或虚假的,可能的或不可能的,并相互抢着鼓动最庸俗的那部分群众的最卑鄙的感情和最无知的成见,就会不间断地喊出高价来吸引或保有选民的选票。阿里斯托芬尼所刻画的克里昂(Cleon)和腊肠卖者之间的竞卖是对这种经常会发生的选举情形的一幅最好的讽刺漫画。这样一个制度,将是适用于人性的最邪恶部分的永恒腐蚀剂。这样一个制度相当于为他的同胞中一群最擅长阿谀奉承的人、最高明的骗子提供658个奖金。在任何专制政府下都不曾出现过这样一种制造大量邪恶的有组织的制作程序。① 当一个完全没有不论来自资产还是职业的独立收入的人,由于具备卓越的条件(这种情况随时都可能碰巧会存在的),应该被选进议会以便提供其他能进议会的人所无法提供的服务的时候,可以有公众捐款的办法;当他在议会时可以像安德鲁·马维尔

---

① 如洛里默先生所评论,给最低等阶级的人从事公共事务制造出金钱的诱惑,煽动家便正式亮相表演了。最应当抨击的,莫过于把促

of his constituents. This mode is unobjectionable, for such an honour will never be paid to mere subserviency: bodies of men do not care so much for the difference between one sycophant and another, as to go to the expense of his maintenance in order to be flattered by that particular individual. Such a support will only be given in consideration of striking and impressive personal qualities, which, though no absolute proof of fitness to be a national representative, are some presumption of it, and, at all events, some guarantee for the possession of an independent opinion and will.

---

gogue would be formally inaugurated. Nothing is more to be deprecated than making it the private interest of a number of active persons to urge the form of government in the direction of its natural perversion, The indications which either a multitude or an individual can give, when merely left to their own weaknesses, afford but a faint idea of what those weaknesses would become when played upon by a thousand flatterers. If there were 658 places of certain, however moderate, emolument, to be gained by persuading the multitude that ignorance is as good as knowledge, and better, it is terrible odds that they would believe and act upon the lesson,'—(Article in *Fraser's Magazine* for April 1859, headed 'Recent Writers on Reform.')

第十章

那样,获得他的选民捐款的支持。这种模式是不应反对的,因为绝不会赋予单纯的阿谀奉承者以这种荣誉。人们并不那么在乎这种人和那个拍马屁者之间的差别,因此不会太关注他的生活费用,以便获得这个人的奉承。只有在考虑到突出的和感人的个人品质时,像这样的支持才会被给予,这种品质尽管不是完全适宜担任国民代表的证明,但却成为这种情况的假定,至少成为具有独立观点和意愿的保证。

使走向自然恶化的政府形式演变为许多积极活动的民众的私人利益这件事。从无论是民众,还是个人所反映出的情况来看,只根据他们自身的弱点,就只能模糊认识到这些弱点被一千个奉承拍马屁的人利用时会变为怎样的情形。倘若要靠游说民众相信无知和有知一样好,甚至更好的话,才能获取 658 个有确定报酬(尽管是中等报酬)的职务,他们很可能会相信并遵照它来指导行动。"(《弗雷泽杂志》1859 年 4 月号中的论文,题目是"近时有关改革的作家。")

CHAPTER XI
Of The Duration Of Parliaments

After how long a term should members of parliament be subject to re-election ? The principles involved are here very obvious; the difficulty lies in their application. On the one hand, the member ought not to have so long a tenure of his seat as to make him forget his responsibility, take his duties easily, conduct them with a view to his own personal advantage, or neglect those free and public conferences with his constituents, which, whether he agrees or differs with them, are one of the benefits of representative government. On the other hand, he should have such a term of office to look forward to, as will enable him to be judged not by a single act, but by his course of action. It is important that he should have the greatest latitude of individual opinion and discretion, compatible with the popular control essential to free government ; and for this purpose it is necessary that the control should be exercised, as in any case it is best exercised, after sufficient time has been given him to show all the qualities he possesses, and to prove that there is some other way than that of a mere obedient voter and advocate of their opinions, by which he can render himself in the eyes of his constituents a desirable and creditable representative.

It is impossible to fix, by any universal rule, the boundary between these principles. Where the democratic power in the constitution is weak or overpassive, and requires stimulation; where the representative, on leaving his constituents, enters, at once into a courtly or aristocratic atmosphere, whose influences all tend to deflect his course into a different direction from the popular one, to tone down any democratic

第十一章　议会的期限

议会成员在多长的任期后就应当改选呢？它涉及的原则在这里是显而易见的，困难在于这些原则的应用。一方面，议员的任期不应当长到使他忘记了他的职责，从而漫不经心地对待他的职务，履行职务时以个人私利为目的，或忽视同他的选民进行自由而公开的协商。而这种协商，不管他对他们的意见同意与否，都是代议制政府的一种好处。另一方面，他应当有这样一个可以期望的任期，使人们能够根据他行为的过程，而不是根据某次单一的行动进行判断。重要的是，他应当拥有与自由政府不可缺少的群众监督相一致的最大程度的个人观点表达权和自由决断权。为此目的，就有必要使这种监督的行使可以像在其行使的任何最好的场合一样，给他充分的时间来展示他所具有的全部品质，并证明除了单纯作为顺从的投票人和选民意见的拥护者之外，他还有其他办法使自己变成选民眼中对其满意和值得信任的代表。

通过某个普遍规则是不可能确定这些原则的界线的。凡是政体中民主力量薄弱或过于消极、需要加以刺激的地方，凡是代表们离开了他们的选民之后就立刻进入到王室或贵族环境的地方，这种环境的影响都使他倾向于偏离民众的方向，使他身上可能具

feelings which he may have brought with him, and make him forget the wishes and grow cool to the interests of those who chose him; the obligation of a frequent return to them for a renewal of his commission, is indispensable to keeping his temper and character up to the right mark. Even three years, in such circumstances, are almost too long a period; and any longer term is absolutely inadmissible. Where, on the contrary, democracy is the ascendant power, and still tends to increase, requiring rather to be moderated in its exercise than encouraged to any abnormal activity; where unbounded publicity, and an ever-present newspaper press, give the representative assurance that his every act will be immediately known, discussed, and judged by his constituents, and that he is always either gaining or losing ground in their estimation —while by the same means, the influence of their sentiments, and all other democratic influences, are kept constantly alive and active in his own mind; less than five years would hardly be a sufficient period to prevent timid subserviency. The change which has taken place in English polities as to all these features, explains why annual parliaments, which forty years ago stood prominently in front of the creed of the more advanced reformers, are so little cared for and so seldom heard of at present. It deserves consideration, that, whether the term is short or long, during the last year of it the members are in the position in which they would always be if parliaments were annual : so that if the term is very brief, there would virtually be annual parliaments during a great proportion of all time. As things now are, the period of seven years, though of unnecessary length, is hardly worth altering for any benefit likely to be produced ; especially since the possibility, always impending, of an earlier dissolution, keeps the motives for standing well with constituents always before the member's eyes.

Whatever may be the term most eligible for the duration of the mandate, it might seem natural that the individual member should vacate his seat at the expiration of that term from the day of his election, and that there should be no general renewal of the whole House. A great deal might be said for this system, if there were any practical object in recommending it. But it is condemned by much stronger reasons than can be alleged in its support. One is, that there would be

第十一章

有的民主情感变得稀少,使他忘记那些选择他的选民的愿望并且对他们的利益变得冷漠的地方,经常进行选举以更新对他的委任,对使他的脾气和性格保持在正确的标准上是必不可少的。在这种情形下,即使是三年一任也显得有些过长,而更长的任期是绝对不允许的。相反,凡是在民主力量处于优势地位,并且仍然处于上升阶段,需要对它的行使加以节制而不是鼓励它达到不正常的活跃程度的地方,凡是极其公开,无处不在的新闻报刊使代表确信,他的任何行动都会为他的选民所了解、讨论和判断,并且他总是在他们的评价中要么提高地位,要么降低地位,而通过同样的手段,选民情绪的影响,以及其他一切的民主影响,都时常闪现在他的头脑中的地方,任期少于五年不足以防止胆小怕事、低声下气。在英国政治中发生的关于这些特征的变化,说明了为什么40年前那些先进的改革家们纲领中所坚持的每年一次的议会,到如今很少有人关心也很少有人提起。值得考虑的是,不管任期是长是短,在任期的最后一年,议员所处的地位与在假设议会每年召开一次时其所处的地位是一样的,所以,如果任期很短,在大部分时间里事实上就是年度议会。就当下而言,七年的任期,尽管有些过长,但也不值得为产生什么好处而加以改变,特别是由于总是有提前解散议会的可能,使得议员的心中总是保有博得选民好感的动机。

无论委任统治的任期持续多长才算是最合适的,很自然,议员在他自当选之日起就拥有的那个任期结束时,就应该腾出他的席位,并且不应该对整个下院的议员进行更换。如果有某个实际的目的要推荐这项制度的话,就可能要花很多笔墨来对它加以论述。但是对它进行责难的理由要比声称支持它的理由有力得多。其中

no means of promptly getting rid of a majority which had pursued a course offensive to the nation. The certainty of a general election after a limited, which would often be a nearly expired, period, and the possibility of it at any time when the minister either desires it for his own sake, or thinks that it would make him popular with the country, tend to prevent that wide divergence between the feelings of the assembly and those of the constituency which might subsist indefinitely if the majority of the House had always several years of their term still to run—if it received new infusions drop by drop, which would be more likely to assume than to modify the qualities of the mass they were joined to. It is as essential that the general sense of the House should accord in the main with that of the nation, as it is that distinguished individuals should be able, without forfeiting their seats, to give free utterance to the most unpopular sentiments. There is another reason, of much weight, against the gradual and partial renewal of a representative assembly. It is useful that there should be a periodical general muster of opposing forces, to gauge the state of the national mind, and ascertain, beyond dispute, the relative strength of different parties and opinions. This is not done conclusively by any partial renewal, even where, as in some of the French constitutions, a large fraction, a fifth or a third, go out at once.

The reasons for allowing to the executive the power of dissolution, will be considered in a subsequent chapter, relating to the constitution and functions of the Executive in a representative government.

一条理由就是,没有什么办法能迅速摆脱与国家舆论相抵触的多数意见。确定在有限的、常常是几乎到期的任期之后进行大选,以及当大臣要么为了自己的目的而希望进行大选,要么认为大选会使他在全国出名时,大选随时都有进行的可能性,这种情况都趋向于防止议会与选民之间情感分歧的加大。如果下院的多数总是还有几年任期的话——如果下院一点一点补充新成员的话,新成员更可能接受议院多数的特质而不是改变这些特质——这种分歧就可能无限期地存在下去。下院的认识应在大体上与国家舆论相一致,这与知名人士应能在不必担心失去其职位的情况下自由表达最不受欢迎的观点,是同样关键的。还有另外一条很有分量的反对逐步地、部分地更换议会议员的理由。为了探测国民的精神状况,以及毫无疑义地确定不同政党和意见的相对分量,对相互对立的力量进行周期性的检阅是有益的。不管进行何种部分的更新都无法完全做到这一点,即使像在法国的某些宪法条文中规定的那样,一大部分议员,占到五分之一或三分之一,同时去职也是这样。

关于允许行政机关拥有解散议会权力的理由,我们将在随后涉及到代议制政府中行政机关的构造和职能的章节中加以论述。

CHAPTER XII
Ought Pledges To Be Required From Members Of Parliament?

Should a member of the legislature be bound by the instruction of his constituents ? Should he be the organ of their sentiments, or of his own ? Their ambassador to a congress, or their professional agent, empowered not only to act for them, but to judge for them what ought to be done ? These two theories of the duty of a legislator in a representative government have each its supporters, and each is the recognised doctrine of some representative governments. In the Dutch United Provinces, the members of the States General were mere delegates; and to such a length was the doctrine carried, that when any important question arose which had not been provided for in their instructions, they had to refer back to their constituents, exactly as an ambassador does to the government from which he is accredited. In this and most other countries which possess representative constitutions, law and custom warrant a member of parliament in voting according to his opinion of right, however different from that of his constituents: but there is a floating notion of the opposite kind, which has considerable practical operation on many minds, even of members of parliament, and often makes them, independently of desire for popularity, or concern for their reelection, feel bound in conscience to let their conduct, on questions on which their constituents have a decided opinion, be the expression of that opinion rather than of their own. Abstractedly from positive law, and from the historical traditions of any particular people, which of these notions of the duty of a representative is the true one ?

第十二章 应当要求议会议员作出保证吗？

一个立法委员要不要受其委托人指示的约束呢？他应该是表达他们情感的喉舌呢，还是仅表达他自己的意见的喉舌？他是他们派往议会的代表呢，还是他们的职业代理人，即不仅拥有为他们行动的权力，而且拥有为他们判断应该做的事情的权力？这两种关于在代议制政府中立法者职责的理论都有它们的支持者，并且每种理论都是某些代议制政府所承认的学说。在荷兰联合省中，国会议员都只是单纯的代表，并且这种理论被贯彻到这样一种程度，即当没有经由选民指令规定的任何重要问题出现时，他们必须转而征询选民的意见，就像大使向任命他的政府所做的那样。在我们这个国家[1]和其他大部分拥有代议制制度的国家，法律和习惯授权其议员根据他认为正确的意见投票，而不管这种意见和他的选民的意见有多么大的不同。但是也有一种不很确定的相反的看法，它对很多人的头脑，甚至是议员，都会有相当大的实际作用，并且常常使他们——这与他们渴望名声和关心再次当选没有关系——感到受道德的约束，让他们在选民有确定意见的问题上使自己的行为表达选民的意见而不是表达他们自己的意见。抽象地从肯定性法律以及任何特定民族的历史传统来看，这些关于代表职责的观念哪一个是对的呢？

---

〔1〕 指英国。

Unlike the questions which we have hitherto treated, this is not a question of constitutional legislation, but of what may more properly be called constitutional morality—the ethics of representative government. It does not so much concern institutions, as the temper of mind which the electors ought to bring to the discharge of their functions ; the ideas which should prevail as to the moral duties of an elector. For, let the system of representation be what it may, it will be converted into one of mere delegation if the electors so choose. As long as they are free not to vote, and free to vote as they like, they cannot be prevented from making their vote depend on any condition they think fit to annex to it. By refusing to elect any one who will not pledge himself to all their opinions, and even, if they please, to consult with them before voting on any important subject not foreseen, they can reduce their representative to their mere mouthpiece, or compel him in honour, when no longer willing to act in that capacity, to resign his seat. And since they have the power of doing this, the theory of the constitution ought to suppose that they will wish to do it; since the very principle of constitutional government requires it to be assumed that political power will be abused to promote the particular purposes of the holder: not because it always is so, but because such is the natural tendency of things, to guard against which is the especial use of free institutions. However wrong, therefore, or however foolish, we may think it in the electors to convert their representative into a delegate, that stretch of the electoral privilege being a natural and not improbable one, the same precautions ought to be taken as if it were certain. We may hope that the electors will not act on this notion of the use of the suffrage ; but a representative government needs to be so framed that even if they do, they shall not be able to effect what ought not to be in the power of any body of persons—class legislation for their own benefit.

When it is said that the question is only one of political morality, this does not extenuate its importance. Questions of constitutional morality are of no less practical moment than those relating to the constitution itself. The very existence of some governments, and all that

第十二章

这和迄今我们所讨论的问题有所不同,这不是一个宪法上的立法问题,而是一个可以更恰当地被称为宪法上的道德问题,即代议制的伦理学问题。它与制度不太相关,而与选民在行使其职能时所应带有的精神气质相关;就他们的道德职责来说,应和占有主要地位的思想相关。因为,不管代议制体系是什么样子,它都可以被转换成一个单纯的代表团,如果选民会这样选择的话。只要他们有不投票的自由以及有按其意愿投票的自由,人们就不能阻止他们使其投票依赖于他们认为适合于附加其上的任何条件。通过拒绝选举那些不能保证顺从他们意志的人,甚至,只要他们高兴,通过拒绝在未预见的任何重要主题投票前不同他们商量的人,他们就能把他们的代表降格为单纯的传声筒,或者强迫他在不愿意那样做的时候放弃他的职位。因为他们有权这样做,宪法理论就应当假设他们会希望这样做,因为宪政政府的一个非常重要的原则是假定政治权力将会被促进权力拥有者的特殊目的而滥用。不是因为情形总是如此,而是因为这就是事物自然的趋向,防止这种趋向是自由制度的特殊用法。因此,不管我们认为选民将其代表转变为代表团是如何错误,或如何愚蠢,选举特权的这种延伸既然是自然的而不是不可能发生的,我们就应当按照好像它一定会发生那样采取防范措施。我们可只希望选民不会这样行使选举权;但是一个代议制政府需要这样架构,以便在即使选民这样做了时,他们也不能够做出任何当权团体都不能做的事情,即为他们自己的利益而进行阶级立法。

当人们说这个问题仅仅是一个政治道德问题时,也不能减轻它的重要性。宪法的道德问题的实际重要性并不亚于那些跟宪法本身相关的问题。某些政府的真实存在以及致使其他政府可

renders others endurable, rests on the practical observance of doctrines of constitutional morality; traditional notions in the minds of the several constituted authorities, which modify the use that might otherwise be made of their powers. In unbalanced governments—pure monarchy, pure aristocracy, pure democracy—such maxims are the only barrier which restrain the government from the utmost excesses in the direction of its characteristic tendency. In imperfectly balanced governments, where some attempt is made to set constitutional limits to the impulses of the strongest power, but where that power is strong enough to overstep them with at least temporary impunity, it is only by doctrines of constitutional morality, recognised and sustained by opinion, that any regard at all is preserved for the checks and limitations of the constitution. In well balanced governments, in which the supreme power is divided, and each sharer is protected against the usurpations of the others in the only manner possible—namely, by being armed for defence with weapons as strong as the others can wield for attack—the government can only be carried on by forbearance on all sides to exercise those extreme powers, unless provoked by conduct equally extreme on the part of some other sharer of power: and in this case we may truly say, that only by the regard paid to maxims of constitutional morality is the constitution kept in existence. The question of pledges is not one of those which vitally concern the existence of representative governments; but it is very material to their beneficial operation. The laws cannot prescribe to the electors the principles by which they shall direct their choice ; but it makes a great practical difference by what principles they think they ought to direct it. And the whole of that great question is involved in the inquiry, whether they should make it a condition that the representative shall adhere to certain opinions laid down for him by his constituents.

No reader of this treatise can doubt what conclusion, as to this matter, results from the general principles which it professes. We have from the first affirmed, and unvaryingly kept in view, the coequal importance of two great requisites of government: responsibility to those for whose benefit political power ought to be, and always professes to be, employed ; and jointly there-

第十二章

以让人忍受的一切，都有赖于对宪法道德学说的实际遵守；有赖于几个宪政政府理念中的传统观念，而这些观念制约着它们权力的行使。在非平衡的政府中，即纯粹的君主制，纯粹的贵族制，纯粹的民主制政府中，这些理念是抑制政府依其特有倾向而趋于极端的唯一措施。在不完善的平衡政府中，尽管人们进行了某种努力，设置宪法上的限制来约束最强大力量的冲动，但权力却强大到足以超越这些限制，至少短时期不会受到惩罚，只有通过由舆论公认和维持的宪法道德学说，才能对宪法中的约束和限制多少保持些尊重。在平衡得很好的政府中，其最高权力是分散的，每个权力分享者都在唯一可能的方式上不受其他权力所有者的篡夺——即用跟其他权力分享者所能用来攻击的武器一样强大的武器来进行武装——政府才可能对各方都保持克制，不行使极端的武力，除非受到了他方同样极端的行为的挑衅。这样，我们才能真正说，只有对宪法道德保持尊重，宪法才能得以继续存在。关于保证的问题，不是那些与代议制政府其的存在关系重大的事情中的一项，但对代议制政府的有益运作来说是非常重要的。法律不能为选民规定用以指导他们选择的原则，但选民认为他们应根据什么原则来指导他们的选择，就有实际上的很大不同。整个重大问题归结到一点，就是：他们是否应该把议员遵守选民为他规定的某些意见作为一项条件。

本文的读者不会有疑问，在这件事情上，本文所表明的一般原则将导致什么结果。我们从一开始就确信，并且在观念上一直坚持，政府有两大同等重要的条件，即对那些为了他们的利益应当，并且常常声称应当运用政治权力的人们负责；与此相联系，为了政府职能的发挥，而以最可能的方法来获取高等智力的好处，而这种

with, to obtain, in the greatest measure possible, for the function of government, the benefits of superior intellects, trained by long meditation and practical discipline to that special task. If this second purpose is worth attaining, it is worth the necessary price. Superior powers of mind and profound study are of no use, if they do not sometimes lead a person to different conclusions from those which are formed by ordinary powers of mind without study: and if it be an object to possess representatives in any intellectual respect superior to average electors, it must be counted upon that the representative will sometimes differ in opinion from the majority of his constituents, and that when he does, his opinion will be the oftenest right of the two. It follows, that the electors will not do wisely, if they insist on absolute conformity to their opinions, as the condition of his retaining his seat.

The principle is, thus far, obvious; but there are real difficulties in its application : and we will begin by stating them in their greatest force. If it is important that the electors should choose a representative more highly instructed than themselves, it is no less necessary that this wiser man should be responsible to them ; in other words, they are the judges of the manner in which he fufils his trust: and how are they to judge, except by the standard of their own opinions ? How are they even to select him in the first instance, but by the same standard ? It will not do to choose by mere brilliancy—by superiority of showy talent. The tests by which an ordinary man can judge beforehand of mere ability are very imperfect : such as they are, they have almost exclusive reference to the arts of expression, and little or none to the worth of what is expressed. The latter cannot be inferred from the former ; and if the electors are to put their own opinions in abeyance, what criterion remains to them of the ability to govern well ? Neither, if they could ascertain, even infallibly, the ablest man, ought they to allow him altogether to judge for them, without any reference to their own opinions. The ablest candidate may be a Tory, and the electors Liberals; or a Liberal, and they may be Tories.

第十二章

智力是经过长期的深思熟虑与对该项特殊任务的实际锻炼而形成的。如果这个第二目的有达到的价值,它就值得付出必要的代价。如果有时高超的思维与深刻的研究不能使一个人得出与普通思维不经研究就得出的结论不相同的结论,那么它们就没有什么作用了。并且如果选出在任何智力方面都要比普通选民优秀的代表是一个目标,那么就必须指望代表们的观点有时与选民的多数有所不同,而且如果这样,他的观点应该常常是两者中正确的意见。由此可知,如果选民坚持以绝对与他们意见相一致作为代表保持其席位的条件,那么他们这样做就是不明智的。

到这里,这个原则就很明显了,但是要将之贯彻下去却存在着现实的困难,因此我们将以讲述这种困难的充分含义作为开始。如果选民应当选择一个有着比他们更高学养的人作代表这一点很重要的话,那么这个更加聪慧的人就有必要对选民负责。换句话说,选民是他信用方式的裁判者。可是除了按照他们自己观点的标准外,他们又怎样判断呢?除了按照这同一标准外,甚至他们怎么全在最初就选择他呢?通过单纯的才华,即炫耀才能的优越感来选择是行不通的。被常人所依据来事先判断一个人单纯能力的那些检验标准是非常不完善的。例如,这些检验标准几乎无一例外地关注表达的技巧,而对所表达内容的价值却很少关心甚至不加关心。后者不能从前者中推导出来。如果选民将他们自己的观点暂时搁置一边,那么还有什么可以使他们判断管理得好坏的标准呢?即使他们能确认,甚至准确无误地确认最有能力的人,他们也不能允许他在丝毫不考虑他们意见的情况下代替他们判断。这个最有才华的人可能是一个托利党人,而选民可能是自由党人;或者他是自由党人,而选民是托利党

The political questions of the day may be Church questions, and he may be a High Churchman, or a Rationalist, while they may be Dissenters, or Evangelicals ; and *vice versâ*. His abilities, in these cases, might only enable him to go greater lengths, and act with greater effect, in what they may conscientiously believe to be a wrong course; and they may be bound by their sincere convictions, to think it more important that their representative should be kept, on these points, to what they deem the dictate of duty, than that they should be represented by a man of more than average abilities. They may also have to consider, not solely how they can be most ably represented, but how their particular moral position and mental point of view shall be represented at all. The influence of every mode of thinking which is shared by numbers, ought to be felt in the legislature : and the constitution being supposed to have made due provision that other and conflicting modes of thinking shall be represented likewise, to secure the proper representation for their own mode may be the most important matter which the electors on the particular occasion have to attend to. In some cases, too, it may be necessary that the representative should have his hands tied, to keep him true to their interest, or rather to the public interest as they conceive it. This would not be needful under a political system which assured them an indefinite choice of honest and unprejudiced candidates ; but under the existing system, in which the electors are almost always obliged, by the expenses of election and the general circumstances of society, to select their representative from persons of a station in life widely different from theirs, and having a different class interest, who will affirm that they ought to abandon themselves to his discretion ? Can we blame an elector of the poorer classes, who has only the choice among two or three rich men, for requiring from the one he votes for, a pledge to those measures which he considers as a test of emancipation from the class-interests of the rich ? It will, moreover, always happen to some members of the electoral body, to be obliged to accept the representative selected by a majority of their own side. But though a candidate of their own choosing would have no chance, their votes may be necessary to the success of the one chosen for them ; and their only means of exerting

第十二章

人。时下的政治问题也许是一个教会问题,他也许是个高教会派或唯理派的人,而选民则是非国教派者或福音主义者,反过来也一样。在这些情形下,他的才能,也许只能使他在选民良心上相信是错误的道路上走得更远或行动得更有效果;选民也许会由于自己的真诚信念而认为,重要的是他们的代表在这些问题上遵守他们认为是责任命令的事情,而不是他们应当由一个更有能力的人来代表。他们也许不得不考虑,不仅仅是他们如何最好地被代表,而是他们特殊的道德立场以及精神信仰如何得到代表。每一种由多数人所共有的思维模式都应在立法机关中有所影响,既然假定宪法对其他的和相互冲突的思维模式同样地凡以体现并对此作了应有的预先安排,那么确保他们自己的观点能得到代表就是选民在选定的场合必须留意的最重要的事情了。同样,在一些场合,也许有必要束缚代表们的手脚,以保证他真正代表选民的利益,或者确切地说保证他真正代表选民们所认为的公共利益。这在一个能够保证他们随意选择诚实而公正的候选人的政治体系下是没有必要的;但是在现存的体系里,选民们由于选举成本和社会一般环境的影响,几乎总是被迫要从身份与他们极不相同、阶级利益不一致的人群中选举他们的代表,那谁能肯定他们应当听任代表们去自由决断呢?一个只能从两到三个富人中选择一个代表的穷苦阶级的选举人,反反因为他要求所选的代表对他认为是试图摆脱富人阶级利益的那些措施提供保证,就要受到责备吗?而且,对某些选举团体的成员来说,会经常不得不接受由他们自己阵营里多数代表选举出来的代表。尽管他们自己所选定的候选人可能没有机会选上,他们的选票也许对于那些为他们的利益而选择的代表的成功是必要的,因而他们对他今后行为发生影响的唯

their share of influence on his subsequent conduct, may be to make their support of him dependent on his pledging himself to certain conditions.

These considerations and counter-considerations are so intimately interwoven with one another; it is so important that the electors should choose as their representatives wiser men than themselves, and should consent to be governed according to that superior wisdom, while it is impossible that conformity to their own opinions, when they have opinions, should not enter largely into their judgment as to who possesses the wisdom, and how far its presumed possessor has verified the presumption by his conduct; that it seems quite impracticable to lay down for the elector any positive rule of duty: and the result will depend, less on any exact prescription, or authoritative doctrine of political morality, than on the general tone of mind of the electoral body, in respect to the important requisite, of deference to mental superiority. Individuals, and peoples, who are acutely sensible of the value of superior wisdom, are likely to recognise it, where it exists, by others signs than thinking exactly as they do, and even in spite of considerable differences of opinion : and when they have recognised it they will be far too desirous to secure it, at any admissible cost, to be prone to impose their own opinion as a law upon persons whom they look up to as wiser than themselves. On the other hand, there is a character of mind which does not look up to any one ; which thinks no other person's opinion much better than its own, or nearly so good as that of a hundred or a thousand persons like itself. Where this is the turn of mind of the electors, they will elect no one who is not, or at least who does not profess to be, the image of their own sentiments, and will continue him no longer than while he reflects those sentiments in his conduct : and all aspirants to political honours will endeavour, as Plato says in the Gorgias, to fashion themselves after the model of the Demos, and make themselves as like to it as possible. It cannot be denied, that a complete democracy has a strong tendency to cast the sentiments of the electors in this mould. Democracy is not favourable to the reverential spirit. That it destroys reverence for mere social

第十二章

一办法,也许就是在他保证某些条件的前提下才对他表示支持。

　　这两方面的考虑如此紧密地相互交织在一起。它是如此重要,以至于选民们应当选择比他们自己更为睿智的人来作他们的代表,并且应当同意按照那个较高的智慧来统治自己。然而,在他们对哪个人具备这种智慧,以及用他的行为进行检验对它假定的拥有者这种假定到何种程度作出判断时,又不可能不在很大程度上考虑到和他们自己的观点(当他们有观点时)是否一致。为选民规定任何实际的义务规则是相当不切实际的。结果将不是依赖于任何确切的规定,或权威性的政治道德学说,而是依赖于有关尊重智力上的优越性这一重要条件方面的选民团体的一般思想状况。对更高智慧的价值异常敏感的个人以及民族,有可能通过它的迹象而非与他们想法完全一样来在这种智慧存在的地方识别它,甚至不管在观点上有多大的不同。并且当他们识别出它时,他们将以任何可以接受的代价去维护它,所以不会倾向于将他们自己的观点当成法律加诸于他们尊之为比他们自己更有智慧的人的头上。另一方面,人有一种不尊重任何其他人的性格,认为没有什么人的观点能比他自己的要高明,或几乎像和他自己那样的一百个人或一千个人的观点一样好。在一个选民性情就是如此的地方,选民们将不会选择那些不能代表,或至少没有明白表示能代表他们情感的人,并且只有他的行动中表现出那些情感时他们才继续支持他。这样,所有对政治荣誉有所企图的人,如同柏拉图在《高尔吉亚斯》中所说的那样,将会努力按照民众的样式去做,并且做得越像越好。不能否认,完全的民主政体有一种强烈的倾向,要把选民的情感塑造成这个样子。民主政治对可敬的精神是不利的。它对单纯的社会地位敬重

position must be counted among the good, not the bad part of its influences ; though by doing this it closes the principal *school* of reverence (as to merely human relations) which exists in society. But also democracy, in its very essence, insists so much more forcibly on the things in which all are entitled to be considered equally, than on those in which one person is entitled to more consideration than another, that respect for even personal superiority is likely to be below the mark. It is for this, among other reasons, I hold it of so much importance, that the institutions of the country should stamp the opinions of persons of a more educated class as entitled to greater weight than those of the less educated : and I should still contend for assigning plurality of votes to authenticated superiority of education, were it only to give the tone to public feeling, irrespective of any direct political consequences.

When there does exist in the electoral body an adequate sense of the extraordinary difference in value between one person and another, they will not lack signs by which to distinguish the persons whose worth for their purposes is the greatest. Actual public services will naturally be the foremost indication : to have filled posts of magnitude, and done important things in them, of which the wisdom has been justified by the results ; to have been the author of measures which appear from their effects to have been wisely planned ; to have made predictions which have been often verified by the event, seldom or never falsified by it; to have given advice, which when taken has been followed by good consequences, when neglected, by bad. There is doubtless a large portion of uncertainty in these signs of wisdom; but we are seeking for such as can be applied by persons of ordinary discernment. They will do well not to rely much on any one indication, unless corroborated by the rest ; and in their estimation of the success or merit of any practical effort, to lay great stress on the general opinion of disinterested persons conversant with the subject matter. The tests which I have spoken of are only applicable to tried men; among whom must be reckoned those who, though untried practically,

第十二章

的破坏必须被算做是好的方面,而不是坏的方面;尽管这样做了它就关闭了存在于社会中的,培养敬重精神的主要学校(仅就人类关系而言)。但同样是民主政治,就其真正本质而言,更加强有力坚持的是一切人有权被平等看待的那些事情,而不是那些一个人有权被看作是比另一个人更值得考虑的事情,甚至对个人优越性的尊重似乎也是不够标准的。除其他理由外,正因为这样,我认为这个国家的制度应该让受过更多教育的阶级成员的观点,拥有比那些受教育较少的阶级成员的观点更多的分量,并且我仍然坚持要给经过鉴定证明受过较高教育的人以相对多数票,即使它仅仅是为了把这种论调诉诸公众舆论,而不管任何直接的政治后果。

当在选举团体中确实存在足够的意识,意识到人与人之间在价值上存在着非同寻常的差别时,他们将会从一些迹象判别出对他们的目的来说具有最大价值的人们。目前的公众服务将自然而然地成为最主要的迹象:担任了重要职位,在职位上做了重要工作,其结果证明了这种智慧;成为方法的创造者,这些方法从其结果来看是经过了明智的筹划的;作出一些常常由事件检验是正确而很少或绝非伪造的预测;提出意见,当这些意见被采纳后会产生好的结果,而被忽视时,结果就是糟糕的。毫无疑问,在这些智慧迹象中存在着大量的不确定因素,但是我们寻找的是能被那些只具有肉眼凡胎的人加以运用的迹象。他们最好不要对某种迹象依赖过多,除非它被其余的迹象所证实;他们在对成功或任何实际努力的价值进行评估时,对熟悉事务而又不偏私的人们的一般意见加以重视。我所提到的检验方法只可适用于受过考验的人士,在他们中间必须包括那些尽管在实践上没有经过考验,但在

have been tried speculatively; who, in public speech or in print, have discussed public affairs in a manner which proves that they have given serious study to them. Such persons may, in the mere character of political thinkers, have exhibited a considerable amount of the same titles to confidence as those who have been proved in the position of practical statesmen. When it is necessary to choose persons wholly untried, the best criteria are, reputation for ability among those who personally know them, and the confidence placed and recommendations given by persons already looked up to. By tests like these, constituencies who sufficiently value mental ability, and eagerly seek for it, will generally succeed in obtaining men beyond mediocrity, and often men whom they can trust to carry on public affairs according to their unfettered judgment; to whom it would be an affront to require that they should give up that judgment at the behest of their inferiors in knowledge. If such persons, honestly sought, are not to be found, then indeed the electors are justified in taking other precautions; for they cannot be expected to postpone their particular opinions, unless in order that they may be served by a person of superior knowledge to their own. They would do well, indeed, even then, to remember, that when once chosen, the representative, if he devotes himself to his duty, has greater opportunities of correcting an original false judgment, than fall to the lot of most of his constituents; a consideration which generally ought to prevent them (unless compelled by necessity to choose some one whose impartiality they do not fully trust) from exacting a pledge not to change his opinion, or, if he does, to resign his seat. But When an unknown person, not certified in unmistakable terms by some high authority, is elected for the first time, the elector cannot be expected not to make, conformity to his own sentiments the primary requisite. It is enough if he does not regard a subsequent change of those sentiments, honestly avowed, with its grounds undisguisedly stated, as a peremptory reason for withdrawing his confidence.

Even Supposing the most tried ability and acknowledged eminence of character in the representative, the private opinions of the

第十二章

理论上却受过考验的人,他们在公开演讲或出版物中讨论过公共事务,这在某种意义上证明他们对这些事务进行过认真的研究。这样的人士,单纯以政治思想家的性质,显示出了与那些在政治实践中被证明了的人一样相当有资格受到信任。当有必要选择完全没有受过考验的人时,最好的标准是他在那些知道他的人当中拥有才能方面的名望,以及由那些德高望重的人士所给予的信任和推荐。通过这样的检验,那些充分重视和急切寻求知识能力的选民一般是能够成功地得到才识过人的人才的,这些人通常是选民能够将公共事务委托他们,让他们自由裁决的人;对他们来说,要求他们按照知识水平不如他们的人的盼咐放弃自己的判断,将会是一种侮辱。如果经过真心实意地寻找没有找到这样的人,那么选民选择其他的防范措施就是正当的了。因为除非他们可以受到比他们更有学识的人的服务,否则不能指望他们将自己特定的意见放在次要的位置上。确实,即使那样,他们也会很好地记住,代表一旦被选出来,如果他忠于职守,就有更多的机会来改正最初的错误判断,而不是由他的大多数选民来决定他怎么做;这种考虑一般说来,应当阻止他的选民要求代表作出不改变他观点的保证,或者如果他改变了观点就要有辞职的保证(除非选民因为有必要而不得不选择一个其公正性并没有得到充分信任的人)。但是当一个没有经过某个高级权威承认的不出名的人第一次当选时,人们不能期望选民不把他们自己的观点当成首要条件。只要他不把后来经过诚实公开宣布的观点(其立场已经公开说明过了)看作是一种断然收回信任的理由,那就够了。

即使假定代表具备最可靠的才能和公认的杰出品质,选民个

electors are not to be placed entirely in abeyance. Deference to mental superiority is not to go the length of self-annihilation —abnegation of any personal opinion. But when the difference does not relate to the fundamentals of politics, however decided the elector may be in his own sentiments, he ought to consider that when an able man differs from him there is at least a considerable chance of his being in the wrong, and that even if otherwise, it is worth while to give up his opinion in things not absolutely essential, for the sake of the inestimable advantage of having an able man to act for him in the many matters in which he himself is not qualified to form a judgment. In such cases he often endeavours to reconcile both wishes, by inducing the able man to sacrifice his own opinion on the points of difference: but, for the able man to lend himself to this compromise is treason against his especial office; abdication of the peculiar duties of mental superiority, of which it is one of the most sacred not to desert the cause which has the clamour against it, nor to deprive of his services those of his opinions which need them the most. A man of conscience and known ability should insist on full freedom to act as he in his own judgment deems best ; and should not consent to serve on any other terms. But the electors are entitled to know how he means to act; what opinions, on all things which concern his public duty, he intends should guide his conduct. If some of these are unacceptable to them, it is for him to satisfy them that he nevertheless deserves to be their representative; and if they are wise, they will overlook, in favour of his general value, many and great differences between his opinions and their own. There are some differences, however, which they cannot be expected to overlook. Whoever feels the amount of interest in the government of his country which befits a freeman, has some convictions on national affairs which are like his life-blood ; which the strength of his belief in their truth, together with the importance he attaches to them, forbid him to make a subject of compromise, or postpone to the judgment of any person however greatly his superior. Such convictions when they exist in a people, or in any appreciable portion of one, are entitled to influence in virtue of their

第十二章

人的观点也不能完全置之不理。尊重智力上的卓越并不意味着要自我放弃即放弃任何个人观点。但当分歧与政治的基本原理没有关系时,不管选民多么坚决地坚持自己的观点,他应当考虑到当一个能人与他不同时,极有可能他自己的观点是错误的,即使不是这样,为了获得让能人在很多他没有能力作出判断的领域替他决策这一非凡的好处,在一些并非绝对关键的事情上放弃自己的观点是值得的。在这种情况下,他常常通过努力诱导能人在分歧点上牺牲自己的观点来调和这两种愿望。但是对能人来说,使自己接受这种妥协就是对他特殊职责的背叛,放弃自己智力优越性所负的特殊责任,这些责任中最为神圣的就是在舆论喧嚣反对的情况下不放弃自己对事业的追求,也不使他那些最可以用来服务的观点得不到表达的机会。一个有良知和才华的人应当坚持要求有充分的自由来根据自己判断是最好的那样去行动,而不应该同意按任何其他的条件来服务。但是选民有资格知道他想要怎样去做,在一切涉及他公共职责范围的事情上,他打算用什么观念来指导他的行动。如果有些观点他们不能接受,那么他就有必要去说服他们,让他们相信他仍然值得做他们的代表;如果他们明智的话,他们将由于他所具有的普遍价值而忽略彼此在观点上的许多巨大分歧。然而,也有些分歧是不能指望他们加以忽略的。凡是感觉到了国家政府中的对一个自由人有利的那部分利益的人,在国家事务方面都具有像他的鲜血一样珍贵的信念;他强烈相信这些信念就是真理,也认为这些信念很重要,这使他不能做任何妥协,或把它们摆在次于任何人意见的地位,不管这个人比他地位高多少。当一个民族或一个民族相当多的部分存有这样的信念时,这些信念借助它们本身的单纯

mere existence, and not solely in that of the probability of their being grounded in truth. A people cannot be well governed in opposition to their primary notions of right, even though these may be in some points erroneous. A correct estimate of the relation which should subsist between governors and governed, does not require the electors to consent to be represented by one who intends to govern them in opposition to their fundamental convictions. If they avail themselves of his capacities of useful service in other respects, at a time when the points on which he is vitally at issue with them are not likely to be mooted, they are justified in dismissing him at the first moment when a question arises involving these, and on which there is not so assured a majority for what they deem right, as to make the dissenting voice of that particular individual unimportant. Thus (I mention names to illustrate my meaning, not for any personal application) the opinions supposed to be entertained by Mr. Cobden and Mr. Bright on resistance to foreign aggression, might be overlooked during the Crimean war, when there was an overwhelming national feeling on the contrary side, and might yet very properly lead to their rejection by the electors at the time of the Chinese quarrel (though in itself a more doubtful question), because it was then for some time a moot point whether their view of the case might not prevail.

As the general result of what precedes, we may affirm that actual pledges should not be required, unless, from unfavourable social circumstances or faulty institutions, the electors are so narrowed in their choice, as to be compelled to fix it on a person presumptively under the influence of partialities hostile to their interest: That they are entitled to a full knowledge of the political opinions and sentiments of the candidate; and not only entitled, but often bound, to reject one who differs from themselves on the few articles which are the foundation of their political belief: That in proportion to the opinion they entertain of the mental superiority of a candidate, they ought to put up with his expressing and acting on opinions different from theirs on any number of things not included in their fundamental articles of belief:

存在,而不仅仅是凭借它们建立在真理之上的可能性,就足以发挥影响。一个民族在遭到统治时其基本权利理念是不能被践踏的,即使这些理念在某些方面是错误的。一个对应当存在于统治者和被统治者之间的关系的正确评价,是不会要求选民同意由一个打算在违反他们根本信念的情况下进行统治的人来做他们的代表。如果他们想要利用他在其他方面提供有用服务的能力时恰好同时他与他们之间的重大分歧很难得到解决,这时他们就有权在涉及这些分歧的一个问题出现,并且在这个问题上还没有一个肯定的多数来支持他们认为正确的东西,使特定个人的意见变得无足轻重的时候,解除他的职务。因此(我在这里提到一些人名是为了说明问题,而不是针对个人的褒贬)那些被认为是为科布登先生和布莱特先生所支持的关于反抗外国入侵的观点在克里米亚战争期间就可能被忽视,在那时,在相反的一面存在着一种压倒性的民族感情,并且在与中国争吵期间(尽管其本身是一个更值得怀疑的问题)这种意见还可能完全导致选民对他们的排斥,因为在当时,他们对这个问题的看法是否就不占优势,还是个值得讨论的问题。

作为上述讨论的一般结论,我们可以肯定,除非由于不利的社会环境或不完善的制度,选民的选择范围被缩小到如此地步,以至于不得不选择一个据推测是被敌视他们利益的偏见所影响的人,否则就不应该要求候选人做实际的保证。他们有权对候选人的政治观点和感情有充分的了解;并且不仅有权,而且必须经常否决一个在作为他们政治信仰基础的少数信条上与他们意见分歧的人;他们越是接受候选人智力上的优越性,就越应当容忍他无论在多少事情上表达与他

That they ought to be unremitting in their search for a representative of such calibre as to be entrusted with full power of obeying the dictates of his own judgment: That they should consider it a duty which they owe to their fellowcountrymen, to do their unmost towards placing men of this quality in the legislature; and that it is of much greater importance to themselves to be represented by such a man, than by one who professes agreement in a greater number of their opinions: for the benefits of his ability are certain, while the hypothesis of his being wrong and their being right on the points of difference is a very doubtful one.

I have discussed this question on the assumption that the electoral system, in all that depends on positive institution, conforms to the principles laid down in the preceding chapters. Even on this hypothesis, the delegation theory of representation seems to me false, and its practical operation hurtful, though the mischief would in that case be confined within certain bounds. But if the securities by which I have endeavoured to guard the representative principle are not recognised by the Constitution; if provision is not made for the representation of minorities, nor any difference admitted in the numerical value of votes according to some criterion of the amount of education possessed by the voters; in that case no words can exaggerate the importance in principle of leaving an unfettered discretion to the representative; for it would then be the only chance, under universal suffrage, for any other opinions than those of the majority to be heard in Parliament. In that falsely called democracy which is really the exclusive rule of the operative classes, all others being unrepresented and unheard, the only escape from class legislation in its narrowest and political ignorance in its most dangerous, form, would lie in such disposition as the uneducated might have to choose educated representatives, and to defer to their opinions. Some willingness to do this might reasonably be expected, and everything would depend upon cultivating it to the highest point. But, once invested with political omnipotence, if the

第十二章

们不同的观点而这些观点只要不与他基本的政治信条相冲突即可;他们应当不懈地寻找这样一个具有才能,可以被授以权力而且只根据自己的判断行事的人来做代表;他们应当将之看作是必须为他们同胞所尽的一项义务,就是要尽他们最大的努力把具备这种品质的人选入立法机关;对他们来说,由这样的人做代表较之由一个声称在许多问题上与他们持同一立场的人做代表要重要得多。因为他的才能所能带来的好处是确定的,而在分歧方面,假定他是错误的而他们是对的,则是一个很值得怀疑的事情。

我已经基于这样一个假设讨论了这个问题,即在一切以实际制度为依据的问题上,选举体系与前面章节所设定的原则是一致的。即使是基于这一假设,在我看来,认为代表是使节的理论也是错误的,并且它在实践上是有害的,尽管在那种场合里,危害将被限制在某个确定的范围内。但是如果我用来努力捍卫代议制原则的防卫措施得不到宪法的承认;如果没有为少数的代表权规定措施,也不容许根据选民的受教育程度来在选票数量上做出区别;那样的话,让代表拥有自由裁量权的原则其重要性怎样夸大也不为过,因为那样一来将是在普遍选举制下的唯一机会让多数人的观点以外的观点在议会中得以表达;在那种虚假地称为民主而实际上却是执政阶级进行排他统治的制度下,所有其他人既没人代表又不能表达意见,避免以最狭隘方式进行阶级立法和最危险的政治无知形式的唯一方法,可能就存在于这样的安排中,即没受过教育的人可能不得不选择受过教育的人做代表,并尊重他们的观点。人们理所当然愿意这样去做,但一切取决于把这种意愿培养到最高的程度。但是,

operative classes voluntarily concurred in imposing upon themselves in this or any other manner, any considerable limitation to their self-opinion and self-will, they would prove themselves wiser than any class, possessed of absolute power, has shown itself, or, we may venture to says is ever likely to show itself, under that corrupting influence.

一旦执政阶级被赋予政治上的无限权力,如果执政阶级自愿同意以这样或那样的方式对他们自己的自负和固执加以相当大的束缚的话,他们将证明自己要比在腐败影响下出现过的,或者我们可以冒昧地说,可能出现的任何拥有绝对权力的阶级更加明智。

CHAPTER XIII
Of A Second Chamber

OF all topics relating to the theory of representative government, none have been the subject of more discussion, especially on the Continent, than what is known as the question of the Two Chambers. It has occupied a greater amount of the attention of thinkers than many questions of ten times its importance, and has been regarded as a sort of touchstone which distinguishes the partisans of limited from those of uncontrolled democracy. For my own part, I set little value on any check which a Second Chamber can apply to a democracy otherwise unchecked; and I am inclined to think that if all other constitutional questions are rightly decided, it is of comparatively little importance whether the Parliament consists of two Chambers, or only of one.

If there are two Chambers, they may either be of similar, or of dissimilar composition. If of similar, both will obey the same influences, and whatever has a majority in one of the Houses will be likely to have it in the other. It is true that the necessity of obtaining the consent of both to the passing of any measure may at times be a material obstacle to improvement, since, assuming both the Houses to be representative, and equal in their numbers, a number slightly exceeding a fourth of the entire representation may prevent the passing of a Bill; while, if there is but one House, a Bill is secure of passing if it has a bare majority. But the case supposed is rather abstractedly possible than likely to occur in practice. It will not often happen that of two Houses similarly composed, one will be almost unanimous, and the other

第十三章 关于第二院

在涉及代议制政府理论的所有话题中,尤其是在欧洲大陆,再也没有比对通常被叫做两院问题的这个话题探讨得更多的了。与其他诸多较它重要十倍的问题相比,这个涉及到两院的问题更是占用了思想家们的大量精力,并且这个问题被视为是一个区分标准,即区分提倡有限制的民主还是提倡无限制的民主的人士的一个标准。就我个人来说,对第二院能对民主施加一种限制,否则,民主便会是不受限制的这样一种看法,是颇不以为然的。我反倒认为,如果所有其他的宪法问题都能正确地得以解决,那么,究竟是由两院组成还只是由一院组成议会,就只是个次要的问题。

如果有两个院,那么,它们的组成要么是一样的要么是不一样的。如果组成一样,两者将顺从同一势力,只要是在其中一院占据多数,在另一院大概也能占据多数。的确,任何议案的通过必须得到两院的赞成,这一种做法时常是改革的重大障碍,因为假定两院都是代议制,代表数量又一样,则稍微超过全部代表的四分之一就可以使法案不能获得通过;反之,如果只存在一院,获得了勉勉强强的超过半数,就确保可以通过法案。但假设的这种情形与其说会在现实中会发生,毋宁说说只是抽象的可能。同样组成的两院中,一院基本上是意见一致的,而另一院差不多是

nearly equally divided: if a majority in one rejects a measure, there will generally have been a large minority unfavourable to it in the other ; any improvement, therefore, which could be thus impeded, would in almost all cases be one which had not much more than a simple majority in the entire body, and the worst consequence that could ensue would be to delay for a short time the passing of the measure, or give rise to a fresh appeal to the electors to ascertain if the small majority in Parliament corresponded to an effective one in the country. The inconvenience of delay, and the advantage of the appeal to the nation, might be regarded in this case as about equally balanced.

I attach little weight to the argument oftenest urged for having two Chambers—to prevent precipitancy, and compel a second deliberation; for it must be a very ill-constituted representative assembly in which the established forms of business do not require many more than two deliberations. The consideration which tells most, in my judgment, in favour of two Chambers (and this I do regard as of some moment) is the evil effect produced upon the mind of any holder of power, whether an individual or an assembly, by the consciousness of having only themselves to consult. It is important that no set of persons should be able, even temporarily, to make their *sic volo* prevail, without asking any one else for his consent. A majority in a single assembly, when it has assumed a permanent character—when composed of the same persons habitually acting together, and always assured of victory in their own House—easily becomes despotic and overweening, if released from the necessity of considering whether its acts will be concurred in by another constituted authority. The same reason which induced the Romans to have two consuls, makes it desirable there should be two Chambers ; that neither of them may be exposed to the corrupting influence of undivided power, even for the space of a single year. One of the most indispensable requisites in the practical conduct of politics, especially in the management of free institutions,

第十三章

势均力敌的,这样的情形是不常出现的。实际情形是,如果一项议案在其中一院被否决,那么,通常说来,在另一院中将存在一支很大的少数派不赞同该议案。因此,能如此被阻止的改革议案,在差不多所有的情况下,将不会获得比整个议会的简单多数更多的票,紧接着出现的最糟糕的结果可能是,使议案的通过延误一段短时间,或者被再一次诉诸选民,以确定议会中的小小多数是否和国家中的有效的多数相当。在这种情形下,延误的不便和诉诸选民的好处可以被视为是大致对等的。

对于设立两院制是为了预防草率,并迫使作第二次考虑这样一种被频繁地提出来支持两院制的论点,我是不怎么重视的。如果它所确立的运作方式没有要求大大超过两次考虑的话,那么这个代议制议会一定是极不完善的。就我自己来说,能支持两院制的最有说服力的理由(而这一点我认为的确是有点重要怯的)是由于意识到只能和自己商量,因而在掌权者心中产生了坏的效果,无论这个掌权者是一个人还是一个议会。重要的是,任何一帮人都不应该在重大事情上,即使是暂时地,使他们自己的意见处于优势地位,而不寻求任何其他人的赞同。在只有一院的议会中的多数,当它获得永久性质的时候,即当它由习惯地在一起工作的同样一些人组成,并始终保证他们在自己的议院中的胜利的时候,很容易变得专制和自负,如果没有必要去考虑它的行动是否要获得另一法定权威的一致同意的话。促使古罗马人设立两个执政官的同一理由,使得两院的存在成为值得期待的:其中任何一个都不会受到专制的腐败势力的影响,即使只在是一年的时间内。在实际的政治管理中,特别是在管理自由制度方面,最不可或缺的条件之一就是和解,即妥协的意愿。也就是

is conciliation; a readiness to compromise ; a willingness to concede something to opponents, and to shape good measures so as to be as little offensive as possible to persons of opposite views; and of this salutary habit, the mutual give-and-take (as it has been called) between two Houses is a perpetual school; useful as such even now, and its utility would probably be even more felt in a more democratic constitution of the Legislature.

But the Houses need not both be of the same composition ; they may be intended as a check on one another. One being supposed democratic, the other will naturally be constituted with a view to its being some restraint upon the democracy. But its efficacy in this respect wholly depends on the social support which it can command outside the House. An assembly which does not rest on the basis of some great power in the country is ineffectual against one which does. An aristocratic House is only powerful in an aristocratic state of society, The House of Lords was once the strongest power in our Constitution, and the Commons only a checking body: but this was when the Barons were almost the only power out of doors. I cannot believe that, in really democratic state of society, the House of Lords would be of any practical value as a moderator of democracy. When the force on one side is feeble in comparison with that on the other, the way to give it effect is not to draw both out in line, and muster their strength in open field over against one another. Such tactics would ensure the utter defeat of the less powerful. It can only act to advantage, by not holding itself apart, and compelling every one to declare himself either with or against it, but taking a position among, rather than in opposition to, the crowd, and drawing to itself the elements most capable of allying themselves with it on any given point; not appearing at all as an antagonist body, to provoke a general rally against it, but working as one of the elements in a mixed mass, infusing its leaven, and often making what would be the weaker part the stronger, by the addition of its influence. The really moderating power in a democratic constitution must act in and through the democratic House.

That there should be, in every polity, a centre of resistance to

第十三章

愿意对反对的一方作出一些让步,并制定出好的方案从而尽可能少地去冒犯持反对意见的一方。两院之间的互让(如人们所说的)是这一有益习惯的永恒学校。作为这样一种学校,这种互让甚至到现在还是有用的,在一个构成成分更加民主的议会中,它的效用也许会更加明显地被感觉到。

但是两院不需要一样的组成,它们可以充当对彼此的一种制衡。其中一院的组成假定具有民主性,而自然地另一院组成的目的是在于对民主施加某种限制。但它在这方面的效用完全取决于它能在议院外获得的社会支持。一个并非植根于国内某种强大力量基础之上的议院,对一个植根于这种基础之上的议院是发挥不了什么作用的。只有在贵族制的社会状态中,一个贵族制议院才是强有力的。上院曾一度成为我们政体中最强大的力量,而下院只是一个制衡团体。但这是发生在贵族几乎是社会上唯一力量的时候。我不相信,在真正民主的社会状态中,充当民主政治调解者的上院会有任何实际价值。当一方的势力比另一方弱的时候,使它发生作用的做法不是把双方队伍进行集合,在战场上互相垒一决高低。这种策略必然使得较弱的一方彻底失败。较弱一方唯一有利的做法是不要把自己和群众相隔离,去强迫每个人表态是支持它还是反对它,而是采取一种站在群众之中而不是和群众相对立的立场,对于在任何一个要点上能和自己联合的人,就把他们吸引到自己里面,一点也不表现为对抗团体而引发普遍的反对,而是作为混合在一起的群众中的一员进行活动,注入它的酵母,通过扩大它的势力,使它的作用由弱变强。民主政体中的真正调解力量,必须在民主议院中并通过民主议院才能产生作用。

在每一种政体里都应该存在一个抵抗宪法上占优势力量的中

the predominant power in the Constitution—and in a democratic constitution, therefore, a nucleus of resistance to the democracy —I have already maintained; and I regard it as a fundamental maxim of government. If any people, who possess a democratic representation, are, from their historical antecedents, more willing to tolerate such a centre of resistance in the form of a Second Chamber or House of Lords than in any other shape, this constitutes a strong reason for having it in that shape. But it does not appear to me the best shape in itself, nor by any means the most efficacious for its object. If there are two Houses, one considered to represent the people, the other to represent only a class, or not to be representative at all, I cannot think that where democracy is the ruling power in society, the second House would have any real ability to resist even the aberrations of the first. It might be suffered to exist, in deference to habit and association, but not as an effective check. If it exercised an independent will, it would be required to do so in the same general spirit as the other House; to be equally democratic with it, and to content itself with correcting the accidental oversights of the more popular branch of the legislature, or competing with it in popular measures.

The practicability of any real check to the ascendancy of the majority, depends henceforth on the distribution of strength in the most popular branch of the governing body : and I have indicated the mode in which, to the best of my judgment, a balance of forces might most advantageously be established there. I have also pointed out, that even if the numerical majority were allowed to exercise complete predominance by means of a corresponding majority in Parliament, yet if minorities also are permitted to enjoy the equal bright due to them on strictly democratic principles, of being represented proportionally to their numbers , this provision will ensure the perpetual presence in the House, by the same popular title as its other members, of so many of the first intellects in the country, that without being in any way banded apart, or invested with any invidious prerogative, this portion of the national representation will have a personal weight much more than in proportion to its numerical strength, and will afford, in a most effective form, the moral centre of resistance which is needed.

第十三章

心——从而在民主政体中应该存在一个抵抗民主的核心——我已经主张过这种观点了,而且我把它视为政府管理的一个基本准则。如果拥有民主代表制的历史经历民众更愿意忍受第二院或上院这种形式的抵抗中心,而不是其他形式,这就会形成一种强有力的理由使得抵抗中心具有第二院这种形式。但就我看来,在本质上,它并不是最好的形式,就它的目的来说,它也绝不是最有效的。如果存在两院,其中一院被认为是代表人民,另一院只是代表一个阶级,或者根本不具代表性,我认为在民主政治占社会统治地位的地方,甚至在第一院偏离轨道时,第二院也不会有进行反抗的真正能力。作为对习惯和同僚关系的尊重,它可能被容许存在,而不是发挥出一种有效的规制作用。如果第二院要行使独立的意志,它就应该遵循和另一院同样的普遍精神去做;必须和后者一样地民主,并满足于修正议会中更有着大众性的那个部门的一些意外疏忽,或者在符合民众需求的议案方面和它进行竞争。

对多数的统治地位进行任何真正制衡的实际可能性,今后将视统治机构中最有大众性的那个部门内部的实力分配而定。根据我的判断,我已经指出了最易于建立起实力平衡的那种模式。我还曾指出,即便基于在议会中相应的多数,而允许人数上的多数拥有完全的优越地位,但如果少数也被许可享有同等权利,即遵循严格的民主原则理应享有的按人数比例选出代表的同等权利,这一规定就将确保这个国家许许多多的第一流的有智有谋之士——和其他议员一样以民众的名义——永远出席议会。我还说,这部分民众代表,在既没有结成单独的帮派,也不具有任何易招妒嫉的特权的情况下,他们将拥有比按照人数比例大得多的个人分量,并且,将以最有效的方式提供所需要的道德层面的抵制

A second Chamber, therefore, is not required for this purpose, and would not contribute to it, but might even, in some conceivable modes, impede its attainment. If, however, for the other reasons aleady mentioned, the decision were taken that there should be such a Chamber, it is desirable that it should be composed of elements which, without being, open to the imputation of class interests adverse to the majority, would incline it to oppose itself to the class interests of the majority, and qualify it to raise its voice with authority against their errors and weaknesses. These conditions evidently are not found in a body constituted in the manner of our House of Lords. So soon as conventional rank and individual riches no longer overawe the democracy, a House of Lords becomes insignificant.

Of all principles on which a wisely conservative body, destined to moderate and regulate democratic ascendancy, could possibly be constructed, the best seems to be that exemplified in the Roman Senate, itself the most consistently prudent and sagacious body that ever administered public affairs. The deficiencies of a democratic assembly, which represents the general public, are the deficiencies of the public itself, want of special training and knowledge. The appropriate corrective is to associate with it a body of which special training and knowledge should be the characteristics. If one House represents popular feeling, the other should represent personal merit, tested and guaranteed by actual public service, and fortified by practical experience. If one is the People's Chamber, the other should be the Chamber of Statesmen ; a council composed of all living public men who have passed through important political offices or employments. Such a chamber would be fitted for much more than to be a merely moderating body. It would not be exclusively a check, but also an impelling force. In its hands, the power of holding the people back would be vested in those most competent, and who would generally be most inclined, to lead them forward in any right course. The council to whom the task would be entrusted of rectifying the people's mistakes, would not represent a class believed to be opposed to their interest, but would consist of their own natural leaders in the path of progress.

第十三章

中心。所以，为了这个目的去设立第二院，这并不需要。而且，对于该目的的实现，设立第二院非但无济于事，反而可能在某些可以想象的情况下，对这一目的的实现甚至会产生妨碍。然而，如果为了我已提及到的其他的理由，决定设立第二院，就期待它由这样一些人组成，由于这些人不牵涉到和多数相对立的任何阶级利益，就使它易于反对多数的阶级利益，并有资格对多数的过失和缺点作有力的评判。在遵循我们上院这种形式组成的团体中，显然是无法满足这些条件的。只要世袭地位和个人财富不再对民主政治产生威慑力，上院也就变得无足轻重了。

在可能借以创立一个缓和和调节民主优势的明智的保守团体的原则中，古罗马的元老院这一例子中所具有的原则似乎是最好的原则。在管理公共事务方面，元老院是曾经出现过的最为善始善终的谨慎而有远见的团体。代表公众的民主议会的缺点就是公众自身的缺点，也就是缺乏特殊训练和知识。适当的补救措施，就是把它和一个以特殊训练和知识为其特点的团体联合在一起。如果一个议院代表着民众诉求的话，另一个就必须代表着个人美德，这种美德是经过实际公共服务的检验和保证，并通过实际经验而得以强化形成的。如果一个是人民的议院的话，另一个就必须是政治家的议院——一个由经过了重要政治职位或雇用关系的一切起作用的政治活动家组成的委员会。这样的议院绝非只是适于作为一个单纯的调解团体。它将不只是一种制衡力量，更是一种促进力量。它手中掌握的限制民众的权力将被赋予那些最有能力，并且通常说来最愿意领导民众沿着正确道路前进的人。赋予修正民众错误的职责的这个委员会，不会代表着被认为和民众利益相对立的阶级，而是由民众自己在进步

No mode of composition could approach to this in giving weight and efficacy to their function of moderators. It would be impossible to cry down a body always foremost in promoting improvements, as a mere obstructive body, whatever amount of mischief it might obstruct.

Were the place vacant in England for such a Senate (I need scarcely say that this is a mere hypothesis), it might be composed of some such elements as the following. All who were or had been members of the Legslative Commission described in a former chapter, and which I regard as an indispensable ingredient in a well constituted popular government. All who were or had been Chief Justice, or heads of any of the superior courts of law or equity. All who had for five years filled the office of puisne judge. All who had held for two years any Cabinet office : but these should also be eligible to the House of Commons, and if elected members of it, their peerage or senatorial office should be held in suspense. The condition of time is needed to prevent persons from being named Cabinet Ministers merely to give them a seat in the Senate ; and the period of two years is suggested, that the same term which qualifies them for a pension might entitle them to a senatorship. All who had filled the office of Commander-in-Chief; and all who, having commanded an army or a fleet, had been thanked by Parliament for military or naval successes. All who had held, during ten years, first-class diplomatic appointments. All who had been Governors-General of India or British America, and all who had held for ten years any Colonial Governorships. The permanent civil service should also be represented; all should be senators who had filled, during ten years, the important offices of Under-Secretary to the Treasury, permanent Under-Secretary of State, or any others equally high and responsible. The functions conferring the senatorial dignity should be limited to those of a legal, political, or military or naval character. Scientific and literary eminence are too indefinite and disputable ; they imply a power of selection, whereas the other qualifications speak for themselves ; if the writings by which reputation has been gained are unconnected with politics, they are no evidence of the

第十三章

道路上的天赋领袖们组成。在有效发挥他们作为调解者职能的方面,任何一种其他构成方式都达不到这种效果。把常常站在促进改革最前沿的团体贬低为单纯妨碍性团体的这种意见是无法接受的,不管这样做可能预防多少危害。

倘若这样一个上院在英国还未曾组成的话(毋庸赘述,这只不过是个假设),它可以由以下这样一些人组成。在我看来,前面的一章中所提及的所有现任或曾任立法委员会委员的人,是一个组织得好的平民政府不可或缺的成分。所有现任或曾任高等法院或衡平法院院长的人;所有曾任陪席法官达五年的人;所有曾任内阁职务达两年的人。但这些人也应有资格被选为下院议员,而如果被选为下院议员,他们的贵族爵位或上院议员的职务应暂时中止。只是为了赋予他们上院席位而把他们提名为内阁阁员,为了防止这种做法,时间条件是必要的,并且作了两年期限的建议。这样,取得退休金资格的同一期限可能使他们有资格获得上院议员职位。还应有所有曾担任总司令职务的人,以及所有指挥过一个军队或一个舰队,并受到议会对其军事或海军的胜利表示感谢的人;所有在十年期间担任过一等外交职务的人;所有曾任印度或英属美洲总督的人,以及所有曾任任何殖民地总督达十年的人。常任文官也应得到代表;所有在十年期间担任过财政副大臣、常任副国务大臣等重要职务或任何其他同等负责高级职务的人都应该是上院议员。应该把那些带有上院尊贵色彩的职务限定在法定的、行政的,或是军事的,或是海军的特征方面。单纯科学上和文学上的卓越是极不确定和有争议性的,因为这些意味着选择能力问题,而其他条件则是不言而喻的;如果获得名誉的著述与政治关系不大,它们就不是所要求的特殊能力的根据;

special qualities required, while if political, they would enable successive Ministries to deluge the House with party tools.

The historical antecedents of England render it all but certain, that unless in the improbable case of a violent subversion of the existing Constitution, any Second Chamber which could possibly exist would have to be built on the foundation of the House of Lords. It is out of the question to think practically of abolishing that assembly, to replace it by such a Senate as I have sketched, or by any other; but there might not be the same insuperable difficulty in aggregating the classes or categories just spoken of to the existing body, in the character of Peers for life. An ulterior, and perhaps, on this supposition, a necessary step, might be, that the hereditary peerage should be present in the House by their representatives instead of personally : a practice already established in the case of the Scotch and Irish Peers, and which the mere multiplication of the order will probably at some time or other render inevitable. An easy adaptation of Mr. Hare's plan would prevent the representative peers from representing exclusively the party which has the majority in the Peerage. If, for example, one representative were allowed for every ten peers, any ten might be admitted to choose a representative, and the peers might be free to group themselves for that purpose as they pleased. The election might be thus conducted: All peers who were candidates for the representation of their order should be required to declare themselves such, and enter their names in a list. A day and place should be appointed at which peers desirous of voting should be present, either in person, or, in the usual parliamentary manner, by their proxies. The votes should be taken, each peer voting for only one. Every candidate who had as many as ten votes should be declared elected. If any one had more, all but ten should be allowed to withdraw their votes, or ten of the number should be selected by lot. These ten would form his constituency, and the remainder of his Voters would be set free to give their votes over again for some one else. This process should be repeated until (so far as possible) every peer present either personally or by proxy was represented. When a number less than ten remained over, if amounting to five they might still be allowed to agree on a representative; if fewer than five their votes must be lost,

第十三章

另一方面,如果是政治的著述,它们就会使得下届内阁用党派斗争的工具充斥在议会中。

就英国历史上的先例而言,差不多可以确信,任何可能存在的第二院必定是以上院的基础为根基的,除非出现以暴力颠覆现行宪法这种不大可能的情况。实际上想废止该院,替换为以我所概述的上院或任何其他的上院,是根本不可能的。但是把刚才提及的各阶级或各类别的人,以终身贵族的特征聚集到现有团体中去,可能并不存在那样不可逾越的困难。将来要采取的,或许基于这一假设必须采取的步骤可能是,世袭贵族将通过他们的代表出席议会,而不是由他们自己出席议会。这一惯例已经在苏格兰和爱尔兰贵族中得以确立,而且随着具有这种情况的人逐渐增加,这一惯例大概终有一天会成为不可避免的。稍微修改黑尔先生的方案,就能防止贵族议员仅仅只代表贵族中占多数的政党。比如,如果在每十个贵族中允许拥有一名代表,那么,任何十个贵族可以挑选出一名代表,为达到这一目的,贵族就可自由地随意组合。选举将以这种方式进行:所有作为代表地位的他们候选人的贵族,应当明确宣布并把姓名写入名单。在指定的日期和地点,希望投票的贵族必须亲自出席,或者遵循通常议会规定的方式由他们的代表出席。开始举行投票,每个贵族只投一个人的票。每个取得十票的候选人需被宣布当选。假如有人票数多于十票,那么,除了这十票之外,可以允许撤回其余的票,或者抽签选定其中十票。这十人组成该次选择的选民,而其余的投票人可以自由地重新对另外的人投票。这一程序反复进行,直到(尽可能)每个亲自或派代表出席的贵族都选出他的代表。当剩下的少于十人时,如果达到五人,他们则仍然被允许一致同意选一名代表;如果达不到五

or they might be permitted to record them in favour of somebody already elected. With this inconsiderable exception, every representative peer would represent ten members of the peerage, all of whom had not only voted for him, but selected him as the one, among all open to their choice, by whom they were most desirous to be represented. As a compensation to the Peers who were not chosen representatives of their order, they should be eligible to the House of Commons ; a justice now refused to Scotch Peers, and to Irish Peers in their own part of the kingdom, while the representation in the House of Lords of any but the most numerous party in the Peerage is denied equally to both.

The mode of composing a Senate, which has been here advocated, not only seems the best in itself, but is that for which historical precedent, and actual brilliant success, can to the greatest extent be pleaded. It is not, however, the only feasible plan that might be proposed. Another possible mode of forming a Second Chamber, would be to have it elected by the First ; subject to the restriction, that they should not nominate any of their own members. Such an assembly, emanating like the American Senate from popular choice, only once removed, would not be considered to clash with democratic institutions, and would probably acquire considerable popular influence. From the mode of its nomination it would be peculiarly unlikely to excite the jealousy of, or to come into any hostile collision with, the popular House. It would moreover (due provision being made for the representation of the minority), be almost sure to be well composed, and to comprise many of that class of highly capable men, who, either from accident or for want of showy qualities, had been unwilling to seek, or unable to obtain, the suffrages of a popular constituency.

The best constitution of a Second Chamber, is that which embodies the greatest number of elements exempt from the class interests and prejudices of the majority, but having in themselves nothing offensive to democratic feeling. I repeat however, that the main reliance for tempering the ascendancy of the majority cannot be placed in a Second Chamber of any kind. The character of a representative government is fixed by the constitution of the popular House. Compared with this, all other questions relating to the form of government are insignificant.

第十三章

人,他们的选票就只好废止,或者允许他们把选票记入某个已被选出的人的名下。除这些无足轻重的例外,每个贵族议员将代表着十个贵族,所有这十个人不仅投了他的票,而且在所有可供选择的人当中,选择他作为他们最希望由他来代表的那个人。作为对没有被选作代表的那些贵族的一种补偿,他们应有资格被选进下院。现在苏格兰贵族得不到这种公正待遇,爱尔兰贵族在他们自己的地区也得不到,而另一方面,除了贵族中人数最多的政党之外,两者都同样得不到在上院中的代表权。

在这里所主张的构成上院的模式,不仅实质上看来是最好的,而且能够在最大程度上获得历史上的先例和实际上辉煌成功的支持。然而,它并非是可能提出的唯一行得通的方案。组成第二院的另一种可能的模式就是通过第一院选出,它的限制条件是他们不能提名他们自己的成员。和美国上院一样,这样一个议院是根植于民众的选择,仅仅是隔了一层,将不会被认为和民主制度相矛盾,并且很可能会获得相当大的民众影响。由于它的提名方式,它尤其不会招致平民议院的嫉妒,或者同它发生敌对的冲突。而且(由于对少数的代表权作了适当的规定),它几乎肯定会组织得很好,并囊括许多能力非凡的人,这些人要么出于偶然,要么由于缺乏炫耀的能力,一直不想去寻求,或者不能获得选民大众的选票。

第二院的最优组成,应当囊括最大数量的不受多数的阶级利益和成见束缚而他们自己又毫不侵犯民主感情的人。但是,我再强调一次,调节多数的统治地位主要不能依赖一个第二院,不管这个第二院是哪一种的。平民议院的组成决定着代议制政府的性质。与这一点相比起来,所有有关政府形式的其他问题都是无关紧要的。

CHAPTER XIV
Of The Executive In A Representative Government

It would be out of place, in this treatise, to discuss the question into what departments or branches the executive business of government may most conveniently be divided. In this respect the exigencies of different governments are different ; and there is little probability that any great mistake will be made in the classification of the duties, when men are willing to begin at the beginning, and do not hold themselves bound by the series of accidents which, in an old government like ours, has produced the existing division of the public business. It may be sufficient to say, that the classification of functionaries should correspond to that of subjects, and that there should not be several departments independent of one another, to superintend different parts of the same natural whole ; as in our own military administration down to a recent period, and in a less degree even at present. Where the object to be attained is single (such as that of having an efficient army), the authority commissioned to attend to it should be single likewise. The entire aggregate of means provided for one end, should be under one and the same control and responsibility. If they are divided among independent authorities, the means, with each of those authorities, become ends, and it is the business of nobody except the head of the Government, who is probably without the appropriate departmental experience, to take care of the real end. The different classes of means are not combined and adapted to one another under the guidance of any leading idea; and while every department pushes forward its own requirements, regardless of those of the rest, the purpose of the work is perpetually sacrificed to the work itself.

As a general rule, every executive function, whether superior or

第十四章　代议制政府拥有的行政权力

在本文中,讨论这样一个问题即政府的行政事务可以最便利地被划分为什么部门或分支是不合适的。在这方面,不同政府的要求是不同的;当人们愿意从最初开始,并且不使他们受一系列约束时那些约束是在像我国那样的旧政府中产生的现存的对公共事务划分事件的约束,那么在划分责任方面就很少会有犯重大错误的可能性。这样说也许就够了,就是职务的划分应当与主题的划分一致,不应该有几个相互独立的部门来管理同样一个自然整体的不同部分,像直到最近,甚至到目前在较小程度上我们自己的军事行政那样。在那个领域,要获取的目标是单一的(例如拥有一支有效率的部队),委托去照管这一目标的政府部门同样也应当是单一的。为一个目标提供的全部手段应当处于同一控制和责任之下,如果它们被互相独立的机构所分开,那么就每个机构来说,手段就变成了目的,它就成了政府首脑一人的事务,他或许没有一定的部门经验来管理好真正的目标。不同种类的手段方法就不在任何主导思想的指导下联合起来并相互适应。当每个部门提出自己的要求而不管其他部门的要求时,工作的目的就永远被牺牲给了工作本身。

作为一条一般规则,每一种不管是上级的还是下级的行政职

subordinate, should be the appointed duty of some given individual. It should be apparent to all the world, who did everything, and through whose default anything was left undone. Responsibility is null, when nobody knows who is responsible. Nor, even when real, can it be divided without being weakened. To maintain it at its highest, there must be one person who receives the whole praise of what is well done, the whole blame of what is ill. There are, however, two modes of sharing responsibility: by one it is only enfeebled, by the other, absolutely destroyed, it is enfeebled, when the concurrence of more than one functionary is required to the same act. Each one among them has still a real responsibility ; if a wrong has been done, none of them can say he did not do it ; he is as much a participant as an accomplice is in an offence: if there has been legal criminality they may all be punished legally, and their punishment needs not be less severe than if there had been only one person concerned. But it is not so with the penalties, any more than with the rewards, of opinion: these are always diminished by being shared. Where there has been no definite legal offence, no corruption or malversation, only an error or an imprudence, or what may pass for such, every participator has an excuse to himself and to the world, in the fact that other persons are jointly involved with him. There is hardly anything, even to pecuniary dishonesty, for which men will not feel themselves almost absolved, if those whose duty it was to resist and remonstrate have failed to do it, still more if they have given a formal assent.

In this case, however, though responsibility is weakened, there still is responsibility ; every one of those implicated has in his individual capacity assented to, and joined in, the act. Things are much worse when the act itself is only that of a majority—a Board, deliberating with closed doors, nobody knowing, or, except in some extreme case, being ever likely to know, whether an individual member voted for the act or against it. Responsibility, in this case, is a mere name.

第十四章

能都应当是委派给某个指定个人的职责。这对任何做过事情,并由于不履行职责而使有些事情没有完成的人来说是显而易见的。当没有人知道谁应负责时,责任就是个零。即使责任真正存在时,它在被分割的时候也不能不被削弱。要把责任放在最高位置,就必须有一个人在事情完成得好的时候独享奖赏,而在事情完成不好时承担全部责任。然而,存在着两种分担责任的方式:一是使责任削弱,二是使之完全遭到破坏,当要求一个以上的官员对同一行为意见一致时,责任就被削弱了。他们中的每一个人仍然有真正的责任;如果做了错事,没有人敢说他自己没有参与;他就像是一个案子中的同案犯那样的参与者;如果有犯罪行为,就应当受到法律的惩罚,并且他们所受的惩罚没有必要比仅仅牵扯到一个人的时候轻。但是对观点的赏罚则不是这样,这些赏罚随着赞同这个观点的人的增多而减轻。在没有确定法律上的犯罪,没有腐败或渎职行为,只有些许过错或大意,或可以被看作是过错或大意的情形下,每个参与者都会因为其他人要和他一起连带负责而替自己找到一个借口。如果那些负责抵制和反对他们找托词的人没有加以抵制和反对的话,如果他们给予了正式的同意,则更会使人们对几乎任何事情,甚至金钱上的欺诈,都可以认为自己几乎是可以免责的。

然而,在这种情形下,尽管责任被削弱了,但是仍然还是有责任的;每个卷入其中的人都以他个人的身份同意和参与了这项行动。当这项行动本身就只是出于多数的行动时,事情就更加糟糕了——关起门来讨论问题的委员会没有人会知道,或除了在某个极端的情形下可能知道,个别成员对这项行动究竟是投了赞成票还是反对票。在这种情形下,责任就仅仅是个名号罢了。边沁

'Boards,' it is happily said by Bentham, 'are screens.' What 'the Board' does is the act of nobody; and nobody can be made to answer for it. The Board suffers, even in reputation, only in its collective character: and no individual member feels this, further than his disposition leads him to identify his own estimation with that of the body—a feeling often very strong when the body is a permanent one, and he is wedded to it for better for worse; but the fluctuations of a modern official career give no time for the formation of such an *esprit de corps*; which, if it exists at all, exists only in the obscure ranks of the permanent subordinates. Boards, therefore, are not a fit instrument for executive business; and are only admissible in it, when, for other reasons, to give full discretionary power to a single minister would be worse.

On the other hand, it is also a maxim of experience, that in the multitude of counsellors there is wisdom, and that a man seldom judges right, even in his own concerns, still less in those of the public, when he makes habitual use of no knowledge but his own, or that of some single adviser. There is no necessary incompatibility between this principle and the other. It is easy to give the effective power, and the full responsibility, to one, providing him when necessary with advisers, each of whom is responsible only for the opinion he gives.

In general, the head of a department of the executive government is a mere politician. He may be a good politician, and a man of merit; and unless this is usually the case, the government is bad. But his general capacity, and the knowledge he ought to possess of the general interests of the country, will not, unless by occasional accident, be accompanied by adequate, and what may be called professional, knowledge of the department over which he is called to preside. Professional advisers must therefore be provided for him. Wherever mere experience and attainments are sufficient—wherever the qualities required in a professional adviser may possibly be united in a single well-selected individual (as in the case, for example, of a law officer), one such person for general purposes, and a staff of clerks to

第十四章

曾恰切地说过,"委员会就是幕布"。"委员会"所做的事情就不是任何个人的行为,任何个人也不能对它负责。委员会甚至在声誉上受到的损害也只是它在集体名声方面,个别成员感觉到的不外是使他自己的判断和该团体的判断结合在一起的意向——当这个团体是永久性的,而他与它休戚与共时,这种感情经常很强烈。但是现代官员的起起落落没有时间去形成这样一种团队精神,如果这种团队精神存在的话,也只存在于职位不高的常任下属职员之中。因此,委员会不是一种适用于行政事务的工具;它只有在因为其他原因,把全部自由裁量权交给一个大臣会更糟糕的时候,才是可以接受的。

另一方面,这也是一条经验法则,即三个臭皮匠顶上一个诸葛亮,并且当一个人习惯应用自己的知识或某个顾问的知识,而不利用任何人的知识的时候,在公众的事情上,甚至是他自己的事情上,都很少能作出正确的判断。这一原则与另一原则之间并不存在必然矛盾。把有效的权力和完全的责任交给一个人,必要的时候为他提供顾问(每个顾问仅仅对他自己提出的意见负责),不是一件很难的事情。

一般情况下,政府部门的首脑是一个纯粹的政治家。他也许是一个好的政治家,一个优秀的人,一般情况下就是这种情形,否则政府就是坏的。但是他除了具备一般才能以及他应当具备的关于国家利益的知识之外,除非出于偶然的机会,将不要求他主管的部门具有足够的、被称为专业知识的东西。因此人们必须为他配备专业顾问。在仅有经验和造诣就足够的情况下——在一个经过精心选择出来的人恰好可能具备专业顾问所具备的知识(例如一位检察官的情形)的情况下,有一个这样为

supply knowledge of details, meet the demands of the case. But, more frequently, it is not sufficient that the minister should consult some one competent person, and, when himself not conversant with the subject, act implicitly on that person's advice. It is often necessary that he should, not only occasionally but habitually, listen to a variety of opinions, and inform his judgment by the discussions among a body of advisers. This, for example, is emphatically necessary in military and naval affairs. The military and naval ministers, therefore, and probably several others, should be provided with a Council, composed, at least in those two departments, of able and experienced professional men. As a means of obtaining the best men for the purpose under every change of administration, they ought to be permanent: by which I mean, that they ought not, like the Lords of the Admiralty, to be expected to resign with the ministry by whom they were appointed: but it is a good rule that all who hold high appointments to which they have risen by selection, and not by the ordinary course of promotion, should retain their office only for a fixed term, unless reappointed; as is now the rule with Staff appointments in the British army. This rule renders appointments somewhat less likely to be jobbed, not being a provision for life, and at the same time affords a means, without affront to any one, of getting rid of those who are least worth keeping, and bringing in highly qualified persons of younger standing, for whom there might never be room if death vacancies, or voluntary resignations, were waited for.

The Councils should be consultative merely, in this sense, that the ultimate decision should rest undividedly with the minister himself: but neither ought they to be looked upon, or to look upon themselves, as ciphers, or as capable of being reduced to such at his pleasure. The advisers attached to a powerful and perhaps self-willed man, ought to be placed under conditions which make it impossible for them, without discredit, not to express an opinion, and impossible

第十四章

了一般目的的人,以及一个为他提供具体知识的参谋机关就满足这种情况下的各种要求了。但是,更多场合下,大臣仅与某个有能力的人商量,而当他本人不熟悉该问题时,无保留地按照那个人的建议行事往往是不够的。他经常有必要不是偶然而是习惯性地听取不同的意见,在经过顾问团体的讨论后形成自己的判断。例如,这一点在陆军和海军事务中尤其重要。因此,陆军大臣和海军大臣可能还有一些其他人士,至少应当在这两个部门里,设立一个由经验丰富的专家组成的委员会。作为一种在每一次政府变动情况下都能网罗到有助于达到目的且有才能的人的方法,成员应当是常任的。我的意思是,他们不应像海军部里的各大臣那样随着任命他的政府内阁进退,但是,所有那些通过选择而不是通过正常途径升迁的位居要职的人,除非经过再次任命,否则只能在一定时期内保有他们的职位,则是一项好的规定,就像目前在英国军队中任命参谋人员的办法那样。这项规定多少减少了假公济私的坏处,任命不是终身的,而同时又提供了一种方法,在不冒犯任何人的情况下,把那些最不值得留下来的人员清除出去,把那些素质极好而资历较轻的人吸收进来,对这些人来说,如果等待因死亡而空缺或因自动去职把职位让出来的话,也许永远也没有机会。

委员会应当只是一个咨询机构,在这种意义上,最后决定权应当由大臣本人掌握。但是不能把他们看成是没有什么影响的人,或者他们自己也不能把自己看作是没什么影响的人,或者看作大臣本人可以随意加以贬低的人。隶属于一个强有力的并且可能很任性的人的那些顾问们应当使他们处于这样的条件下,即对他们来说为了保持信誉而不可能不发表意见,要使他们的上

for him not to listen to and consider their recommendations, whether he adopts them or not. The relation which ought to exist between a chief and this description of advisers is very accurately hit by the constitution of the Council of the Governor-General and those of the different Presidencies in India. These Councils are composed of persons who have professional knowledge of Indian affairs which the Governor-General and Governors usually lack, and which it would not be desirable to require of them. As a rule, every member of Council is expected to give an opinion, which is of course very often a simple acquiescence ; but if there is a difference of sentiment, it is at the option of every member, and is the invariable practice, to record the reasons of his opinion ; the Governor-General, or Governor, doing the same. In ordinary cases the decision is according to the sense of the majority ; the Council, therefore, has a substantial part in the government: but if the Governor-General, or Governor, thinks fit, he may set aside even their unanimous opin, recording his reasons. The result is, that the chief is individually and effectively responsible for every act of the Government. The members of Council have only the responsibility of advisers ; but it is always known, from documents capable of being produced, and which if called for by Parliament or public opinion always are produced, what each has advised, and what reasons he gave for his advice: while, from their dignified position, and ostensible participation in all acts of government, they have nearly as strong motives to apply themselves to the public business, and to form and express a well-considered opinion on every part of it, as if the whole responsibility rested with themselves.

This mode of conducting the highest class of administrative business is one of the most successful instances of the adaptation of means to ends, which political history, not hitherto very prolific in works of skill and contrivance, has yet to show. It is one of the acquisitions with which the art of politics has been enriched by the experience of the East India Company's rule; and, like most of the other wise contrivances by which India has been preserved to this country, and an amount of good government produced which is truly wonderful considering the circumstances and the materials, it is probably destined to perish in the general holocaust which the traditions of Indian government seem fated to undergo, since they have been placed at the mercy of public ignorance, and the presumptuous vanity of political men.

第十四章

级不能不听取他们的建议,不管他采纳与否。存在于首领和如此描述的顾问之间的关系和印度总督与省长之下委员会的组成相当符合。委员会由那些具备总督和地方长官通常所不熟悉的、也不要求他们具备的有关印度事务的专业知识的人士组成。通常,每个委员会成员都需具备有关印度事务专业知识的人组成,而这些知识是总督和地方长官通常所不熟悉的,也不能要求他们具备的,当然这只是一条不成文的规定。但是如果有不同的观点,每个成员可以选择,并且这也是个惯例,把他的理由记录下来,总督或地方长官也可以这样做。在一般场合,决定是根据多数人的意见做出的,因此,顾问委员会在政府中起着很大的作用。但是如果总督或地方长官认为合适,他可以把他们全体一致的意见撇在一边,而把自己的理由记录下来。其结果是,首脑独自而且有效地承担政府每一次行为的责任,委员会的成员只承担顾问的责任。但是从可以得到的文件以及在由于议会或舆论要求而出示的文件中,人们常常可以发现,员全的成员提出了什么建议以及他所提建议的理由。而且,由于他们地位尊贵,并且在表面上参加了政府的所有事务,所以他们有着强烈的动机将整个身心投入到公共事务当中去,并且对公共事务的每个部分都要形成和表达经过深思熟虑的观点,好像整个责任都落在了他们身上似的。

  这种处理最高行政事务的模式是在政治史上,而不是在当今关于设计发明的著作中,曾经展现的将手段适用于目的的最成功的事例之一。它是从丰富了政治艺术的东印度公司的统治经验中获得的;并且,像大部分其他我国保存的印度的智慧设计,以及所产生的从当时情况和特定条件来看,是真正奇妙的好政府那样,它有可能注定要在政府传统似乎无法避免的普遍灾难中毁灭,因为它们是受公众的无知和政治人物的专横和虚荣所支配

Already an outcry is raised for abolishing the Councils, as a superfluous and expensive clog on the wheels of government; while the clamour has long been urgent, and is daily obtaining more countenance in the highest quarters, for the abrogation of the professional civil service, which breeds the men that compose the Councils, and the existence of which is the sole guarantee for their being of any value.

A most important principal of good government in a popular constitution, is that no executive functionaries should be appointed by popular election: neither by the votes of the people themselves, nor by those of their representatives. The entire business of government is skilled employment; the qualifications for the discharge of it are of that special and professional kind, which cannot be properly judged of except by persons who have themselves some share of those qualifications, or some practical experience of them. The business of finding the fittest persons to fill public employment—not merely selecting the best who offer, but looking out for the absolutely best, and taking note of all fit persons who are met with, that they may be found when wanted—is very laborious, and requires a delicate as well as highly conscientious discernment; and as there is no public duty which is in general so badly performed, so there is none for which it is of greater importance to enforce the utmost practicable amount of personal responsibility, by imposing it as a special obligation on high functionaries in the several departments. All subordinate public officers who are not appointed by some mode of public competition, should be selected on the direct responsibility of the minister under whom they serve. The ministers, all but the chief, will naturally be selected by the chief; and the chief himself, though really designated by Parliament, should be, in a regal government, officially appointed by the Crown. The functionary who appoints should be the sole person empowered to remove a subordinate officer who is liable to removal ; which the far greater number ought not to be, except for personal misconduct; since it would be vain to expect that the body of persons by whom the whole detail of the public business is transacted, and whose qualifications are generally of much more importance to the public than those of the minister himself, will devote themselves to their profession, and acquire the knowledge and skill on which the minister must often place entire dependence, if they are liable at any moment to be turned adrift for no fault, that the minister may gratify himself, or promote his political interest, by appointing somebody else.

第十四章

的。早就有人提出要废除委员会,把它当作政府车轮上多余和昂贵的累赘;而同时,取消职业的文官制度的呼声早已甚嚣尘上,并且日益得到最上层人物的支持。文官制度培养着组成委员会所需要的人才,而它的存在则是委员会有价值的唯一保障。

在人民政体中,良好政府最重要的原则是政务官员都不应当根据普选来任命:既不由人民亲自投票任命,也不由人民代表的投票来任命。政府的整个事务都属于技术工作,完成这项工作需要特殊的和专业的资格,只有那些本身具备这种资格或有这方面实践经验的人,才能对这种资格作出恰当的评估。寻找最适合从事政府事务人士的工作——不仅仅是从提出申请的人中挑选最优秀的,而且要物色绝对优秀的,并要留意碰到的所有合适的人,以便当需要时能找到他们——是非常艰苦的,这需要细致而且高度负责的洞察力,因为一般不存在履行得很糟糕的公共职责,所以不存在像对一些部门中的高级官员那样强加以特殊义务那种为它规定极大可行的个人责任的作法。那些不是通过某种公开竞选方式上台的下级公务官员,应当由他们为之服务对其直接负责的那个大臣来挑选,各大臣除首相外,自然将由首相来任命,而首相本人尽管实际上是由议会指派的,在一个王国政府里则要由国王来正式任命。解除一个本该免职的下级官员的职务只能由有权任命官员的人来进行。绝大部分官员除了其本人行为不端外都不应该被免职,因为如果他们随时都有可能无辜地被辞退,而大臣们又通过任命其他人来满足自己的要求或提升他的政治利益,那么要期望这些负责处理公共事务全部细节,其资格对公众而言一般要比大臣本人重要得多的人忠于职守,并去获得大臣常常必须依赖的那种知识和技能,就将是徒然的。

To the principle which condemns the appointment of executive officers by popular suffrage, ought the chief of the executive, in a republican government, to be an exception ? Is it a good rule, which, in the American Constitution, provides for the election of the President once in every four years by the entire people ? The question is not free from difficulty. There is unquestionably some advantage, in a country like America, where no apprehension needs be entertained of a *coup d'état*, in making the chief minister constitutionally independent of the legislative body, and rendering the two great branches of the government, while equally popular both in their origin and in their responsibility, an effective check on one another. The plan is in accordance with that sedulous avoidance of the concentration of great masses of power in the same hands, which is a marked characteristic of the American Federal Constitution. But the advantage, in this instance, is purchased at a price above all reasonable estimate of its value. It seems far better that the chief magistrate in a republic should be appointed avowedly, as the chief minister in a constitutional monarchy is virtually, by the representative body. In the first place, he is certain, when thus appointed, to be a more eminent man. The party which has the majority in Parliament would then, as a rule, appoint its own leader ; who is always one of the foremost, and often the very foremost person in political life: while the President of the United States, since the last survivor of the founders of the republic disappeared from the scene, is almost always either an obscure man, or one who has gained any reputation he may possess in some other field than politics. And this, as I have before observed, is no accident, but the natural effect of the situation. The eminent men of a party, in an election extending to the whole country, are never its most available candidates. All eminent men have made personal enemies, or have done something, or at the lowest professed some opinion, obnoxious to some local or other considerable division of the community, and likely to tell with fatal effect upon the number of votes; whereas a man without antecedents, of whom nothing is known but that he professes the creed of the party, is readily voted for by its entire strength. Another important consideration is the great mischief of unintermitted electioneering. When the highest dignity in the State is to be conferred by popular election once in every few years, the whole intervening

第十四章

对于反对通过选举来任命行政官员的这一原则来说,共和制政府里的行政首脑应当是个例外吗?美国宪法规定每四年举行一次由全国人民投票的总统选举,这是一个好的制度吗?要回答这个问题不是没有困难。在像美国这样一个不用担心会有政变的国家里,使政府首脑在宪法上独立于立法机关,并且使这两个在起源和责任方面同样深得人心的政府部门,能相互有效地进行牵制,这毫无疑问是有某种好处的。这样做的目的是要避免权力过分地集中在同一个人的手中,它是美国联邦宪法的一个显著特点。但在这种情况下,其好处是用高于对其价值的一切合理估计的代价买来的。在一个共和制国家里,其行政首脑公然地由立法机关来任命似乎要好得多,就像在君主立宪制国家里,首相实际上是由代议团体任命的那样。首先,如果是这样任命的话,他肯定是一个非常杰出的人。在议会中占多数的政党通常会任命自己的领袖;他在政治生活中总是重要人物之一,并且常常是处于风口浪尖的人物。可是,美国总统,自从那些共和国的奠基人淡出人们的视界后,几乎总是那么要么是不怎么出名的人物,要么就是在政治以外有些名望的人物。正如我前面评论过的那样,这一点并不是什么巧合,而是形势变化的自然结果,在一个遍全国的大选中,一个政党的杰出人物从来就不是这个政党最有希望的候选人。任何杰出人物都会有个人的政敌,或做过某些事情,或至少讲过某个观点,让社会某个地方其他某个重要部门的人感到不满,可能对选票数目产生致命的效果。可是一个没有什么经历的人——人们对他的了解也只是停留在他对党的纲领的叙述方面——就容易得到该党全体的选票。另外一个重要的考虑就是不间断的选举所带来的巨大麻烦。当国家的最高职位要由数年

time is spent in what is virtually a canvass. President, ministers, chiefs of parties, and their followers, are all electioneerers ; the whole community is kept intent on the mere personalities of politics, and every public question is discussed and decided with less reference to its merits than to its expected bearing on the presidential election. If a system had been devised to make party spirit the ruling principle of action in all public affairs, and create an inducement not only to make every question a party question, but to raise questions for the purpose of founding parties upon them, it would have been difficult to contrive any means better adapted to the purpose.

 I will not affirm that it would at all times and places be desirable, that the head of the executive should be so completely dependent upon the votes of a representative assembly as the Prime Minister is in England, and is without inconvenience. If it were thought best to avoid this, he might, though appointed by Parliament, hold his office for a fixed period, independent of a parliamentary vote : which would be the American system, minus the popular election and its evils. There is another mode of giving the head of the administration as much independence of the legislature as is at all compatible with the essentials of free government. He never could be unduly dependent on a vote of Parliament, if he had, as the British prime minister practically has, the power to dissolve the House and appeal to the people; if, instead of being turned out of office by a hostile vote, he could only be reduced by it to the alternative of resignation or dissolution. The power of dissolving Parliament is one which I think it desirable he should possess, even under the system by which his own tenure of office is secured to him for a fixed period. There ought not to be any possibility of that deadlock in politics, which would ensue on a quarrel breaking out between a President and an Assembly, neither of whom, during an interval which might amount to years, would have any legal means of ridding itself of the other. To get through such a period without *a coup d' état* being attempted, on either side or on both, requires such a combination of the love of liberty and the habit of self-restraint, as very few nations have yet shown themselves capable of: and though this extremity were avoided, to expect that

第十四章

一次的选举来决定时,两次选举期间的整个时间实际上都将花在竞选运动当中。总统、部长们、政党领袖们,以及他们的追随者们,都在从事竞选活动。整个社会都只关注着政治人物,人们在针对每个公共问题进行讨论和决策时关心的不是其本身的价值,而是看它对总统选举的预期影响。如果人们要设计一种制度,使得党的精神成为任何公共事务中行动的支配原则,并创造一种诱导因素,不仅使每个问题成为政党问题,而且使人们为了给政党提供根据而提出问题,那么就很难想出要比这更合乎这个目的的手段了。

我不想断言,行政首脑应当像英国首相那样完全由一个代表大会投票选出,随时随地都让人渴望并且没有什么不便之处。如果人们认为最好避免这一点,那么尽管他是由议会来任命的,但却可以不依赖议会的投票在一个确定的时间内主持政事,这样就成了美国的政治制度,而省却了普选和它带来的麻烦。还有一种方式可以使政府首脑与立法机关保持很大的独立性,而与自由政府的各要素相一致。如果他像英国首相实际拥有的那样,拥有解散议会、诉诸人民的权力,那么他从来就不必过分依赖议会的表决。如果他不想被政敌的表决赶下台,那么他就只能辞职或解散议会。解散议会的权力在我看来,是他值得保留的权力,即使是处在这样一种在确定的时间内能保障他任期的制度下也是如此。不应当存在任何政治僵局的可能性,这种僵局将接着引发总统和议会之间的争吵,在长达数年的时期内任何一方都没有什么法律手段除掉对方。要经历这样一个时期而任何一方都没有政变的意图,就要求把对自由的热爱与自我约束的习惯结合起来,就像极少国家曾表明能够做到的那样。即使撇开这种极端的情

the two authorities would not paralyse each other's operations, is to suppose that the political life of the country will always be pervaded by a spirit of mutual forbearance and compromise, imperturbable by the passions and excitements of the keenest party struggles. Such a spirit may exit, but even where it does, there is imprudence in trying it too far.

Other reasons make it desirable that some power in the state (which can only be the executive) should have the liberty of at any time, and at discretion, calling a new parliament. When there is a real doubt which of two contending parties has the stronger following, it is important that there should exist a constitutional means of immediately testing the point, and setting it at rest. No other political topic has a chance of being properly attended to while this is undecided : and such an interval is mostly an interregnum for purposes of legislative or administrative improvement; neither party having sufficient confidence in its strength, to attempt things likely to provoke opposition in any quarter that has either direct or indirect influence in the pending struggle.

I have not taken account of the case in which the vast power centralized in the chief magistrate, and the insufficient attachment of the mass of the people to free institutions, give him a chance of success in an attempt to subvert the Constitution, and usurp sovereign power. Where such peril exists, no first magistrate is admissible whom the Parliament cannot, by a single vote, reduce to a private station. In a state of things holding out any encouragement to that most audacious and profligate of all breaches of trust, even this entireness of constitutional dependence is but a weak protection.

Of all officers of government, those in whose appointment any participation of popular suffrage is the most objectionable are judicial officers. While there are no functionaries whose special and professional qualifications the popular judgment is less fitted to estimate, there are none in whose case absolute impartiality, and freedom from connexion with politicians or sections of politicians, are of anything like equal importance. Some thinkers, among others Mr. Bentham, have been of opinion that, although it is better that judges should not be appointed by popular election, the people of their district ought to have the power after sufficient experience, of removing them from their

第十四章

况不说,期望这两个权力部门不至于使彼此的运转陷于瘫痪,就是假定这个国家的政治生活中总是弥漫着相互容忍与妥协的精神,保持镇定不为最尖锐的政党斗争的激情所动。这样的精神也许存在,但即使在它存在的地方,对它的考验也是轻率的。

还有其他的理由使人们期望国家的某些权力(这只能是行政权力)应当在任何时候都拥有根据自己的判断来决定召开新的议会的自由。当对竞争的双方究竟哪一方拥有更多的追随者存在真正的怀疑时,重要的就是应当有一种宪法手段来立即加以检验并制止纷争。在这一点没有确定以前,人们就不可能对其他政治话题加以适当的注意,并且在这样的一段时期内立法或行政改革方面的目的通常都是空白,没有什么政党对自己的力量有足够的信心从而去做那些可能导致对当前斗争有直接间接影响的人们反对的事情。

我没有考虑这样一种情形,即巨大的权力集中在行政首脑的手中,而人民却并不热衷于自由制度,使他有机会尝试成功地破坏宪法和篡夺最高权力。当有这样的危险时,就不容许存在议会不能通过投票表决将他加以罢免的行政首脑了。在鼓励这种最大胆放肆的背信弃义的状态下,即使是完全宪法意义上的依赖关系也只不过是一种脆弱的保障。

在所有政府官员中,那些最不应该用普选方式来加以任命的官员就是司法官员。尽管对一切官员的特殊和专业的条件,群众都适合做出评价,但是却没有任何官员在绝对公正和不与政治家或各派政治家发生联系方面是像司法官员那样重要的。有些思想家,其中包括边沁先生认为,尽管法官最好不要由大选来任命,但是法官所在的那个区的人民在拥有足够的经

trust. It cannot be denied that the irremovability of any public officer, to whom great interests are entrusted, is in itself an evil. It is far from desirable that there should be no means of getting rid of a bad or incompetent judge, unless for such misconduct as he can be made to answer for in a criminal court ; and that a functionary on whom so much depends, should have the feeling of being free from responsibility except to opinion and his own conscience. The question however is, whither in the peculiar position of a judge, and supposing that all practicable securities have been taken for an honest appointment, irresponsibility, except to his own and the public conscience, has not on the whole less tendency to pervert his conduct, than responsibility to the government, or to a popular vote. Experience has long decided this point in the affirmative, as regards responsibility to the executive; and the case is quite equally strong when the responsibility sought to be enforced is to the suffrages of electors. Among the good qualities of a popular constituency, those peculiarly imcumbent upon a judge, calmness and impartiality, are not numbered. Happily, in that intervention of popular suffrage which is essential to freedom, they are not the qualities required. Even the quality of justice, though necessary to all human beings, and therefore to all electors, is not the inducement which decides any popular election. Justice and impartiality are as little wanted for electing a member of parliament, as they can be in any transaction of men. The electors have not to award something which either candidate has a right to, nor to pass judgment on the general merits of the competitors, but to declare which of them has most of their personal confidence, or best represents their political convictions. A judge is bound to treat his political friend, or the person best known to him, exactly as he treats other people; but it would be a breach of duty as well as an absurdity if an elector did so. No argument can be grounded on the beneficial effect produced on judges, as on all other functionaries, by the moral jurisdiction of opinion; for even in this respect, that which really exercises a useful control over the proceedings of a judge, when fit for the judicial office, is not (except sometimes in political eases) the opinion of the community generally, but that of the only public by whom his conduct or qualifications can be duly estimated, the bar of his own court. I must

第十四章

验后,应当有权将他们免职。不能否认,如果对任何被委以重任的官员没有将他们免职的方法,那本身就是一个祸害。人们绝不希望看到一个糟糕的或不称职的法官除非是其错误行为触犯了刑律,否则就没有将他罢免的办法;一个人们如此依赖的官员,除非受舆论以及他自己良心约束以外就无需对其行为负责。然而,问题是,从法官的特殊地位来看,并且假定人们在对他进行公正任命时采取了一切可行的保障措施,那么仅仅使他对自己和公众的良心负责,是否大体上要比对政府或公民投票负责更可能不使他的行为堕落呢?关于对行政主管负责这一点,经验早已经作了肯定回答。就加强对选民负责方面来说,情形也是一样的。在一个选区选民的良好品质中,并不包括法官所需要的特殊品质,即冷静和公正无私。幸亏在作为自由所必不可少的人民选举中,这些品质并不是必需的。甚至公正的品质,尽管对一切人,从而也对一切选民是必要的,但却不是决定任何大众选举的因素。正如人们之间的任何交易那样,在选举一个议员的过程中,公正与公平并非是必不可少的。选民不需要对候选人有权得到的东西作出裁决,也不需要对竞选者的一般优点进行判断,只需要宣布他们中的哪一个最受他们个人的信任,或最能代表他们的政治信念。而法官对待他从事政治的友人或他最了解的人则必须完全像对待其他人一样。可是如果一个选民这样做,那他就将是失职的和荒谬的。舆论对法官的道义裁判所产生的有益影响,就像它对其他官员所产生的情形一样,不能作为论据,因为即使在这方面,对法官——当他适合从事司法工作时——的诉讼程序真正实施有益控制的不是(除了有时在政治案件上的情形)社会的一般舆论外,而仅仅是对他的行为和资质能予以恰当评估的那部分人,即他自己法庭上的人

not be understood to say that the participation of the general public in the administration of justice is of no importance; it is of the greatest: but in what manner ? By the actual discharge of a part of the judicial office, in the capacity of jurymen. This is one of the few cases in politics, in which it is better the people should act directly and personally than through their representatives; being almost the only case in which the errors that a person exercising authority may commit, can be better borne than the consequences of making him responsible for them. If a judge could be removed from office by a popular vote, whoever was desirous of supplanting him would make capital for that purpose out of all his judicial decisions ; would carry all of them, as far as he found practicable, by irregular appeal before a public opinion wholly incompetent, for want of having heard the case, or from having heard it without either the precautions or the impartiality belonging to a judicial hearing; would play upon popular passion and prejudice where they existed, and take pains to arouse them where they did not. And in this, if the case were interesting, and he took sufficient trouble, he would infallibly be successful, unless the judge or his friends descended into the arena, and made equally powerful appeals on the other side. Judges would end by feeling that they risked their office upon every decision they gave in a case susceptible of general interest, and that it was less essential for them to consider what decision was just, than what would be most applauded by the public, or would least admit of insidious misrepresentation. The practice introduced by some of the new or revised State Constitutions in America, of submitting judicial officers to periodical popular re-election, will be found, I apprehend, to be one of the most dangerous errors ever yet committed by democracy: and, were it not that the practical good sense which never totally deserts the people of the United States, is said to be producing a reaction, likely in no long time to lead to the retractation of the error, it might with reason be regarded as the first great downward step in the degeneration of modern democratic government. ①

---

① I have been informed, however, that in the States. which have made their judges elective, the choice is not really made by the people, With regard

第十四章

们的意见。人们不要以为我是说一般公众参加司法活动是不重要的,它非常重要,但是以什么方式呢？就是要以陪审员的身份履行部分司法工作。这是政治上少有的情形之一,在这种情形中,人们最好直接行动而不是通过他们的代表行动,这几乎是行使权力的人可能犯的错误比他由于要对错误负责而产生的后果更能忍受的唯一情形。如果法官可以通过公众投票加以免职,希望替代他的人将为了这一目的而利用他所做的一切判决;他将以他认为可行的方式,不通过规定的程序把所有的判决摆在缺乏鉴别能力的公众舆论面前,因为公众没有审理过案子,或者缺乏审案所必要的审慎与公正;他将利用存在于公众间的激情与偏见,在没有这些激情与偏见的地方则尽力去煽动他们。这样,如果人们对这个案子感兴趣,而他又下了相当大的功夫,他无疑会取得成功,除非这个法官或法官的朋友奋起反击,从另一方面向公众发出了同等强大的呼吁。法官最终会觉得他对易受公众影响的案子的每个判决都会使他冒丢官的危险,并且会觉得考虑什么最容易受到公众赞扬和最不会受到恶意曲解要比考虑什么样的判决是公正的更为重要。美国某些新的或修正的州宪法规定司法官员定期由人民重新选举的做法,我觉得这将是民主政治所犯过的最危险的错误之一。并且,如果不是据说美国民众从来没有完全遗弃的实际良知正在产生一种反作用,这种反作用可能不久会消除这种错误,就有理由认为它是在现代民主政体的衰败中倒退的第一大步了。①

---

① 然而,人们告诉我,在其法官是通过选举产生的美国各州中,法官不是真正由人民选出的,而是由各政党领袖选出,选民从来没有考虑过选

To that large and important body which constitutes the permanent strength of the public service, those who do not change with changes of politics, but remain, to aid every ministet by their experience and traditions, inform him by their knowledge of business, and conduct official details under his general control ; those in shorts who form the class of professional public servants, entering their profession as others do, while young, in the hope of rising progressively to its higher grades as they advance in life ; it is evidently inadmissible that these should be liable to be turned out, and deprived of the whole benefit of their previous service, except for positive, proved, and serious misconduct. Not, of course, such delinquency only as makes them amenable to the law; but voluntary neglect of duty, or conduct implying untrustworthiness for the purposes for which their trust is given them. Since, therefore, unless, in case of personal culpability, there is no way of getting rid of them except by quartering them on the public as pensioners, it is of the greatest importance that the appointments should be well made in the first instance ; and it remains to be considered, by what mode of appointment this purpose can best be attained.

In making first appointments, little danger is to be apprehended from want of special skill and knowledge in the choosers, but much from partiality, and private or political interest. Being, as a rule, appointed at the commencement of manhood, not as having learnt, but in order that they may learn, their profession, the only thing by which the best candidates can be discriminated, is proficiency in the ordinary branches of liberal education: and this can be ascertained without

---

but by the leaders of parties ; no elector ever thinking of voting for any one out the party candidate ; and that, in consequence, the person elected is usually in effect the same who would have been appointed to the office by the President or by a Minister of Justice. Thus one bad practice limits and corrects another: and that habit of voting *en masse* under a party banner, which is so full of evil in all cases in which the function of electing is rightly vested in the people, tends to alleviate a still greater mischief in a case where the officer to be elected is one who *ought* to be chosen not by the people but for them.

第十四章

关于形成公共事务常备力量的那个庞大的、重要群体,那些不随政局的变化而变化的人,则留了下来去用他们的经验和惯例帮助每一位部长,向他们提供处理政务的知识,并在他一般的控制之下来处理具体公务;简而言之,那些构成了职业公务员阶层的人,他们在年轻的时候像其他人一样开始他们的职业生涯,希望随着年龄的增长职位也得到相应的增长,除非能证明他们确实犯有严重的过错,显然不能允许轻易地把这些人开除,将他们因以前的服务而享有的整个好处都加以剥夺。当然,这不限于那种根据法律应当加以处理的渎职行为,也包括玩忽职守的行为,或者就其受委托的意图来说是不值得信任的行为。因此,既然除非由于他们个人的过失就无法将他们开除(除了把他们作为支取年金者交给社会外),那么最为重要的就是在当初任命他们的时候应当相当审慎;现在仍然需要思考通过什么方式来任命官员才能最好地达到这一目的。

在作最初的任命时,人们要担心的不是任命官员的人缺乏特殊的技能和知识,而是他们的偏心、个人的或政治利益。通常,由于在成年伊始就接受任命,不是作为学习过职业技能的人,而是为了他们可以学习这个职业的技能,所以能判别最佳候选人的唯一一件事情就是对文科教育的一般学科的精通程度。并且,

---

举政党以外的候选人。因此由选举产生的法官通常与那些由总统或司法部长任命的法官同样有效。这样,一个坏的做法限制和改正另一个坏的做法:在政党旗帜下进行整体投票这一在各种场合(其中选举职能正当地归属于人民)都有害的习惯,却倾向于减轻在所选官员不应由人民选出而应当为人民而选出的场合中的更大的害处。

difficulty, provided there be the requisite pains and the requisite impartiality in those who are appointed to inquire into it. Neither the one nor the other can reasonably be expected from a minister ; who must rely wholly on recommendations, and however disinterested as to his personal wishes, never will be proof against the solicitations of persons who have the power of influencing his own election, or whose political adherence is important to the ministry to which he belongs. These considerations have introduced the practice of submitting all candidates for first appointments to a public examination, conducted by persons not engaged in politics, and of the same class and quality with the examiners for honours at the Universities. This would probably be the best plan under any system ; and under our parliamentary government it is the only one which affords a chance, I do not say of honest appointments, but, even of abstinence from such as are manifestly and flagrantly profligate.

It is also absolutely necessary that the examinations should be competitive, and the appointments givento those who are most successful. A mere pass examination never, in the long run, does more than exclude absolute dunces. When the question, in the mind of the examiner, lies between blighting the prospects of an individual, and performing a duty to the public which, in the particular instance, seldom appears of first-rate importance; and when he is sure to be bitterly reproached for doing the first; while in general no one will either know or care whether he has done the latter ; the balance, unless he is a man of very unusual stamp, inclines to the side of good-nature. A relaxation in one instance establishes a claim to it in others, which every repetition of indulgence makes it more difficult to resist; each of these in succession becomes a precedent for more, until the standard of proficiency sinks gradually to something almost contemptible. Examinations for degrees at the two great Universities have generally been as slender in their requirements, as those for honours are trying and serious. Where there is no inducement to exceed a certain minimum, the minimum comes to be the maximum : it becomes the general practice not to aim at more, and as in everything there are some who do not attain all they aim at , however low the standard may be

第十四章

只要那些负责考核的人不怕辛苦、内心公正,那么这一点是不难确定的。但人们不能指望部长能合理地做到这点,他必须完全依赖别人的推荐,不管他个人的愿望是怎样的无私,都不能证明他能抵制那些对他的选举有影响能力的人或其政治忠诚对他所属政府部门关系重大的人们的请求。这些考虑使得人们采取了将初次任命的候选人全部由公开举行的考试来选拔的做法,这种考试由不从事政治、具备与在大学负责优等生考试的考官同样级别和素养的人来进行。这或许是任何制度下的最好计划,在我们的议会制政府下,我且不说这是诚实的任命,但恰好这是提供一个机会来弃绝那些明显确实品行不端的人的唯一办法。

另外,绝对必要的是这种考试应该是竞争性的,考试成绩最好的人才能得到任命。长远看来,单纯的通过考试只是把那些绝对愚笨的人挡在了门外。当考官脑子里所想的问题是介于毁掉一个人的前程和履行对公众的一项责任(这在特定情况下很少表现出头等的重要性)这两者之间时,当他毁人前程时必定会遭到严厉的谴责,而他是否履行职责则无人知晓或关心时,除非他是一个具有非同寻常的性格的人,否则他将倾向于做一个老好人。对一个人放宽条件就会招致别的人也要求这样对待,而每次重复这样的迁就行为则使人难以抵制。每件接连发生的这种事情都会变成更多类似事情的先例,直到精通学业的标准渐渐堕落到几乎让人瞧不起的地步。两个主要大学的学位考试一般说来要求都不高,不像对优等生的考试那样难度很大并很严格。如果没有超过某种最低限度的诱因,那么这个最低限度就会变成最高限度;不想达到更高目标就会成为一般的习惯,正如在每件事情上都有不指望达到他们所设定的目标的人一样,不管标准定得有多

pitched, there are always several who fall short of it. When, on the contrary, the appointments are given to those, among a great number of candidates, who most distinguish themselves, and where the successful competitors are classed in order of merit, not only each is stimulated to do his very utmost, but the influence is felt in every place of liberal education throughout the country. It becomes with every schoolmaster an object of ambition, and an avenue to success, to have furnished pupils who have gained a high place in these competitions; and there is hardly any other mode in which the State can do so much to raise the quality of educational institutions throughout the country. Though the principle of competitive examinations for public employment is of such recent introduction in this country, and is still so imperfectly carried out, the Indian service being as yet nearly the only case in which it exists in its completeness, a sensible effect has already begun to be produced on the places of middle-class education; notwithstanding the difficulties which the principle has encountered from the disgracefully low existing state of education in the country, which these very examinations have brought into strong light. So comtemptible has the standard of acquirement been found to be, among the youths who obtain the nomination from a minister, which entitles them to offer themselves as candidates, that the competition of such candidates produces almost a poorer result than would be obtained from a mere pass examination ; for no one would think of fixing the conditions of a pass examination so low as is actually found sufficient to enable a young man to surpass his fellow-candidates. Accordingly, it is said that successive years show on the whole a decline of attainments, less effort being made, because the results of former examinations have proved that the exertions then used were greater than would have been sufficient to attain the object. Partly from this decrease of effort, and partly because, even at the examinations which do not require a previous nomination, conscious ignorance reduces the number of competitors to a mere handful, it has so happened that though there have always been a few instances of great proficiency, the lower part of the list of successful candidates represents but a very moderate amount of acquirement ; and we have it on the word of the Commissioners that nearly all who have been unsuccessful have owed their failure to ignorance not of the higher branches of instruction, but of its very humblest elements—spelling and arithmetic.

么低,总是会有一些人达不到这个标准。相反,当从为数众多的候选人中任命那些最杰出的人,最成功的竞争者被按照优点分了等级时,则不仅每个人都会被激励去做得最好,而且整个国家每个地方的文科教育都会受到这样的影响。培养出在这些竞争中取得更高位置的学生就成为每个校长的一个雄心勃勃的目标、成功的途径;在这个国家再没有别的什么方式能比这更能提高全国的教育水平了。尽管招考公职人员的这种竞争性考试的原则最近才被介绍到这个国家,而且实施得仍然不很完善,到现在为止只有在印度实施的文官制度是较为完善的唯一例子,但早就对中等阶级教育地位产生了明显的效果。尽管由于这个国家水平低得大失体统的教育状况,这项原则遭遇到巨大的困难,这些考试本身已经将这些困难充分暴露出来了。在这些获得了部长提名(这使得他们作为候选人的资格)的年轻人当中,学识的标准被发现遭到如此轻视,以至于这样的候选人考试的结果比那种单纯过关考试的结果还要糟糕。因为没有人想到把考试及格的条件定得那样低,实际上使一个年轻人能胜过其他竞争伙伴就行。因此,据说连续几年都表明大体上学识水平是下降的,努力程度也在下降,因为以前的考试结果已经证明不需要作太多的努力就可以达到目的。部分地因为努力程度下降了,部分地因为,甚至在不要求事先提名的考试中,自我意识到的无知将竞争者减少到少而又少的数量,这样一来,尽管总是有少数几个饱学之士,但在他们之下的成功的候选人则只达到中等程度的水平,并且委员们曾说过,几乎所有没有通过考试的人,其失败的原因不是因为他们对高等学科的无知,而是因为对最基础的知识——拼写和算术的无知。

The outcries which continue to be made against these examinations, by some of the organs of opinion, are often, I regret to say, as little creditable to the good faith as to the good sense of the assailants. They proceed partly by misrepresentation of the kind of ignorance, which, as a matter of fact, actually leads to failure in the examinations. They quote with emphasis the most recondite questions① which can be shown to have been ever asked, and make it appear as if unexceptional answers to all these were made the *sine quânon* of success. Yet it has been repeated to satiety, that such questions are not put because it is expected of every one that he should answer them, but in order that whoever is able to do so may have the means of proving and availing himself of that portion of his knowledge. It is not as a ground of rejection, but as an additional means of success, that this opportunity is given. We are then asked whether the kind of knowledge supposed in this, that, or the other question, is calculated to be of any use to the candidate after he has attained his object. People differ greatly in opinion as to what knowledge is useful. There are persons in existence, and a late Foreign Secretary of State is one of them, who think English spelling a useless accomplishment in a diplomatic attach , or a clerk in a Government office. About one thing the objectors seem to be unanimous, that general mental cultivation is not useful in these employments, whatever else may be so. If, however (as I presume to think), it is useful, or if any education at all is useful, it must be tested by the tests most likely to show whether the candidate possesses it or not, To ascertain whether he has been well educated, he must be interrogated in the things which he is likely to know if he has been well educated, even though not directly pertinent to the work to which he is to be appointed . Will those who object to

---

① Not always, however, the most recondite; for a late denouncer of competitive examination in the House of Commons had the naïveté to produce a set of almost elementary questions in algebra, history and geography, as a proof of the exorbitant amount of high scientific attainment which the Commissioners were so wild as to exact.

第十四章

有些舆论机构继续有人不断呼吁取消这些考试,我很抱歉地说,这些呼声就攻击者们的真诚性和判断力来说,往往是不值得一提的。他们部分地靠歪曲事实上导致在考试中失败的那种无知来达到目的。他们着重提出的显然是曾经问过的最深奥的问题[1],并弄得好像能够回答这些问题被看成是成功的必不可少的条件似的。但已经重复过多次的是,出这样的问题并不是因为期待每个人都能答对,而是为了让那些能回答的人有办法证明和利用他的那部分知识。提供这样的机会不是用来排斥人才,而是用来作为成功的补充手段。于是,人们就会问,假定在这个或别的问题上包含的知识,是否考虑过它在候选人达到其目的之后还会有什么用处。在什么知识是有用的这个问题上,人们的观点是各异的。现在有些人,并且已故的一位外交大臣就是其中之一,竟然认为英语拼写对一位外交随员或政府职员来说是一门无用的技艺。反对者似乎对一件事情是意见一致的,即对这些职业来说,不管别的什么职业是否也可能如此,一般的智力修养是没有用的。然而(我冒昧地认为),如果这种智力修养有用的话,或者如果任何教育至少是有些用处的话,它就必须通过最可能说明是否候选人拥有这种修养的测试来加以检验。要确信他是否受过良好教育,就必须以如果他受过良好教育就可能知道的东西来考问他,即使这些东西与他将被任命去做的工作没有直接的关系。在一个通常只教授古典文学和数学的国家里,那些反对对他

---

[1] 然而,也并非常常是最深奥的,因为在国会下院,最近一个反对选拔性考试的人天真地提出了一套关于代数、历史和地理方面的几乎最为基础的问题,作为考试委员们盲目地强求达到的高等科学造诣的过分要求的证明。

his being questioned in classics and mathematics, in a country where the only things regularly taught are classics and mathematics, tell us what they would have him questioned in ? There seem, however, to be equal objection to examining him in these, and to examining him in anything *but* these; If the Commissioners—anxious to open a door of admission to those who have not gone through the routine of a grammar-school, or who make up for the smallness of their knowledge of what is there taught, by greater knowledge of something else allow marks to be gained by proficiency in any other subject of real utility, they are reproached for that too. Nothing will satisfy the objectors, but free admission of total ignorance.

We are triumphantly told, that neither Clive nor Wellington could have passed the test which is prescribed for an aspirant to an engineer cadetship. As if, because Clive and Wellington did not do what was not required of them, they could not have done it if it had been required. If it be only meant to inform us that it is possible to be a great general without these things, so it is without many other things which are very useful to great generals. Alexander the Great had never heard of Vauban's rules, nor could Julius Cæsar speak French. We are next informed that bookworms, a term which seems to be held applicable to whoever has the smallest tincture of book-knowledge, may not be good at bodily exercises, or have the habits of gentlemen. This is a very common line of remark with dunces of condition ; but whatever the dunces may think, they have no monopoly of either gentlemanly habits or bodily activity. Wherever these are needed, let them be inquired into, and separately provided for, not to the exclusion of mental qualifications, but in addition. Meanwhile, I am credibly informed, that in the Military Academy at Woolwich, the competition cadets are as superior to those admitted on the old system of nomination, in these respects as in all others ; that they may learn even their drill more quickly ; as indee d might be expected , for an intelligent

第十四章

提关于古典文学和数学问题的人,能告诉我们他们会用什么样的问题来考察他吗?然而看来似乎是,他们反对用古典文学和数学知识来考察他,同样也反对用古典文学和数学知识以外的任何知识来考察他。如果考试委员——因为急于接纳那些没有正常读完语法学校,或者以更多其他方面的知识来弥补在那里学到很少的知识的人——允许通过对任何其他实用科目的精通得到分数的话,他们也会受到责备。除了让完全无知的人自由入选之外,是没有什么能让反对者满意的。

他们洋洋得意地告诉我们,就算是克莱夫和惠林顿这类有抱负的人也没法通过军校工兵的考试。仿佛由于克莱武与惠林顿没有做过并未要求他们做的事情,假如要求他们做他们也做不了似的。如果这只是意味着要告诉我们,没有这些知识也可能成为一名将军,因此,同样没有其他许多对伟大的将军们来说很有用的知识,也可能成为伟大的将军。亚历山大大帝从来没有听说过沃班法则,朱利亚·恺撒也不会说法语。接下来,他们还告诉我们,书呆子——这似乎被认为是适用于那些染有丁点儿书本知识痕迹的人的一个术语——可能不善于运动锻炼,或可能不具绅士习惯。这是有地位的傻瓜们极其普遍的评语,但是不管这些傻瓜们可能怎样去想,他们也不能垄断绅士习惯和身体活动。凡是需要这些条件的地方,不妨进行考察并另作规定,不排除智力条件,而是附加智力条件。同时,有人如实地告诉我,在伍尔韦奇军事学院,那些经过竞争进来的学生在这些方面和其他方面一样,跟那些按老办法通过推荐进来的学生一样优秀,甚至他们可能在操练方面学得更快;人们确实会期望聪明的学生学什么都要

person learns all things sooner than a stupid one : and that in general demeanour they contrast so favourably with their predecessors, that the authorities of the institution are impatient for the day to arrive when the last remains of the old leaven shall have disappeared from the place. If this be so, and it is easy to ascertain whether it is so, it is to be hoped we shall soon have heard for the last time that ignorance is a better qualification than knowledge, for the military, and *àfortiori* for every other, profession; or that any one good quality, however little apparently connected with liberal education, is at all likely to be promoted by going without it.

Though the first admission to government employment be decided by competitive examination, it would in most cases be impossible that subsequent promotion should be so decided: and it seems proper that this should take place, as it usually does at present, on a mixed system of seniority and selection. Those whose duties are of a routine character should rise by seniority to the highest point to which duties merely of that description can carry them ; while those to whom functions of particular trust, and requiring special capacity, are confided, should be selected from the body on the discretion of the chief of the office. And this selection will generally be made honestly by him, if the original appointments take place by open competition : for under that system, his establishment will generally consist of individuals to whom, but for the official connexion, he would have been a stranger. If among them there be any in whom he, or his political friends and supporters, take an interest, it will be but occasionally, and only when, to this advantage of connexion, is added, as far as the initiatory examination could test it, at least equality of real merit. And, except when there is a very strong motive to job these appointments, there is always a strong one to appoint the fittest person ; being the one who gives to his chief the most useful assistance; saves him most trouble, and helps most to build up that reputation for good management of public business, which necessarily and properly redounds to the credit of the minister, however much the qualities to which it is immediately owing may be those of his subordinates.

第十四章

比愚笨的学生来得快。并且在一般举止方面,他们表现得要比他们的前任学员要好,以至于学校当局急于盼望老办法的最后残余从那个地方消失的那一天早日到来。如果事情真是这样,并且很容易确定是否是这样,就可以企盼我们很快就再也听不到,说无知对军队以及其他每一种职业来说,要比有知识更好、或者说任何一种好的品质,不管它表面上与文科教育联系怎样地少,都完全可能在没有文科教育的情况下培养完成这样的言论了。

尽管初次能否进入政府工作应由竞争性的考试来决定,但在绝大多数场合下随后的升迁不可能也用同样的方法来决定。因为这种升迁,似乎要像目前惯常做法那样,将资历和选拔两者结合起来进行才是适当的。那些担任日常职务的人应当按照资历条件升迁到这项职务能使他升到的最高位置,而那些被委托担任怀有特殊期盼的职位,或需要特殊能力的职位的人,则应按照部门首脑的周到考虑从工作人员中选拔。如果最初的录用是根据公开竞争决定的,那么一般说来进行这种选拔时他将秉持公正之心,因为在那种制度下,他的工作班子一般由那些要不是因为工作关系,他将会很陌生的人组成。如果在他们中间有他或他的政友感兴趣的人,那也只是出于偶然,并且这时除这种关系外还至少具有经过录用考试检验的真正的优点。除了存在着极强烈的动机去利用任命人员的机会营私舞弊外,总是存在着任用最合适的人员这种强烈动机;因为只有这个人才能给他的上级以最有用的帮助,帮他解决最麻烦的问题,最有助于他在公共事务管理方面树立良好的声誉,不管这种声誉品质有多少是直接属于其部下的,它都必然地、正当地促进部长的威望。

CHAPTER XV
Of Local Representative Bodies

It is but a small portion of the public business of a country, which can be well done, or safely attempted, by the central authorities; and even in our own government, the least centralized in Europe, the legislative portion at least, of the governing body busies itself far too much with local affairs, employing the supreme power of the state in cutting small knots which there ought to be other and better means of untying, The enormous amount of private business which takes up the time of Parliament, and the thoughts of its individual members, distracting them from the proper occupations of the great council of the nation, is felt by all thinkers and observers as a serious evil, and what is worse, an increasing one.

It would not be appropriate to the limited design of this treatise, to discuss at large the great question, in no way peculiar to representative government, of the proper limits of governmental action. I have said elsewhere①what seemed to me most essential respecting the principles by which the extent of that action ought to be determined. But after subtracting from the functions performed by most European governments, those which ought not to be undertaken by public authorities at all, there still remains so great and various an aggregate of duties, that, if only on the principle of division of labour, it is indispensable to share them between central and local authorities. Not solely are separate executive officers required for purely local duties (an amount of separation which exists under all governments), but the popular control over those officers can only be advantageously exerted through a separate organ. Their original appointment, the function of

---

① 'On Liberty,' concluding chapter: and, at greater length, in the final chapter of 'Principles of Political Economy.'

第十五章　地方代表机关

无论是中央政府所能执行好的,还是有把握努力去做好的,只不过占国家事务的一小部分;甚至就欧洲而言,在我们这样一个中央集权程度最低的政府里,至少作为统治集团的立法部门是过多地热衷于地方性的事务,迫不及待地行使国家的最高权力去解决那些小而复杂的难题,而这原本应当用其他更好的方法去应对。议会的时间被大量的私人事务消耗了,议会中各个议员的思想偏离了国家重大会议的本职工作,对于这一点,所有的思想家和观察家都觉得是一种严重的弊端,并且更糟的是,这是一种日益严重的弊端。

对于这篇论著的有限篇幅来说,要详尽探讨这样一个大问题,即政府作为范围界限这个并非代议制政府所专有的大问题,是不适当的。对于有关需凭借以决定政府作为的边界的那些原则最根本的东西,我在别处已经提到过。①但是,从多数欧洲政府行使的职责中清除那些根本不应当由政府机关去做的事情之后,依然还存在着诸多的各种职责,如果只是遵循分工原则,那

---

① 《论自由》,结尾一章;更详尽的地方参见《政治经济学原理》的最后一章。

watching and checking them, the duty of providing, or the discretion of withholding, the supplies necessary for their operations, should rest not with the national Parliament or the national executive, but with the people of the locality. That the people should exercise these functions directly and personally, is evidently inadmissible. Administration by the assembled people is a relic of barbarism, opposed to the whole spirit of modern life : yet so much has the course of English institutions depended on accident, that this primitive mode of local government remained the general rule in parochial matters up to the present generation; and, having never been legally abolished, probably subsists unaltered in many rural parishes even now. There remains the plan of representative sub-Parliaments for local affairs ; and these must henceforth be considered as one of the fundamental instituitions of a free government. They exist in England, but very incompletely, and with great irregularity and want of system : in some other countries much less popularly governed, their constitution is far more rational. In England there has always been more liberty, but worse organization, while in other countries there is better organization, but less liberty. It is necessary, then, that in addition to the national representation, there should be municipal and provincial representations: and the two questions which remain to be, resolved are, how the local representative bodies should be constituted, and what should be the extent of their functions.

In considering these questions, twopoints require an equal degree of our attention: how the local business itself can be best done; and how its transaction can be made most instrumental to the nourishment of public spirit and the development of intelligence. In an earlier part of this inquiry I have dwelt in strong language—hardly any language is strong enough to express the strength of my conviction—on the importance of that portion of the operation of free institutions which may be called the public education of the citizens. Now, of this operation the local administrative institutions are the chief instrument. Except by

么,把这些职责分派给中央和地方权力机构就很有必要。不仅需要个别的行政官员负责纯属地方性的事务(在所有政府中这种划分都是存在的),而且,只有凭借另外的机关,才能有利地对这些官员进行民众监督。对这些官员最初的任命,对他们进行监督和制约的职能,为他们职能的行使提供必要拨款的职责,或扣压这种拨款的自由裁决权,都不应由全国的议会或中央行政机关来行使,而应由当地的人民来行使。显而易见,不容许民众直接地、个别地行使这些职能,由集聚在一起的民众来管理是一种野蛮习惯的残余,它与现代文明精神是相违背的。这种英国政府制度的演变进程是如此受偶然因素的影响,以致直到如今,这种地方治理的简单模式还是处理许多乡村教区事务中的一个根本原则,而且,由于这一作法在法律上从未被取消,所以直到现在,这种模式在许多乡村教区事务中仍被一成不变地保持着。处理地方性事务的下一级的议会代表性方案还保留着,从而这被认为是构成自由政府的基本制度之一。这种议会在英国是存在的,只是很不完全,有着很大的不规则性和体系缺失。在其他一些更少民众统治的国家里,它们的宪法却合理得多。在英国,自由总是较多但组织却较坏,然而,其他国家有着较好的组织但自由却较少。因此,除了全国代表制以外,还需要有市和省的代表制。地方代表机关应怎么样组成,以及它们的职责界线应怎样确立仍然是两个尚待解决的问题。

在考虑这些问题时,我们要对以下两点予以同等程度的关注:其一,地方事务本身怎样才能被处理得最好;其二,如何通过对地方事务的处理,来达到最有益于培育公共精神和发展智力方面的目的。在本论著前面一个部分中,我曾用强有力的语言——几

the part they may take as jurymen in the administration of justice, the mass of the population have very little opportunity of sharing personally in the conduct of the general affairs of the community. Reading newspapers, and perhaps writing to them, public meetings, and solicitations of different sorts addressed to the political authorities, are the extent of the participation of private citizens in general politics, during the interval between one parliamentary elation and another. Though it is impossible to exaggerate the importance of these various liberties, both as securities for freedom and as means of general cultivation, the practice which they give is more in thinking than in action, and in thinking without the responsibilities of action; which with most people amounts to little more than passively receiving the thoughts of some one else. But in the case of local bodies, besides the function of electing, many citizens in turn have the chance of being elected, and many, either by selection or by rotation, fill one or other of the numerous local executive offices. In these positions they have to act, for public interests, as well as to think and to speak, and the thinking cannot all be done by proxy. It may be added, that these local functions, not being in general sought by the higher ranks, carry down the important political education which they are the means of conferring, to a much lower grade in society. The mental discipline being thus a more important feature in local concerns than in the general affairs of the State, while there are not such vital interests dependent on the quality of the administration, a greater weight may be given to the former consideration, and the latter admits much more frequently of being postponed to it, than in matters of general legislation, and the conduct of imperial affairs.

  The proper constitution of local representative bodies does not

第十五章

乎没有什么语言足够强有力来表达我信念的强度——阐述了自由制度的那部分作用的重要性,也就是可以被称之为公民的公共教育的重要性。如今,达到这一目标的主要手段是地方行政制度。除了可能充当司法方面的陪审员而起作用之外,人民大众亲自参加普通社会事务管理的机会是很少的。阅读报纸或者写信给报刊,公共集会以及向政府当局发出各种呼吁,是普通公民在两届议会选举之间的间隔期间参政的范围。尽管强调作为自由保障,以及一般教养手段的各种自由的重要性加以强调一点也不过分,但这些自由所提供的实践与其说是在行动方面,还不如说是在思想方面,甚至体现在没有行动责任的思想方面;与被动地接纳某个别人的思想相比照,对于大多数人而言,这种自由也好不到哪里去。不过,地方团体的情形则是不一样的,除了选举职能之外,许多公民还有轮流当选的机会,还有许多人通过选拔或者通过轮流的办法,履行诸多地方行政职务中的这个或那个职务。在这些职位上,他们必须为公共利益而行动,至于他们思考和说话就更是如此了,而且代表人是不能完全包办这种思考的。可以进一步补充说,一般而论,地位较高的人对这些地方职位是不怎么有兴趣的,因而这些职位作为一种媒介,继而把重要的行政训练扩展到社会中地位更低的阶层了。因此,与一般国家事务相比较而言,智力训练是地方事务中更重要的特点。另一方面,行政能力的大小与地方事务的关系又不大,因而对智力训练的考虑就可能更多一些,而在这种情形下,与一般立法和帝国事务管理等事项相比起来,对行政能力的考虑常常可以被置于低于智力训练的地位。

地方代表机关的适当组成没有表现出多大困难。与适用于

present much difficulty. The principles which apply to it do not differ in any respect from those applicable to the national representation. The same obligation exists, as in the case of the more important function, for making the bodies elective; and the same reasons operate as in that case, but with still greater force, for giving them a widely democratic basis: the danger being less, and the advantages, in point of popular education and cultivation, in some respects even greater. As the principal duty of the local bodies consists of the imposition and expenditure of local taxation, the electoral franchise should vest in all who contribute to the local rates, to the exclusion of all who do not. I assume that there is no indirect taxation, no *octroi* duties, or that if there are, they are supplementary only ; those on whom their burthen falls being also rated to a direct assessment. The representation of minorities should be provided for in the same manner as in the national Parliament, and there are the same strong reasons for plurality of votes. Only, there is not so decisive an objection, in the inferior as in the higher body, to making the plural voting depend (as in some of the local elections of our own country) on a mere money qualification: for the honest and frugal dispensation of money forms so much larger a part of the business of the local, than of the national body, that there is more justice as well as policy in allowing a greater proportional influence to those who have a larger money interest at stake.

In the most recently established of our local representative institutions, the Boards of Guardians, the justices of peace of the district sit *ex officio* along with the elected members, in number limited by law to a third of the whole. In the peculiar constitution of English society, I have no doubt of the beneficial effect of this provision. It secures the presence, in these bodies, of a more educated class than it would perhaps be practicable to attract thither on any other terms; and while the limitation in number of the *ex officio* members precludes them from acquiring predominance by mere numerical strength, they, as a virtual representation of another class, having sometimes a different interest from the rest, are a check upon the class interests of the farmers or petty shopkeepers who form the bulk of the elected

第十五章

全国代表制的原则相比,地方代表机关所适用的原则没有丝毫的不同。与在更重要职能的情形下一样,通过选举程序,这种机关得以产生;并且基于同样的但更有说服力的理由,这种机关被赋予广泛的民主基础,也就是说,这种机关的危险较少,而且在平民教育和教养等某些方面,甚至有更多益处。由于地方代表机关的主要职责是征收和支出地方税,所有对地方赋税做出贡献的人应被赋予选举权,而对此没有做出贡献的人则不应被赋予这种权利。我假定没有任何间接税,也没有货物入市税,或者如果有,它们也只是附加的;负担这类税的人仍应征收直接的地方税。好比全国性议会的情形一样,少数的代表权需予以规定,并且对于复数投票的实施有着同样强有力的理由。只是在低级的代表机关,不像高级代表机关那样断然反对复数投票取决于单纯的金钱条件(恰似我国的某些地方选举的情形那样)。与全国性团体相比较而言,由于正直而节俭地管理财政是地方代议制团体中较重要的一部分事务,因此许可那些具有较多金钱利益关系的民众发挥出较大比例的影响,是更睿智同时也是更公允的。

在最近设置的地方代表机关贫民救济委员会中,地区的治安法官当然和选出的成员坐在一起,但按照法规,其人数不能超过总数的三分之一。在英国社会的特殊体制,我相信这一规定会发挥有益的作用。比起其他实际可行的方法,这一规定可以确保这些机构能吸引到更为有教养的阶级;另外,由于这些当然成员受到人数方面的限制,所以不会出现单纯的人数居多而使他们处于占上风的情形。作为另一阶级的事实上的代表,他们有时具有和其他人不同的利益,所以他们对于小农场主或小店主的阶级利益是一种制约,而正是这些人构成被选救济委员的大多数。我们现

Guardians. A similar commendation cannot be given to the constitution of the only provincial boards we possess, the Quarter Sessions, consisting of the justices of peace alone; on whom, over and above their judicial duties, some of the most important parts of the administrative business of the country depend for their performance. The mode of formation of these bodies is most anomalous, they being neither elected, nor, in any proper sense of the term, nominated, but holding their important functions, like the feudal lords to whom they succeeded, virtually by right of their acres: the appointment vested in the Crown (or, speaking practically, in one of themselves, the Lord Lieutenant) being made use of only as a means of excluding any one who it is thought would do discredit to the body, or, now and then, one who is on the wrong side in politics. The institution is the most aristocratic in principle which now remains in England; far more so than the House of Lords, for it grants public money and disposes of important public interests, not in conjunction with a popular assembly, but alone. It is clung to with proportionate tenacity by our aristocratic classes; but is obviously at variance with all the principles which are the foundation of representative government. In a country Board there is not the same justification as in Boards of Guardians for even an admixture of *ex officio* with elected members: since the business of a county being on a sufficiently largo scale to be an object of interest and attraction to country gentleman, they would have no more difficulty in getting themselves elected to the Board, than they have in being returned to Parliament as county members.

In regard to the proper circumscription of the constituencies which elect the local representative bodies; the principle which, when applied as an exclusive and unbending rule to Parliamentary representation is inappropriate, namely community of local interests, is here the only just and applicable one. The very object of having a local representation, is in order that those who have any interest in common, which they do not share with the general body of their countrymen, may manage that joint interest by themselves: and the purpose is contradicted, if the distribution of the local representation follows any other rule than the grouping of those joint interests. There are local

第十五章

有的唯一的地方委员会则不带有这样的优点,它是一个单独由治安法官组成的地方法庭,这个法庭每个季度开审,除了履行司法职务之外,这些法庭还应完成某些非常重要的国家行政事务。这些机构的组成方式是很不规则的,它们既不是由选举产生,也不是通过在任何严格意义上的提名,而是像他们所继承的封建贵族那样,事实上是依照他们对土地的权利而享有重要职位。英国国王享有对他们的任命权(或者实际上是隶属于他们自己当中的一个,也就是相当于地方的代理长官),这种任命要么只被用来作为排除被认为会有损于该机构声誉的人的一种手段,要么被用来清除有时在政治上站错队的人的一种手段。这一机构是英国现在保持下来的原则上最贵族式的机构,比起英国上议院来,该机构的贵族式做法是有过之而无不及。因为拨款也好,处理重要的公共利益也罢,这个机构都不是与平民议会商讨,而只是单独地决断。贵族阶级相当顽固地抱着这种制度不放,但显而易见,它和作为代议制政府基础的一切原则是相冲突的。在郡委员会,即使只是实行当然成员和被选成员的混合,也不存在与贫民救济委员会同样的理由。因为在相当大的程度上,一个郡的事务是地方绅士所关注和被吸引的对象,比起作为郡的议员被选入议会中,他们被选入郡委员会是不会有更大困难的。

至于选举地方代表机关的选民的应有限制条件,对议会代表制而言,这样一个不适于当作唯一和可坚持的规则加以适用的原则,即地方利益共享的原则,在这里就是唯一公正和可适用的原则。地方代表权的目的,本身就是让那些具有和普通人利益不一致的共同利益的人们可以自行协调好共同的利益,如果地方代表权的分配遵循任何其他的规则,而不遵循共同利益的组合的话,那么

interests peculiar to every town, whether great or small, and common to all its inhabitants: every town, therefore, without distinction of size, ought to have its municipal council. It is equally obvious, that every town ought to have but one. The different quarters of the same town have seldom or never any material diversities of local interest; they all require to have the same things done, the same expenses incurred: and, except as to their churches, which it is probably desirable to leave under simply parochial management, the same arrangements may be made to serve for all. Paving, lighting, water supply, drainage, port and market regulations, cannot without great waste and inconvenience be different for different quarters of the same town. The subdivision of London into six or seven independent districts, each with its separate arrangements for local business (several of them without unity of administration even within themselves), prevents the possibility of consecutive or well regulated co-operation for common objects, precludes any uniform principle for the discharge of local duties, compels the general government to take things upon itself which would be best left to local authorities if there were any whose authority extended to the entire metropolis; and answers no purpose but to keep up the fantastical trappings of that union of modern jobbing and antiquated foppery, the Corporation of the City of London.

Another equally important principle is, that in each local circumscription there should be but one elective body for all local business, not different bodies for different parts of it. Division of labour does not mean cutting up every business into minute fractions; it means the union of such operations as are fit to be performed by the same persons, and the separation of such as can be better performed by different persons. The executive duties of the locality do indeed require to be divided into departments, for the same reasons as those of the state ; because they are of diverse kinds, each requiring knowledge peculiar to itself, and needing, for its due performance,

第十五章

这种做法就和要达到的目的南辕北辙了。每个市,不分大小,都有自身特殊的利益,而且,这个市的全部市民都共同分享该利益。因此,每个市,无论大小,都应当设立市议会。同样明显的是,每个市应该只有一个市议会。对于同一个市的各个区来说,地方利益上的重大分歧很少甚至根本不存在;它们被要求做相同的事情,承担相同的开支;并且,除了最好让教区去管理它们的教会这件事务之外,它们要求作同样的安排以便能服务所有的人。铺路、照明、供水、排水装置、港口和市场规范,同一个市的各区不能各搞各的,否则就会造成很大的浪费和不便。伦敦市被划分为六七个独立的区,对地方事务都作出了自己的安排(其中有几个区甚至在其本区内也缺乏行政的统一),导致既不可能对共同目的进行连贯的或有条不紊的合作,也排除了行使地方职责方面的任何统一的原则,并迫使通常的政府不得不担负起那些本应地方政府。去做的那些,而这些事情本来最好是由一个假定的人权力覆盖到全市的地方政府去做,并且除了保持那个作为现代的假公济私和陈旧的纨绔习气的混合的奇异装饰——伦敦市自治体之外,这个机构实现不了任何目的。

　　另外一个同样重要的原则是,在每一地方界限内,只能有一个管理所有的地方性事务的被选出的机关,而不是因为要处理该地区不同部分的事务就去设立不同的机关。劳动分工并不就是把每件事情都划分为细小的部分,而是意味着把适合由同一个人做的事情合起来让这个人去做,而把能由不同的人做得更好的事情加以分割让不同的人去做。基于与国家的行政职务同样的理由,地方的行政职务的确要求划分为不同的部门,因为它们的性质是多种多样的,每种职务都需要特定的知识,并且需要任命特别有

the undivided attention of a specially qualified functionary. But the reasons for subdivision, which apply to the execution, do not apply to the control.

The business of the elective body is not to do the work, but to see that it is properly done, and that nothing necessary is left undone. This function can be fulfilled for all departments by the same superintending body ; and by a collective and comprehensive far better than by a minute and miscroscopic view. It is as absurd in public affairs as it would be in private, that every workman should be looked after by a superintendent to himself. The Government of the Crown consists of many departments, and there are many ministers to conduct them, but those ministers have not a Parliament apiece to keep them to their duty. The local, like the national parliament, has for its proper business to consider the interest of the locality as a whole, composed of parts all of which must be adapted to one another, and attended to in the order and ratio of their importance. There is another very weighty reason for uniting the control of all the business of a locality under one body. The greatest imperfection of popular local institutions, and the chief cause of the failure which so often attends them, is the low calibre of the men by whom they are almost always carried on. That these should be of a very miscellaneous character is, indeed, part of the usefulness of the institution; it is that circumstance chiefly which renders it a school of political capacity and general intelligence. But a school supposes teachers as well as scholars : the utility of the instruction greatly depends on its bringing inferior minds into contact with superior, a contact which in the ordinary course of life is altogether exceptional, and the want of which contributes more than anything else to keep the generality of mankind on one level of contented ignorance. The school, moreover, is worthless, and a school of evil instead of good, if through the want of due surveillance, and of the presence within itself of a higher order of characters,

第十五章

资格的官员一心一意去履行职务,以便使职务得到适当的执行。但是适用于行政职务的详细划分的理由并不适用于监督职务。

由选举产生的机关,它的职务不是做工作,而是竭力把工作做好,不遗漏本该做却还没有做的事情。对所有的部门来说,这项监督职务能够通过同一个监督机关来执行,并且与遵循细小的和微观的看法相比,遵循集体的和全面的看法要好得多。就公共事务而言,与私人事务一样,让每个监工去负责监督每一个工人的做法是可笑的。英王政府由许多部门组成,并且让许多部长去领导,但并不是让每一个个别议会都去监督那些部长履行职务。和全国的议会一样,地方议会的分内职责是把地方利益作为一个整体加以权衡,这个整体由各个部分组成,各个部分需互相协调,并按照它们重要性的次序和比例,把它们再加以组合。让一个机关对一个地方的全部事务进行监督还有另外一个重要理由。平民地方机关的最大缺陷,以及它们经常遭受失败的主要原因,在于几乎总是由才智欠缺的人掌管这些机关。他们应该是全面发展的人,这一点正是该机关的有用之处;大体上,正是由于这种状况,才使它成为行政能力和平常智力的学校。但是,如果它是一个学校,就应假定不但要有学生,而且更要有老师。教育的效用极大地取决于它使文化差的人和文化好的人进行交流,然而,这样的交流,在一般的生活过程中是完全不常见的,而缺乏这种交流就只会把大多数人停留在自我陶醉的无知水平上。另外,如果由于缺乏到位的监管,缺少在它本身内较高级人物的存在,那么,这个学校不但没有任何价值,而且会成为一个邪恶的而不是善良的学校,这个机关的所作所为就可能,也常常会堕落到追逐其成员的私利那种既肆无忌惮又愚蠢的地步。并且,要说

the action of the body is allowed, as it so often is, to degenerate into an equally unscrupulous and stupid pursuit of the self-interest of its members. Now, it is quite hopeless to induce persons of a high class, either socially or intellectually, to take a share of local administration in a cozener by piecemeal, as members of a Paving Board or a Drainage Commission. The entire local business of their town is not more than a sufficient object, to induce men whose tastes incline them and whose knowledge qualifies them for national affairs, to become members of a mere local body, and devote to it the time and study which are necessary to render their presence anything more than a screen for the jobbing of inferior persons, under the shelter of their responsibility. A mere Board of Works, though it comprehend the entire metropolis, is sure to be composed of the same class of persons as the vestries of the London parishes; nor is it practicable or even desirable, that such should not form the majority; but it is important for every purpose which local bodies are designed to serve, whether it be the enlightened and honest performance of their special duties, or the cultivation of the political intelligence of the nation, that every such body should contain a portion of the very best minds of the locality: who are thus brought into perpetual contact, of the most useful kind, with minds of a lower grade, receiving from them what local or professional knowledge they have to give, and in return inspiring them with a portion of their own more enlarged ideas, and higher and more enlightened purposes.

A mere village has no claim to a municipal representation, By a village I mean a place whose inhabitants are not markedly distinguished by occupation or social relations from those of the rural districts adjoining, and for whose local wants the arrangements made for the surrounding territory will suffice. Such small places have rarely a sufficient public to furnish a tolerable municipal council: if they contain any talent or knowledge applicable to public business, it is apt to be all concentrated in some one man, who thereby becomes the dominator of the place. It is better that such places should be merged in a larger circumscription. The local representation of rural districts will naturally be determined by geographical considerations;

服无论是在社会地位上还是在智力上属于上等阶层的人参加地方行政,就好比铺路委员会或排水委员会委员那样,在一个角落里做些琐碎的事情,这是根本不能指望的。城市的整个地方事务才是一项目标,这项目标才足以来说服有志投身于全国事务的人们,或其学识有资格承担全国事务的人们,成为单纯的地方机关的成员,并为这个地方机关奉献出时间和学识,以便使他们的参政不仅仅是在他们的责任掩盖下营私舞弊任用劣等人员的屏障。单纯一个市政工程局,尽管它包括整个伦敦市,肯定要由组成伦敦教区的教区委员会那样的人员组成;排斥这种人构成多数是不现实的,或者甚至是不值得期待的。但是重要的是,就地方机关要提供服务的每一个目的而言,无论它对这些机关的特殊职务的开明而正直的履行也好,还是它对民族的政治智慧的培育也好,每个机关都要由一部分该地区最优秀的人组成。这些人就这样和较低级的民众进行非常有益的持久的交流,他们从而接受这些民众所能给予的涉及到地方和职业的知识,作为对此的一种积极回应,他们再用自己更开阔的思想和更高、更开明的目的对这些民众加以启发。

单纯的乡村不能对市的代表权提出要求。我所提及的乡村意味着这样一个场所,就职业或社会关系而言,这个乡村的居民同附近农村居民并没有什么明显的区别,而且,当地的需要通过对周围地区所作的安排就足以得到满足。在这样的小地方中,几乎没有足够的公众来组成一个体面的市议会。假如这种地方需要任何的才智或知识以履行公共事务的话,就常常集中于某一个人,因此,这个人就是这个地方的统治者。把这种地方合并到较大地区较好。农村地区的地方代表权将自然地由地理情况决定,

with due regard to those sympathies of feeling by which human beings are so much aided to act in concert, and which partly follow historical boundaries, such as those of countries or provinces, and partly community of interest and occupation, as in agricultural, maritime, manufacturing, or mining districts. Different kinds of local business may require different areas of representation. The Unions of parishes have been fixed on as the most appropriate basis for the representative bodies which superintend the relief of indigence ; while, for the proper regulation of highways, or prisons, or police, a larger extent, like that of an average county, is not more than sufficient. In these large districts, therefore, the maxim, that an elective body constituted in any locality should have authority over all the local concerns common to the locality, requires modification from another principle; as well as from the competing consideration, of the importance of obtaining for the discharge of the local duties the highest qualifications possible. For example, if it be necessary (as I believe it to be) for the proper administration of the Poor Laws, that the area of rating should not be more extensive than most of the present Unions, a principle which requires a Board of Guardians for each Union; yet, as a much more highly qualified class of persons is likely to be obtainable for a County Board, than those who compose an average Board of Guardians, it may on that ground be expedient to reserve for the County Boards some higher descriptions of local business, which might otherwise have been conveniently managed within itself by each separate Union.

Besides the controlling Council, or local sub-Parliament, local business has its executive department. With respect to this, the same questions arise, as with respect to the executive authorities in the State ; and they may, for the most part, be answered in the same manner. The principles applicable to all public trusts are in substance the same. In the first place, each executive officer should be single, and singly responsible for the whole of the duty committed to his charge. In the next place, he should be nominated, not elected. It is ridiculous that a surveyor, or a health officer, or even a collector of rates, should be appointed by popular suffrage. The popular choice usually depends on interest with a few local leaders, who, as they are not supposed to make the appointment, are not responsible for it;

第十五章

适当地关注有益于人类一致行动的共同感情,沿着历史的边界,比如郡或者省的边界,这种感情部分得以形成。此外,这种感情部分是源于共同的利益和职业,如在农业、海运、制造业或矿业地区。不同类别的地方事务可能需要不同范围的代表权。教区协会被确立为监督救济穷困的代表机关的最合适的基础;另一方面,要求有一个像一般的郡那样大的区域,以便对公路、监狱或警察进行适当监管。因此,在这些大地区中,这一原则,即任何由地方组成的按照选举产生的机关,就要求由另一原则以及通过对获得最高资格的人行使地方职责的重要性的权衡来作出修正。应当有管理该地方共通的一切地方事务的权力,举一个例子来讲,如果就济贫法的适当管理而言,赋税范围有必要(对此我是认可的)不超过多数现有教区协会的区域的话,这一原则就需要在每个协会中设置一个贫民救济委员会。但是,和组成一般贫民救济委员会的成员相比起来,郡委员会可能获得资格高得多的人,由于这种根据,在郡委员会中,保留某些较高一类的地方事务或许是适宜的,否则这些事务就可能由各个协会便利地地加以处理。

除了负责监督的议会或下级地方议会之外,地方事务有它自己的行政部门。对这个部门来讲,和国家行政部门一样的问题便产生了,这些问题大部分可作同样的答复。适用于一切公众委托的原则本质上是同样的。第一,每个行政官员必须是单一的,并单独负责委托给他的整个职务。第二,行政官员必须通过提名而不是通过选举产生。一律通过普选来对每一个检查员,或卫生官员,或甚至收税员作出任命,将是非常可笑的。大众的选择一般受制于少数地方首脑产生的影响,这些地方首脑,由于他们并没有作这种任命的职责,所以对这种任命是不负责任的,或

or on an appeal to sympathy, founded on having twelve children, and having been a rate-payer in the parish for thirty years. If in cases of this description election by the population is a farce, appointment by the local representative body is little less objectionable. Such bodies have a perpetual tendency to become joint stock associations for carrying into effect the private jobs of their various members. Appointment should be made on the individual responsibility of the Chairman of the body, let him be called Mayor, Chairman of Quarter Sessions, or by whatever other title. He occupies in the locality a position analogous to that of the prime minister in the State, and under a well-organized system the appointment and watching of the local officers would be the most important part of his duty: he himself being appointed by the council from its own number, subject either to annual re-election, or to removal by a vote of the body.

From the constitution of the local bodies, I now pass to the equally important and more difficult subject of their proper attributions. This question divides itself into two parts : what should be their duties, and whether they should have full authority within the sphere of those duties, or should be liable to any, and what, interference on the part of the central government.

It is obvious, to begin with, that all business purely local-all which concerns only a single locality—should devolve upon the local authorities. The paving, lighting, and cleansing of the streets of a town, and in ordinary circumstances the draining of its houses, are of little consequence to any but its inhabitants. The nation at large is interested in them in no other way, than that in which it is interested in the private well-being of all its individual citizens. But among the duties classed as local, or performed by local functionaries, there are many which might with equal propriety be termed national, being the share, belonging to the locality, of some branch of the public administration in the efficiency of which the whole nation is alike interested: the gaols, for instance, most of which in this country are under county

第十五章

者大众的选择受同情的诉求的影响,这种诉求所依据的是有12个孩子,以及在这教区中担任了30年的纳税人。如果在这种情况下,公众的选举是一种闹剧的话,那么,也同样应该反对地方代表机关所作出的这种任命。这样的机关永远存在着这样一种倾向,即把它演变为实施其各种成员私人营利事业的合股公司的倾向。必须由该机关的主席个人作出任命,这个人可称做市长、地方法庭庭长或不管什么别的名称都可以。他在当地所拥有的地位,与首相在国家中的地位相类似,在组织井井有条的制度下,对地方官员的任命和监督就成为他最重要的一部分职责。他本人通过郡议会从其成员中获得任命,每年改选一次,或者由郡议会决定免职。

在阐述了地方机关组成的问题之后,我现在要转到地方机关的正当职权这个问题,这个问题不但是同样重要,而且尤为困难。可以把这个问题划分成两个部分:它们的职责有哪些,以及在那些职责的范围之内,它们是否应享有充分的权力,或者是否要受到中央政府的某种干涉和什么样的干涉。

首先,显而易见的是,纯属地方的一切事务——一切只是牵涉到单个地区的事务——应由地方当局负责。铺路、照明和一个市的街道保洁工作,以及在一般情况下对房屋的排水,所有这些事务只对其居民关系重大,而对其他人则无关痛痒。通常国家对这些事感兴趣,不外乎是源于它对所有市民的个人福利的关心。但是,隶属于地方的事务或通过地方官员行使的事务中,有许多事务同样可以被正当地称之为国家的事务,这些事务是公共行政某些部门从属于地方的那部分,全体民众也是一样地关注它的效率。比如监狱,我国大多数的监狱是处在郡管理之下。

management; the local police; the local administration of justice, much of which, especially in corporate towns, is performed by officers elected by the locality, and paid from local funds. None of these can be said to be matters of local, as distinguished from national importance. It would not be a matter personally indifferent to the rest of the country, if any part of it became a nest of robbers or a focus of demoralization, owing to the maladministration of its police; or if, through the bad regulations of its gaol, the punishment which the courts of justice intended to inflict on the criminals confined therein (who might have come from, or committed their offences in, any other district) , might be doubled in intensity, or lowered to practical impunity. The points, moreover, which constitute good management of these things, are the same everywhere ; there is no good reason why police, or gaols, or the administration of justice, should be differently managed in one part of the kingdom and in another ; while there is great peril that in things so important, and to which the most instructed minds available to the State are not more than adequate, the lower average of capacities which alone can be counted of for the service of the localities, might commit errors of such magnitude as to be a serious blot upon the general administration of the country. Security of person and property, and equal justice between individuals, are the first needs of society, and the primary ends of government: if these things can be left to any responsibility below the highest, there is nothing, except war and treaties, which requires a general government at all. Whatever are the best arrangements for securing these primary objects should be made universally obligatory, and, to secure their enforcement, should be placed under central superintendence, It is often useful, and with the institutions of our own country even necessary, from the scarcity, in the localities, of officers representing the general government, that the execution of duties imposed by the central authority should be entrusted to functionaries appointed for local purposes by the locality. But experience is daily forcing upon the public a conviction of the necessity of having at least inspectors appointed by the general government, to see that the local officers do their duty. If prisons are under local management, the central government appoints inspectors of prisons, to take care that the rules laid down by Parliament are

第十五章

地方警察,地方司法,特别是在自治城市,很多是通过地方选出的官员来执行,并从地方专款中拨付薪水。不能说这些只是从属地方重要性的事务,而不是从属全国重要性的事务。倘若由于某地方的治安形势严重恶化,这地方变成了盗贼的安乐窝或道德败坏的中心,那么,对国家其余的人而言,这就不是一件与个人无关、可以置之不理的事情。或者,如果由于监狱的不适当管理,法院对监禁在其中的罪犯(他们可能来自其他地区,或在其他地区犯了罪)的惩处,重罚一倍或减轻到事实上不受惩罚的地步,情形也是相同的。此外,构成这些事务的良好管理的标准在哪里都是同样的。在王国的这一部分和另一部分,以不同的方式对警察、监狱或司法进行管理,这是没有根据的。同时应当让国家最有教养的人来做的如此重要的事情,却只能由能力较差的人来为地方服务,就可能是铸成国家一般行政方面的严重污点的重大错误,这是非常危险的。人身和财产的安全以及个人之间的平等公正,是社会的第一需要,也是政府的首要目的。因此,如果把这些事情都不交给最高的负责机关,那么除了战争和条约之外,就没有什么事情需要一个全国性的政府去做了。要是保证这些首要目的的最好的安排,都必须带有强制性,并且,为了确保它们的贯彻实施,都必须把这些事务置于中央监督之下。基于各地区缺少代表全国性政府的官员的因素,把中央政府所规定的职责的执行,委托给该地区为地方的目的任命的官员,常常是有益处的,就我国制度来说,它甚至是必要的。但是经验正在天天促使民众相信,必须至少有全国性政府任命的监察官,在他们的监督之下使地方官员恪守他们的职责。如果监狱是处在地方管辖之下,对于议会所制定的规则,中央政府任命的监狱监察官就要注意遵守,如果

observed, and to suggest others if the state of the gaols shows them to be requisite: as there are inspectors of factories, and inspectors of schools, to watch over the observance of the Acts of Parliament relating to the first, and the fulfilment of the conditions on which State assistance is granted to the latter.

But, if the administration of justice, police and gaols included, is both so universal a concern, and so much a matter of general science independent of local peculiarities, that it may be, and ought to be, uniformly regulated throughout the country, and its regulation enforced by more trained and skilful hands than those of purely local authorities ; there is also business, such as the administration of the poor laws, sanitary regulation, and others, which, while really interesting to the whole country, cannot consistently with the very purposes of local administration, be managed otherwise than by the localities. In regard to such duties, the question arises, how far the local authorities ought to be trusted with discretionary power, free from any superintendence or control of the State.

To decide this question, it is essential to consider what is the comparative position of the central and the local authorities, as to capacity for the work, and security against negligence or abuse. In the first place, the local representative bodies and their officers are almost certain to be of a much lower grade of intelligence and knowledge, than Parliament and the national executive. Secondly, besides being themselves of inferior qualifications, they are watched by, and accountable to, an inferior public opinion. The public under whose eyes they act, and by whom they are criticised, is both more limited in extent, and generally far less enlightened, than that which surrounds and admonishes the highest authorities at the capital; while the comparative smallness of the interests involved, causes even that inferior public to direct its thoughts to the subject less intently, and with less solicitude. Far less interference is exercised by the press and by public discussion, and that which is exercised may with much more impunity be disregarded, in the proceedings of local, than in those of national authorities. Thus far, the advantage seems wholly on the side of management by the central government. But, when we

第十五章

监狱的状况表明有必要的话,可建议其他的规则,就像工厂督察,和学校督学一样,监管着议会有关工厂法令的遵守情况,以及国家对学校给予资助的条件的履行状况。

但是,如果司法行政部门,包括警察和监狱,既然是民众普遍关心的事情,又是不受地方特点约束的一般科学问题,那么可以也应当在全国范围内统一作出规定,并且,应由比纯属地方政府的人更训练有素和更娴熟的人贯彻执行有关规定;另一方面,还有其他一些事务如济贫法、卫生规则,以及其他的管理,尽管全国民众也真正关心这些事务,但不能在与地方行政的目的相适应的情况下,通过地方管理以外的办法进行管理。关于这样一些职责,产生了这样的问题:地方政府应当被授予的自由裁量权,应法可何种程度内不受国家的监督或控制。

要决定这个问题,就有必要对中央当局和地方当局有关做这工作的能力,以及防止玩忽职守或滥用职权方面所处的相对地位加以考虑。首先,在智力和知识程度方面,地方代表机关和它的官员几乎肯定逊于议会和中央行政部门。其次,除了他们自身条件较差之外,对他们进行监督的,以及他们需对其负责的舆论也较弱。与围绕和警告着首都最高当局的公众相比较而言,无论是对他们的作为进行监督的公众,还是对他们提出批评的公众,范围较小而且通常说来更不开明得多。同时,在所涉及的比较狭小的利益的影响下,甚至使得那些较低级的民众对问题的思考也不那么专心,也不那么热情。由报刊和公开讨论所作出的干预就更是少得多,比起对中央当局的行动所作出的干预来,对地方当局的行动所作出的干预可能遭到尤为漠然的忽视。上面所提及的,似乎完全是中央政府管理这方面占有优势。但是,当我们

look more closely, these motives of preference are found to be balanced by others fully as substantial. If the local authorities and public are inferior to the central ones in knowledge of the principles of administration, they have the compensating advantage of a far more direct interest in the result. A man's neighbours or his landlord may be much cleverer than himself, and not without an indirect interest in his prosperity, but for all that, his interests will be better attended to in his own keeping than in theirs. It is further to be remembered, that even supposing the central government to administer through its own officers, its officers do not act at the centre, but in the locality; and however inferior the local public may be to the central, it is the local public alone which has any opportunity of watching them, and it is the local opinion alone which either acts directly upon their own conduct, or calls the attention of the government to the points in which they may require correction. It is but in extreme cases that the general opinion of the country is brought to bear at all upon details of local administration, and still more rarely has it the means of deciding upon them with any just appreciation of the case. Now, the local opinion necessarily acts far more forcibly upon purely local administrators. They, in the natural course of things, are permanent residents, not expecting to be withdrawn from the place when they cease to exercise authority in it; and their authority itself depends, by supposition, on the will of the local public. I need not dwell on the deficiencies of the central authority in detailed knowledge of local persons and things, and the too great engrossment of its time and thoughts by other concerns, to admit of its acquiring the quantity and quality of local knowledge necessary even for deciding on complaints, and enforcing responsibility from so great a number of local agents. In the details of management, therefore, the local bodies will generally have the advantage; but in comprehension of the principles even of purely local management, the superiority of the central government, when rightly constituted, ought to be prodigious : not only by reason of

第十五章

更加审慎地探讨这些问题的时候,就发现其他一些同等重要的动机把这些选择的动机抵消了。如果就行政管理原则方面的知识而言,地方当局和地方的公众比起中央当局和公众来要差一些,但他们却对结果有更直接的利害关系,从而他们可以获得这一个补偿的好处。一个人的邻居或他的房东或许比他本人要聪明得多,对他的事业发达也不是没有间接的影响,但尽管如此,通过他自己的管理,他的利益将比在他们的管理下维护得更好。此外还要铭记,即使假定中央政府是通过它自己的官员来进行管理,它的官员也不是在中央行动,而是在地方上行动。不管比起中央的公众,地方的公众有多差,只有地方的公众才有机会监督这些官员,只有地方的舆论才能直接影响这些官员的行为,或者引起政府注意作必要的修正。只有在极端的情形下,地方行政的细节才会为国家的一般舆论所关注,至于通过对这些事情的公正判断,这种舆论有办法去决定这种细节的情况就更加罕见了。而且,地方舆论必然更强劲地影响纯属地方的行政官员。在事情的自然状态下,这些官员是永久的居民,不要指望当他们不再行使权力时会离开这个地方;并且依照假定,他们的权力本身要受制于当地公众的意志。中央当局缺乏对地方上的人和事的具体了解,以及其他一些事情过多地挤占了它的时间和思想,以至于中央当局甚至不能获得一定数量和质量的地方知识,而这种地方知识对于申诉作出决定和迫使为数众多的地方代理人负起责任是必要的。对所有这些缺陷,我没有必要详细展开来说。因此,通常说来,在管理的细节方面,地方机关是占有优势的;但是在对甚至纯属地方管理的原则的理解方面,如果中央政府组织得好,这方面的优越性应该是巨大的;不仅由于组成中

the probably great personal superiority of the individuals composing it, and the multitude of thinkers and writers who are at all times engaged in pressing useful ideas upon their notice, but also because the knowledge and experience of any local authority is but local knowledge and experience, confined to their own part of the country and its modes of management, whereas the central government has the means of knowing all that is to be learnt from the united experience of the whole kingdom, with the addition of easy access to that of foreign countries.

The practical conclusion from these premises is not difficult to draw. The authority which is most conversant with principles should be supreme over principles, while that which is most competent in details should have the details left to it. The principal business of the central authority should be to give instruction, of the local authority to apply it. Power may be localized, but knowledge to be most useful, must be centralized ; there must be somewhere a focus at which all its scattered rays are collected, that the broken and coloured lights which exist elsewhere may find there what is necessary to complete and purify them. To every branch of local administration which affects the general interest, there should be a corresponding central organ, either a minister, or some specially appointed functionary under him; even if that functionary does no more than collect information from all quarters, and bring the experience acquired in one locality to the knowledge of another where it is wanted. But there is also something more than this for the central authority to do. It ought to keep open a perpetual communication with the localities: informing itself by their experience, and them by its own; giving advice freely when asked, volunteering it when seen to be required ; compelling publicity and recordation of proceedings, and enforcing obedience to every general law which the legislature has laid down on the subject of local management. That some such laws ought to be laid down few are likely to deny. The localities may be allowed to mismanage their own interest, but not to prejudice those of others, nor violate those principles of justice between

第十五章

央政府的人具有也许很大的个人优越性,以及有着许多思想家和政论家,他们常常促使这些人关注有益的意见,而且由于任何地方当局的知识和经验只是限定在地方的知识和经验之内,受到他们自己的那部分地区以及它的管理方式的限制,而中央政府则有办法获知一切知识和经验,这些东西必须从整个王国的整体经验中才能获得,此外,中央政府还易于接触到外国的经验。

通过这些前提,我们不难得出实际的结论。在原则问题上,最洞悉原则的当局应该是最高的权威;在具体问题上,最有能力的当局需负责管理具体问题。中央当局的主要职责应该是发出指示,地方当局的主要职责则是具体运用指示。权力可以地方化,但最有用的知识必须集中。在某个地方必须有一个焦点,这个焦点可以集中一切分散的光线,从而使得别处的不完整和有色的光线,可以在那个焦点找到使它们变得完整和纯化所必要的东西。对牵涉到公众利益的每个地方行政部门,应该设立一个相应的中央机关,负责该机关的可以是一个部长,或者是经特别任命的、比他职务低的某个官员。即便这个官员所做的只不过是从各个地方收集情报,并把从一地区获得的经验下发给需要这经验的另一地区。但是除了这些事之外,中央当局还要做其他一些事。它必须经常和地方保持自由沟通:对各地的经验进行收集,并把自己的经验下发到各地;当受到咨询时要立即提出意见,当看到有这种要求时就主动提出意见;要求把诉讼程序公开化并做下记录,强制遵守立法机关对地方管理问题所制定的每一项普遍通行的法律。应当制定这样一些法律,很少人会对此表示否认。各个地区对其本身的利益管理失当是可以允许的,但不允许侵害其他地区的利益,也不允许侵犯那些人与人之间的公平原则,因

one person and another, of which it is the duty of the State to maintain the rigid observance. If the local majority attempts to oppress the minority, or one class another, the State is bound to interpose. For example, all local rates ought to be voted exclusively by the local representative body; but that body, though elected solely by ratepayers, may raise its revenues by imposts of such a kind, or assess them in such a manner, as to throw an unjust share of the burthen on the poor, the rich, or some particular class of the population : it is the duty, therefore, of the legislature, while leaving the mere amount of the local taxes to the discretion of the local body, to lay down authoritatively the modes of taxation, and rules of assessment, which alone the localities shall be permitted to use. Again in the administration of public charity, the industry and morality of the whole labouring population depends, to a most serious extent, upon adherence to certain fixed principles in awarding relief. Though it belongs essentially to the local functionaries to determine who, according to those principles, is entitled to be relieved, the national parliament is the proper authority to prescribe the principles themselves ; and it would neglect a most important part of its duty if it did not, in a matter of such grave national concern, lay down imperative rules, and make effectual provision that those rules should not be departed from. What power of actual interference with the local administrators it may be necessary to retain, for the due enforcement of the laws, is a question of detail into which it would be useless to enter. The laws themselves will naturally define the penalties, and fix the mode of their enforcement. It may be requisite, to meet extreme cases, that the power of the central authority should extend to dissolving the local representative council, or dismissing the local executive: but not to making new appointments, or suspending the local institutions. Where Parliament has not interfered, neither ought any branch of the executive to interfere with authority ; but as an adviser and critic, an enforcer of the laws, and a denouncer to Parliament or the local constituencies, of conduct which it deems condemnable, the functions of the executive are of the greatest possible value.

Some may think that, however much the central authority surpasses the local in knowledge of the principles of administration,

第十五章

为这个原则是国家有责任严格遵循的。如果地方的多数派妄图压迫少数派,或者一个阶级压迫另一个阶级,国家就不得不干预。比如,地方代表机关应当专门对一切地方税进行表决,但是这个机关,尽管完全是通过纳税人得以选出的,也许征收这样一些税以增加收入,或通过这样的方法来征税,结果使得穷人、富人或某个特定阶级承担了不公平的份额。因此,尽管地方机关可以自由决定地方税的单纯数量,但是立法机关有义务强制规定只允许地方行使的征税方式和估量税额的规则。又比如,在公共慈善事业的管理方面,整个劳动人民的勤勉和道德品质,在很大程度上取决于遵循接受救济的某些确定原则的情况。尽管遵循那些规则以确定谁有资格获得救济的事务实际上是由地方官员所作出的,但全国议会是制定那些原则的正当权威。如果在这一举国上下严重关注的事情上,全国议会没有规定强制性原则,并作出不应违背这些规则的有效规定,它就疏忽了最重要的一部分职责。至于为了法律的正当执行,它有必要保留怎样的实际干涉地方行政官员的权力,则是一个没有必要涉及到的枝节问题。毋庸置疑,法律自身将对惩罚作出规定,并确定其实施方法。为处理极端的情况,中央当局享有解散地方议会或把地方行政长官罢免的权力,这样做或许是必要的,但不能有作出新的任命或中止地方机关运作的权力。在议会没有加以干涉的地方,任何行政部门也不应当有干涉的权力,而是充当一个顾问和批评者,一个法律执行者以及把中央当局认为应该谴责的行为,在议会中或当着地方选民的面进行谴责,这样的行政职能是具有非常大的价值的。

有些人或许认为,无论中央当局在对管理原则的熟悉程度上如

the great object which has been so much insisted on, the social and political education of the citizens, requires that they should be left to manage these matters by their own, however imperfect, lights. To this it might be answered, that the education of the citizens is not the only thing to be considered ; government and administration do not exist for that alone, great as its importance is. But the objection shows a very imperfect understanding of the function of popular institutions as a means of political instruction. It is but a poor education that associates ignorance with ignorance, and leaves them, if they care for knowledge, to grope their way to it without help, and to do without it if they do not. What is wanted is, the means of making ignorance aware of itself, and able to profit by knowledge; accustoming minds Which know only routine, to act upon, and feel the value of, principles; teaching them to compare different modes of action, and learn, by the use of their reason, to distinguish the best. When we desire to have a good school, we do not eliminate the teacher. The old remark. ' as the schoolmaster is, so will be the school, ' is as true of the indirect schooling of grown people by public business, as of the schooling of youth in academies and colleges. A government which attempts to do everything, is aptly compared by M. Charles de Rémusat to a schoolmaster who does all the pupils' tasks for them ; he may be very popular with the pupils, but he will teach them little. A government, on the other hand, which neither does anything itself that can possibly be done by any one else, nor shows any one else how to do anything, is like a school in which there is no schoolmaster, but only pupil-teachers who have never themselves been taught.

第十五章

何胜过地方当局,公民的社会政治教育——人们经常坚持的一项伟大目标——要求能按照公民自己的见解处理这些事情,而不管他们的见解是如何不完善。对此,我可以做这样的回答,对公民的教育并不是唯一应该考虑的事情;尽管公民教育是很重要的,然而,政府和行政并不是单单为它而存在。但是,从这种反对意见中可以表明一点:即对平民机关作为政治教化的手段的这种职能,尚缺乏完全地理解。把无知者和愚昧者搁在一块,假如他们想要知识,就让他们在缺乏别人帮助的情况下摸索前进,假如他们不想要知识,就让他们没有知识,这不过是一种贫乏的教育。我们所要做的是如何使无知者自己洞察到自己的无知,并能从知识中获得教益;使只知道例行公事的人习惯于遵循原则行动,并感觉到原则的价值;教他们对不同的行动方式作比较,并运用他们的理性,去学会辨别哪一种是最好的。当我们期待有一个好学校时,我们并不是把教师排除在外。俗话说,"老师是什么样,学校就会是什么样",对青年的学校教育是这样,对成年人的公共事务教育也是如此。查尔斯·德·瑞穆沙先生非常恰到好处地把企图做一切事情的政府比作帮学生做全部作业的老师。在学生那里,他可能很受欢迎,但是,他教给学生的东西却少得可怜;另一方面,只要是可能让别人做的事它就不去做,也不去教别人做事方法的政府,就好比一所没有老师的学校,在这所学校中,只有自己就从来就没有受过教育的学生老师。

CHAPTER XVI
Of Nationality, As Connected With Representative Government

A Portion of mankind may be said to constitute a Nationality, if they are united among themselves by common sympathies, which do not exist between them and any others—which make them cooperate with each other more willingly than with other people, desire to be under the same government, and desire that it should be government by themselves or a portion of themselves, exclusively. This feeling of nationality may have been generated by various causes. Sometimes it is the effect of identity of race and descent. Community of language, and community of religion, greatly contribute to it. Geographical limits are one of its causes. But the strongest of all is identity of political antecedents; the possession of a national history, and consequent community of recollections ; collective pride and humiliation, pleasure and regret, connected with the same incidents in the past. None of these circumstances however are either indispensable, or necessarily sufficient by themselves. Switzerland has a strong sentiment of nationality, though the cantons are of different races, different languages, and different religions. Sicily has hitherto felt itself quite distinct in nationality from Naples, notwithstanding identity of religion, almost identity of language, and a considerable amount of common historical antecedents. The Flemish and the Walloon provinces of Belgium, notwithstanding diversity of race and language, have a much greater feeling of common nationality, than the former have with Holland, or the latter with France. Yet in general the national feeling is proportionally weakened by the failure of any of the causes which contribute to it.

第十六章　与代议制政府有关的民族问题

　　如果人类的一部分人由共同情感联合在一起,而在他们与任何别人之间不存在这种情感,那么就可以说这些人组成了一个民族——这种情感使他们更愿意互相合作,而不是跟别的民族合作,希望相处在同一个政府之下,并且希望那个政府是由他们自己或他们中的一部分人来管理。形成这种民族情感可能有多方面的原因。有时它是种族与血统的身份认同的结果。共同的语言、共同的宗教对民族情感的形成作用不小。地理边界也是它的原因之一。但最重要的原因是对共同的政治经历的认同、拥有民族的历史,以及从而产生的共同的民族记忆、与过去同一事件相联系的集体的骄傲和耻辱、快乐和悔恨。然而这些情况既不是不可或缺的,也不是必然足够的。瑞士各州尽管有着不同的种族,不同的语言,不同的宗教,却有着强烈的民族情感,西西里尽管与那不勒斯有着共同的宗教,几乎相同的语言,并且有着相当多的共同历史,但却至今认为它和那不勒斯属于不同的民族。比利时的佛兰芒省和瓦龙省尽管种族和语言差异很大,但较之前者同荷兰,或后者同法国,却有更多共同的民族情感。可是一般说来,民族情感由于缺乏其形成的某种原因而遭到相对削弱。对语言、文学以及在某种程度上

Identity of language, literature, and, to some extent, of race and recollections, have maintained the feeling of nationality in considerable strength among the different portions of the German name, though they have at no time been really united under the same government ; but the feeling has never reached to making the separate states desire to get rid of their autonomy. Among Italians an identity far from complete, of language and literature, combined with a geographical position which separates them by a distinct line from other countries, and, perhaps more than everything else, the possession of a common name, which makes them all glory in the past achievements in arts, arms, politics, religious primacy, science, and literature, of any who share the same designation, give rise to an amount of national feeling in the population, which, though still imperfect, has been sufficient to produce the great events now passing before us: notwithstanding a great mixture of races, and although they have never, in either ancient or modern history, been under the same government, except while that government extended or was extending itself over the greater part of the known world.

Where the sentiment of nationality exists in any force, there is a *primâ facie* case for uniting all the members of the nationality under the same government, and a government to themselves apart. This is merely saying that the question of government ought to be decided by the governed. One hardly knows what any division of the human race should be free to do, if not to determine, with which of the various collective bodies of human beings they choose to associate themselves. But, when a people are ripe for free institutions, there is still a more vital consideration. Free institutions are next to impossible in a country made up of different nationalities. Among a people without fellowfeeling, especially if they read and speak different languages, the united public opinion, necessary to the working of representative government, cannot exist. The influences which form opinions and decide political acts, are different in the different sections of the country. An altogether different set of leaders have the confidence of one part of the country and of another. The same books, newspapers, pamphlets, speeches, do not reach them. One section does not know what opinions, or what instigations, are circulating in another.

第十六章

的种族和回忆的认同,维持着德意志不同部分相当强烈的民族情感,尽管它们绝没有真正地联合在同一个政府下面;但是这种情感从来没有达到使各州希望放弃它们自治的程度。在意大利人中,不完全的语言和文学方面的认同,加上以明显的分界线将他们与其他国家区分开来的地理位置,以及也许更为重要的是,他们同一名称的人所共有的称号(这使得他们为过去在艺术、军事、政治、教皇权力、科学和文学等方面的成就而自豪),在人民中间引发了相当程度的民族情感,这些民族情感尽管仍然不很完全,但却足够产生现在我们看到的伟大事件。尽管存在种族方面的重大混杂,尽管除了当那个政府曾经扩张或正在扩张到那个已知世界的大部分的时候,他们不论在古代还是近代历史上,从来没有处于同一个政府之下。

凡是在民族感情有效存在的地方,似乎就证明有把所有民族的成员组成一个政府,并且是只有他们自己成员的政府的根据。这只是说政府的问题应当由被统治者来决定。一个人,如果人们不决定在各种的人类集体组织中他们愿意参加哪一类集体组织的话,就无法知道某一部分人应自由地做些什么。但是当一个民族采用自由制度的时机成熟的时候,仍然有更为关键的东西要考虑。在一个多民族的国家里,自由制度几乎是不可能的。在一个缺乏认同,特别是语言不同的民族里,不存在代议制政府运转所必需的一致的公共舆论。形成舆论以及决定政治行为的势力在国家的不同地区各不相同。得到国家这一地区信赖的领导班子与得到另一地区信赖的领导班子是完全不同的。同样的书籍、报纸、宣传手册、演讲到不了这些地方。一个地方不知另一个地方正在流行怎样的舆论,进行怎样的宣传鼓

The same incidents, the same acts, the same system of government, affect them in different ways; and each fears more injury to itself from the other nationalities, than from the common arbiter, the state. Their mutual antipathies are generally much stronger than jealousy of the government. That any one of them feels aggrieved by the policy of the common ruler, is sufficient to determine another to support that policy. Even if all are aggrieved, none feel that they can rely on the others for fidelity in a joint resistance ; the strength of none is sufficient to resist alone, and each may reasonably think that it consults its own advantage most by bidding for the favour of the government against the rest. Above all, the grand and only reliable security in the last resort against the despotism of the government, is in that case wanting: the sympathy of the army with the people. The military are the part of every community in whom, from the nature of the case, the distinction between their fellow-countrymen and foreigners is the deepest and strongest. To the rest of the people, foreigners are merely strangers ; to the soldier, they are men against whom he may be called, at a week's notice, to fight for life or death. The difference to him is that between friends and foes—we may almost say between fellow-men and another kind of animals : for as respects the enemy, the only law is that of force, and the only mitigation, the same as in the case of other animals—that of simple humanity. Soldiers to whose feelings half or three-fourths of the subjects of the same government are foreigners, will have no more scruple in mowing them down, and no more desire to ask the reason why, than they would have in doing the same thing against declared enemies. An army composed of various nationalities has no other patriotism than devotion to the flag. Such armies have been the executioners of liberty through the whole duration of modern history. The sole bond which holds them together is their officers, and the government which they serve ; and their only idea, if they have any, of public duty, is obedience to orders. A government thus supported, by keeping its Hungarian regiments in Italy and its Italian in

第十六章

动。同一事件,同一行为,同一政府体制,对它们的影响各不相同;每个民族害怕受到其他民族带来的伤害更甚于害怕受到共同的主宰,即国家带来的伤害。它们相互的厌恶一般要比对政府的猜忌更强烈得多。只要它们中的任何一个感得受到了共同统治者政策的不法侵害就足以决定另一个民族去支持那个政策。即使都受到了侵害,它们也认为不能忠诚地互相依靠来奋起反抗。每个民族的力量都不足以单独地进行反抗,并且每个民族都会合理地认为最有利的办法就是赢得政府的好感以反对其他的民族。最为重要的是,作为反抗专制政府的重要的和唯一有效的保证在那种情况下是不存在的,即军队对人民的同情。军队是每个社会的一部分,在这一部分中,按照事情的性质来说,他们的同胞与外国人之间的区别是最深刻、最明显的。对其余的人民来说,外国人仅仅是陌生人,而对士兵来说,外国人是他可能在一周简报中被征召过来要与之进行生死搏斗的人。对他来说,这种区别犹如朋友和敌人——我们几乎可以这样说——犹如同胞与另一种类动物之间的区别。因为关于敌人,唯一的法律就是暴力,并且唯一的缓解办法就是和对其他动物的情形一样,单纯的人道。士兵们如果觉得处于同一政府下的一半或四分之三的国民都是外国人,他将像对付公开宣布的敌人那样毫不犹豫地摧毁它,并且不愿意问这样做的理由。由多个民族组成的军队只忠于所属的军旗,毫无爱国之心。在整个近代历史进程中,这样的军队一直就是绞杀自由的刽子手。把他们团结起来的唯一纽带就是他们的长官,以及他们所效力的政府。他们唯一的公共责任观——如果他们有的话——就是服从命令。政府通过保持它的匈牙利军团于意大利和保持它的意大利军团于匈牙利,有了军队这样的支持,它就能用

Hungary, can long continue to rule in both places with the iron rod of foreign conquerors.

If it be said that so broadly marked a distinction between what is due to a fellow-countryman and what is due merely to a human creature, is more worthy of savages than of civilized beings, and ought, with the utmost energy, to be contended against, no one holds that opinion more strongly than myself. But this object, one of the worthiest to which human endeavour can be directed, can never, in the present state of civilization, be promoted by keeping different nationalities of anything like equivalent strength under the same government. In a barbarous state of society, the case is sometimes different. The government may then be interested in softening the antipathies of the races, that peace may be preserved, and the country more easily governed. But when there are either free institutions, or a desire for them, in any of the peoples artificially tied together, the interest of the government lies in an exactly opposite direction. It is then interested in keeping up and envenoming their antipathies; that they may be prevented from coalescing, and it may be enabled to use some of them as tools for the enslavement of others. The Austrian Court has now for a whole generation made these tactics its principal means of government ; with what fatal success, at the time of the Vienna insurrection and the Hungarian contest, the world knows too well. Happily there are now signs that improvement is too far advanced to permit this policy to be any longer successful.

For the preceding reasons, it is in general a necessary condition of free institutions, that the boundaries of governments should coincide in the main with those of nationalities. But several considerations are liable to conflict in practice with this general principle. In the first place, its application is often precluded by geographical hindrances. There are parts even of Europe, in which different nationalities are so locally intermingled, that it is not practicable for them to be under separate governments. The population of Hungary is composed of Magyars, Slovacks, Croats, Serbs, Roumans, and in some districts, Germans, so mixed up as to be incapable of local separation ;

第十六章

外国征服者的铁鞭继续长期统治这两个地方。

如果有人说,如此宽泛地在什么人必定是同胞而什么人只是单纯的人类之间作出区分,是野蛮人的做法而非文明人所为,并且应当竭力加以反对,那么,再没有什么人比我更强烈地支持这种观点了。但是这个目标,这个人类能够去努力的最有价值的目标,在当前的文明发展水平下,绝不能通过保持在同一政府下各个民族力量相当的办法来达到。在野蛮的社会状态下,情形有时不同。在那时政府可能关心缓和民族之间的憎恶,从而和平可以保持,国家更易于统治。但是当存在自由制度时,或者有得到自由制度的愿望时,在任何人为地捆绑在一起的民族里,政府关心的就完全是相反的方面。那时它将关心维持并且强化它们之间的憎恶,从而可以防止它们联合,使它能够利用其中的某些民族作为奴役其他民族的工具。奥地利法庭目前在整整一代人中间把这些策略作为他们统治的主要手段;全世界都十分清楚,这些策略在维也纳起义和与匈牙利角逐中取得了何等重要的成功。令人高兴的是,现在有迹象表明,人类的进步已经使得这种政策不会再有成功的机会了。

根据上述理由,政府的范围应该大体上与民族的范围一致,这在一般情况下是自由制度的一个必要条件。但在实践中某些考虑事项与这条一般原则容易发生冲突。首先,地理阻碍常常使它难以适用。即使在欧洲也有这样的地方,不同的民族混居在一起,要把它们置于个别的民族管理之下是不可能的。匈牙利的人口由马扎尔人、斯洛伐克人、克罗地亚人、塞尔维亚人、罗马尼亚人以及在某些地区的德意志人组成,混杂到这种地步,以至于无

and there is no course open to them but to make a virtue of necessity, and reconcile themselves to living together under equal rights and laws. Their community of servitude, which dates only from the destruction of Hungarian independence in 1849, seems to be ripening and disposing them for such an equal union. The German colony of East Prussia is cut off from Germany by part of the ancient Poland, and being too weak to maintain separate independence, must, if geographical continuity is to be maintained, be either under a non-German government, or the intervening Polish territory must be under a German one. Another considerable region in which the dominant element of the population is German, the provinces of Courland, Esthonia, and Livonia, is condemned by its local situation to form part of a Slavonian state. In Eastern Germany itself there is a large Slavonic population: Bohemia is principally Slavonic, Silesia and other districts partially so. The most united country in Europe, France, is far from being homogeneous: independently of the fragments of foreign nationalities in its remote extremities, it consists, as language and history prove, of two portions, one occupied almost exclusively by a Gallo-Roman population, while in the other the Frankish, Burgundian, and other Teutonic races form a considerable ingredient.

When proper allowance has been made for geographical exigencies, another more purely moral and social consideration offers itself. Experience proves, that it is possible for one nationality to merge and be absorbed in another: and when it was originally an inferior and more backward portion of the human race, the absorption is greatly to its advantage. Nobody can suppose that it is not more beneficial to a Breton, or a Basque of French Navarre, to be brought into the current of the ideas and feelings of a highly civilized and cultivated people— to be a member of the French nationality, admitted on equal terms to all the privileges of French citizenship, sharing the advantages of French

第十六章

法按地区把它们分开;并且他们别无他法,只能不得已而甘愿这样,在平等权利和法律下心平气和地生活在一起。它们受奴役的一致性可追溯到1849年匈牙利人丧失独立的时候,似乎正在成熟到使他们倾向于这种平等的联合。德意志人聚居地东普鲁士被古波兰从德意志分割出来,并且由于太弱而不能维持独立,必须——如果要保持地理上的连接的话——要么被置于非德意志政府之下,要么夹在当中的波兰领土被置于德意志政府之下。另一个相当大的、其主要居民是德意志人的地区是库尔兰、爱沙尼亚和里窝尼亚诸省,由于当地的形势被宣布为斯拉夫国家的一部分,在东德意志本身就有大量的斯拉夫人口:波希米亚主要是斯拉夫人,西里西亚和其他地区部分地是斯拉夫人。欧洲最统一的国家法国也绝不是清一色的,除了在其极边远的地方还居住着零星的外族之外,正如语言和历史表明的,它包括两部分,一部分主要居住着几乎清一色的高卢—罗马人,而另一部分则是由法兰克人、勃艮第人,以及其他条顿民族的人(Teutonic)占据了相当大的成分。

当我们对地理上的情况作了适当的考虑后,另外一种更纯粹的关于道德和社会的考虑就出现了。经验证明,有可能一个民族融入另一个民族并为之同化,并且当它原来就是一个低级并且更为落后的种族时,这种同化对它就大为有利。没有人会认为假如一个法国布里多尼人或一个法国纳瓦拉的巴斯克人被带入一个高度文明和有教养的民族的思想和情感的洪流之中——成为法兰西民族的一员,在平等条件下享有法国公民的一切特权,享受法国保护的有利条件,以

protection, and the dignity and *prestige* of French power—than to sulk on his own rocks, the half-savage relic of past times, revolving in his own little mental orbit, without participation or interest in the general movement of the world. The same remark applies to the Welshman or the Scottish Highlander, as members of the British nation.

Whatever really tends to the admixture of nationalities, and the blending of their attributes and peculiarities in a common union, is a benefit to the human race. Not by extinguishing types, of which, in these cases, sufficient examples are sure to remain, but by softening their extreme forms, and filling up the intervals between them. The united people, like a crossed breed of animals (but in a still greater degree, because the influences in operation are moral as well as physical), inherits the special aptitudes and excellences of all its progenitors, protected by the admixture from being exaggerated into the neighbouring vices. But to render this admixture possible, there must be peculiar conditions. The combinations of circumstances which occur, and which affect the result are various.

The nationalities brought together under the same government, may be about equal in numbers and strength, or they may be very unequal. If unequal, the least numerous of the two may either be the superior in civilization, or the inferior, Supposing it to be superior, it may either, through that superiority, be able to acquire ascendancy over the other, or it may be overcome by brute strength, and reduced to subjection. This last is a sheer mischief to the human race, and one which civilized humanity with one accord should rise in arms to prevent. The absorption of Greece by Macedonia was one of the greatest misfortunes which ever happened to the world: that of any of the principal countries of Europe by Russia would be a similar one.

If the smaller nationality, supposed to be the more advanced in improvement, is able to overcome the greater, as the Macedonians, reinforced by the Greeks, did Asia, and the English India, there is

第十六章

及法国实力的尊严和威望——与结束过去时代的半野蛮的遗迹,绕着自己狭小的精神生活轨道旋转,不参加也不关心世界的一般活动相比,会更为无益。同样的评论也适用于成为英国民族成员的威尔士人或英格兰高地人的情形。

凡是倾向于民族融合,并且将它们民族的属性和特性调和进一个共同的联合体中,对人类都是有益的。不是通过消灭不同的类型(这种例子在这些场合中肯定会存在着),而是通过软化它们最极端的形式,并缩小它们之间的差距。融合起来的人民像杂交繁殖的动物那样(但这是在更大程度上,因为起作用的影响既是肉体的也是道德的),继承其一切先代的特质和优点,融合的结果使这些特质和优点不至于趋于极端而变成缺陷。但是要使这种融合成为可能,必须要有特殊的条件。发生并影响到结果的各种条件的结合是多样的。

处于同一个政府下的各个民族,可以在人数上和力量上大致相当,也可以很不相当。如果不相当,两个民族中人数最少的在文明方面可以是较高的,也可以是较低的。假定它是较高的,那么尽管在其文明上有优越感,从而可能能够取得对另一个民族的支配权,但也可能被野蛮力量所征服并被降至从属地位。后者对人类来说是完全有害的,是文明人类应一致起来用武力来防止的。马其顿吞并希腊就是世界上曾发生过的最大的灾难之一,而欧洲任何一个主要国家若被俄罗斯吞并也将是类似的灾难。

如果较小的民族(假设它在改良方面取得了更大的进步),像马其顿人那样在希腊人的增援下能够征服亚洲,和英国人征服英属印度一样,常常有益于增进文明。但是在这种情形下,征服者

often a gain to civilization; but the conquerors and the conquered cannot in this case live together under the same free institutions. The absorption of the conquerors in the less advanced people would be an evil: these must be governed as subjects, and the state of things is either a benefit or a misfortune, according as the subjugated people have or have not reached the state in which it is an injury not to be under a free government, and according as the conquerors do or do not use their superiority in a manner calculated to fit the conquered for a higher stage of improvement. This topic will be particularly treated of in a subsequent chapter.

When the nationality which succeeds in overpowering the other, is both the most numerous and the most improved ; and especially if the subdued nationality is small, and has no hope of reasserting its independence ; then, if it is governed with any tolerable justice, and if the members of the more powerful nationality are not made odious by being invested with exclusive privileges, the smaller nationality is gradually reconciled to its position, and becomes amalgamated with the larger. No BasBreton, nor even any Alsatian, has the smallest wish at the present day to be separated from France. If all Irishmen have not yet arrived at the same disposition towards England, it is partly because they are sufficiently numerous to be capable of constituting a respectable nationality by themselves ; but principally because, until of late years, they had been so atrociously governed, that all their best feelings combined with their bad ones in rousing bitter resentment against the Saxon rule. This disgrace to England, and calamity to the whole empire, has, it may be truly said, completely ceased for nearly a generation. No Irishman is now less free than an Anglo-Saxon, nor has a less share of every benefit either to his country or to his individual fortunes, than if he were sprung from any other portion of the British dominions. The only remaining real grievance of Ireland, that of the State Church, is one which half, or nearly half, the people of the larger island have in common with them. There is now next to nothing, except the memory of the past, and the difference in the predominant religion, to keep apart two races,

第十六章

和被征服者不能在同样的自由制度下生活在一起。征服者被较不发达的民族同化将会是一种不幸,因为这些落后的人必须作为臣民被统治着,而事态是有益还是不幸,需根据被征服者是否已达到不处在自由政府之下就会有害的状态,以及根据是否利用他们的优越性在某种意义上使被征服者适于更高的发展阶段而定。这个话题将在接下来的一章中加以特别的讨论。

当成功地制服了另一个民族的民族既是人口众多,又是最为先进的时候,特别是当被征服的民族是个弱小的民族,没有希望恢复其独立的时候,那么,如果统治尚且公正,如果更为强大民族的成员不因拥有排他性的特权而让人讨厌的话,较弱小的民族就渐渐地接受了其地位,为较大的民族所吞并了。巴斯—布里多尼亚人,甚至任何阿尔萨斯人如今都不会有哪怕是一丁点脱离法国的想法。如果所有的爱尔兰人在对待英国方面仍未达到相同的意向,那部分原因是它有足够的人数使它能够形成一个让人尊敬的民族,但主要原因是直到最近几年,他们被如此残酷地统治着,以至于他们所有的最好情感都与坏的情感结合起来,煽动起仇恨来反对撒克逊人的统治。这种让英国感到耻辱、让整个帝国感到是个灾难的事,可以真正地说,花了几乎一代人的时间才得以完全平息。现在每个爱尔兰人不管他来自英国版图内的任何地方,都跟盎格鲁—撒克逊人一样享有自由,享有国家以及他个人财产给他带来的每一份利益。爱尔兰人唯一留下来的真正不满,是国家教会,这也是一半或几乎一半的大岛岛民和他们所共有的不满。除了对过去的回忆,以及居支配地位的宗教方面的不同外,现在差不多没有什么能把这两个民族

perhaps the most fitted of any two in the world to be the completing counterpart of one another. The consciousness of being at last treated not only with equal justice but with equal consideration, is making such rapid way in the Irish nation, as to be wearing off all feelings that could make them insensible to the benefits which the less numerous and less wealthy people must necessarily derive, from being fellow-citizens instead of foreigners to those who are not only their nearest neighbours, but the wealthiest and one of the freest, as well as most civilized and powerful, nations of the earth.

The cases in which the greatest practical obstacles exist to the blending of nationalities, are when the nationalities which have been bound together are nearly equal in numbers, and in the other elements of power. In such cases, each confiding in its strength, and feeling itself capable of maintaining an equal struggle with any of the others, is unwilling to be merged in it : each cultivates with party obstinacy its distinctive peculiarities ; obsolete customs, and even declining languages, are revived, to deepen the separation ; each deems itself tyrannized over if any authority is exercised within itself by functionaries of a rival race ; and whatever is given to one of the conflicting nationalities, is considered to be taken from all the rest. When nations, thus divided, are under a despotic government which is a stranger to all of them, or which though sprung from one, yet feeling greater interest in its own power than in any sympathies of nationality, assigns no privilege to either nation, and chooses its instruments indifferently from all ; in the course of a few generations, identity of situation often produces harmony of feelings, and the different races come to feel towards each other as fellow-countrymen ; particularly if they are dispersed over the same tract of country. But if the era of aspiration to free government arrives before this fusion has been effected, the opportunity has gone by for effecting it. From that time, if the unreconciled nationalities are geographically separate, and especially if their local position is such that there is no natural fitness or convenience in their being under the same government (as in the

第十六章

分开了,这是也许世界上两个相互配合得最好的民族了。感觉到不仅得到同等的公平对待而且得到了同等的关注,使得爱尔兰人迅速地消除所有可能使他们对所得好处麻木不仁的感情,使他们感觉到,人数较少、不很富裕的民族必须作为同胞而不是外国人从那个不仅是他们的近邻,而且是地球上最富裕并且最自由的民族之一,同时也是最文明和最强大的民族那里寻得好处。

在民族合并中最大的实际障碍是当这些已经结合在一起的民族在人数以及其他实力因素都几乎相等的时候。在这些情况下,每一个民族都相信自己的实力,认为自己能够与其他任何民族相抗衡,因而不愿意被融合。每个民族以政党的偏执性来培养自己与众不同的特性,陈旧的习俗甚至没落的语言,都被加以复兴,以加深这种分离。每个民族都认为如果自己由来自敌对种族的官员统治必定会招致暴政,并且认为凡是互相冲突的民族融合以后,一个民族所得到只是所有其余民族所失。当如此互相分离的民族处于一个专制政府的统治之下,而这个专制政府对所有成员来说都是陌生的,或者尽管它源出其中一个民族,然而却由于过分关注自己的权力、对任何民族情感不感兴趣,而不给别的民族以特权,并且中立地从它们中间挑选自己的傀儡时,在经历了几代之后,对处境的认同经常会产生出情感的和谐来,从而不同的种彼此将对方当作同胞来看待,特别是如果他们散居在同一个地方时。但是假如渴望自由政府的时代要早于这种民族融合完成之时到来的话,完成这种融合的机会就随之失去了。从那时起,假如不和谐一致的民族在地理上是分离的,特别是如果它们在地方的地位就是如此,不是自然地适合或方便处在同一个政府下面(例如意大利的

case of an Italian province under a French or German yoke), there is not only an obvious propriety, but, if either freedom or concord is cared for, anecessity, for breaking the connexion altogether. There may be cases in which the provinces, after separation, might usefully remain united by a federal tie : but it generally happens that if they are willing to forgo complete independence, and become members of a federation, each of them has other neighbours with whom it would prefer to connect itself, having more sympathies in common, if not also greater community of interest.

一个省处在法国或德国支配下的场合），不存在明显的适当性,而且如果人们在乎自由或在乎和谐的话，那么就有打破这种联系的必要了。存在着这样的例子，即一个省份在分离之后，可能通过联邦的纽带有效地联合起来。但一般情况是，如果它们愿意放弃完全的独立，变成联邦的成员，那么它们中的每一个都有其他它们愿意与之连接的邻居，具有更多的共同情感，如果不是也具有更大的共同利益的话。

CHAPTER XVII
Of Federal Representative Governments

Portions of mankind who are not fitted, or not disposed, to live under the same internal government, may often with advantage be federally united, as to their relations with foreigners: both to prevent wars among themselves, and for the sake of more effectual protection against the aggression of powerful States.

To render a federation advisable, several conditions are necessary. The first is, that there should be a sufficient amount of mutual sympathy among the populations. The federation binds them always to fight on the same side; and if they have such feelings towards one another, or such diversity of feeling towards their neighbours, that they would generally prefer to fight on opposite sides, the federal tie is neither likely to be of long duration, nor to be well observed while it subsists. The sympathies available for the purpose are those of race, language, religion, and above all, of political institutions, as conducing most to a feeling of identity of political interest. When a few free states, separately insufficient for their own defence, are hemmed in on all sides by military or feudal monarchs, who hate and despise freedom even in a neighbour, those states have no chance for preserving liberty and its blessings, but by a federal union. The common interest arising from this cause has in Switzerland, for several centuries, been found adequate to maintain efficiently the federal bond, in spite not only of difference of religion when religion was the grand source of irreconcilable political enmity throughout Europe, but also in spite of great weakness in the constitution of the federation itself. In America, where all the conditions for the maintenance of union existed at the

第十七章　联邦的代议制政府

在对外关系方面，不适于或不情愿在同一国内政府下生活的几部分人，组成联邦常常是有益处的，因为这样做的话，既能防止他们彼此之间的战争，又能更有效地防御强国的侵略。

要使结盟成为可能，以下几个条件是必备的：第一个条件是，民众之间需具备足够多的彼此的认同。由于受到联盟的约束，他们总是要为同一方而战斗；如果他们互相之间的感情，或对待他们的邻居方面所带有的不同感情，是通常愿意为相反的一方而战斗，那么，这种联盟的纽带是不可能长久持续的，即使在它存在之时，也不会得到好的遵循。在这种意义上的认同，就是源于种族、语言、宗教，尤其是政治制度方面的认同，它对于政治利益的共同感的生成是最为有利的。当几个没有足够实力去单独自我防御的自由国家，像铁桶一样被军事的或封建的君主所包围，而这些君主又仇恨和藐视甚至邻国的自由时，那么这些国家除非结成联盟，否则不可能保持其自由和幸福。在瑞士，基于这种原因产生的共同利益，几个世纪以来被认为是适宜于有效地维护联盟的纽带，尽管该国不仅有着宗教方面的差异，而宗教在当时是整个欧洲不可调和的政治冲突的主要根源，而且联盟自身的构造上也具有重大的缺点。在美国，那里最大程度上具备着保持联盟的

highest point, with the sole drawback of difference of institutions in the single but most important article of Slavery, this one difference has gone so far in alienating from each other's sympathies the two divisions of the Union, as to be now actually effecting the disruption of a tie of so much value to them both.

The second condition for the stability of a federal government, is that the separate states be not so powerful, as to be able to rely, for protection against foreign encroachment, on their individual strength. If they are, they will be apt to think that they do not gain, by union with others, the equivalent of what they sacrifice in their own liberty of action : and consequently, whenever the policy of the Confederation, in things reserved to its cognizance, is different from that which any one of its members would separately pursue, the internal and sectional breach will, through absence of sufficient anxiety to preserve the Union, be in danger of going so far as to dissolve it.

A third condition, not less important than the two others, is that there be not a very marked inequality of strength among the several contracting states. They cannot, indeed, be exactly equal in resources : in all federations there will be a gradation of power among the members ; some will be more populous, rich, and civilized than others. There is a wide difference in wealth and population between New York and Rhode Island; between Berne, and Zug or Glaris. The essential is, that there should not be any one State so much more powerful than the rest, as to be capable of vying in strength with many of them combined. If there be such a one, and only one, it will insist on being master of the joint deliberations : if there be two, they will be irresistible when they agree ; and whenever they differ, everything will be decided by a struggle for ascendancy between the rivals. This cause is alone enough to reduce the German Bund to almost a nullity, independently of its wretched internal constitution. It effects none of the purposes of a confederation. It has never bestowed on Germany an

第十七章

一切条件,唯一的缺陷是在奴隶条款方面的制度上的分歧,这一分歧虽然只是单独一个但却最为重要,因为这一分歧在疏远联盟的两个部分相互之间的感情上走得这么远,导致了对双方都有极大价值的纽带的断裂。

联邦政府稳定性的第二个条件是,个别的国家不能强大到能依靠它们各自的力量抵抗外国的侵略的程度。否则它们就很容易认为,它们在牺牲行动自由方面的坏处,不能从它们与其他别的国家联盟所得到的好处中得到补偿;因此,只要是联邦在其有权管辖的事情上的政策迥异于任何一个成员各自实施的政策,那么,由于缺乏维护联邦的饱满热情,内部的和地区之间的不协调就存在着演变到联邦解体的危险。

其重要性不逊于上面两个条件的第三个条件是,在缔约的各个国家中,实力的不平等并不是特别显著。当然,它们的资源也是不可能绝对均等的,在一切联邦中各邦之间的实力总是有差异的;有些邦人口较稠密,较富有,也较文明。纽约州和罗得岛州之间在财富和人口方面的差距是巨大的;伯尔尼州和楚格州或格拉利斯州之间的情况也是一样。最关键的一点是,不应存在任何一个这样的邦国,它的力量比其他各邦国都强大,以至强大到能有力量和很多个邦国联合在一起的力量相对抗的地步。如果有这样一个邦国,而且是唯一的一个,它坚持要控制共同的商议;假如有两个这样的邦,当它们见解达到共识时,那么将是不可抵抗的;而一旦它们观点不一致,一切都将取决于它们在斗争之后占优势的一方。就凭这一原因就足以把德意志联邦瓦解,更不用提它极差的内部构成了。它一点也没有实现联邦的真正目的。它从来没有赋予德意志统一的

uniform system of customs, nor so much as an uniform coinage; and has served only to give Austria and Prussia a legal right of pouring in their troops to assist the local sovereigns in keeping their subjects obedient to despotism : while in regard to external concerns, the Bund would make all Germany a dependency of Prussia, if there were no Austria, and of Austria if there were no Prussia : and in the meantime each petty prince has little choice but to be a partisan of one or the other, or to intrigue with foreign governments against both.

There are two different modes of organizing a Federal Union. The federal authorities may represent the Governments solely, and their acts may be obligatory only on the Governments as such, or they may have the power of enacting laws and issuing orders which are binding directly on individual citizens. The former is the plan of the German so-called Confederation, and of the Swiss Constitution previous to 1847. It was tried in America for a few years immediately following the War of Independence. The other principle is that of the existing Constitution of the United States, and has been adopted within the last dozen years by the Swiss Confederacy. The Federal Congress of the American Union is a substantive part of the government of every individual State. Within the limits of its attributions, it makes laws which are obeyed by every citizen individually, executes them through its own officers, and enforces them by its own tribunals. This is the only principle which has been found, or which is ever likely, to produce an effective federal government. An union between the governments only, is a mere alliance, and subject to all the contingencies which render alliances precarious. If the acts of the President and of Congress were binding solely on the Governments of New York, Virginia, or Pennsylvania, and could only be carried into effect through orders issued by those Governments to officers appointed by them under responsibility to their own courts of justice, no mandates of the Federal Government which were disagreeable to a local majority would ever be executed. Requisitions issued to a government have no

第十七章

关税制度,也没有就统一的货币制度作出规定;它只是有利于赋予奥地利和普鲁士合法权力,从而派遣它们的军队去协助各地方的君主压迫其臣民服从专制制度;另一方面,在对外关系方面,假如没有奥地利的话,联邦将把全德意志变成普鲁士的属国;而假如没有普鲁士的话,联邦则将把全德意志变成奥地利的属国。这时候,每个小君主除了依附这国或那国,或者和外国政府互相勾结以反对两者之外,几乎没有更多的选择。

在联邦的构成上,有两种不同的模式。第一种模式是,联邦当局只是代表着各个政府,它的行为只对作为政府的各邦政府有强制力;第二种模式是,联邦当局有权制定法律和颁布法令,这些法律和法令将直接对各个公民有强制力。前者是德意志所谓联邦的方案,以及在1847年之前瑞士宪法的方案。紧挨着独立战争之后的数年里,这种方案也曾被美国试行过。另一种模式是美国现行宪法的原则,并且在最近12年中,瑞士联邦也采纳了这一模式。美国联邦的联邦国会是每一个州政府的实体部分。在它的职权范围内,它颁布每个公民都须自觉遵守的法律,通过它自己的官员加以执行,并把强制执行该项法律的权力交给它自己的法院。这是人们已经发现或确曾有可能构建有效的联邦政府的唯一模式。单单政府之间的联合只不过是一种联盟,而且它容易受到一切偶然事件的影响从而使得联盟变得不稳定。倘若美国总统和国会的法令只对纽约、维吉尼亚或宾夕法尼亚等各州的政府有强制力,并且那些法令的执行,只能通过这些政府给各自所任命的官员发布的命令加以施行,而这些政府只对它们各自的法院负责,那么联邦政府的任何命令,如果无法获得多数州的同意就得不到执行了。向州政府发

other sanction, or means of enforcement, than war: and a federal army would have to be always in readiness, to enforce the decrees of the Federation against any recalcitrant State ; subject to the probability that other States, sympathizing with the recusant, and perhaps sharing its sentiments on the particular point in dispute, would withhold their contingents, if not send them to fight in the ranks of the disobedient State. Such a federation is more likely to be a cause than a preventive of internal wars: and if such was not its effect in Switzerland until the events of the years immediately preceding 1847, it was only because the Federal Government felt its weakness so strongly, that it hardly ever attempted to exercise any real authority. In America, the experiment of a Federation on this principle broke down in the first few years of its existence ; happily while the men of enlarged knowledge and acquired ascendancy, who founded the independence of the Republic, were still alive to guide it through the difficult transition. The 'Federalist,' a collection of papers by three of these eminent men, written in explanation and defence of the new Federal Constitution while still awaiting the national acceptance, is even now the most instructive treatise we possess on federal government. In Germany, the more imperfect kind of federation, as all know, has not even answered the purpose of maintaining an alliance. It has never, in any European war, prevented single members of the Confederation from allying themselves with foreign powers against the rest. Yet this is the only federation which seems possible among monarchical states. A king, who holds his power by inheritance, not by delegation, and who cannot be deprived of it, nor made responsible to any one for its use, is not likely to renounce having a separate army, or to brook the exercise of sovereign authority over his own subjects, not through him directly, but by another power. To enable two or more countries under kingly government to be joined together in an effectual confederation,

第十七章

出的征用物资的命令,除了诉诸战争之外也就没有其他制裁或强制手段了。在这种情形之下,联邦军队将不得不常常准备着对桀骜不驯的州强制执行联邦的法令。还有这样一种可能性:其他的州,对老唱反调的州怀有同情之心,或许在有争议的某一个观点上对它有同感,因而,如果不把其军队派去和不服从的州的军队一起作战的话,这些州将不会派遣它们的军队。这样的联邦与其说是防止内战的手段,毋宁说是引发内战的原因。如果说这并非是瑞士联邦直到1847年前几年发生的事件以前的情况,那不过是因为联邦政府感到本身力量很弱小,以致几乎不曾企图行使任何真正权力的结果。在美国,遵循这一模式的联邦的试验,在其存在的最初几年里就归于失败,幸运的是,当时具有广博知识和占有权势的先驱们——他们奠定了共和国的独立——仍然活着来引领共和国度过困难的过渡期《联邦党人文集》这本书,是在新的联邦宪法还没有得到全民认可的时候,为了对这一宪法作说明和辩护而写的。这本书是由三个杰出的联邦主义者所写文章的汇编,迄今仍是我们关于联邦政府所具有的最富教益的论述。正如大家所知晓的,德意志,这个更为不完善的联邦,甚至尚未达到维护同盟的目的。在任何一次欧洲战争中,它都未曾防止联邦的单个成员和外国联合起来反对其他成员。尽管如此,这种联邦似乎是君主国家之间唯一可能的联盟。如果一个君主,他权力的获得是基于继承关系而不是根据委托关系的话,那么,在既不能剥夺他的权力,又无法使他就权力的行使对任何人负责的情况下,要让这个君主放弃控制一支独立的军队,或者容忍任何国家不通过他而直接对他的臣民行使主权,都是不可能的。要把两个以上的君主政府的国家联合在一个有效的联盟之

it seems necessary that they should all be under the same king. England and Scotland were a federation of this description, during the interval of about a century between the union of the Crowns and that of the Parliaments. Even this was effected, not through federal institutions, for none existed, but because the regal power in both Constitutions was during the greater part of that time so nearly absolute, as to enable the foreign policy of both to be shaped according to a single will.

Under the more perfect mode of federation, where every citizen of each particular State owns obedience to two Governments, that of his own State, and that of the federation, it is evidently necessary not only that the constitutional limits of the authority of each should be precisely and clearly defined, but that the power to decide between them in any case of dispute should not reside in either of the Governments, or in any functionary subject to it, but in an umpire independent of both. There must be a Supreme Court of Justice, and a system of subordinate Courts in every State of the Union, before whom such questions shall be carried, and whose judgment on them, in the last stage of appeal, shall be final, Every State of the Union, and the Federal Government itself, as well as every functionary of each, must be liable to be sued in those Courts for exceeding their powers, or for non-performance of their federal duties, and must in general be obliged to employ those Courts as the instrument for enforcing their federal rights. This involves the remarkable consequence, actually realized in the United States, that a Court of Justice the highest federal tribunal, is supreme over the various Governments, both State and Federal; having the right to declare that any law made, or act done by them, exceeds the powers assigned to them by the Federal Constitution, and, in consequence, has no legal validity. It was natural to feel strong doubts, before trial had been made, how such a provision would work; whether the tribunal would have the courage to exercise its constitutional power ; if it did, whether it would exercise it wisely, and whether the Governments would consent to submit peaceably to its decision. The discussions on the American Constitution, before its final adoption , give evidence that these natural apprehensions

第十七章

内,使该联盟处在同一国王管辖之下,看起来是很有必要的。在国王的联合和议会的联合之间存在的约一世纪的时间内,英格兰和苏格兰就属于这样一种联盟。甚至这种联盟之所以有效果,也并非是源于联邦制度——因为那时这种制度根本不存在——而是由于在那段时期的大部分时间内,两国宪法中的王权都差不多是绝对的,导致两国遵循一个意志使其对外政策得以形成。

在更完善的联邦模式下,每个特定州的公民必须服从两个政府,一个是他自己的州政府,另一个是联邦的政府,不仅应该对每个政府在宪法上的权限作出明确规定,而且当出现争议时,裁决权不应由其中任何一个政府去决定,也不应由各政府的任何官员去决定,而应由超脱于两者之外的仲裁者去决定。应该有一个最高法院和在各州内的下级法院系统,把有争议的问题递交给这些法院,它们对争议作出的终审判决将是不能更改的。和联邦及各州政府的每个官员一样,联邦的每个州,以及联邦政府本身,当超越了它们的权限,或者没有行使其联邦职责时,都应受到这些法院的控诉,并且通常说来不得不利用这些法院作为实现它们联邦利益的手段。这牵涉到实际上出现在美国的那种极不寻常的后果,即作为联邦最高法庭的法院的权威是要高于各个州及联邦政府的;它有权宣布它们所颁布的法律或其行为不具备法律效力,因为这些法律或行为超出了联邦宪法赋予它们的权限。在经过检验之前,对于这样的规定会发挥怎样的作用,法庭是否会有行使其宪法权力的勇气,如果有这种勇气的话,它是否能明智地运用这种权力,以及对于它作出的判决各个政府是否会同意平静地服从,民众自然而然会感到强烈的怀疑。在最终表决通过美国宪法之前,有关这一规定的讨论表明,这种种自然会有的担

were strongly felt; but they are now entirely quieted, since, during the two generations and more which have subsequently elapsed, nothing has occurred to verify them, though there have at times been disputes of considerable acrimony, and which became the badges of parties, respecting the limits of the authority of the Federal and State Governments. The eminently beneficial working of so singular a provision, is probably, as M. de Tocqueville remarks, in a great measure attributable to the peculiarity inherent in a Court of Justice acting as such—namely, that it does not declare the law *eo nomine* and in the abstract, but waits until a case between man and man is brought before it judicially, involving the point in dispute: from which arises the happy effect, that its declarations are not made in a very early stage of the controversy ; that much popular discussion usually precedes them; that the Court decides after hearing the point fully argued on both sides by lawyers of reputation ; decides only as much of the question at a time as is required by the case before it, and its decision, instead of being volunteered for political purposes, is drawn from it by the duty which it cannot refuse to fulfil, of dispensing justice impartially between adverse litigants. Even these grounds of confidence would not have sufficed to produce the respectful submission with which all authorities have yielded to the decisions of the Supreme Court on the interpretation of the Constitution, were it not that complete reliance has been felt, not only on the intellectual pre-eminence of the judges composing that exalted tribunal, but on their entire superiority over either private or sectional partialities. This reliance has been in the main justified ; but there is nothing which more vitally imports the American people, than to guard with the most watchful solicitude against everything which has the remotest tendency to produce deterioration in the quality of this great national institution. The confidence on which depends the stability of federal institutions was for the first time impaired, by the judgment declaring slavery to be of common right, and consequently lawful in the Territories while not yet constituted as States, even against the will of a majority of their inhabitants. This memorable decision has probably done more than anything else to bring the sectional division to the crisis which is now issuing

第十七章

忧已经被民众强烈地感受到;但是现在对其种种的担心已完全没有必要,因为在那以后所经历过的六十多年里,这种种担心的事情已被证实并没有发生,尽管有时关于联邦和州政府权限的辩论是相当尖锐的,而且这种辩论成为了政党的标记。这样一项单个的规定之所以具有显著有益的作用,在德·托克维尔先生看来,很大程度上可以把它归功于法院作为一个法院所内在的特性——即它不是从其名义和抽象方面去宣告法律,而是在出现人和人之间涉及争议问题的案件时,把这个案件列入法院中行使司法权力:在那里,绝妙的结果得以产生,法律的宣告并不在争议一开始就作出,在其以前一般先有很多民众性的讨论,在听取双方有声誉的律师就争议问题充分辩论之后,法院才会作出判决,每一次只依据案件所要求的问题作出裁决,而且它的裁决并非是为了政治上的目的而自愿作出的,而是源于这一不能拒绝履行的职责——法院应对原被告双方进行公平审判。甚至这些信任的理由也不足以产生那种毕恭毕敬的服从,这种服从是从所有政府当局对最高法院关于宪法解释中可以看出来的,如果不是因为它们不仅对组成这个尊贵法庭的法官们的卓越才能,而且对他们完全优于个人的或地区的偏见有完全的信赖的话。这种信赖基本上是正当的;但是对于美国人民而言,再也没有比谨小慎微地预防一切哪怕是稍微倾向于在这一伟大的国家制度的性质上产生退化变质的事情更重要的了。决定着联邦制度稳定性基础的信任,第一次受到削弱是源于这样一个裁决,它宣称奴隶制是一种公民权利,因而即使这种奴隶制是违背该地区多数居民的意志的,它在还没有成为州的地区内也是合法的。比起任何其他的事情来,这一值得注意的裁决或许更使地方性的分裂产生内战结果的危

in separation. The main pillar of the American Constitution is scarcely strong enough to bear many more such shocks.

The tribunals which act as umpires between the Federal and the State Governments, naturally also decide all disputes between two States, or between a citizen of one State and the government of another. The usual remedies between nations, war and diplomacy, being precluded by the federal union, it is necessary that a judicial remedy should supply their place. The Supreme Court of the Federation dispenses international law, and is the first great example of what is now one of the most prominent wants of civilized society, a real International Tribunal.

The powers of a Federal Government naturally extend not only to peace and war, and all questions which arise between the country and foreign governments, but to making any other arrangements which are, in the opinion of the States, necessary to their enjoyment of the full benefits of union. For example, it is a great advantage to them that their mutual commerce should be free, without the impediment of frontier duties and customhouses. But this internal freedom cannot exist, if each State has the power of fixing the duties on interchange of commodities between itself and foreign countries; since every foreign product let in by one State, would be let into all the rest. And hence all custom duties and trade regulations, in the United States, are made or repealed by the Federal Government exclusively. Again, it is a great convenience to the States to have but one coinage, and but one system of weights and measures ; which can only be ensured, if the regulation of these matters is entrusted to the Federal Government. The certainty and celerity of Post Office communication is impeded, and its expense increased, if a letter has to pass through half a dozen sets of public offices, subject to different supreme authorities: it is convenient, therefore, that all Post Offices should be under the Federal Government. But on such questions the feelings of different communities are liable to be different. One of the American States, under the guidance of a man who has displayed powers as a speculative political thinker superior to any who has appeared in American politics since the authors of the 'Federalist', [①] claimed a veto for each State on the

---

① Mr. Calhoun.

机。美国宪法的主要支柱的确没有强大到足以经受得起更多这样的打击。

法院,作为联邦政府和州政府之间的仲裁者,自然也对一切争议进行裁决,这种争议可以发生在两个州之间,或这一州的公民和另一州的政府之间。既然国家之间的一般救济手段即战争和外交被联邦的结合所排除,那么,用司法救济来取代它们就颇有必要。联邦的最高法院行使着国际法,因而是迄今作为文明社会最凸显的需要之一的真正的国际法庭的第一个杰出典范。

联邦政府的权力不仅自然延伸到战争与和平,和这个国家与外国政府之间产生的一切问题,而且延伸到根据各州由于享有联合的充分利益而需要作出的其他的安排意冗。比如,它们之间的贸易自由不受过境税和海关的阻碍,对它们是一大便利。如果每一个州有权确定该州和外国之间商品交换的税率,国内的自由是不可能存在的,但是这种由一个州准入的每种外国产品都将进入所有其他的州。因此,在美国一切关税和贸易规则都专由联邦政府制定或废除。此外,只有一种币制,一种度量衡制度,对各州也是一大便利。而这只有当这些事项被委托给联邦政府时才能得到保证。如果一封信必须通过很多套隶属于不同的最高当局的公共机关的话,邮政通讯的准确和迅速就会遭受妨碍,其费用也会增加,因此所有的邮局应该被置于联邦政府管理之下就应该。但是在这种问题上,不同的社会容易产生不同的感受。美国的一个州,在自从《联邦党人文集》的作家们以来在美国政治中出现过的最深思熟虑的政治家①的指导下,呼吁每个州对

---

① 卡尔霍恩先生。

custom laws of the Federal Congress: and that statesman, in a posthumous work of great ability, which has been printed and widely circulated by the legislature of South Carolina, vindicated this pretension on the general principle of limiting the tyranny of the majority, and protecting minorities by admitting them to a substantial participation in political power. One of the most disputed topics in American politics, during the early part of this century, was whether the power of the Federal Government ought to extend, and whether by the Constitution it did extend, to making roads and canals at the cost of the Union. It is only in transactions with foreign powers that the authority of the Federal Government is of necessity complete. On every other subject, the question depends on how closely the people in general wish to draw the federal tie ; what portion of their local freedom of action they are willing to surrender, in order to enjoy more fully the benefit of being one nation.

Respecting the fitting constitution of a federal government within itself, much needs not be said. It of course consists of a legislative branch and an executive, and the constitution of each is amenable to the same principles as that of representative governments generally. As regards the mode of adapting these general principles to a federal government, the provision of the American Constitution seems exceedingly judicious, that Congress should consist of two Houses, and that while one of them is constituted according to population, each State being entitled to representatives in the ratio of the number of its inhabitants, the other should represent not the citizens, but the State Governments, and every State, whether large or small, should be represented in it by the same number of members. This provision precludes any undue power from being exercised by the more powerful States over the rest, and guarantees the reserved rights of the State Governments, by making it impossible, as far as the mode of representation can prevent, that any measure should pass Congress, unless approved not only by a majority of the citizens, but by a majority of the States. I have before adverted to the further incidental advantage obtained, of raising the standard of qualifications in one of the Houses. Being nominated by select bodies, the Legislatures of the various States, whose choice, for reasons already indicated, is more likely to fall on eminent men than any popular election—who have not only the

第十七章

联邦国会的海关税法享有否决权,并且,这位政治家在一本具有杰出才华的遗著中(由南卡罗莱纳州议会出版和广泛发行),根据这样一个通常原则,即要限制多数的暴政和允许少数实际上参政来保护少数,论证了这一主张。在本世纪初期,美国政治中一个最富有争议性的议题是,联邦政府的权力是否应该延伸和遵照美国宪法是否已经延伸到让联邦承担费用修公路和开运河。只有在同外国处理事务方面,联邦政府的权力才是有必要完全的。在其他所有问题上,则应取决于民众对把联邦的纽带拉得有多紧的期待;取决于为更充分地享有作为一个国家的利益他们愿意让与他们地方的行动自由到什么程度。

对于一个联邦政府在其本身内的适当构成这样一个问题,没有必要赘言太多。毋庸置疑,联邦政府是由一个立法部门和一个行政部门构成,而每一部门又是基于和一般代议制政府原则相同的原则组合而成。至于把这些原则适应于联邦政府的模式,美国宪法的规定似乎是极为明智的:由上下两院构成国会,其中一院按人口组成,遵照其居民的人数比例,每个州被赋予选出代表的权利;另一院则不是代表公民而是代表州政府,并且,无论这个州是大州还是小州,需在其中有同等人数的代表。这一规定为排除更强大的州对其他各州行使任何不适当的权力提供了保证,并且在代表方式所能防止的范围内,防止任何议案在国会通过,除非它不仅得到公民多数的认可,而且得到多数的州的认可,从而保证各州政府所保留的权利。我在前面曾提到,还有由于提高两院之一的资格条件而获得的额外附带好处。既然这些代表是由各个州议会提名选出,它们的选择,正如已经指出的理由那样,比任何平民选举更可能选择杰出人物——它们不仅有权选择

power of electing such, but a strong motive to do so, because the influence of their State in the general deliberations must be materially affected by the personal weight and abilities of its representatives ; the Senate of the United States, thus chosen, has always contained nearly all the political men of established and high reputation in the Union: while the Lower House of Congress has, in the opinion of competent observers, been generally as remarkable for the absence of conspicuous personal merit, as the Upper House for its presence.

When the conditions exist for the formation of efficient and durable Federal Unions, the multiplication of such is always a benefit to the world. It has the same salutary effect as any other extension of the practice of co-operation, through which the weak, by uniting, can meet on equal terms with the strong. By diminishing the number of those petty states which are not equal to their own defence, it weakens the temptations to an aggressive policy, whether working directly by arms, or through the *prestige* of superior power. It of course puts an end to war and diplomatic quarrels, and usually also to restrictions on commerce, between the States composing the Union ; while, in reference to neighbouring nations, the increased military strength conferred by it is of a kind to be almost exclusively available for defensive, scarcely at all for aggressive, purposes. A federal government has not a sufficiently concentrated authority, to conduct with much efficiency any war but one of self-defence, in which it can rely on the voluntary co-operation of every citizen : nor is there anything very flattering to national vanity or ambition in acquiring, by a successful war, not subjects, nor even fellowcitizens, but only new, and perhaps troublesome. independent members of the confederation. The warlike proceedings of the Americans in Mexico were purely exceptional, having been carried on principally by volunteers, under the influence of the migratory propensity which prompts individual Americans to possess themselves of unoccupied land ; and stimulated, if by any public motive, not by that of national aggrandizement, but by the purely sectional purpose of extending slavery. There are few signs

第十七章

这种人物,而且带着强烈的动机去这样做,因为,毋庸置疑,州代表的个人的分量和才能将会极大地对各州在全体会议的讨论产生重大影响。这样选出的美国参议院,往往囊括几乎全国所有的被公认的享有盛誉的政治人物;而另一方面,在有资格的观察家看来,国会众议院的特点,通常说来缺乏显著的个人美德,这正与参议院相反。

当生成有效而持久的联邦的条件存在时,这种联邦数目的增加对世界来说总是有好处的。和任何其他扩大合作的做法相比,它产生同样的有益效果,依赖这种联合,弱的一方就能和强的一方处于平等地位。通过减少那些不能自我防御的小国的数量,它就削弱了对侵略性政策的诱惑,不管这种政策是直接动用武力还是通过强势实力的威慑。毋庸置疑,它终结了组成联邦的各国之间的战争和外交争吵,并且常常也结束了它们之间的贸易限制;而在有关邻国方面,由于组成了联盟因而其军事实力得以增加,然而,这个联盟的性质几乎完全是用于防卫的目的,而很少用于侵略的目的。联邦政府没有足够集中的权力使得其能有效地发动任何战争,除非这是一场自卫战争,在这种战争中,它能够依赖每一个公民的主动合作。而在一场胜利的战争之后,所获得的不是驯服的臣民,甚至也不是同辈的公民,而只是不同于以往的,或许是麻烦的、独立的联邦成员,这对民族的虚荣或野心来讲也是不值得高兴的。美国人对墨西哥的好战的行为,纯粹是一个例外,这场战争主要是由志愿兵参与的,这些志愿兵受到刺激各个美国人占据无主土地的那种迁移倾向的影响;如果说这场战争带有任何公开的目的,那也不是源于民族扩张的目的,而是源于纯粹地区性的扩充奴隶制目的的刺激。很少有证据

in the proceedings of Americans, nationally or individually, that the desire of territorial acquisition for their country as such, has any considerable power over them. Their hankering after Cuba is, in the same manner, merely sectional, and the Northern States, those opposed to slavery, have never in any way favoured it.

The question may present itself (as in Italy at its present uprising) whether a country, which is determined to be united, should form a complete, or a merely federal union. The point is sometimes necessarily decided by the mere territorial magnitude of the united whole. There is a limit to the extent of country which can advantageously be governed, or even whose government can be conveniently superintended, from a single centre. There are vast countries so governed; but they, or at least their distant provinces, are in general deplorably ill administered, and it is only when the inhabitants are almost savages that they could not manage their affairs better separately. This obstacle does not exist in the case of Italy, the size of which does not come up to that of several very efficiently governed single states in past and present times. The question then is, whether the different parts of the nation require to be governed in a way so essentially different, that it is not probable the same Legislature, and the same ministry or administrative body, will give satisfaction to them all. Unless this be the case, which is a question of fact, it is better for them to be completely united. That a totally different system of laws, and very different administrative institutions, may exist in two portions of a country without being any obstacle to legislative unity, is proved by the case of England and Scotland. Perhaps, however, this undisturbed co-existence of two legal systems, under one united legislature, making different laws for the two sections of the country in adaptation to the previous differences, might not be so well preserved, or the same confidence might not be felt in its preservation, in a country whose legislators were more possessed (as is apt to be the case on the Continent) with the mania for uniformity. A people having that

第十七章

表明,在美国人的做法中,无论对于全国来说还是就个人而言,为他们的国家本身获取领土的愿望对他们没有什么大的吸引力。他们对古巴的垂涎同样仅仅是区域性的,而反对奴隶制的北方各州从来没有支持过这种做法。

这样的一个问题可能全被提出(正如当前意大利发生的暴动那样):在一个国家决定联合起来时,究竟应该组成一个完全的联邦还是组成一个单纯的联邦。这问题有时必然单纯由联合整体的领土大小来确定。能够从一个中心进行有利的治理,或者甚至对其政府易于施加监督的国家的范围,有着一种界限。对一些广袤国家的统治就是这样的;但是这些国家,或者至少这些国家的遥远的外省,通常说来对它们的治理都是极差的,而且只有在他们的居民几乎是野蛮人的情况下,他们才能各自把自己的事情管理得最好。就意大利而言,这种障碍并不存在,与过去和现在若干管理得极有成效的单一国家相比,它的面积没有那么大。因此问题是,这个国家的各个部分是否需要用截然不同的方式来进行治理,因为同一议会和同一政府或行政部门不可能满足它们全体的需求。除非情况本身是这样,而这是个事实问题,它们完全联合起来便是最好的模式。截然不同的法律制度,以及极不相同的行政制度都可以共存于国家的两个部分,而且它们不会妨碍立法的统一,这一点已经被英格兰和苏格兰的情况加以证实。然而,在一个统一的立法机构领导下,为国家的两个部分制定出不同的法律以适应以前分歧,这样现存的两种法律制度的彼此不妨碍的共存状态,也许在其立法者更着迷于整齐划一的国家里(恰似在欧洲大陆上容易出现的情形),可能不会得到很好的保持,或者对保持共存缺乏同等的信任。只要有利害关系的人们不觉得其利益受

unbounded toleration which is characteristic of this country, for every description of anomaly, so long as those whose interests it concerns do not feel aggrieved by it, afforded an exceptionally advantageous field for trying this difficult experiment. In most countries, if it was an object to retain different systems of law, it might probably be necessary to retain distinct legislatures as guarnians of them ; which is perfectly compatible with a national Parliament and King, or a national Parliament without a King, supreme over the external relations of all the members of the body.

Whenever it is not deemed necessary to maintain permanently, in the different provinces, different systems of jurisprudence, and fundamental institutions grounded on different principles, it is always practicable to reconcile minor diversities with the maintenance of unity of government. All that is needful is to give a sufficiently large sphere of action to the local authorities. Under one and the same central government there may be local governors, and provincial assemblies for local purposes. It may happen, for instance, that the people of different provinces may have preferences in favour of different modes of taxation. If the general legislature could not be depended on for being guided by the members for each province in modifying the general system of taxation to suit that province, the Constitution might provide that as many of the expenses of government as could by any possibility be made local, should be defrayed by local rates imposed by the provincial assemblies, and that those which must of necessity be general, such as the support of an army and navy, should, in the estimates for the year, be apportioned among the different provinces according to some general estimate of their resources, the amount assigned to each being levied by the local assembly on the principles most acceptable to the locality, and paid *en bloc* into the national treasury. A practice approaching to this existed even in the old French monarchy, so far as regarded the *pays d' états*; each of which, having consented or being required to furnish a fixed sum, was left to assess it upon the inhabitants by its own officers, thus escaping the grinding despotism of the royal *intendants* and *subdélégués*; and this privilege is always mentioned as one of the advantages which mainly contributed to render them, as some of them were, the most flourishing provinces of France.

Identity of central government is compatible with many different

第十七章

到侵害,那么,我国人民将对任何反常情况都能容忍(这正是我国民众的特点),这就为尝试这一困难的实验提供了一个特别有益的场所。在多数国家中,如果目的是要维护不同的法律制度,就极有可能有必要去保留独特的议会以保护好这些制度;这和一个同时存在全国议会和国王,或一个没有国王的全国议会,在所有成员的对外关系上高于一切,是根本不冲突的。

只要民众有这样一种想法,即认为没有必要在不同的省份长久保留不同的法律制度以及基于不同原则的根本制度,那么,把次要的分歧同维护政府的统一相协调总是可以行得通的。唯一要做的是把足够广泛的活动范围赋予地方当局。在接受同一个中央政府的领导下,可以有各省省长和为地方目的尽责的省议会。或许有这样的情形,例如,各省的民众可能偏爱选择不同的征税模式。倘若不能指望全国议会能得到各个省的议员的指导,从而修正总的税收制度以适合各个省份,宪法不妨作出这样的规定:只要是可调整为地方开支的政府开支,都应遵照各省议会规定的地方税率付税,而务必列为全国性的开支,如维持陆军和海军的开支,必须在当年的财政预算中,遵照各省资源大体上的估计分配到各省,分配到各省的数额,由地方议会遵循当地最能认可的原则征收,汇总起来缴纳到国家财政部。对国家的各个省来说,和这相接近的做法,甚至出现在古老的法国君主国;其中每一个省一旦认可或者被要求上交一定的金额,就被允许任用它自己的官员向居民进行征税,从而避免皇室监督官及其代表的暴敛;而这一特别待遇常常被说成是其中的一种好处——主要有利于使它们成为——有些省也的确曾成为——法国最繁华的省份。

维持同一个中央政府和确保有程度不等的集权,包括在行政

degrees of centralization, not only administrative, but even legislative. A people may have the desire, and the capacity, for a closer union than one merely federal, while yet their local peculiarities and antecedents render considerable diversities desirable in the details of their government. But if there is a real desire on all hands to make the experiment successful, there needs seldom be any difficulty in not only preserving these diversities, but giving them the guarantee of a constitutional provision against any attempt at assimilation, except by the voluntary act of those who would be affected by the change.

方面而且甚至立法方面的集权是并不冲突的。一国民众或许有意愿并且有能力维持一个比单纯联合更紧密的联邦,但另一方面,他们的地方特异性和先前的经历又使得在政府管理方面的细节上保持着巨大的差异,这一点也成为值得期待的。但是,如果民众都有真正的意愿使这种实验取得成功,那么,不仅在保留这种多样性方面,而且在赋予这种多样性以宪法规定的保障,从而防止任何同化的企图(除了有关的民众自愿这样做之外)方面,就不会存在任何困难。

CHAPTER XVIII
Of The Government Of Dependencies By A Free State

Free States, like all others, may possess dependencies, acquired either by conquest or by colonization: and our own is the greatest instance of the kind in modern history. It is a most important question, how such dependencies ought to be governed.

It is unnecessary to discuss the case of small posts, like Gibraltar, Aden, or Heligoland, which are held only as naval or military positions. The military or naval object is in this case paramount, and the inhabitants cannot, consistently with it, be admitted to the government of the place ; though they ought to be allowed all liberties and privileges compatible with that restriction, including the free management of municipal affairs ; and, as a compensation for being locally sacrificed to the convenience of the governing State, should be admitted to equal rights with its native subjects in all other parts of the empire.

Outlying territories of some size and population, which are held as dependencies, that is, which are subject, more or less, to acts of sovereign power on the part of the paramount country, without being equally represented (if represented at all) in its legislature, may be divided into two classes. Some are composed of people of similiar civilization to the ruling country ; capable of, and ripe for, representative government: such as the British possessions in America and Australia. Others, like India, are still at a great distance from that state.

In the case of dependencies of the former class, this country has at length realized, in rare completeness, the true principle of government. England has always felt under a certain degree of obligation to

第十八章 自由国家的附属国政府

像所有类型的国家一样,自由国家可能通过征服或者殖民而拥有属国,我们自己的属国则是近代历史中最为主要的例子。而最为重要的一个问题是应当如何去统治这些属国。

这里没有必要去讨论一些仅仅作为海军或陆军驻地如直布罗陀、亚丁港或黑利戈兰等的小海港城市的情况。在这种情况下,陆军或海军的军事目标是最为重要的,因此居民一向不被允许去管理这些地方,尽管他们被允许享有与这些限制相符合的自由和特权,包括自由管理市政,并且,作为一种对为了当地统治便利所作出的牺牲的补偿,他们应当被允许在帝国所有其他地方享有跟当地臣民一样的权利。

具有一定面积和人口的边远领土,它们作为附属国,也就是说,它们或多或少地服从于最高母国的国家主权行为,而在其议会中却没有同等的代表权(如果有代表权的话),它们可以被分成两类情况,一些领地,如英国在美洲或澳洲的领地的人民具有与宗主国家相似的文明,能够实行代议制并且具备实行代议制的条件;另外一些领地(例如印度)的人民距离那种状态却仍然很远。

就前一类附属国来说,我国最终少见地完全实现了政府的真正原则。英国总是在某种程度上感到有责任给予这种与自己有

bestow on such of her outlying populations as were of her own blood and language, and on some who were not, representative institutions formed in imitation of her own ; but until the present generation, she has been on the same bad level with other countries as to the amount of self-government which she allowed them to exercise through the representative institutions that she conceded to them. She claimed to be the supreme arbiter even of their purely internal concerns, according to her own, not their, ideas of how those concerns could be best regulated. This practice was a natural corollary from the vicious theory of colonial policy—once common to all Europe, and not yet completely relinquished by any other people—which regarded colonies as valuable by affording markets for our commodities, that could be kept entirely to ourselves: a privilege we valued so highly that we thought it worth purchasing by allowing to the colonies the same monopoly of our market for their own productions, which we claimed for our commodities in theirs. This notable plan for enriching them and ourselves, by making each pay enormous sums to the other, dropping the greatest part by the way, has been for some time abandoned. But the bad habit of meddling in the internal government of the colonies, did not at once terminate when we relinquished the idea of making any profit by it. We continued to torment them, not for any benefit to ourselves, but for that of a section or faction among the colonists: and this persistence in domineering cost us a Canadian rebellion, before we had the happy thought of giving it up. England was like an ill brought-up elder brother, who persists in tyrannizing over the younger ones from mere habit, till one of them, by a spirited resistance, though with unequal strength, gives him notice to desist. We were wise enough not to require a second warning. A new era in the colonial policy of nations began with Lord Durham's Report ; the imperishable memorial of that nobleman's courage, patriotism, and enlightened liberality, and of the intellect and practical sagacity of its joint authors, Mr. Wakefield

第十八章

血缘或语言渊源的人民,以及一些没有这种渊源的边远人民以模仿它自己制度而形成的代议制度。但是直到这一代为止,就它允许他们通过它给予他们的代议制度进行管理的程度而言,它与其他国家处在同样糟糕的层次上,甚至在纯属他们内部的事务上,它也只是从自己的角度而不是从他们的角度来考虑如何最好地加以管理,声称自己才是这些事务的最高主宰。这种做法是那种错误的殖民理论的必然结果。这种理论曾在整个欧洲流行,而现在还没有被任何一个民族完全加以抛弃。这种理论认为殖民地的价值在于为我们提供商品市场,是我们可以完全据为己有的市场,一种我们如此看重的特权,以至于我们认为可以允许殖民地用它们自己的产品来对我们的市场同样地加以垄断,正如我们的商品在它们的市场上享有垄断地位那样。这种通过使一方向另一方支付巨大金额,并把其中最大部分留在流通过程中,以使它们和我们自己都富裕的方案,在某个时期被废弃了。但是当我们放弃通过这个方法使彼此都受益的想法时,干涉殖民地内部事务的坏习惯却没有停止。我们不是为了自己的任何利益,而是为了殖民地的某个部门或派系的利益去继续折磨它们,而这种坚持对殖民地专权的做法,在我们产生放弃它的可喜想法之前,就使我们付出了加拿大叛乱的代价。英国就像一个缺乏教养的兄长,仅仅因为习惯而不断欺压那些小兄弟们,直到它们之间有一个不顾力量悬殊而奋起反抗,以警告它停止欺压行为。我们还算聪明,不需要来第二次警告。德拉姆勋爵报告开始了殖民政策的新时期。这是那个贵族的勇气、爱国心和开明态度以及报告的共同作者——韦克菲尔德(Wakefield)先生和已故的查尔斯·布勒——的才智和实际工作的敏锐的不可磨灭

and the lamented Charles Bullet. ①

It is now a fixed principle of the policy of Great Britain, professed in theory and faithfully adhered to in practice, that her colonies of European race, equally with the parent country, possess the fullest measure of internal self-government. They have been allowed to make their own free representative constitutions, by altering in any manner they thought fit, the already very popular constitutions, which we had given them. Each is governed by its own legislature and executive, constituted on highly democratic principles. The veto of the Crown and of Parliament, though nominally reserved, is only exercised (and that very rarely) on questions which concern the empire, and not solely the particular colony. How liberal a construction has been given to the distinction between imperial and colonial questions, is shown by the fact, that the whole of the unappropriated lands in the regions behind our American and Australian colonies have been given up to the uncontrolled disposal of the colonial communities ; though they might, without injustice, have been kept in the hands of the Imperial Government, to be administered for the greatest advantage of future emigrants from all parts of the empire. Every Colony has thus as full power over its own affairs, as it could have if it were a member of even the loosest federation; and much fuller than would belong to it under the Constitution of the United States, being free even to tax at its pleasure the commodities imported from the mother country. Their union with Great Britain is the slightest kind of federal union; but not a strictly equal federation, the mother country retaining to itself the powers of a Federal Government, though reduced in practice to their very narrowest limits. This inequality is, of course, as far as it goes, a disadvantage to the dependencies, which have no voice inforeign policy, but are bound by the decisions of the superior country. They are compelled to join England in war , without being in any way consulted previous to

---

① I am speaking here of the *adoption* of this improved policy, not, of course, of its original suggestion. The honour of having been its earliest champion belongs unquestionably to Mr. Roebuck.

第十八章

的纪念碑。①

目前,英国在理论上公开宣布、在实践上忠实坚持的一项政策的确定原则是:它那些属于欧洲种族的殖民地与母国同等地拥有对内部事务最充分的自治。这些殖民地被允许通过它们认为合适的任何方式来修改我们给予它们的早已深入人心的宪法,以制定自己的自由的代议制宪法。每个殖民地都由自己的立法机关和行政机关来管理,而这些机关是按照高度民主原则组成的。国王和议会名义上保留的否决权,只有在议题涉及帝国而不仅仅是某个特定的殖民地时,才会行使,而且这样的机会很少出现。对帝国问题和殖民地问题所做解释的自由度有多大,可以由这样的事实加以说明,即在我们美洲和澳洲殖民地后方的广大区域内的整个未经占有的土地都归各殖民地任意处置;尽管这些土地会被帝国政府毫不利己地控制在手中加以管理,以便使今后来自欧洲各国的移民受惠。因此,每个殖民地都拥有处置自己事务的全部权力,就如作为最松散的联邦成员所拥有的权力那样;并且比在美国宪法下享有的权利还要充分,自由到了甚至可以根据自己喜好来决定自母国进口商品税款程度。它们与大不列颠的联合就是最松散的联邦,但并非是严格意义上的平等联邦。母国保留着联邦政府的权力,尽管在实践上这种权力被限定在最狭窄的范围内。这种不平等就目前的情形来说对附属国当然是不利的,使得它们在外交政策上没有发言权却又受制于母国的决策。它们被迫在事前没有得到任何磋商的情况下加入英国

---

① 我在此所提到的对这一改进政策的采用,当然不是它最初的建议。最早提倡这一建议的荣誉毫无疑问应当属于罗巴克(Roebuck)先生。

engaging in it.

Those (now happily not a few) who think that justice is as binding on communities as it is on individuals, and that men are not warranted in doing to other countries, for the supposed benefit of their own country, what they would not be justified in doing to other men for their own benefit—feel even this limited amount of constitutional subordination on the part of the colonies to be a violation of principle, and have often occupied themselves in looking out for means by which it may be avoided. With this view it has been proposed by some, that the colonies should return representatives to the British legislature ; and by others, that the powers of our own, as well as of their Parliaments, should be confined to internal policy, and that there should be another representative body for foreign and imperial concerns, in which last the dependencies of Great Britain should be represented in the same manner, and with the same completeness, as Great Britain itself. On this system there would be a perfectly equal federation between the mother country and her colonies, then no longer dependencies.

The feelings of equity, and conceptions of public morality, from which these suggestions emanate, are worthy of all praise ; but the suggestions themselves are so inconsistent with rational principles of government, that it is doubtful if they have been seriously accepted as a possibility by any reasonable thinker. Countries separated by half the globe do not present the natural conditions for being under one government, or even members of one federation. If they had sufficiently the same interests, they have not, and never can have, a sufficient habit of taking counsel together. They are not part of the same public ; they do not discuss and deliberate in the same arena, but apart, and have only a most imperfect knowledge of what passes in the minds of one another. They neither know each other's objects, nor have confidence in each other's principles of conduct. Let any Englishman ask himself how he should like his destinies to depend on an assembly of which one-third was British-American, and another third South African and Australian. Yet to this it must come, if there were anything like fair or equal representation ; and would not every one feel

第十八章

阵营进行战斗。

有些人(令人高兴的是这种人不在少数)认为社会应当像个人那样保持公正,并且认为人没有理由为了自己国家假定的利益而对付别的国家,正如人为了自己的利益而对付他人是不正当的,这些人甚至觉得这种有限的宪法上的从属关系也是违反原则的,并常常致力于寻求避免这种从属关系的办法。本着这样的观点,一些人建议殖民地应当向英国议会派出代表;另一些人则建议,我们的权力以及殖民地议会的权力,应当限于处理内部事务,而对于外交和帝国事务,则应有另外一个代议机关负责。在这个代议机关里,殖民地应当有和大不列颠同样方式、同样充分的代表权。在这个体系中,母国和它的殖民地之间就将形成一个完美的同盟,那时就不再有附属国了。

产生这些建议的公平感以及公共道德观念是值得称颂的;但这些建议本身和理性的统治原则如此不一致,以至于是否会有某个通情达理的思想家真诚地认为它们是可做的事情,是值得怀疑的。相距半个地球之遥的国家不具备处在同一政府统治下的自然条件,甚至不具备作为联邦成员的自然条件,如果它们充分具备同样的利益,那么它们没有也不可能具备坐在一起协商的习惯。这些国家的人民不属于相同的群体;他们不是在相同的平台上,而是各自地进行讨论与协商问题,并且对彼此心中所想的事情只有极不充分的了解。他们既不知道彼此的目标,对彼此的行为原则也缺乏信任。任何一个英国人都可以问自己是否愿意让他的命运由其中三分之一是英属美洲人,而另外三分之一是南非人和澳大利亚人组成的议会来决定。然而,如果存在任何公平或平等的代表权的话,就一定会是这样。并且,我们每个人难道不觉

that the representatives of Canada and Australia, even in matters of an imperial character, could not know, or feel any sufficient concern for, the interests, opinions, or wishes of English, Irish, and Scotch ? Even for strictly federative purposes, the conditions do not exist, which we have seen to be essential to a federation. England is sufficient for her own protection without the colonies ; and would be in a much stronger, as well as more dignified position, if separated from them, than when reduced to be a single member of an American, African, and Australian confederation. Over and above the commerce which she might equally enjoy after separation, England derives little advantage, except in *prestige*, from her dependencies ; and the little she does derive is quite outweighed by the expense they cost her, and the dissemination they necessitate of her naval and military force, which in case of war, or any real apprehension of it, requires to be double or treble what would be needed for the defence of this country alone.

But though Great Britain could do perfectly well without her colonies, and though on every principle of morality and justice she ought to consent to their separation, should the time come when, after full trial of the form of union, they deliberately desire to be dissevered; there are strong reasons for maintaining the present slight bond of connexion, so long as not disagreeable to the feelings of either party. It is a step, as far as it goes, towards universal peace, and general friendly co-operation among nations. It renders war impossible among a large number of otherwise independent communities ; and moreover hinders any of them from being absorbed into a foreign state, and becoming a source of additional aggressive strength to some rival power, either more despotic or closer at hand, which might not always be so unambitious or so pacific as Great Britain. It at least keeps the markets of the different countries open to one another, and prevents that mutual exclusion by hostile tariffs, which none of the great communities of mankind, except England, have completely outgrown. And in the case of the British possessions it has the advantage, specially valuable at the present time, of adding to the moral influence, and weight in the councils of the world, of the Power which, of all in existence,

第十八章

得加拿大与澳大利亚的代表们甚至在涉及帝国性质的问题上,对英国人、爱尔兰人和苏格兰人的利益、想法或愿望都不甚了解或关心不够吗?即使是严格地限于联邦目的,这些在我们看来是联邦存在所必不可少的条件也不存在。英国没有殖民地也足以保护自己,并且,如果跟这些殖民地分离,比将自己降格为有美洲、非洲和澳大利亚参加的联邦的一个单纯成员要处于更为强大和更有尊严的位置。英国在与它们分离之后,在同样享有的贸易方面从附属国那里得到的好处,除了在威望方面是少而又少的。英国得到的好处与它为它们所花的费用相比,简直是少得可怜,而且它们离不开英国的海陆军力量,一旦发生战争或有战争的真实危险时,英国为它们不得不作的布防就达到仅仅为保护本土所需的两倍或三倍。

但是尽管大不列颠在没有殖民地时也会相当不错,并且尽管按照任何道义和公正的原则它应当同意与它们分离,但经过联盟形式的完全实验之后,它们却还审慎地希望在分离的时刻来临之前,只要不引起任何一方反感,却又有强有力的理由来维持当前这种轻微的联系。就当前情况而言,这种联系是走向国家间普遍和平和友好合作的一步。它使得战争在一大堆否则就是独立的社会之间成为不可能;并且防止了它们中间任何一个被外国所兼并,成为某个更为专制或更为临近的敌对国家的额外的侵略力量的源泉,而这个国家可能不总是像大不列颠那样没有野心或爱好和平。它至少使得不同国家的市场向彼此开放,并且防止了通过敌对的关税来互相排斥,这种关税,除了英国,还没有一个伟大的人类社会得以完全摆脱。就英国的领地而言,它有这样的优势(在当前特别有价值),即增加这个最理解自由的强国在世界会议中

best understands liberty—and whatever may have been its errors in the past, has attained to more of conscience and moral principle in its dealings with foreigners, than any other great nation seems either to conceive as possible, or recognise as desirable. Since, then, the union can only continue, while it does continue, on the footing of an unequal federation, it is important to consider by what means this small amount of inequality can be prevented from being either onerous or humiliating to the communities occupying the less exalted position.

The only inferiority necessarily inherent in the case is, that the mother country decides, both for the colonies and for herself, on questions of peace and war. They gain, in return, the obligation on the mother country to repel aggressions directed against them ; but, except when the minor community is so weak that the protection of stronger power is indispensable to it, reciprocity of obligation is not a full equivalent for non-admission to a voice in the deliberations. It is essential, therefore, that in all wars, save those which, like the Caffre or New Zealand wars, are incurred for the sake of the particular colony, the colonists should not (without their own voluntary request) be called on to contribute anything to the expense, except what may be required for the specific local defence of their own ports, shores, and frontiers against invasion. Moreover, as the mother country claims the privilege, at her sole discretion, of taking measures or pursuing a policy which may expose them to attack, it is just that she should undertake a considerable portion of the cost of their military defence even in time of peace; the whole of it, so far as it depends upon a standing army.

But there is a means, still more effectual than these, by which, and in general by which alone, a full equivalent can be given to a smaller community for sinking its individuality, as a substantive power among nations, in the greater individuality of a wide and powerful empire. This one indispensable, and at the same time sufficient, expedient, which meets at once the demands of justice and the growing exigencies of policy, is, to open the service of government in all its departments, and in every part of the empire, on perfectly equal terms, to the inhabitants of the Colonies . Why does no one ever hear a

第十八章

的道义影响和分量。并且这个国家不管在过去犯过什么错,在对待外国人方面,所达到的良心和道德原则要超过任何其他大国认为可以达到或承认值得向往的程度。因此,这种联盟只能维系下去,而一旦得以维系,就只能建立在不平等的基础上。重要的是,要考虑一下用什么方法才能使这些地位较低的社会不感到负担过重或觉得丢脸。

在这种情况下,必然会有的唯一不平等就是,母国有权替自己和殖民地就战争与和平问题作出决策。作为回报,母国有义务击退直接针对殖民地的侵略。但是除了较小的殖民地弱到离不开强大国家的保护这样的情况以外,作为互恶的义务与在协商中不承认发言权并不完全相等。因此,关键是,在所有的战争中,除了那些为了特定殖民地而引起的战争如加夫里和新西兰战争外,殖民地的人民如果不是自愿要求,就不能被强迫承担任何费用,除非这些费用是用来保护他们的港口、海岸以及边界不被侵犯的。而且,由于母国有权仅仅根据自己的判断而采取措施或奉行某种政策,使殖民地暴露在可能受攻击的地位,所以即使在和平时期,由母国承担大部分殖民地的军事防御开支,如果是常备军则负担全部开支,则是公平合理的。

但是有一种方法要比这些方法更为有效,通过这种方法,并且一般只有通过这种方法,较小的附属国才能在把自己作为独立存在的国家的个性融入到一个幅员辽阔的强大帝国的较大个性中时得到完全相等的东西。这个必不可少的,同时也是充分、有利的办法(它既能够满足公正的要求又能够满足日益增长的政策上的迫切需求),就是以完全平等的条件,将政府的服务在它的所有部门以及在帝国的每一部分,向殖民地的居民开放。为什

breath of disloyalty from the islands in the British Channel ? By race, religion, and geographical position they belong less to England than to France. But, while they enjoy, like Canada and New South Wales, complete control over their internal affairs and their taxation, every office or dignity in the gift of the Crown is freely open to the native of Guernsey or Jersey. Generals, admirals, peers of the United Kingdom, are made, and there is nothing which hinders prime ministers to be made, from those insignificant islands. The same system was commenced in reference to the Colonies generally, by an enlightened Colonial Secretary, too early lost, Sir William Molesworth, when he appointed Mr. Hinckes, a leading Canadian politician, to a West Indian government. It is a very shallow view of the springs of political action in a community, which thinks such things unimportant because the number of those in a position actually to profit by the concession might not be very considerable. That limited number would be composed precisely of those who have most moral power over the rest: and men are not so destitute of the sense of collective degradation, as not to feel the withholding of an advantage from even one person, because of a circumstance which they all have in common with him, an affront to all. If we prevent the leading men of a community from standing forth to the world as its chiefs and representatives in the general councils of mankind, we owe it both to their legitimate ambition, and to the just pride of the community, to give them in return an equal chance of occupying the same prominent position in a nation of greater power and importance. Were the whole service of the British Crown open to the natives of the Ionian Islands, we should hear no more of the desire for union with Greece. Such an union is not disirable for the people, to whom it would be a step backward in civilization ; but it is no wonder if Corfu, which has given a minister of European reputation to the Russian Empire , and a President to Greece itself before the arrival

第十八章

么人们从来没有听过英吉利海峡中各岛屿中有丝毫不忠的声音呢？从种族、宗教以及地理位置的角度看，在它们更应该属于法国而不是英国才对。但是，当它们像加拿大和新南威尔士那样，对内政和税收拥有完全的控制权的同时，国王授予的每一个职位和荣誉都自由地向格恩西和泽西的居民开放。那些微不足道的岛屿也可以向联合王国输送将军、海军将领和贵族，并且不存在妨碍首相从这些岛屿中产生的任何障碍。一般说来，在殖民地实施这一制度始于过早死去的那个开明的殖民大臣威廉·莫尔思沃斯爵士，当时他任命杰出的加拿大籍政治家辛克斯（Hinckes）先生到西印度群岛的一个政府任职。如果认为由于在这样的让步中实际受益的人可能不是很多，因此这样的事情就不重要，么这就是对社会中政治行为的动力的一种极为肤浅的看法。那些受益的少数恰恰是由相对于其余的人来说拥有最强大的道义力量的人们组成的，并且人们并非如此缺乏集体倒退的感觉，以至于领会不到由于他们处于相同的境地，不给他们中哪怕是一个人某种好处，就是对他们全体的公开侮辱。如果我们不让一个社会的杰出人物作为人类全体大会中的领袖和代表出现在世人面前，那么我们就对他们合法的进取心以及社会应有的自尊心负有回报的义务，让他们在一个更加强大和更加重要的国家里拥有取得同等显要位置的机会。假如英国国王提供的一切服务都向爱奥尼亚群岛的居民开放，那么我们就不再会听到与希腊结盟的愿望了。这样的联盟不是人民想要的，对他们来说，这就是文明的倒退；但是如果科孚岛——这个岛屿在巴伐利亚人到来之前向俄罗斯帝国输送了一位具有欧洲声望的大臣，并为希腊本身提供了一名总

of the Bavarians, should feel it a grievance that its people are not admissible to the highest posts in some government or other.

Thus far, of the dependencies whose population is in a sufficiently advanced state to be fitted for representative government. But there are others which have not attained that state, and which, if held at all, must be governed by the dominant country, or by persons delegated for that purpose by it. This mode of government is as legitimate as any other, if it is the one which in the existing state of civilization of the subject people, most facilitates their transition to a higher stage of improvement. There are, as we have already seen, conditions of society in which a vigorous despotism is in itself the best mode of government for training the people in what is specifically wanting to render them capable of a higher civilization. There are others, in which the mere fact of despotism has indeed no beneficial effect, the lessons which it teaches having already been only too completely learnt ; but in which, there being no spring of spontaneous improvement in the people themselves, almost their only hope of making any stops in advance depends on the chances of a good despot. Under a native despotism, a good despot is a rare and transitory accident : but when the dominion they are under is that of a more civilized people, that people ought to be able to supply it constantly. The ruling country ought to be able to do for its subjects all that could be done by a succession of absolute monarchs, guaranteed by irresistible force against the precariousness of tenure attendant on barbarous despotisms, and qualified by their genius to anticipate all that experience has taught to the more advanced nation. Such is the ideal rule of a free people over a barbarous or semi-barbarous one. We need not expect to see that ideal realized ; but unless some approach to it is, the rulers are guilty of a dereliction of the highest moral trust which can devolve upon a nation : and if they do not even aim at it, they are selfish usurpers, on a par in criminality with any of those whose ambition and rapacity have sported from age to age with the destiny of masses of mankind.

第十八章

统——会因为它的人民没有在某个政府或其他地方得到最高职位的机会而感到自己处境悲惨,是不足为怪的。

到这里,我讲的都是那些其人民处于一个相当进步的状态、能够适应代议制政府的属地的情形。但还有一些属地没有达到这样的水平,如果要加以控制的话,必须由支配国或者由它派出的代表来直接加以统治。如果这种统治模式在被统治人民已有的文明状况下,最能推动他们向进步的更高阶段过渡的话,那么这种统治模式就和其他的任何统治模式一样是合法的。正如我们早已经看到的那样,在有些社会条件下,强大的专制政府本身就是在训练人民适应较高文明时所需要方面时的最好的统治模式。还有一些社会,在这些社会中单纯的专制统治确实已经不具备任何有益的效果,专制统治所给予的教训早已完全为人所知了,可是在人民当中却不存在自发的进步动力,他们进步的几乎是唯一的希望就是依赖于有一个好的专制君主。在一个本土的专制政府下,开明的专制君主是罕见的,是一个稍纵即逝的意外事件,但是当他们处于一个更为文明的民族统治之下时,这个民族就应该能够持续不断地提供这种统治。统治国应该能够为它的臣民们做那些世袭专制君主所能做的一切事情,通过不可抗拒的力量来保证避免没有野蛮专制统治所带来的不稳定性,通过他们的聪明才智来期望他们具有先进国家的一切经验。这就是自由民族对野蛮或半野蛮民族的理想统治。我们不必期待这种理想统治会实现,但是除非在某种程度上接近于这种理想,统治者就犯有玩忽职守的罪行,辜负了国家所担负的最崇高的道德委托。如果统治者甚至不以这种理想为目标,他们就是自私的篡位者,跟那些世世代代把民众的命运当儿戏、充满野心和贪婪的人

As it is already a common, and is rapidly tending to become the universal, condition of the more backward populations, to be either held in direct subjection by the more advanced, or to be under their complete political ascendancy ; there are in this age of the world few more important problems than how to organize this rule, so as to make it a good instead of an evil to the subject people, providing them with the best attainable present government, and with the conditions most favourable to future permanent improvement. But the mode of fitting the government for this purpose, is by no means so well understood as the conditions of good government in a people capable of governing themselves. We may even say, that it is not understood at all.

The thing appears perfectly easy to superficial observers. If India (for example) is not fit to govern itself, all that seems to them required is, that there should be a minister to govern it: and that this minister, like all other British ministers, should be responsible to the British Parliament. Unfortunately this, though the simple mode of attempting to govern a dependency, is about the worst ; and betrays in its advocates a total want of comprehension of the conditions of good government. To govern a country under responsibility to the people of that country, and to govern one country under responsibility to the people of another, are two very different things. What makes the excellence of the first, is that freedom is preferable to despotism : but the last is despotism, The only choice the case admits, is a choice of despotisms: and it is not certain that the despotism of twenty millions is necessarily better than that of a few, or of one. But it is quite certain, that the despotism of those who neither hear, nor see, nor knew anything about their subjects, has many chances of being worse than that of those who do. It is not usually thought that the immediate agents of authority govern better because they govern in the name of an absent master, and of one who has a thousand more pressing interests

第十八章

所犯的罪过没什么两样。

处于落后状态的人民要么将由更为先进的人民来统治,要么就处于他们完全的政治支配之下,这已经是很平常的事,并且正在迅速趋于普遍。在当今世界很少有什么问题要比如何着手组织这样的统治更为重要,以使这种统治成为臣属人民的好的统治而不是坏的统治,为他们提供最好的可以达到的现实政府和最有利于未来持久进步的条件。但是使政府适合于这一目的的模式,决不像能够管理自己人民的好政府所具备的条件那样为人们所充分理解。我们甚至可以说它根本就没有被人们所理解。

对于肤浅的观察家来说事情似乎相当简单。如果印度(打个比方)管理不了自己,那么在他们看来所要做的不外是应当有一位大臣去管理它,并且这位大臣要像所有其他英国大臣那样对英国议会负责。而不幸的是,尽管这是试图统治一个附属国的简单模式,但却是最糟糕的模式,并且这表明拥护它的人对良好政府的条件根本就缺乏理解。以对一个国家的人民负责任的态度来管理那个国家,以及以对另一国人民负责任的态度去管理一个国家,是两件极为不同的事情。要使前一种情况变得卓越的话,自由要比专制更为可取;而对于后一种情况,则专制更为可取。在后一种情况下,唯一的选择是不同的专制方式的选择。并且我们还不能确定对两千万人口的专制是否优于对少数或者一个人的专制。但可以肯定的是,对于其臣民不闻、不见、知之甚少的人所施行的专制更有可能比那些对其臣民有所了解的人所施行的专制更加糟糕。通常人们并不认为权威统治的直接代理人会因为他们是以一个并不在场的主人(而且这个主人还有上千种更为迫切的利益需要去关注)的名义进行统治,就统治得更好。主人

toattend to. The master may hold them to a strict responsibility, enforced by heavy penalties ; but it is very questionable of those penalties will often fall in the right place.

It is always under great difficulties, and very imperfectly, that a country can be governed by foreigners ; even when there is no extreme disparity, in habits and ideas, between the rulers and the ruled. Foreigners do not feel with the people. They cannot judge, by the light in which a thing appears to their own minds, or the manner in which it affects their feelings, how it will affect the feelings or appear to the minds of the subject population. What a native of the country, of average practical ability, knows as it were by instinct, they have to learn slowly, and after all imperfectly, by study and experience. The laws, the customs, the social relations, for which they have to legislate, instead of being familiar to them from childhood, are all strange to them. For most of their detailed knowledge they must depend on the information of natives ; and it is difficult for them to know whom to trust. They are feared, suspected, probably disliked by the population ; seldom sought by them except for interested purposes ; and they are prone to think that the servilely submissive are the trustworthy. Their danger is of despising the natives ; that of the natives is, of disbelieving that anything the strangers do can be intended for their good. These are but a part of the difficulties that any rulers have to struggle with, who honestly attempt to govern well a country in which they are foreigners. To overcome these difficulties in any degree, will always be a work of much labour, requiring a very superior degree of capacity in the chief administrators, and a high average among the subordinates: and the best organization of such a government is that which will best ensure the labour, develop the capacity, and place the highest specimens of it in the situations of greatest trust. Responsibility to an authority which has gone through none of the labour, acquired none of the capacity, and for the most part is not even aware that either, in any peculiar degree,

第十八章

也许会以严刑苛法来要求这些代理人尽职尽能,但很值得怀疑的是,这些处罚往往是否是恰当的。

一个国家要由外国人来统治往往是非常困难的,而且极不完善。即使统治者和被统治者之间在习惯和观念上不存在极端的差异,也是这样。外国人与当地人民之间很难有相同的情感。他们不能凭借一件事情浮现于自己头脑中的情况,或者凭借这件事情影响他们情感的情形,来判断这件事情将如何影响其臣属人民的情感,或者将如何浮现在这些人的头脑里面。这个国家具有一般实践能力的当地人民似乎通过本能就能了解的东西,这些外国人就必须通过学习和经验慢慢地加以了解,并且学得还很不完善。他们必须通过立法来加以确立的法律、风俗习惯和社会关系,对他们来说全都是陌生的,而不是从幼年起就熟悉的事物。他们大部分详细的知识都必须依靠当地人提供的信息才能获得,而困难的是他们不知道应该信任谁。人民害怕他们,怀疑他们,甚至可能讨厌他们,除非因为利害关系,否则很少找他们,于是他们认为奴性服从的人就是可以信赖的人。他们的危险在于轻视本地人,而本地人的危险则是不相信陌生人所做的任何事情会是为了他们的利益。这些只是任何作为外国人而真心想统治好这个国家的统治者必须加以克服的困难中的一小部分。要想在某种程度上克服这些困难是一件需要费很多力气去做的事情,要求其主要的行政长官具有超凡的能力,而他们的部属则需要中等水平的能力,而且要组织好这样的政府,就必须确保这种劳动,发展这种能力,并且对这种能力的最高典范给予最大的信任。向一个没有经历过这样的劳动、不具备这样的能力、而且在某种特别程度上多半甚至不知道这种劳动和能力是必须的,这样的一个权

is required, cannot be regarded as a very effectual expedient for accomplishing these ends.

The government of a people by itself has a meaning, and a reality ; but such a thing as government of one people by another, does not and cannot exist. One people may keep another as a warren or preserve for its own use, a place to make money in, a human cattle farm to be worked for the profit of its own inhabitants. But if the good of the governed is the proper business of a government, it is utterly impossible that a people should directly attend to it. The utmost they can do is to give some of their best men a commission to look after it ; to whom the opinion of their own country can neither be much of a guide in the performance of their duty, nor a competent judge of the mode in which it has been performed. Let any one consider how the English themselves would be governed, if they knew and cared no more about their own affairs, than they know and care about the affairs of the Hindoos. Even this comparison gives no adequate idea of the state of the case: for a people thus indifferent to politics altogether, would probably be simply acquiescent, and let the government alone : whereas in the case of India, a politically active people like the English, amidst habitual acquiescence, are every now and then interfering, and almost always in the wrong place. The real causes which determine the prosperity or wretchedness, the improvement or deterioration, of the Hindoos, are too far off to be within their ken. They have not the knowledge necessary for suspecting the existence of those causes, much less for judging of their operation. The most essential interests of the country may be well administered without obtaining any of their approbation, or mismanaged to almost any excess without attracting their notice. The purposes for which they are principally tempted to interfere, and control the proceedings of their delegates, are of two kinds. One is, to force English ideas down the throats of the natives ; for instance, by measures of proselytism, or acts intentionally or unintentionally offensive to the religious feelings of the people. This misdirection of opinion in the ruling country is instructively

第十八章

威负责,不能认为是为了达到这些目的的比较有效的对策。

由一个国家自己进行统治具有某种意义以及现实性,但是一个国家由另一个国家来进行管理,则是不存在并且不可能存在的事情。一个国家可能将另一个国家当成自己所用的养殖场和私人领域,是一个可以赚钱的地方,一个为自己居民福利而运转的人畜的农场。但是如果被统治者的好处正是政府固有的职能,那么绝对不可能由一国人民直接去加以关注。他们能做的顶多就是委托他们中间最优秀的人去管理这个国家;对这些人来说,他们自己国家的观念既不能作为他们履行职责的指导,他们自己也不是胜任对履行该项职责的方式作出判断的裁判者。任何一个人都可以设想一下,如果英国人对自己的事情像他们对印度人的事情那样一无所知、漠不关心的话,那么他们自己将怎样进行管理。即使是这样进行比较,也不能给予这一事态以恰当的看法,因为对政治如此冷漠的一国人民,将有可能只是默许,并且对政府听之任之。而对于印度的情况,像英国人这样一个在政治上积极而在习惯上却保持默许的民族,却时常进行几乎总是错误的干涉。决定印度是繁荣还是处境悲惨,是进步还是退步的真正原因远在他们的视线范围之外。他们没有足够的知识来怀疑那些原因的存在,而用来判断这些原因所起作用的知识就更加少了。这个国家最本质的利益可以在没有得到他们任何许可的情况下得到良好的管理,或者在几乎管理得一塌糊涂的情况下也不致引起他们的注意。诱惑他们去干涉以及控制他们代表的行动的意图主要有以下两类:一是,比如说,通过改变当地人的宗教信仰,或者有意或无意地冒犯他们宗教情感的手段,将他们的英国观念强行灌输给当地人。在统治国家中,这种观念的错误指导通过目前普遍存

exemplified (the more so, because nothing is meant but justice and fairness, and as much impartiality as can be expected from persons really convinced) by the demand now so general in England for having the Bible taught, at the option of pupils or of their parents, in the Government schools. From the European point of view nothing can wear a fairer aspect, or seem less open to objection on the score of religious freedom. To Asiatic eyes it is quite another thing. No Asiatic people ever believes that a government puts its paid officers and official machinery into motion unless it is bent upon an object; and when bent upon an object, no Asiatic believes that any government, except a feeble and contemptible one, pursues it by halves. If Government schools and schoolmasters taught Christianity, whatever pledges might be given of teaching it only to those who spontaneously sought it, no amount of evidence would ever persuade the parents that improper means were not used to make their children Christians, or at all events, outcasts from Hindooism. If they could, in the end, be convinced of the contrary, it would only be by the entire failure of the schools, so conducted, to make any converts. If the teaching had the smallest effect in promoting its object, it would compromise not only the utility and even existence of the government education, but perhaps the safety of the government itself. An English Protestant would not be easily induced, by disclaimers of proselytism, to place his children in a Roman Catholic seminary: Irish Catholics will not send their children to schools in which they can be made Protestants: and we expect that Hindoos, who believe that the privileges of Hindooism can be forfeited by a merely physical act, will expose theirs to the danger of being made Christians !

Such is one of the modes in which the opinion of the dominant country tends to act more injuriously than beneficially on the conduct of its deputed governors. In other respects, its interference is likely to be oftenest exercised where it will be most pertinaciously demanded,

第十八章

在于英国的、在公办学校根据学生或家长的选择教授《圣经》的要求得到富有启发意义的例证(尤其是因为除了正义和公平,以及能期待于真正深信无疑的人们的那种公正无私以外没别的意思)。从欧洲的观点看,没有什么比这更显得公平,或者没有什么会比这更不至于会因为宗教自由而遭到反对了。而在亚洲人眼里,情况则又是另外一种样子。在亚洲不会有人相信政府会让它花钱雇佣的官员或者官僚机器运转起来,除非它是为了达到某个目的,并且当政府致力于达到某个目的时,没有亚洲人会相信它会半途而废,除非它是一个虚弱而且卑劣的政府。如果公办学校及其教师们开设基督教课程,则无论如何要保证这些课程只对那些自愿选择学习它的人开放,也没有证据显示可以说服学生家长相信不会使用不当的手段使他们的小孩变成基督教徒,或不管怎样都会被印度教所排斥的人。如果他们最终相信不是这样,那也只能是由于这样管理的学校完全失败了,没能产生出任何皈依者。如果教授《圣经》在促进其目的方面起到丝毫的作用,它就不仅会危害政府教育的效用以至其存在,而且也许会危害政府本身。一个英国新教徒不会轻易地被那些否认诱使改变宗教信仰的人所引诱,将其子女送入罗马天主教神学院学习,爱尔兰天主教徒不会将他们的子女送入可能把他们变成新教徒的学校,可是我们却期待印度人,那些认为仅仅因为一次粗野的行为就能够使印度教特权丧失的印度人,会让他们的子女处于被变成基督教教徒的危险之中!

这就是其中的一种模式,在这种模式中,统治国家的舆论倾向于认为其委托的总督的行为起更有害而不是更有利的作用。在其他方面,统治国家可能会在英国殖民者的坚决要求下,

and that is, on behalf of some interest of the English settlers. English settlers have friends at home, have organs, have access to the public; they have a common language, and common ideas with their countrymen: any complaint by an Englishman is more sympathetically heard, even if no unjust preference is intentionally accorded to it. Now, if there be a fact to which all experience testifies, it is that when a country holds another in subjection, the individuals of the ruling people who resort to the foreign country to make their fortunes, are of all others those who most need to be held under powerful restraint. They are always one of the chief difficulties of the government. Armed with the *prestige* and filled with the scornful overbearingness of the conquering nation, they, have the feelings inspired by absolute power, without its sense of responsibility. Among a people like that of India, the utmost efforts of the public authorities are not enough for the effectual protection of the weak against the strong: and of all the strong, the European settlers are the strongest. Wherever the demoralizing effect of the situation is not in a most remarkable degree corrected by the personal character of the individual, they think the people of the country mere dirt under their feet: it seems to them monstrous that any rights of the natives should stand in the way of their smallest pretensions : the simplest act of protection to the inhabitants against any act of power on their part which they may consider useful to their commercial objects, they denounce, and sincerely regard, as an injury. So natural is this state of feeling in a situation like theirs, that even under the discouragement which it has hitherto met with from the ruling authorities, it is impossible that more or less of the spirit should not perpetually break out. The Government, itself free from this spirit, is never able sufficiently to keep it down in the young and raw even of its own civil and military officers, over whom it has so much more control than over the independent residents. As it is with the English in India, so, according to trustworthy testimony, it is with the French in Algiers ; so with the Americans in the countries conquered from Mexico ; so it seems to be with the Europeans in China, and already

第十八章

为了他们的某种利益而经常进行干涉。英国殖民者在其家乡会有朋友,会有跟公众相通的舆论机关,他们与其同胞有相同的语言,相同的观念。英国人的任何投诉都会得到更多的同情,即使在这种同情中不存在故意的、不公正的偏爱。现在,如果存在被一切经验所证明的事实的话,那么这个事实就是当一个国家使另外一个国家附属于它时,那些到这个附属国寻求发财致富的统治国的人民,就是最需要以强力加以约束的人。他们始终是附属国政府的主要困难之一。由于他们凭借征服国家的威望,心中充满着征服国家的专横跋扈,他们抱有由绝对权力所激发的情感,却毫无责任意识。在像印度这样的国家的人民中,权力机关尽最大努力也不足以有效地保护弱势群体去与强势群体对抗,而欧洲殖民者是强势群体中最强的。不管在哪里,只要这种令人沮丧的形势没有通过个人本身的品质在最显著的程度上加以纠正,他们就会认为附属国的人民只是他们脚下的泥土。在他们看来,当地人的任何要求要是妨碍他们哪怕是一丁点要求的话也是令人难以置信的。对于当地居民最轻微的保护措施以对抗作为殖民者的他们认为有利于他们商业目的的任何权力行动,他们都加以谴责,并且真心认为,这是损害他们利益的行为。在像他们所处的那种情形下,他们有这样的情感是如此的自然,以至于到目前即使仍为统治当局所阻止,这种情绪还或多或少会爆发出来,政府本身是不受这种情绪影响的,但却永远做不到抑制它的那些年轻的没有经验的文职人员和军官们的这种情绪,而和那些相对独立的侨民相比,政府对他们的控制力要强得多。和英国人在印度一样,根据可信赖的证据表明,法国人在阿尔及尔也是这样的,美国人在从墨西哥那夺来的土地上也是这样的,似乎跟欧洲人在中国

even in Japan; there is no necessity to fecal how it was with the Spaniards in South America. In all these cases, the government to which these private adventurers are subject, is better than they. and does the most it can to protect the natives against them. Even the Spanish Government did this, sincerely and earnestly, though ineffectually, as is known to every reader of Mr. Helps' instructive history. Had the Spanish Government been directly accountable to Spanish opinion, we may question if it would have made the attempt: for the Spaniards, doubtless, would have taken part with their Christian friends and relations rather than with Pagans. The settlers, not the natives, have the ear of the public at home; it is they whose representations are likely to pass for truth, because they alone have both the means and the motive to press them perseveringly upon the inattentive and uninterested public mind. The distrustful criticism with which Englishmen, more than any other people, are in the habit of scanning the conduct of their country towards foreigners, they usually reserve for the proceedings of the public authorities. In all questions between a government and an individual, the presumption in every Englishman's mind is, that the government is in the wrong. And when the resident English bring the batteries of English political action to bear upon any of the bulwarks erected to protect the natives against their encroachments, the executive, with their real but faint velleities of something better, generally find it safer to their parliamentary interest, and at any rate less troublesome, to give up the disputed position, than to defend it.

  What makes matters worse is, that when the public mind is invoked (as, to its credit, the English mind is extremely open to be) in the name of justice and philanthropy, in behalf of the subject community or race, there is the same probability of its missing the mark. For in the subject community also there are oppressors and oppressed; powerful individuals or classes, and slaves prostrate before them;

第十八章

的情形差不多,甚至在日本也是这样。没有必要回顾西班牙人当年在南美洲的情况是怎样,在所有的这些场合,这些私人冒险家所属的政府都要比他们自己好得多,并尽自己最大的努力来保护本地人不受他们的侵扰。正如每个读过赫尔普斯先生那富有启发意义的历史著作的读者所知道的那样,甚至西班牙政府也这样做了,尽管没有什么效果,但却是满心诚恳、充满热情的。假如西班牙政府曾直接对西班牙的舆论负责的话,那么我们就要质疑它是否会做这样的努力,因为毫无疑问,西班牙人会站在他们的基督教朋友以及亲戚们那一边而不会去支持异教徒。国内的公众听取的是殖民者的意见而不是当地人的意见,只有他们的陈述才可能被看成是真实的,因为只有他们才既有手段又有动机去坚定不移地迫使那些疏忽大意和漠不关心的公众接受他们的陈述。英国人要比其他任何国家的人民对政府更具不信任的批评精神,他们形成了审视其国家对待外国人的所作所为的习惯,这些批评通常是针对公共当局的行动的。在所有政府和个人之间的问题上,英国人的头脑中总是假定错误在政府方面。并且当英国居民将英国人政治行动的炮火对准任何竖立起来的用来保护当地土著不受他们侵害的壁垒时,行政部门虽然有真正想使事情做得更好的却很微弱的单纯愿望,但却通常会发现放弃受争议的立场要比捍卫这种立场对其议会的利益更为安全,至少是麻烦要少些。

更糟糕的是,当舆论为了从属的社会或种族的利益,以正义和博爱的名义发动起来的时候(因为英国舆论很容易被发动是出了名的),同样可能偏离靶心。因为在从属社会中同样也存在着压迫和被压迫者,存在着强有力的个人或阶级以及匍匐在他们面前

and it is the former; not the latter, who have the means of access to the English public. A tyrant or sensualist who has been deprived of the power he had abused, and instead of punishment, is supported in as great wealth and splendour as he ever enjoyed ; a knot of privileged landholders, who demand that the State should relinquish to them its reserved right to a rent from their lands, or who resent as a wrong any attempt to protect the masses from their extortion; these have no difficulty in procuring interested or sentimental advocacy in the British Parliament and press. the silent myriads obtain none.

The preceding observations exemplify the operation of a principle—which might be called an obvious one, were it not that scarcely anybody seems to be aware of it—that, while responsibility to the govererned is the greatest of all securities for good government, responsibility to somebody else not only has no such tendency, but is as likely to produce evil as good. The responsibility of the British rulers of India to the British nation is chiefly useful because, when any acts of the government are called in question, it ensures publicity and discussion; the utility of which does not require that the public at large should comprehend the point at issue, provided there are any individuals among them who do ; for a merely moral responsibility not being responsibility to the collective people, but to every separate person among them who forms a judgment, opinions may be weighed as well as counted, and the approbation or disapprobation of one person well versed in the subject, may outweigh that of thousands who know nothing about it at all,It is doubtless a useful restraint upon the immediate rulers that they can be put upon their defence, and that one or two of the jury will form an opinion worth having about their conduct, though that of the remainder will probably be several degrees worse than none. Such as it is, this is the amount of benefit to India from the control exercised over the Indian government by the British Parliament and people.

第十八章

的奴隶,而且只有前者而不是后者才有办法接触到英国大众。一个暴君或耽于声色的人,他那曾经滥用的权力被剥夺了,可是却不会遭到惩罚,而是得到与他曾经享有的同样巨大的财富和显赫名声的支持。一群拥有特权的地主,他们要求国家把所保留的在他们土地上征收地租的权力让给他们,或者憎恨国家为保护大众不受他们敲诈勒索而采取的任何尝试,并将斥之错误。正是这些人,可以毫无困难地从英国议会和新闻舆论中得到充满偏见或意气用事的支持。而无数沉默的大众却得不到任何支持。

以上的论述证明了这样一条原则——如果不是几乎没有人知道这样一条原则的话,那么就可以称它是一条显而易见的原则了——也即是说,对被统治者负责是良好政府的最大保证,但是对个别的某个人负责就不仅不会有这样的趋势,而且既可能产生有利因素也可能产生有害因素。印度的英国统治者向英国负责基本上是有益的,因为当政府的任何行为遭到质疑时,它可以保证公开讨论。公开讨论的功用并不是要求一般公众应该理解讨论的要点,只要公众中有人能够理解就行。因为纯粹道德上的责任不是对全体人民负责任,而是对他们中形成了判断的每个独立的个人负责,各种观点既可以按数量来计算,也可以按它的价值来计算,一个精通于某个领域问题的人赞同或不赞同,可能要比成千上万的一无所知的人的赞同或不赞同的分量要重得多。毫无疑问这是对直接统治者的一种有效约束,他们可以被放在被告席上,一个或者两个陪审团的成员将就他的行为提出有价值的意见,尽管其他人的意见在不同程度上有要比没有更坏。情形就是如此,这就是从由英国议会和人民对印度政府行使的控制中得来的对印度的好处。

It is not by attempting to rule directly a country like India, but by giving it good rulers, that the English people can do their duty to that country; and they can scarcely give it a worse one than an English Cabinet Minister, who is thinking of English not Indian politics ; who seldom remains long enough in office to acquire an intelligent interest in so complicated a subject; upon whom the factitious public opinion got up in Parliament, consisting of two or three fluent speakers, acts with as much force as if it were genuine ; while he is under none of the influences of training and position which would lead or qualify him to form an honest opinion of his own. A free country which attempts to govern a distant dependency, inhabited by a dissimiliar people, by means of a branch of its own executive, will almost inevitably fail. The only mode which has any chance of tolerable success, is to govern through a delegated body, of a comparatively permanent character; allowing only a right of inspection, and a negative voice, to the changeable Administration of the State. Such a body did exist in the case of India ; and I fear that both India and England will pay a severe penalty for the shortsighted policy by which this intermediate instrument of government was done away with.

It is of no avail to say that such a delegated body cannot have all the requisites of good government, above all, cannot have that complete and ever-operative identity of interest with the governed, which it is so difficult to obtain even where the people to be ruled are in some degree qualified to look after their own affairs. Real good government is not compatible with the conditions of the case. There is but a choice of imperfections. The problem is, so to construct the governing body that, under the difficulties of the position, it shall have as much interest as possible in good government, and as little in bad. Now these conditions are best found in an intermediate body. A delegated administration has always this advantage over a direct one, that it has, at all events, no duties to perform except to the governed. It has no interests to consider except theirs. Its own power of deriving

第十八章

英国人民不是通过试图去直接统治像印度这样的国家,而是通过向它提供好的统治者来履行他们对印度的责任的。并且他们给予印度的统治者不会比内阁大臣差到哪儿去,他想的是英国的政治而不是印度的政治;他很少能有足够长的任期可以使他对于一个如此复杂的问题养成明智的兴趣。议会中起来针对他的虚假的舆论是由两三个能言善辩的人士形成的,这种舆论力量很大,就好像是真的一样。而他却不会受到能引导他或使他有能力形成他自己的真正意见的训练和职位的影响。一个试图通过自己行政部门的分支机构去统治一个遥远的、居住着不同人民的附属国的自由国家,将几乎不可避免地要遭到失败。唯一有机会获得相当成功的模式是通过一个具有相对长久性质的,经过授权的代表团体进行统治,对于容易变更的国家行政部门只给予审查权和否决权。这样的统治团体确实在印度存在过,但是我担心印度和英国都会因为废除这一中介的统治手段的短视政策而受到严重的惩罚。

无需说明,这样的代表团体不能具备良好政府的一切条件,首先,它具有和被统治者完全相同和永远起作用的利益认同,这种利益认同甚至在被统治者有某种程度的能力来管理自己事务的地方也难以得到。真正良好的政府与这里所说的各种情况是不同的,只能在不完美的状态中进行选择。问题是,统治集团应如此组成,使它能在所处困难的情形下,尽可能多地保持对良好的政府的兴趣以及尽可能少地对糟糕的政府感兴趣。现在,一个中间团体最具备这些条件。一个经过授权的行政部门与一个直接的行政部门相比总是有这种好处,即无论如何,它除了对被统治者负有责任之外,就不存在什么责任了。它没有兴趣去考虑

profit from misgovernment may be reduced—in the latest constitution of the East India Company it was reduced to a singularly small amount: and it can be kept entirely clear of bias from the individual or class interests of any one else. When the home government and Parliament are swayed by those partial influences in the exercise of the power reserved to them in the last resort, the intermediate body is the certain advocate and champion of the dependency before the imperial tribunal. The intermediate body, moreover is, in the natural course of things, chiefly composed of persons who have acquired professional knowledge of this part of their country's concerns; who have been trained to it in the place itself, and have made its administration the main occupation of their lives. Furnished with these qualifications, and not being liable to lose their office from the accidents of home politics, they identify their character and consideration with their special trust, and have a much more permanent interest in the success of their administration, and in the prosperity of the country which they administer, than a member of a cabinet under a representative constitution can possibly have in the good government of any country except the one which he serves. So far as the choice of those who carry on the management on the spot devolves upon this body, the appointments are kept out of the vortex of party and parliamentary jobbing. and freed from the influence of those motives to the abuse of patronage, for the reward of adherents, or to buy off those who would otherwise be opponents, which are always stronger, with statesmen of average honesty, than a conscientious sense of the duty of appointing the fittest man. To put this one class of appointments as far as possible out of harm's way, is of more consequence than the worst which can happen to all other offices in the state; for, in every other department, if the officer is unqualified, the general opinion of the community directs him in a certain degree what to do ; but in the position of the administrators of a dependency where the people are not fit to have the control in their own hands, the character of the government entirely depends on the qualifications, moral and intellectual, of the individual functionaries.

第十八章

除他们之外的利益。它本身源自恶政所得来的权力可以被减少到——在最近的东印度公司的章程中这项权力被削减到——一个异乎寻常的微小数量,并且它能完全摆脱来自任何个人利益或阶级利益所产生的偏见。当母国政府和议会在行使作为最后手段保留给它们的权力时受到片面的影响而产生摇摆时,中间团体在帝国法庭面前就必定是这个附属国确定的拥护者和支持者。而且,自然而然,中间团体主要由那些具有他们国家所关心的这部分事务的专门知识的人们组成,他们为适应团体中的位置而受过训练,并且将行政工作作为他们终生的主要职业。具备这样的资质,并且不容易由于国内政治事件而丢掉饭碗,因此他们就将自己的声誉和思想与他们的特殊责任等同起来,并且他们对在行政方面取得成功,对他们管理的国家的繁荣,所抱有的兴趣,要比代议制政体中的内阁成员所抱有的对除他所服务的国家之外的任何国家的良好政府兴趣更为持久。只要选择具体负责管理的人员的权力由这个团体掌握,那么对这些人员的任命就可以远离政党和议会假公济私的漩涡之中,也不至于受到为了答谢支持者而滥用任命权,或者为了收买那些否则就会成为反对者的人的动机等的影响,这些动机对于具备一般诚实的政治家来说,总是要比任命最合适的官员这种发自内心的责任感更加强有力。将这一类任命尽可能置于安全地带,与可能发生于国家所有其他部门的最糟糕的情况相比要重要得多。因为在任何其他部门,如果官员是不合格的,那么社会普遍舆论在某种程度上指导他应该做些什么,可是当处于附属国的管理者的位置,而那里的百姓不适于通过自己的双手来进行控制,那么政府的声誉就完全取决于各个官员的道德和智力上的资质了。

It cannot be too often repeated, that in a country like India everything depends on the personal qualities and capacities of the agents of government. This truth is the cardinal principle of Indian administration. The day when it comes to be thought that the appointment of persons to situations of trust from motives of convenience, already so criminal in England, can be practised with impunity in India, will be the beginning of the decline and fall of our empire there. Even with a sincere intention of preferring the best candidate, it will not do to rely on chance for supplying fit persons. The system must be calculated to form them. It has done this hitherto; and because it has done so, our rule in India has lasted, and been one of constant, if not very rapid, improvement in prosperity and good administration. As much bitterness is now manifested against this system, and as much eagerness displayed to overthrow it, as if educating and training the officers of government for their work were a thing utterly unreasonable and indefensible, an unjustifiable interference with the rights of ignorance and inexperience. There is a tacit conspiracy between those who would like to job in first-rate Indian offices for their connexions here, and those who, being already in India, claim to be promoted from the indigo factory or the attorney's office, to administer justice or fix the payments due to government from millions of people. The ' monopoly' of the Civil Service, so much inveighed against, is like the monopoly of judicial offices by the bar ; and its abolition would be like opening the bench in Westminster Hall to the first comer whose friends certify that he has now and then looked into Blackstone. Were the course ever adopted of sending men from this country, or encouraging them in going out, to get themselves put into high appointments without having learnt their business by passing through the lower ones, the most important offices would be thrown to Scotch cousins and adventurers, connected by no professional feeling with the country or the work, held to no previous knowledge, and eager only to make money rapidly and return home. The safety of the country is, that those by whom it is administered be sent out in youth, as candidates only, to

第十八章

在像印度这样的国家,一切都取决于政府代理人的个人禀赋和能力,这一点需要反复加以说明。这一事实是印度行政的基本原理。当有一天人们认为出于便利的目的任命处于负责岗位的官员的做法(这种做法在英国已经算是犯罪了),可以安然无恙地施行于印度的时候,就将是我们帝国在那儿的衰落的开始。即使有选择最优秀的候选人的真诚意图,依靠偶然的机会提供合适人选也是行不通的。体制必须适合培养这样的人选,到现在为止一直是这样做的;并且正是因为这样做了,我们在印度的统治才得以延续,并且在繁荣和善治方面,即使不是速度很快,也算是持续不断地取得进步。现在这个体制遭到了激烈的反对,人们热衷于推翻它,似乎教育和培训政府官员以适应他们的工作是一件极其不可理喻和无法自辩的事情,是对无知者和无经验者权利的不合理的干涉。在那些想为他们的亲戚谋求印度最好职位的人以及那些早已经在印度宣扬他们将在靛青厂或律师事务所中获得升职的人之间暗中隐藏着的某种阴谋,来进行司法活动或确定千百万老百姓应向政府缴纳的款额。受到人们猛烈抨击的对于文职的"垄断"与律师界对于司法职位的垄断是一样的,而这种垄断的废除就像是将英国国会议事厅的法官职位向第一个进来的并经过其朋友证明他曾经偶尔浏览布莱克斯通的法律书籍的人开放。假如采取将人们从这个国家送出去,或鼓励他们出去的做法,以使他们不通过较低的职位学习业务就被委以高级职位,那么最重要的职位就拱手让给了远亲和冒险家们,他们与这个国家或工作没有多少职业上的感情联系,也没有什么事先的了解,只是想尽快发财后回家过日子。这个国家的安全在于,那些管理这个国家的人在年轻的时候就被送过来,只是作为候选人,

begin at the bottom of the ladder, and ascend higher or not, as, after a proper interval, they are proved qualified, The defect of the East India Company's system was, that though the best men were carefully sought out for the most important posts, yet if an officer remained in the service, promotion, though it might be delayed, came at last in some shape or other, to the least as well as to the most competent. Even the inferior in qualifications, among such a corps of functionaries, consisted, it must be remembered, of men who had been brought up to their duties, and had fulfilled them for many years, at lowest without disgrace, under the eye and authority of a superior. But though this diminished the evil, it was nevertheless considerable. A man who never becomes fit for more than an assistant's duty, should remain an assistant all his life, and his juniors should be promoted over him. With this exception, I am not aware of any real defect in the old system of Indian appointments. It had already received the greatest other improvement it was susceptible of, the choice of the original candidates by competitive examination: which, besides the advantage of recruiting from a higher grade of industry and capacity, has the recommendation, that under it, unless by accident, there are no personal ties between the candidates for offices and those who have a voice in conferring them.

It is in no way unjust, that public officers thus selected and trained should be exclusively eligible to offices which require specially Indian knowledge and experience. If any door to the higher appointments, without passing through the lower, be opened even for occasional use, there will be such incessant knocking at it by persons of influence that it will be impossible ever to keep it closed. The only excepted appointment should be the highest one of all. The Viceroy of British India should be a person selected from all Englishmen for his great general capacity for government. If he have this, he will be able to distinguish in others, and turn to his own use, that special knowledge and judgment in local affairs which he has not himself had the opportunity of acquiring. There are good reasons why the Viceroy should not be a member of the regular service. All services have, more or less, their class prejudices, from which the supreme ruler

第十八章

从职位阶梯的最底层开始,经过一段时间,在他们合格之后才逐步晋升。东印度公司体制上的缺陷在于,尽管最优秀的人被精心挑选出来担任最重要的职位,然而,如果一个官员仍然在职,那么尽管会有所耽搁,然而最差的和最有能力的官员一样,都会以这种或那种方式得到提升。在这样的一个官员群体中,必须记住,即使是低级官员,也是由那些受过职业训练、并且在那些岗位上呆了好多年,职位虽然卑微但却未丢脸,并且处在上级的监视和权威之下的人组成的。但尽管这样使不幸得以减少,不幸的事件的数量还是相当可观的。一个只适合充当助手的人,就应当一辈子做他的助手去,职位比他低的人应当越过他得到提拔。除了这个例外,我就不知道在印度旧的任命制度中还有什么真正的缺点。它早已得到它所能容许的最大的改进,即通过竞争性的考试来选择最初的候选人。这种考试除了具备录取得分较高的勤勉、有能力的人的优势之外,还具备一项优势,即在这种制度下,除非出于偶然,职位的候选人与有权给予这种职位的人之间不存在个人的联系。

经过如此选择与训练的公职人员应当是唯一适合担任特别需要具备有关印度的知识与经验的职务,如果任何通向较高级别职务的大门,在没有经过较低职务之门的情况下,即使是由于偶然使用而被打开,那将不断会有权势人物来叩门,以致不再可能把门关上。唯一的例外应当是最高级人物的任用。英属印度的总督应当是一个由全体英国人选出来的、具有超常的、全面的统治能力的人。如果他具备这样的能力,那么他就能把别人所具有的、而他却没有机会学习的,对于地方事务的特殊知识和判断力鉴别出来,并为自己所用。我们有很好的理由解释为什么总督不应该是一个处理日常事务的官员,所有的部门,或多或少都带

ought to be exempt. Neither are men, however able and experienced, who have passed their lives in Asia, so likely to possess the most advanced European ideas in general statesmanship, which the chief ruler should carry out with him, and blend with the results of Indian experience. Again, being of a different class, and especially if chosen by a different authority, he will seldom have any personal partialities to warp his appointments to office. This great security for honest bestowal of patronage existed in rare perfection, under the mixed government of the Crown and the East India Company. The supreme dispensers of office, the Governor-General and Governors, were appointed, in fact though not formally, by the Crown, that is, by the general Government, not by the intermediate body; and a great officer of the Crown probably had not a single personal or political connexion in the local service: while the delegated body, most of whom had themselves served in the country, had, and were likely to have, such connexions. This guarantee for impartiality would be much impaired, if the civil servants of Government, even though sent out in boyhood as mere candidates for employment, should come to be furnished, in any considerable proportion, by the class of society which supplies Viceroys and Governors. Even the initiatory competitive examination would then be an insufficient security. It would exclude mere ignorance and incapacity; it would compel youths of family to start in the race with the same amount of instruction and ability as other people; the stupidest son could not be put into the Indian service, as he can be into the Church ; but there would be nothing to prevent undue preference afterwards. No longer all equally unknown and unheard of by the arbiter of their lot, a portion of the service would be personally, and a still greater number politically, in close relation with him. Members of certain families, and of the higher classes and influential connexions generally, would rise more rapidly than their competitors, and be often kept in situations for which they were unfit, or placed in those for which others were fitter. The same influences would be brought

第十八章

有部门偏见,这是最高统治者应该加以避免的。在亚洲生活了多年的人,不管他多有能力,多有经验,也不可能具备一般政治才能中所要求的最先进的欧洲思想,而这种思想主要是统治者应当加以落实、并和印度经验的成果融会贯通在一起的。此外,由于他属于不同的阶级,特别是如果他是由不同的权力机关任命的话,他将不会有个人的偏好来影响他对于官员的任命。这种对官员任命的诚实安排其巨大保障在国王和东印度公司的混合政府里达到了罕见的完美状态。对职务进行委派的高级人员,即总督和地方长官,实际上在形式上是由国王来任命,即由全国政府进行委任的,而不是由代议机关来进行委任的。而且国王的一位高级官员可能在地方部门里没有任何个人或政治上的联系,而代议团体的成员,他们中大多数人在那个国家服务,就存在和极可能存在这种联系。如果政府的公务员,即使在少年时期就被当成后备人员送出去,而结果却在相当可观的比例上由提供总督和地方长官的那个社会的阶级来提供,那么对于公正的保证就会遭到削弱。甚至初次的竞争性考试也会是不充分的保障。这项考试只能排除无知的以及能力不够的人,它将迫使名门望族的年轻人以与其他人同样程度的教育和能力展开竞赛,最蠢笨的子弟不能像可以进入教会担任神职那样,允许他进入印度政界担任官职,但是在此以后无法防止不恰当的偏爱。不再是所有人不知道或从未听说过他们的命运主宰者,一部分官员和他会有密切的个人联系,还有更大一部分人则和他在政治上有密切的联系。某些家族成员和一般与上等阶级及其权势人物有亲戚关系的人员,提拔的速度要比他们的竞争者更快,并且常常被放在他们不适合担任的职位上,或放在别人更能胜任的职位上。在部队中同样的势力

into play, which affect promotions in the army: and those alone, if such miracles of simplicity there be, who believe that these are impartial, would expect impartiality in those of India. This evil is, I fear, irremediable by any general measures which can be taken under the present system. No such will afford a degree of security comparable to that which once flowed spontaneously from the so-called double government.

What is accounted so great an advantage in the case of the English system of government at home, has been its misfortune in India—that it grew up of itself, not from preconceived design, but by successive expedients, and by the adaptation of machinery originally created for a different purpose. As the country on which its maintenance depended, was not the one out of whose necessities it grew, its practical benefits did not come home to the mind of that country, and it would have required theoretic recommendations to render it acceptable. Unfortunately, these were exactly what it seemed to be destitute of: and undoubtedly the common theories of government did not furnish it with such, framed as those theories have been for states of circumstances differing in all the most important features from the case concerned. But in government, as in other departments of human agency, almost all principles which have been durable were first suggested by observation of some particular case, in which the general laws of nature acted in some new or previously unnoticed combination of circumstances. The institutions of Great Britain, and those of the United States, have had the distinction of suggesting most of the theories of government which, through good and evil fortune, are now, in the course of generations, reawakening political life in the nations of Europe. It has been the destiny of the government of the East India Company to suggest the true theory of the government of a semi-barbarous dependency by a civilized country, and after having done this, to perish. It would be a singular fortune if, at the end of two or three more generations, this speculative result should be the only remaining

第十八章

也会起作用,这将影响到人员的提拔。只有那些相信——如果还会有如此不可思议的天真的话——这些负责提拔的是公正无私的人,才会期望在印度的提拔中也会有公正。在现有的体制下,我认为这种弊端通过所能采取的任何措施,恐怕也无法纠正。没有什么办法可提供能达到曾经一度自发地出现于所谓双重政府的保证的那种程度。

英国国内的政府体制被认为是一个如此巨大的优势,可是在印度这种优势却成为这种体制的不幸。英国政府体制是自发生成的,不是通过预先想好的设计,而是通过连续的权宜之计,通过改造原先为不同目的创立的机构发展起来的。由于需要依赖这项制度的国家不是这项制度根据需要发展起来的那个国家,因此这个国家就感觉不到这个制度的好处,需要有理论上的介绍以便使它能接受。不幸的是,这样的介绍似乎恰恰就是所缺少的。毋庸置疑,关于政府的一般理论并没有给它提供所需要的东西,因为那些理论是为那些其环境在所有最重要的特征上都与现在所关注的情形不相同的国家设计出来的。但是在政府里,正如人类机构的其他部门一样,几乎所有的持久原则最先都是在基于对某个特别事例的观察基础上提出来的,在这个事例中,一般自然法则在某些新的或之前不被注意的综合环境中起作用。大不列颠的制度,以及美国的制度,都因为其中提出了很多政府理论而享有殊荣,这些理论,尽管经历了好运和厄运,在历经几代之后,现在正唤醒着欧洲各国的政治生活。东印度公司的命运就是提出由一个文明国家统治一个半野蛮附属国的真正理论,并且在完成这项工作之后,就终结了自己。在两代或三代之后,如果这种经过深思熟虑得来的成果会成为我们在印度统治所剩下的唯一果

fruit of our ascendancy in India; if posterity should say of us, that having stumbled accidentally upon better arrangements than our wisdom would ever have devised, the first use we made of our awakened reason was to destroy them, and allow the good which had been in course of being realized to fall through and be lost, from ignorance of the principles on which it depended. *Di meliora*: but if a fate so disgraceful to England and to civilization can be averted, it must be through far wider political conceptions than merely English or European practice can supply, and through a much more profound study of Indian experience, and of the conditions of Indian government, than either English politicians, or those who supply the English public with opinions, have hitherto shown any willingness to undertake.

第十八章

实,那么这将是一笔独特的财富;如果后人会说我们,在意外发现了比我们智慧所能设想的更好的安排之后,我们第一次利用我们觉醒了的理智就是去破坏这种安排,并且由于对于美好事物所依赖的原则的无知,而让美好事物在实现过程中遭到失败或丧失。改进方案:如果对英国以及对文明如此可耻的命运是可以预防的话,那么就必定要通过形成比单纯英国或欧洲的实践所能提供的更为广泛的政治观念,要对印度经验和印度政府的情况进行更加深入的研究,而且这种研究一定要比英国政治家或那些为英国公众提供建议的人们迄今所愿意进行的研究要深入得多才行。

译者后记

约翰·斯图亚特·穆勒(John Stuart Mill, 1806~1873)是英国近代著名的思想家,他思想深邃,富有远见,在政治、经济、哲学、逻辑学、宗教、伦理等诸多领域均作出了杰出的理论贡献,因而,西方学界甚至称之为"19世纪英国不列颠民族精神的象征"、"理性主义的圣人"。穆勒的政治思想对后世的影响更是深远,尤其是他在1861年发表的《代议制政府》更是西方政治思想发展史上的一部里程碑式的著作,穆勒在这部书里,根据英国议会改革的历史经验,在总结前人关于代议制理论的基础上,系统地阐述了代议制的种种问题,主要包括代议制政府的形式、职能、民主制、选举权、议会以及地方代表机关和民族等问题,并针对当时英国的议会改革提出了大量有建设意义的看法,这些看法,对英国及欧美各国政治制度的进一步完善具有持久的影响,成为资产阶级政治理论的重要组成部分。该书自出版以来,就成为研究代议制度的一本重要的书籍,是政治学专业学生必读的西方经典书目之一。作为一名刚刚进入政治学研究领域的学生,本人翻译此书的最初目的也就是希望通过对本书的翻译,以这种方式,来把握这位思想大师的政治观念;同时,也希望通过翻译此书,能为学习西方政治学理论的研究者或学生提供更为精确的译本,以尽自己的一点绵薄之力。

出于这一目的,译者在翻译过程中严格忠实于原文,对所译文字进行仔细推敲,反复修改,力求用语准确,行文流畅。力求使读者在阅读该书的过程中,不会出现太大的理解偏差,能较好地领会穆勒所要表达的意思。为了方便读者阅读,对于这些词汇以及常用的政治学术语也尽量采用通用的翻译方法,以便读者理解。

在着手翻译之前,译者注意到商务印书馆在1982年就推出了由汪瑄主译的《代议制政府》,但随着时代的发展和政治学研究的深入,我们发现这个译本在概念推敲、行文与理解等诸多方面已经与时代有了一定的差距,需要后来者在此基础上作些改进和突破,以求完善。重译此书的必要性就在于此。但在此仍要向这位学界前辈表示谢意,他的译本给译者在翻译本书时提供了很好的借鉴,使译者能够把有限的精力用在如何作进一步改进方面的努力上来。

在此书的翻译过程中,译者得到了很多人士的热情帮助,在此表示感谢。尤其要感谢中共中央党校博士研究生钟雪生,他在本书的翻译完成后,对译稿进行了细致的校对,帮助改进了许多翻译不当之处;感谢中央党校博士研究生姚仁权,他在具体的一些翻译问题上给了我很大的启发。

由于译者才疏学浅,水平有限,译文中仍然不免要出现一些纰漏与失误,恳请广大读者朋友批评指正。

段小平
2006年9月